Hands-On Selenium
WebDriver with Java

*A Deep Dive into the Development of
End-to-End Tests*

Boni García

Beijing · Boston · Farnham · Sebastopol · Tokyo

Hands-On Selenium WebDriver with Java

by Boni García

Published by O'Reilly Media, Inc., 1005 Gravenstein Highway North, Sebastopol, CA 95472.

O'Reilly books may be purchased for educational, business, or sales promotional use. Online editions are also available for most titles (*https://oreilly.com*). For more information, contact our corporate/institutional sales department: 800-998-9938 or *corporate@oreilly.com*.

Acquisitions Editor: Suzanne McQuade

Development Editor: Rita Fernando

Production Editor: Kristen Brown

Copyeditor: Piper Editorial Consulting, LLC

Proofreader: JM Olejarz

Indexer: Sam Arnold-Boyd

Interior Designer: David Futato

Cover Designer: Karen Montgomery

Illustrator: Kate Dullea

April 2022:   First Edition

Revision History for the First Edition

2022-03-31:   First Release

See *https://oreilly.com/catalog/errata.csp?isbn=9781098110000* for release details.

978-1-098-11000-0

[LSI]

To the most precious thing to me in the world: my children, Pablo and Carlos.

I love you more than anything.

Table of Contents

Part II.   The Selenium WebDriver API

Part III.   Advanced Concepts

Foreword

In 1999, Kent Beck wrote *Extreme Programming Explained*. This introduced the world to Extreme Programming (XP). For many people this was the way they first heard about Agile software development. Over the next 20 years, many of the ideas behind the book faded away, but there was one idea that stuck: we should be writing automated tests that verify our code is working as it should. XP expected these tests to be written before the app logic, leading to Test Driven Development (TDD).

Today, while strict TDD is seldom practiced, the idea of writing tests is prevalent (though not always popular!). Most companies now acknowledge the need for some kind of automated testing. Many of us actually write tests! Even "regular" QA roles now frequently require people to write code.

In 2004, Jason Huggins started Selenium at a software development consultancy called Thoughtworks, which specialized in Agile development. Employees were steeped in XP and were keen proponents of TDD. From the very beginning, Selenium has been closely associated with testing.

Back then, testing websites in a browser was relatively simple. These were the olden days, when there were dozens of browsers to choose between and JS was still spelled "JavaScript." Sites were small, functionality limited, and the interactions the user could have via the browser were limited too: maybe just filling out a form and clicking a "submit" button. This is the world that Selenium was born into, and the APIs and functionality it offered were as focused as the platform it tested.

Then the world discovered XMLHttpRequest hiding in Internet Explorer, it was implemented in Firefox, and suddenly "Web 2.0" became the hot new buzzword. Google Maps showed the world what browsers could do, and the world loved it! Websites started offering more functionality, driven by carefully handcrafted JS. Selenium adapted and evolved too. I wrote the WebDriver APIs, and these came to the fore. Although they aimed to lead people in a certain direction, the underlying complexity of what Selenium was trying to automate meant that it became a more complicated tool.

As I write this, browsers are more capable, powerful, and flexible than ever before. We don't write "websites" any more. We write "web apps," the current ultimate expression of that being the "Single Page App" or SPA. These push browsers harder than ever, but they're a natural evolution. Fortunately, once again, Selenium has evolved and grown to allow these kinds of apps to be automated, adding a range of new features in Selenium 4 to help cope with the new testing needs. Adding this functionality has made Selenium an even more complicated tool.

But despite having grown more complicated over the years, Selenium is a tool used by people of all levels of programming comfort and ability. There's more to writing a successful Selenium test than "just" learning the APIs. There's a wealth of technology that surrounds it, from the test frameworks you can use, to the Design Patterns you can (and should!) follow when writing the tests, to how we manage the binary dependencies required by our tests. If we want our tests to run in a reasonable amount of time, we need to have access to infrastructure that supports this.

There's just so much to learn, and there's surprisingly little guidance for how all the pieces fit together.

That's why I'm so glad that Boni has written this book. It starts by explaining what Selenium is, and the various components within it, and then each chapter builds on the previous ones, gradually introducing more ideas and concepts in a way that feels natural and obvious.

Better yet, Boni goes further than just discussing how to use the raw APIs. He also describes the ecosystem of services, tools, and test runners that people need to understand to get the most from the tool. His experience using Selenium and providing some of these supporting tools shines through: you're in the hands of a master here.

The way this book is structured allows anyone using Selenium to dive in at the point that feels right to them. Just getting started? Then start at the beginning of the book, as Boni lays out the basics for you in an engaging and approachable way. Maybe you're familiar with Selenium but want to know what's new in Selenium 4, or some of the less well-known features it offers? Then just jump into the middle of the book; there's so much there, even I learned a few things!

One thing that I hope people take away from this book is that Selenium is only part of the puzzle that is automated testing. Boni covers this too, introducing readers (you!) to how to integrate it into your test frameworks, to the various unit testing libraries you might want to use, and to Design Patterns that can help keep your tests maintainable and fresh. After all, although it may take time to write an automated test in the first place, it can live for years, and being able to work on it with ease is important.

This book paves the road to mastering Selenium and using it effectively. I sincerely hope that this makes using it easier and—dare I say it?—more enjoyable.

— Simon Mavi Stewart
Creator of WebDriver,
Selenium Project Lead 2009–2021,
and coeditor of the W3C WebDriver and
WebDriver BiDi specifications
London, January 2022

Preface

Selenium is an open source umbrella project that enables the automation of web browsers. The core component of the Selenium project is Selenium WebDriver, a library for controlling browsers (e.g., Chrome, Firefox, Edge, Safari, or Opera) programmatically. Selenium WebDriver provides a cross-browser Application Programming Interface (API) in several programming languages (officially supported in Java, JavaScript, Python, C#, or Ruby).

Although we can use Selenium WebDriver for multiple purposes related to browser automation, its primary use is implementing end-to-end tests for web application verification. Thousands of organizations and testers now use Selenium worldwide, and it is one of the leading solutions for end-to-end testing, supporting a multi-million-dollar industry.

Who Should Read This Book

This book provides a comprehensive summary of the main features of Selenium WebDriver version 4, using Java as language binding. It reviews the main aspects of automated web navigation, browser manipulation, web element interaction, user impersonation, automated driver management, the Page Object Model (POM) design pattern, use of remote and cloud infrastructure, integration with Docker and third-party tools, and much more.

The primary audience of this book includes Java coders of different levels (from beginner to advanced), such as developers, testers, QA engineers, etc. Thus, you need a basic knowledge of the Java language and object-oriented programming. The final goal is to have a comprehensive understanding of the main aspects of Selenium WebDriver to create end-to-end tests in Java using different testing frameworks of your choice (e.g., JUnit or TestNG).

Why I Wrote This Book

Test automation is a software testing technique that leverages automation tools to control test execution. It allows increased efficiency and effectiveness while ensuring the overall quality of a software system. In this arena, Selenium WebDriver is the de facto standard library to develop end-to-end tests for web applications. This book provides the first complete review of Selenium 4 to date.

The book follows a learn-by-doing approach. To that aim, we review the main features of Selenium WebDriver through ready-to-be-executed test examples. These examples are publicly available in a GitHub open source repository (*https://github.com/bonigarcia/selenium-webdriver-java*). For the sake of completeness, this repository contains each test example in different flavors of the embedding testing framework: JUnit 4, JUnit 5 (alone or with Selenium-Jupiter), and TestNG.

Navigating This Book

The content of this book is divided into 3 parts and 10 chapters:

Part I, Introduction

Part I provides technological background on Selenium, test automation, and project setup. This part, more theoretical than practical, is composed of two chapters:

- Chapter 1, "A Primer on Selenium", presents the core components of the Selenium project (WebDriver, Grid, and IDE) and its ecosystem (i.e., the tools and technologies around Selenium). In addition, this chapter reviews the principles of end-to-end testing related to Selenium.

- Chapter 2, "Preparing for Testing", explains how to set up a Java project (Maven and Gradle) containing end-to-end tests that use the Selenium WebDriver API. Then, you will learn how to develop your first WebDriver tests using different testing frameworks: JUnit 4, JUnit 5 (alone or in conjunction with Selenium-Jupiter), and TestNG.

Part II, The Selenium WebDriver API

Part II provides practical insight into the Selenium WebDriver API. This part is guided by tests available in the examples repository and includes the following chapters:

- Chapter 3, "WebDriver Fundamentals", describes the primary aspects of the Selenium WebDriver API for carrying out automated interaction with web applications. Thus, this chapter reviews several strategies for locating and waiting for web elements. In addition, you will discover how to impersonate user actions (i.e., automated interactions using the keyboard and mouse) in a browser.

- Chapter 4, "Browser-Agnostic Features", reviews those aspects of the Selenium WebDriver API that are interoperable in different browsers. Hence, this chapter shows how to execute JavaScript, create event listeners, manage windows, make screenshots, handle the shadow DOM, manipulate cookies, access the browser history or web storage, or interact with windows, tabs, and iframes, among other elements.

- Chapter 5, "Browser-Specific Manipulation", explains those aspects of the Selenium WebDriver API particular to specific browsers. This group of features covers browser capabilities (options, arguments, preferences, etc.), the Chrome DevTools Protocol (CDP), geolocation functions, basic and web authentication, printing pages to PDF, or the WebDriver BiDi API.

- Chapter 6, "Remote WebDriver", describes how to use the Selenium WebDriver API to control remote browsers. Then, you will learn how to set up and use Selenium Grid version 4. Finally, you will discover how to use advanced infrastructure for Selenium tests in cloud providers (e.g., Sauce Labs, BrowserStack, or CrossBrowserTesting, among others) and browsers in Docker containers.

Part III, Advanced Concepts

Part III focuses on leveraging the Selenium WebDriver API in different ambits and use cases. This part includes the following chapters:

- Chapter 7, "The Page Object Model (POM)", introduces POM, a popular design pattern used in conjunction with Selenium WebDriver. This pattern allows users to model web pages using object-oriented classes to ease test maintenance and reduce code duplication.

- Chapter 8, "Testing Framework Specifics", reviews several particular features of the unit testing framework used together with Selenium WebDriver that allow improvements to different aspects of the overall testing process. To that aim, this chapter first explains how to carry out cross-browser testing (i.e., reusing the same test logic for verifying web applications using different browsers) using parameterized tests and test templates. Then, you will learn how to split tests into different categories for execution filtering, ordering tests, failure analysis (i.e., collecting and analyzing data to determine the cause of a failure), retrying tests, parallel test execution, test listeners, or disabling tests.

- Chapter 9, "Third-Party Integrations", reviews different technologies you can use to enhance your Selenium WebDriver tests, such as reporting tools, test data generation, and other frameworks (e.g., Cucumber or Spring). Moreover, this chapter describes how to use external libraries with Selenium to implement specific use cases, such as file downloading or nonfunctional tests (such as load, security, or accessibility).

- Chapter 10, "Beyond Selenium", presents a couple of automation frameworks related to Selenium: Appium (for mobile testing) and REST Assured (for testing REST web services). To conclude, we review some of the most relevant current alternatives to Selenium WebDriver, such as Cypress, WebDriverIO, TestCafe, Puppeteer, or Playwright.

Conventions Used in This Book

The following typographical conventions are used in this book:

Italic

Indicates new terms, URLs, email addresses, filenames, and file extensions.

`Constant width`

Used for program listings, as well as within paragraphs to refer to program elements such as variable or function names, databases, data types, environment variables, statements, and keywords.

`Constant width bold`

Shows commands or other text that the user should type literally.

`Constant width italic`

Shows text that should be replaced with user-supplied values or by values determined by context.

 This element signifies a tip or suggestion.

 This element signifies a general note.

 This element indicates a warning or caution.

Using Code Examples

Code examples are available for download at *https://github.com/bonigarcia/selenium-webdriver-java*. If you have a technical question or a problem using the code examples, please email *bookquestions@oreilly.com*.

This book is here to help you get your job done. In general, if example code is offered with this book, you may use it in your programs and documentation. You do not need to contact us for permission unless you're reproducing a significant portion of the code. For example, writing a program that uses several chunks of code from this book does not require permission. Selling or distributing examples from O'Reilly books does require permission. Answering a question by citing this book and quoting example code does not require permission. Incorporating a significant amount of example code from this book into your product's documentation does require permission.

We appreciate, but generally do not require, attribution. An attribution usually includes the title, author, publisher, and ISBN. For example: "*Hands-On Selenium WebDriver with Java* by Boni García (O'Reilly). Copyright 2022 Boni García, 978-1-098-11000-0."

If you feel your use of code examples falls outside fair use or the permission given above, feel free to contact us at *permissions@oreilly.com*.

O'Reilly Online Learning

 For more than 40 years, *O'Reilly Media* has provided technology and business training, knowledge, and insight to help companies succeed.

Our unique network of experts and innovators share their knowledge and expertise through books, articles, and our online learning platform. O'Reilly's online learning platform gives you on-demand access to live training courses, in-depth learning paths, interactive coding environments, and a vast collection of text and video from O'Reilly and 200+ other publishers. For more information, visit *https://oreilly.com*.

How to Contact Us

Please address comments and questions concerning this book to the publisher:

O'Reilly Media, Inc.
1005 Gravenstein Highway North
Sebastopol, CA 95472

800-998-9938 (in the United States or Canada)
707-829-0515 (international or local)
707-829-0104 (fax)

We have a web page for this book, where we list errata, examples, and any additional information. You can access this page at *https://oreil.ly/handsOn_SeleniumWDJ*.

Email *bookquestions@oreilly.com* to comment or ask technical questions about this book.

For news and information about our books and courses, visit *https://oreilly.com*.

Find us on Facebook: *https://facebook.com/oreilly*.

Follow us on Twitter: *https://twitter.com/oreillymedia*.

Watch us on YouTube: *https://www.youtube.com/oreillymedia*.

Acknowledgments

First, I want to thank the team at O'Reilly for making this book a reality. Their editorial support has been exemplary through every stage of this journey.

I also want to recognize the technical reviewers who helped with this book. Their valuable feedback and expert advice improved its quality significantly: Diego Molina (staff software engineer at Sauce Labs and technical lead of the Selenium project), Filippo Ricca (associate professor of computer science at Università di Genova), Andrea Stocco (postdoctoral researcher at Software Institute in Università della Svizzera italiana), Ivan Krutov (software developer at Aerokube), and Daniel Hinojosa (independent consultant, programmer, instructor, speaker, and author)—thank you very much.

Lastly, I would like to acknowledge the contribution of Simon Stewart (creator of WebDriver and Selenium project lead until 2021). Thanks a lot, Simon, for writing the foreword on this book and for your priceless feedback about its content. But mainly, I want to recognize your work during all these years leading the Selenium project. Your contributions to the automation testing community are already part of software history.

Introduction

Selenium is an open source umbrella project composed of three core components: WebDriver, Grid, and IDE. Selenium provides advanced capabilities for browser automation that practitioners typically use for implementing end-to-end tests for web applications. This first part of the book is a comprehensive overview of the Selenium project and its ecosystem. Moreover, it provides a primer on the software testing theory, focusing on its practical applications for Selenium WebDriver. Finally, you will discover how to set up a project (using Maven or Gradle) for developing WebDriver tests. For the sake of completeness, I cover different alternatives regarding the unit testing framework used to embed the calls to the Selenium WebDriver API, namely, JUnit 4, JUnit 5 (alone or extended by Selenium-Jupiter), and TestNG.

CHAPTER 1

A Primer on Selenium

Selenium (*https://www.selenium.dev*) is an open source suite composed of a set of libraries and tools that enable the automation of web browsers. We can see Selenium as an umbrella project with three core components: WebDriver, Grid, and IDE (Integrated Development Environment). Selenium WebDriver is a library that allows the driving of browsers programmatically. Thus, we can use Selenium WebDriver to navigate websites and interact with web pages (e.g., clicking on links, filling in forms, etc.) as a real user would do, in an automated fashion. The primary use of Selenium WebDriver is the automated testing of web applications. Other Selenium uses include the automation of web-based administration tasks or web scraping (automated web data extraction).

This chapter provides a comprehensive overview of the Selenium core components: WebDriver, Grid, and IDE. Then, it reviews the Selenium ecosystem, i.e., other tools and technologies around it. Finally, it analyzes the foundations of software testing related to Selenium.

Selenium Core Components

Jason Huggins and Paul Hammant created Selenium in 2004 while working in Thoughtworks. They chose the name "Selenium" as a counterpart to Mercury, an existing testing framework developed by Hewlett-Packard. The name is significant because the chemical selenium is known for reducing the toxicity of mercury.

That initial version of Selenium (known today as *Selenium Core*) is a JavaScript library that impersonates user actions in web applications. Selenium Core interprets the so-called *Selenese* commands to achieve this task. These commands are encoded as an HTML table composed of three parts: *command* (action executed in a web browser, such as opening a URL or clicking a link), *target* (locator that identifies a web element, such as the attribute of a given component), and *value* (optional data, such as the text typed into a web-form field).

Huggins and Hammant added a scripting layer to Selenium Core in a new project called *Selenium Remote Control* (RC). Selenium RC follows a client-server architecture. Clients use a binding language (such as Java or JavaScript) to send Selenese commands over HTTP to an intermediate proxy called the *Selenium RC Server*. This server launches web browsers on demand, injecting the Selenium Core library into a website and proxying requests from clients to Selenium Core. In addition, the Selenium RC Server masks the target website to the same local URL of the injected Selenium Core library to avoid same-origin policy concerns. This approach was a game-changer for browser automation at that time, but it had significant limitations. First, because JavaScript is the underlying technology to support automation, some actions are not permitted since JavaScript does not allow them—for instance, uploading and downloading files or handling pop-ups and dialogs, to name a few. Besides, Selenium RC introduces a relevant overhead that impacts its performance.

In parallel, Simon Stewart created the project *WebDriver* in 2007. WebDriver and Selenium RC were equivalent from a functional perspective, i.e., both projects allow programmers to impersonate web users using a programming language. Nevertheless, WebDriver uses the native support of each browser to carry out the automation, and therefore, its capabilities and performance are far superior to RC. In 2009, after a meeting between Jason Huggins and Simon Stewart at the Google Test Automation Conference, they decided to merge Selenium and WebDriver in a single project. The new project was called *Selenium WebDriver* or Selenium 2. This new project uses a communication protocol based on HTTP combined with the native automation support on the browser. That approach is still the basis of Selenium 3 (released in 2016) and Selenium 4 (released in 2021). Now we refer to Selenium RC and Core as "Selenium 1," and its use is discouraged in favor of Selenium WebDriver. This book focuses on the latest version of Selenium WebDriver to date, i.e., version 4.

 Appendix A summarizes the novelties shipped with Selenium 4. This appendix also contains a migration guide for bumping from Selenium 3 to 4.

Today, Selenium is a well-known automation suite composed of three subprojects: WebDriver, Grid, and IDE. The following subsections present the main characteristics of each one.

Selenium WebDriver

Selenium WebDriver is a library that allows the controlling of web browsers automatically. To that aim, it provides a cross-platform API in different language bindings. The official programming languages supported by Selenium WebDriver are Java, JavaScript, Python, Ruby, and C#. Internally, Selenium WebDriver uses the native support implemented by each browser to carry out the automation process. For this reason, we need to place a component called *driver* between the script using the Selenium WebDriver API and the browser. Table 1-1 summarizes the browsers and drivers officially supported by Selenium WebDriver.

 The name *Selenium* is widely used to refer to the library for browser automation. Since this term is also the name of the umbrella project, I use *Selenium* in this book to identify the browser automation suite, which is composed of three components: Selenium WebDriver (library), Selenium Grid (infrastructure), and Selenium IDE (tool).

Table 1-1. Browsers and drivers supported by Selenium WebDriver

Browser	Driver	Operating system	Maintainer	Download
Chrome/Chromium	chromedriver	Windows/macOS/Linux	Google	*https://chromedriver.chromium.org*
Edge	msedgedriver	Windows/macOS/Linux	Microsoft	*https://developer.microsoft.com/en-us/microsoft-edge/tools/webdriver*
Firefox	geckodriver	Windows/macOS/Linux	Mozilla	*https://github.com/mozilla/geckodriver*
Opera	operadriver	Windows/macOS/Linux	Opera Software AS	*https://github.com/operasoftware/operachromiumdriver*
Internet Explorer	IEDriverServer	Windows	Selenium project	*https://www.selenium.dev/downloads*
Safari	safaridriver	macOS	Apple	Built-in

Drivers (e.g., chromedriver, geckodriver, etc.) are platform-dependent binary files that receive commands from a WebDriver script and translate them into some browser-specific language. In the first releases of Selenium WebDriver (i.e., in Selenium 2), these commands (also known as the *Selenium protocol*) were JSON messages over HTTP (the so-called *JSON Wire Protocol*). Nowadays, this communication (still JSON over HTTP) follows a standard specification named *W3C WebDriver* (*https://www.w3.org/TR/webdriver*). This specification is the preferred Selenium protocol as of Selenium 4.

Figure 1-1 summarizes the basic architecture of Selenium WebDriver we have seen so far. As you can see, this architecture has three tiers. First, we find a script using the Selenium WebDriver API (Java, JavaScript, Python, Ruby, or C#). This script sends W3C WebDriver commands to the second layer, in which we find the drivers. This figure shows the specific case of using chromedriver (to control Chrome) and geckodriver (to control Firefox). Finally, the third layer contains the web browsers. In the case of Chrome, the native browser follows the *DevTools Protocol* (*https://chromedevtools.github.io/devtools-protocol*). DevTools is a set of developer tools for browsers based on the Blink rendering engine, such as Chrome, Chromium, Edge, or Opera. The DevTools Protocol is based on JSON-RPC messages and allows inspecting, debugging, and profiling these browsers. In Firefox, the native automation support uses the *Marionette* (*https://firefox-source-docs.mozilla.org/testing/marionette*) protocol. Marionette is a remote protocol based on JSON, allowing instrumenting and controlling web browsers based on the Gecko engine (such as Firefox).

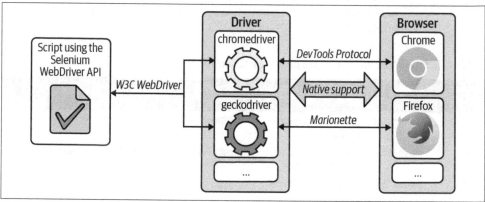

Figure 1-1. Selenium WebDriver architecture

Overall, Selenium WebDriver allows controlling web browsers as a user would, but programmatically. To that aim, the Selenium WebDriver API provides a wide variety of features to navigate web pages, interact with web elements, or impersonate user actions, among many other capabilities. The target application is web-based, such as static websites, dynamic web applications, Single Page Applications (SPA), complex enterprise systems with a web interface, etc.

Selenium Grid

The second project of the Selenium family is *Selenium Grid*. Philippe Hanrigou started the development of this project in 2008. Selenium Grid is a group of networked hosts that provides browser infrastructure for Selenium WebDriver. This infrastructure enables the (parallel) execution of Selenium WebDriver scripts with remote browsers of a different nature (types and versions) in multiple operating systems.

Figure 1-2 shows the basic architecture of Selenium Grid. As you can see, a group of nodes provides browsers used by Selenium scripts. These nodes can use different operating systems (as we saw in Table 1-1) with various installed browsers. The central entry point to this Grid is the *Hub* (also known as *Selenium Server*). This server-side component keeps track of the nodes and proxies requests from the Selenium scripts. Like in Selenium WebDriver, the W3C WebDriver specification is the standard protocol for the communication between these scripts and the Hub.

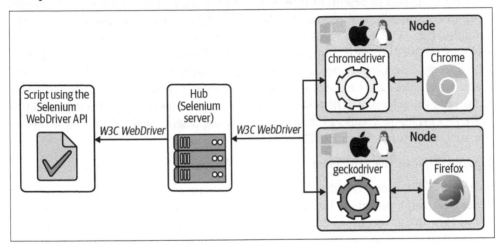

Figure 1-2. Selenium Grid hub-nodes architecture

The hub-nodes architecture in Grid has been available since Selenium 2. This architecture is also present in Selenium 3 and 4. Nevertheless, this centralized architecture can lead to performance bottlenecks if the number of requests to the Hub is high. Selenium 4 provides a fully distributed flavor of Selenium Grid to avoid this problem. This architecture implements advanced load balancing mechanisms to avoid overloading any component.

 Chapter 6 describes how to set up Selenium Grid following the classical approach (based on a hub and set of nodes). This chapter also covers the *standalone* mode (i.e., hub and node(s) hosted in the same machine) and the fully distributed architecture.

Selenium IDE

Selenium IDE (*https://www.selenium.dev/selenium-ide*) is the last core component of the Selenium suite. Shinya Kasatani created this project in 2006. Selenium IDE is a tool that implements the so-called *Record and Playback* (R&P) automation technique. As the name suggests, this technique has two steps. First, in Selenium IDE, the *record* part captures user interactions with a browser, encoding these actions as Selenium commands. Second, we use the generated Selenium script to execute a browser session automatically (*playback*).

This early version of Selenium IDE was a Firefox plug-in that embedded Selenium Core to record, edit, and play back Selenium scripts. These early versions were XPI modules (i.e., a technology used to create Mozilla extensions). As of version 55 (released in 2017), Firefox migrated support for add-ons to the W3C Browser Extension specification (*https://browserext.github.io/browserext*). As a result, Selenium IDE was discontinued, and for some time, it has not been possible to use it. The Selenium team rewrote Selenium IDE following the Browser Extensions recommendation to solve this problem. Thanks to this, we can now use Selenium IDE in multiple browsers, such as Chrome, Edge, and Firefox.

Figure 1-3 shows the new Selenium IDE GUI (Graphical User Interface).

Using this GUI, users can record interactions with a browser and edit and execute the generated script. Selenium IDE encodes each interaction in different parts: a command (i.e., the action executed in the browser), a target (i.e., the locator of the web element), and a value (i.e., the data handled). Optionally, we can include a description of the command. Figure 1-3 shows a recorded example of these steps:

1. Open website (*https://bonigarcia.dev/selenium-webdriver-java*). We will use this website as the practice site in the rest of the book.

2. Click on the link with the text "GitHub." As a result, the navigation moves to the examples repository source code.

3. Assert that the book title (*Hands-On Selenium WebDriver with Java*) is present on the web page.

4. Close the browser.

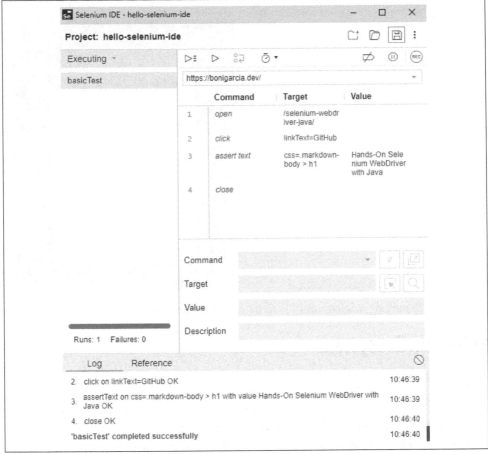

Figure 1-3. Selenium IDE showing an example of a recorded script

Once we have created a script in Selenium IDE, we can export this script as a Selenium WebDriver test. For instance, Figure 1-4 shows how to convert the presented example as a JUnit test case. Finally, we can save the project on our local machine. The resulting project for this sample is available in the examples GitHub repository (*https://github.com/bonigarcia/selenium-webdriver-java/tree/master/selenium-ide*).

 The Selenium project is porting Selenium IDE to Electron (*https:// www.electronjs.org*) at the time of this writing. Electron is an open source framework based on Chromium and Node.js that allows desktop application development.

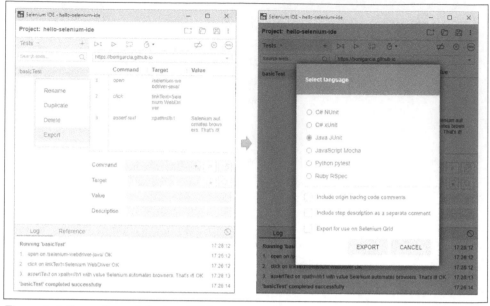

Figure 1-4. Exporting a Selenium IDE script to a JUnit test case

Selenium Ecosystem

Software ecosystems are collections of elements interacting with a shared market underpinned by a common technological background. In the case of Selenium, its ecosystem involves the official core projects and other related projects, libraries, and actors. This section reviews the Selenium ecosystem, divided into the following categories: language bindings, driver managers, frameworks, browser infrastructure, and community.

Language Bindings

As we already know, the Selenium project maintains various language bindings for Selenium WebDriver: Java, JavaScript, Python, Ruby, and C#. Nevertheless, other languages are also available. Table 1-2 summarizes these language bindings for Selenium WebDriver maintained by the community.

Table 1-2. Unofficial language bindings for Selenium WebDriver

Name	Language	License	Maintainer	Website
hs-webdriver	Haskell	BSD-3-Clause	Adam Curtis	*https://github.com/kallisti-dev/hs-webdriver*
php-webdriver	PHP	MIT	Facebook, community	*https://github.com/php-webdriver/php-webdriver*
RSelenium	R	AGPLv3	rOpenSci	*https://github.com/ropensci/RSelenium*

Name	Language	License	Maintainer	Website
Selenium	Go	MIT	Miki Tebeka	*https://github.com/tebeka/selenium*
Selenium-Remote-Driver	Perl	Apache 2.0	George S. Baugh	*https://github.com/teodesian/Selenium-Remote-Driver*
webdriver.dart	Dart	Apache 2.0	Google	*https://github.com/google/webdriver.dart*
wd	JavaScript	Apache 2.0	Adam Christian	*https://github.com/admc/wd*

Driver Managers

Drivers are mandatory components to control web browsers natively with Selenium WebDriver (see Figure 1-1). For this reason, before using the Selenium WebDriver API, we need to manage these drivers. *Driver management* is the process of downloading, setting up, and maintaining the proper driver for a given browser. The usual steps in the driver management procedure are:

1. *Download*

    Each browser has its own driver. For example, we use chromedriver for controlling Chrome or geckodriver for Firefox (see Table 1-1). The driver is a platform-specific binary file. Therefore, we need to download the proper driver for a given operating system (typically, Windows, macOS, or Linux). In addition, we need to consider the driver version since a driver release is compatible with a given browser version (or range). For example, to use Chrome 91.x, we need to download chromedriver 91.0.4472.19. We usually find the browser-driver compliance in the driver documentation or release notes.

2. *Setup*

    Once we have the proper driver, we need to make it available in our Selenium WebDriver script.

3. *Maintenance*

    Modern web browsers (e.g., Chrome, Firefox, or Edge) upgrade themselves automatically and silently, without prompting the user. For this reason, and concerning Selenium WebDriver, we need to maintain the browser-driver version compatibility in time for these so-called *evergreen* browsers.

As you can see, the driver maintenance process can be time-consuming. Furthermore, it can cause problems for Selenium WebDriver users (e.g., failed tests due to browser-driver incompatibility after an automatic browser upgrade). For this reason, the so-called *driver managers* aim to carry out the driver management process in an automated fashion to some extent. Table 1-3 summarizes the available driver managers for different language bindings.

Table 1-3. Driver managers for Selenium WebDriver

Name	Language	License	Maintainer	Website
WebDriverManager	Java	Apache 2.0	Boni García	*https://github.com/bonigarcia/webdrivermanager*
webdriver-manager	JavaScript	MIT	Google	*https://www.npmjs.com/package/webdriver-manager*
webdriver-manager	Python	Apache 2.0	Serhii Pirohov	*https://pypi.org/project/webdriver-manager*
WebDriverManager.Net	C#	MIT	Aliaksandr Rasolka	*https://github.com/rosolko/WebDriverManager.Net*
webdrivers	Ruby	MIT	Titus Fortner	*https://github.com/titusfortner/webdrivers*

In this book, I recommend using WebDriverManager because it automates the entire driver maintenance process (i.e., download, setup, and maintenance). See Appendix B for further information about automated and manual driver management.

Locator Tools

The Selenium WebDriver API provides different ways to locate web elements (see Chapter 3): by attribute (id, name, or class), by link text (complete or partial), by tag name, by CSS (Cascading Style Sheets) selector, or by XML Path Language (XPath). Specific tools can help to identify and generate these locators. Table 1-4 shows some of these tools.

Table 1-4. Locators tools summary

Name	Type	License	Maintainer	Website
Chrome DevTools	Built-in browser tool	Proprietary freeware, based on open source	Google	*https://developer.chrome.com/docs/devtools*
Firefox Developer Tools	Built-in browser tool	MPL 2.0	Mozilla	*https://developer.mozilla.org/en-US/docs/Tools*
Cropath	Browser extension	Freeware	AutonomIQ	*https://autonomiq.io/deviq-chropath.html*
SelectorsHub	Browser extension	Freeware	Sanjay Kumar	*https://selectorshub.com*
POM Builder	Browser extension	Freeware	LogiGear Corporation	*https://pombuilder.com*

Frameworks

In software engineering, a *framework* is a set of libraries and tools used as a conceptual and technological base and support for software development. Selenium is the foundation for frameworks that wrap, enhance, or complement its default features. Table 1-5 contains some of these frameworks and libraries based on Selenium.

Table 1-5. Testing frameworks and libraries based on Selenium

Name	Language	Description	License	Maintainer	Website
CodeceptJS	JavaScript	Multi-backend testing framework that models browser interactions as simple steps from a user perspective	MIT	Michael Bodnarchuk	https://codecept.io
FluentSelenium	Java	Fluent API for Selenium WebDriver	Apache 2.0	Paul Hammant	https://github.com/Selenium HQ/fluent-selenium
FluentLenium	Java	Website and mobile automation framework to create readable and reusable WebDriver tests	Apache 2.0	FluentLenium team	https://fluentlenium.com
Healenium	Java	Library for improving the stability of Selenium tests by using machine learning algorithms to analyze web and mobile web elements	Apache 2.0	Anna Chernyshova and Dmitriy Gumeniuk	https://healenium.io
Helium	Python	High-level API based on Selenium WebDriver	MIT	Michael Herrmann	https://github.com/mherrma nn/selenium-python-helium
QAF (QMetry Automation Framework)	Java	Test automation platform for web and mobile applications	MIT	Chirag Jayswal	https://qmetry.github.io/qaf
Lightning	Java	Lightweight Selenium WebDriver client for Java	Apache 2.0	FluentLenium	https://github.com/aerokube /lightning-java
Nerodia	Python	Python port of the Watir Ruby gem	MIT	Lucas Tierney	https://nerodia.readthedocs.i o
Robot Framework	Python, Java, .NET, and others	Generic automation framework based on human-readable test cases	Apache 2.0	Robot Framework Foundation	https://robotframework.org
Selenide team	Java	Fluent, concise API for Selenium WebDriver	MIT	Selenide team	https://selenide.org
SeleniumBase	Python	Browser automation framework based on WebDriver and pytest	MIT	Michael Mintz	https://seleniumbase.io
Watir (Web Application Testing in Ruby)	Ruby	Gem library based on WebDriver for automating web browsers	MIT	Titus Fortner	http://watir.com
WebDriverIO	JavaScript	Test automation framework based WebDriver and Appium	MIT	Christian Bromann	https://webdriver.io
Nightwatch.js	JavaScript	Integrated end-to-end testing framework based on the W3C WebDriver	MIT	Andrei Rusu	https://nightwatchjs.org

Name	Language	Description	License	Maintainer	Website
Applitools	Java, JavaScript, C#, Ruby, PHP, Python	Test automation framework for visual user interface regression and A/B testing. It provides SDKs for Selenium, Appium, and others	Commercial	Applitools team	*https://applitools.com*
Katalon Studio	Java, Groovy	Test automation platform leveraging Selenium WebDriver, Appium, and cloud providers	Commercial	Katalon team	*https://www.katalon.com*
TestProject	Java, C#, Python	Test automation platform for web and mobile apps built on top of Selenium and Appium	Commercial	TestProject team	*https://testproject.io*

Browser Infrastructure

We can use Selenium WebDriver to control local browsers installed in the machine running the WebDriver script. Also, Selenium WebDriver can drive remote web browsers (i.e., those executed in other hosts). In this case, we can use Selenium Grid to support the remote browser infrastructure. Nevertheless, this infrastructure can be challenging to create and maintain.

Alternatively, we can use a *cloud provider* to outsource the responsibility for supporting the browser infrastructure. In the Selenium ecosystem, a cloud provider is a company or product that supplies managed services for automated testing. These companies typically offer commercial solutions for web and mobile testing. The users of a cloud provider request on-demand browsers of different types, versions, and operating systems. Also, these providers typically offer additional services for easing the testing and monitoring activities, such as access to session recordings or analysis capabilities, to name a few. Some of the most relevant cloud providers for Selenium nowadays are Sauce Labs (*https://saucelabs.com*), BrowserStack (*https://www.browserstack.com*), LambdaTest (*https://www.lambdatest.com*), CrossBrowser-Testing (*https://crossbrowsertesting.com*), Moon Cloud (*https://aerokube.com/moon-cloud*), TestingBot (*https://testingbot.com*), Perfecto (*https://www.perfecto.io*), or Testinium (*https://testinium.com*).

Another solution we can use to support the browser infrastructure for Selenium is *Docker* (*https://www.docker.com*). Docker is an open source software technology that allows users to pack and run applications as lightweight, portable containers. The Docker platform has two main components: the *Docker Engine*, a tool for creating and running containers, and the *Docker Hub* (*https://hub.docker.com*), a cloud service for distributing Docker images. In the Selenium domain, we can use Docker to pack and execute containerized browsers. Table 1-6 presents a summary of relevant projects using Docker in the Selenium ecosystem.

Table 1-6. Docker resources for Selenium

Name	Description	License	Maintainer	Website
docker-selenium	Official Docker images for Selenium Grid	Apache 2.0	Selenium project	https://github.com/seleniumhq/docker-selenium
Selenoid	Lightweight Golang implementation of Selenium Hub running browsers in Docker (images available on Docker Hub)	Apache 2.0	Aerokube	https://aerokube.com/selenoid
Moon	Enterprise Selenium cluster that use Docker and Kubernetes	Commercial	Aerokube	https://aerokube.com/moon
Callisto	Open source Kubernetes-native implementation of Selenium Grid	MIT	Aerokube	https://github.com/wrike/callisto

Community

Due to its collaborative nature, software development needs the organization and interaction of many participants. In the open source domain, we can measure the success of a project by the relevance of its community. Selenium is supported by a large community of many different participants worldwide. Table 1-7 presents a summary of several Selenium resources grouped into the following categories: official documentation, development, support, and events.

Table 1-7. Selenium community resources

Category	Description	Website
Official documentation	User guide	https://www.selenium.dev/documentation
	Blog	https://www.selenium.dev/blog
	Wiki	https://github.com/seleniumhq/selenium/wiki
	Ecosystem	https://www.selenium.dev/ecosystem
Development	Source code	https://github.com/seleniumhq/selenium
	Issues	https://github.com/seleniumhq/selenium/issues
	Governance	https://www.selenium.dev/project
Support	User group	https://groups.google.com/group/selenium-users
	Slack	https://seleniumhq.slack.com
	IRC	https://webchat.freenode.net/#selenium
	StackOverflow	https://stackoverflow.com/questions/tagged/selenium
	Reddit	https://www.reddit.com/r/selenium
Events	Conference	https://www.selenium.dev/categories/conference
	Meetups	https://www.meetup.com/topics/selenium

Software Testing Fundamentals

Software testing (or simply *testing*) consists of the dynamic evaluation of a piece of software, called *System Under Test* (SUT), through a finite set of test cases (or simply *tests*), giving a verdict about it. Testing implies the execution of SUT using specific input values to assess the outcome or expected behavior.

At first glance, we distinguish two separate categories of software testing: manual and automated. On the one hand, in *manual testing*, a person (typically a software engineer or the final user) evaluates the SUT. On the other hand, in *automated testing*, we use specific software tools to develop tests and control their execution against the SUT. Automated tests allow the early detection of defects (usually called *bugs*) in the SUT while providing a large number of additional benefits (e.g., cost savings, fast feedback, test coverage, or reusability, to name a few). Manual testing can also be a valuable approach in some cases, for example, in *exploratory testing* (i.e., human testers freely investigate and evaluate the SUT).

 There is no universal classification for the numerous forms of testing presented in this section. These concepts are subject to continuous evolution and debate, just like software engineering. Consider it a proposal that can fit into a large number of projects.

Levels of Testing

Depending on the size of the SUT, we can define different *levels of testing*. These levels define several categories in which software teams divide their testing efforts. In this book, I propose a stacked layout to represent the different levels (see Figure 1-5). The lower levels of this structure represent the tests aimed at verifying small pieces of software (called *units*). As we ascend in the stack, we find other tiers (e.g., *integration*, *system*, etc.) in which the SUT integrates more and more components.

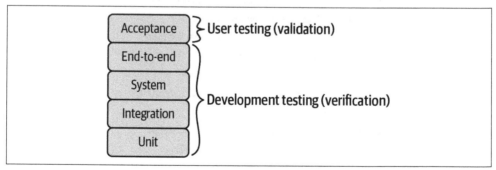

Figure 1-5. Stack representation of the different levels of testing

The lowest level of this stack is *unit testing*. At this level, we assess individual units of software. A unit is a particular observable element of behavior. For instance, units are typically methods or classes in object-oriented programming and functions in functional programming. Unit testing aims to verify that each unit behaves as expected. Automated unit tests usually run very fast since each test executes a small amount of code in isolation. To achieve this isolation, we can use *test doubles*, pieces of software that replace the dependent components of a given unit. For example, a popular type of test double in object-oriented programming is the *mock object*. A mock object mimics an actual object using some programmed behavior.

The next level in Figure 1-5 is *integration testing*. At this level, different units are composed to create composite components. Integration testing aims to assess the interaction between the involved units and expose defects in their interfaces.

Then, at the *system testing* and *end-to-end* (E2E) levels, we test the software system as a whole. We need to deploy the SUT and verify its high-level features to carry out these levels. The difference between system/end-to-end and integration testing is that the former involves all the system components and the final user (typically impersonated). In other words, system and end-to-end testing assess the SUT through the User Interface (UI). This UI can be graphical (GUI) or nongraphical (e.g., text-based or other types).

The Test Pyramid

The *test pyramid* is a classical representation of the levels of testing. Mike Cohn first coined this concept in 2009. In his original conception, Cohn recommended a large number of unit tests as the basis of testing efforts. The following levels (e.g., integration tests) are less numerous in each stage but typically more expensive (in terms of development and maintenance effort) and slow (in terms of execution time). This proposal might be impractical for many projects because unit tests are not always from a comprehensive testing suite. For this reason, other authors define different shapes for the levels of testing, such as the *testing trophy* (in which the intermediate layer, i.e., the integration test, is the largest). Since the relevance of the different test categories can vary from one project to another, I use a basic stack structure to represent the different levels of testing.

Figure 1-6 illustrates the difference between system and end-to-end testing. As you can see, on the one hand, end-to-end testing involves the software system and its dependent subsystems (e.g., database or external services). On the other hand, system testing comprises only the software system, and these external dependencies are typically mocked.

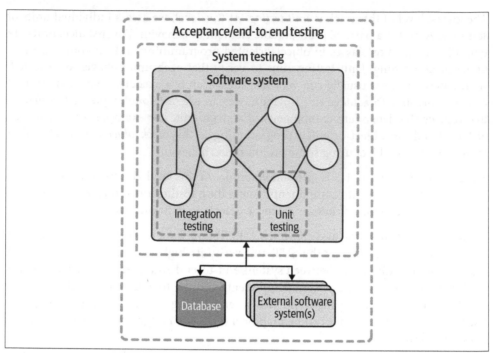

Figure 1-6. Component-based representation of the different levels of testing

Acceptance testing is the top tier of the presented stack. At this level, the final user participates in the testing process. The objective of acceptance testing is to decide whether the software system meets end-user expectations. As you can see in Figure 1-6, like end-to-end testing, acceptance testing validates the whole system and its dependencies. Therefore, acceptance tests also use the UI to carry out the SUT validation.

 The primary purpose of Selenium WebDriver is to implement end-to-end tests. Nevertheless, we can use WebDriver to carry out system testing when mocking the backend calls made by the website under test. Moreover, we can use Selenium WebDriver in conjunction with a Behavior-Driven Development (BDD) tool to implement acceptance tests (see Chapter 9).

Verification and Validation

The down levels of the test stack we have seen (unit, integration, system, and end-to-end testing) belong to *development testing*. Development testing is a process carried out by the team that produces the software system (i.e., developers, testers, etc.) during the construction phase of the software development lifecycle. Development testing is a type of *verification* since we assess that the software meets its stated functional and nonfunctional requirements (i.e., its specification). Using the classical definition stated by Barry Boehm in 1984, verification allows answering the following question: "*Are we building the product right?*"

The top level of the test stack represented in Figure 1-5 (i.e., acceptance testing) belongs to *user testing* since it involves the final user in the testing process. Acceptance testing is a type of *validation* because its objective is to prove the software system meets end-user expectations. Validation is a more general process than verification since the system specification does not always reflect the user's real wishes or needs. Thus, according to Boehm, validation allows answering the question "*Are we building the right product?*"

Types of Testing

Depending on the strategy for designing test cases, we can implement different types of tests. The two principal types of testing are:

Functional testing (also known as behavioral or closed-box testing)
> Evaluates the compliance of a piece of software with the expected behavior (i.e., its functional requirements).

Structural testing (also known as clear-box testing)
> Determines if the program-code structure is faulty. To that aim, testers should know the internal logic of a piece of software.

The difference between these testing types is that functional tests are responsibility-based, while structural tests are implementation-based. Both types can be performed at any test level (unit, integration, system, end-to-end, or acceptance). Nevertheless, structural tests are commonly done at the unit or integration level since these levels enable more direct control of the code execution flow.

 Black-box and *white-box* testing are other names for functional and structural testing, respectively. Nevertheless, these designations are not recommended since the tech industry is trying to adopt more inclusive terms and use neutral terminology instead of potentially harmful language.

There are different flavors of functional testing. For example:

UI testing (known as GUI testing when the UI is graphical)
> Evaluates if the visual elements of an application meet the expected functionality. Note that UI testing is different from the system and end-to-end testing levels since the former tests the interface itself, and the latter evaluates the whole system through the UI.

Negative testing
> Evaluates the SUT under unexpected conditions (e.g., expected exceptions). This term is the counterpart of the regular functional testing (sometimes called *positive testing*), in which we assess if the SUT behaves as expected (i.e., its *happy path*).

Cross-browser testing
> This is specific for web applications. It aims to verify the compatibility of websites and applications in different web browsers (types, versions, or operating systems).

A third miscellaneous testing type, *nonfunctional testing*, includes testing strategies that assess the quality attributes of a software system (i.e., its nonfunctional requirements). Common methods of nonfunctional testing include, but are not limited to:

Performance testing
> Assesses different metrics of software systems, such as response time, stability, reliability, or scalability. The objective of performance testing is not finding bugs but finding system bottlenecks. There are two common subtypes of performance testing:

Load testing
> Increases the usage on the system by simulating multiple concurrent users to verify if it can operate in the defined boundaries.

Stress testing
> Exercises a system beyond its operational capacity to identify the actual limits at which the system breaks.

Security testing
> Tries to evaluate security concerns, such as confidentiality (disclosure of information protection), authentication (ensuring the user identity), or authorization (determining user rights and privileges), among others.

Usability testing
> Evaluates how user-friendly a software application is. This assessment is also called User eXperience (UX) testing. A subtype of usability testing is:

A/B testing
> Compares different variations of the same application to determine which one is more effective for its end users.

Accessibility testing
> Evaluates if a system is usable by people with disabilities.

 We use Selenium WebDriver primarily to implement functional tests (i.e., interacting with a web application UI to assess the application behavior). It is unlikely to use WebDriver to implement structural tests. In addition, although it is not its principal usage, we can use WebDriver to implement nonfunctional tests, e.g., for load, security, accessibility, or localization (assessment of specific locale settings) testing (see Chapter 9).

Testing Methodologies

The *software development lifecycle* is the set of activities, actions, and tasks required to create software systems in software engineering. The moment at which software engineers design and implement test cases in the overall development lifecycle depends on the specific development process (such as iterative, waterfall, or agile, to name a few). Two of the most relevant testing methodologies are:

Test Driven Development (TDD)
> TDD is a methodology in which we design and implement tests before the actual software design and implementation. At the beginning of the 21st century, TDD became popular with the rise of *agile* software development methodologies, such as Extreme Programming (XP). In TDD, a developer first writes an (initially failing) automated test for a given feature. Then, the developer creates a piece of code to pass that test. Finally, the developer refactors the code to achieve or improve readability and maintainability.

Test Last Development (TLD)
> TLD is a methodology in which we design and implement tests after implementing the SUT. This practice is typical in traditional software development processes, such as waterfall (sequential), incremental (multi-waterfall), spiral (risk-oriented multi-waterfall), or Rational Unified Process (RUP).

Another relevant testing methodology is *Behavior-Driven Development* (BDD). BDD is a testing practice derived from TDD, and consequently, we design tests at the early stages of the software development lifecycle in BDD. To that aim, conversations occur between the final user and the development team (typically with the project leader, manager, or analysts). These conversations formalize a common understanding of the desired behavior and the software system. As a result, we create acceptance tests in terms of one or more *scenarios* following a *Given-When-Then* structure:

Given

Initial context at the beginning of the scenario

When

Event that triggers the scenario

Then

Expected outcome

 TLD is a common practice used to implement Selenium Web-Driver. In other words, developers/testers do not implement a WebDriver test until the SUT is available. Nevertheless, different methodologies are also possible. For instance, BDD is a common approach when using WebDriver with Cucumber (see Chapter 9).

Closely related to the domain of testing methodologies, we find the concept of *Continuous Integration* (CI). CI is a software development practice where members of a software project build, test, and integrate their work continuously. Grady Booch first coined the term CI in 1991. Now it is a popular strategy to create software.

As Figure 1-7 shows, CI has three separate stages. First, we use a *source code repository*, a hosting facility to store and share the source code of a software project. We typically use a *version control system* (VCS) to manage this repository. A VCS is a tool that keeps track of the source code, who made each change, and when (sometimes called *patch*).

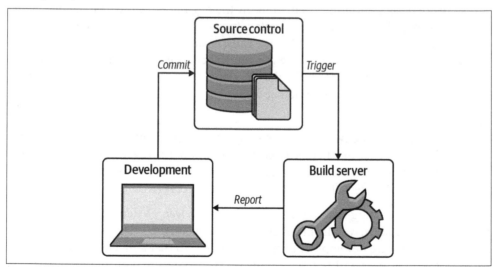

Figure 1-7. CI generic process

Git, initially developed by Linus Torvalds, is the preferred VCS today. Other alternatives are a *concurrent versions system* (CVS) or Subversion (SVN). On top of Git, several *code hosting platforms* (such as GitHub, GitLab, or Bitbucket) provide collaborative cloud repository hosting services for developing, sharing, and maintaining software.

Developers synchronize a local repository (or simply, *repo*) copy in their local environments. Then, they do the coding work using that local copy, committing new changes to the remote repository (typically daily). The basic idea of CI is that every commit triggers the build and test of the software with the new changes. The test suite executed to assess that a patch does not break the build is called a *regression test*. A regression suite can contain tests of different types, including unit, integration, end-to-end, etc.

When the number of tests is too large for regression testing, we typically choose only a part of the relevant tests from the whole suite. There are different strategies to select these tests, for instance, *smoke testing* (i.e., tests that ensure the critical functionality) or *sanity testing* (i.e., tests that evaluate the basic functionality). Lastly, we can execute the complete suite as a scheduled task (typically nightly).

We need to use a server-side infrastructure called a *build server* to implement a CI pipeline. The build server usually reports a problem to the original developer when the regression tests fail. Table 1-8 provides a summary of several build servers.

Table 1-8. Build servers

Name	Description	License	Maintainer	Website
Bamboo	Easy use with Jira (issue tracker) and Bitbucket	Commercial	Atlassian	*https://www.atlassian.com/software/bamboo*
GitHub Actions	Integrated build server in GitHub	Free for public repositories	Microsoft	*https://github.com/features/actions*
GitLab CI/CD	Integrated build server in GitLab	Free for public repositories	GitLab	*https://docs.gitlab.com/ee/ci*
Jenkins	Open source automation server	MIT	Jenkins team	*https://www.jenkins.io*

I use a GitHub repository (*https://github.com/bonigarcia/selenium-webdriver-java*) to publish and maintain the test examples presented in this book. GitHub Actions is the build server for this repo (see Chapter 2).

We can extend a typical CI pipeline in two ways (see Figure 1-8):

Continuous Delivery (CD)
> After CI, the build server deploys the release to a staging environment (i.e., a replica of a production environment for testing purposes) and executes the automated acceptance tests (if any).

Continuous Deployment
> The build server deploys the software release to the production environment as the final step.

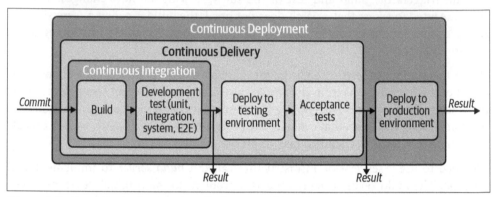

Figure 1-8. Continuous Integration, Delivery, and Deployment pipeline

Close to CI, the term DevOps (development and operations) has gained momentum. DevOps is a software methodology that promotes communication and collaboration between different teams in a software project to develop and deliver software efficiently. These teams include developers, testers, QA (quality assurance), operations (infrastructure), etc.

Test Automation Tools

We need to use some tooling to implement, execute, and control automated tests effectively. One of the most relevant categories for testing tools is the *unit testing framework*. The original framework in the unit testing family (also known as *xUnit*) is SmalltalkUnit (or SUnit). SUnit is a unit test framework for the Smalltalk language created by Kent Beck in 1999. Erich Gamma ported SUnit to Java, creating JUnit. Since then, JUnit has been very popular, inspiring other unit testing frameworks. Table 1-9 summarizes the most relevant unit testing frameworks in different languages.

Table 1-9. Unit testing frameworks

Name	Language	Description	License	Maintainer	Website
JUnit	Java	Reference implementation of xUnit family	EPL	JUnit team	https://junit.org
TestNG	Java	Inspired by JUnit and NUnit, including extra features	Apache 2.0	Cedric Beust	https://testng.org
Mocha	JavaScript	Test framework for Node.js and the browser	MIT	OpenJS Foundation	https://mochajs.org
Jest	JavaScript	Focused on simplicity with a focus on web applications	MIT	Facebiij	https://jestjs.io
Karma	JavaScript	Allows you to execute JavaScript tests in web browsers	MIT	Karma team	https://karma-runner.github.io
NUnit	.Net	Unit testing framework for all .Net languages (C#, Visual Basic, and F#)	MIT	.NET Foundation	https://nunit.org
unittest	Python	Unit testing framework included as a standard library as of Python 2.1	PSF License	Python Software Foundation	https://docs.python.org/library/unittest.html
minitest	Ruby	Complete suite of testing utilities for Ruby	MIT	Seattle Ruby Brigade	https://github.com/settlers/minitest

An important common characteristic of the xUnit family is the test structure, composed of four phases (see Figure 1-9):

Setup
   The test case initializes the SUT to exhibit the expected behavior.

Exercise
   The test case interacts with the SUT. As a result, the test gets an outcome from the SUT.

Verify
   The test case decides if the obtained outcome from the SUT is as expected. To that aim, the test contains one or more assertions. An *assertion* (or predicate) is a boolean-value function that checks if an expected condition is true. The execution of the assertions generates a test verdict (typically, pass or fail).

Teardown
   The test case puts the SUT back into the initial state.

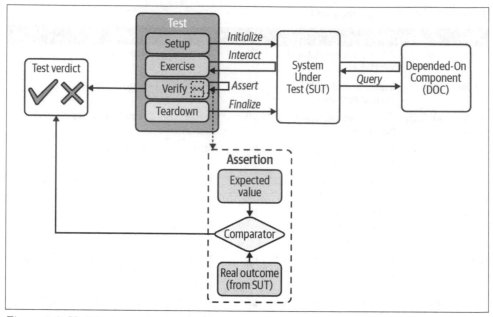

Figure 1-9. Unit test generic structure

 We can use unit testing frameworks in conjunction with other libraries or utilities to implement any test type. For example, as explained in Chapter 2, we use JUnit and TestNG to embed the call to the Selenium WebDriver API, implementing end-to-end tests for web applications.

The stages of setup and teardown are optional in a unit test case. Although it is not strictly mandatory, verifying is highly recommended. Even if unit testing frameworks include capabilities to implement assertions, it is common to incorporate third-party *assertions libraries*. These libraries aim to improve the test code's readability by providing a rich set of fluent assertions. In addition, these libraries offer enhanced error messages to help testers understand the cause of a failure. Table 1-10 contains a summary of some of the most relevant assertion libraries for Java.

Table 1-10. Assertion libraries for Java

Name	Description	License	Maintainer	Website
AssertJ	Fluent assertions Java library	Apache 2.0	AssertJ team	*https://assertj.github.io/doc*
Hamcrest	Java library of matchers aimed to create flexible assertions	BSD	Hamcrest team	*http://hamcrest.org*
Truth	Fluent assertions for Java and Android	Apache 2.0	Google	*https://truth.dev*

As you can see in Figure 1-9, the SUT usually can query another component, named the *Depended-On Component* (DOC). In some cases (e.g., at the unit or system testing level), we might want to isolate the SUT from the DOC(s). We can find a wide variety of mock libraries to achieve this isolation.

Table 1-11 shows a comprehensive summary of some of these mock libraries for Java.

Table 1-11. Mock libraries for Java

Name	Level	Description	License	Maintainer	Website
EasyMock	Unit	It allows mocking objects for unit testing using Java annotations	Apache	EasyMock team	*https://easymock.org*
Mockito	Unit	Mocking Java library for mock creation and verification	MIT	Mockito team	*https://site.mockito.org*
JMockit	Integration	It allows out-of-container integration testing for Java EE and Spring-based apps	Open	JMockit team	*https://jmockit.github.io*
MockServer	System	Mocking library for any system integrated via HTTP or HTTPS with Java clients	Apache 2.0	James Bloom	*https://www.mock-server.com*
WireMock	System	Tool for simulating HTTP-based services	Apache 2.0	Tom Akehurst	*https://wiremock.org*

The last category of testing tools we analyze in this section is BDD, a development process that creates acceptance tests. There are plenty of alternatives to implement this approach. For instance, Table 1-12 shows a condensed summary of relevant BDD frameworks.

Table 1-12. BDD frameworks

Name	Language	Description	License	Maintainer	Website
Cucumber	Ruby, Java, JavaScript, Python	Testing framework to created automated acceptance tests following a BDD approach	MIT	SmartBear Software	*https://cucumber.io*
FitNesse	Java	Standalone collaborative wiki and acceptance testing framework	CPL	FitNesse team	*http://fitnesse.org*
JBehave	Java, Groovy, Kotlin, Ruby, Scala	BDD framework for all JVM languages	BSD-3-Clause	JBehave team	*https://jbehave.org*
Jasmine	JavaScript	BDD framework for JavaScript	MIT	Jasmine team	*https://jasmine.github.io*
Capybara	Ruby	Web-based acceptance test framework that simulates scenarios for user stories	MIT	Thomas Walpole	*https://teamcapybara.github.io/capybara*

Name	Language	Description	License	Maintainer	Website
Serenity BDD	Java, Javascript	Automated acceptance testing library	Apache 2.0	Serenity BDD team	https://serenity-bdd.info

Summary and Outlook

Selenium has come a long way since its inception in 2004. Many practitioners consider it the de facto standard solution to develop end-to-end tests for web applications, and it is used by thousands of projects worldwide. In this chapter, you have seen the foundations of the Selenium project (made up of WebDriver, Grid, and IDE). In addition, Selenium has a rich ecosystem and active community. WebDriver is the heart of the Selenium project, and it is a library that provides an API to control different web browsers (e.g., Chrome, Firefox, Edge, etc.) programmatically. Table 1-13 contains a comprehensive overview of the primary and secondary uses of Selenium WebDriver.

Table 1-13. Selenium WebDriver primary and secondary usages

	Primary	Secondary (other usages)
Purpose	Automated testing	Web scraping, web-based administration tasks
Test level	End-to-end testing	System testing (mocking backend calls) Acceptance testing (e.g., using with Cucumber)
Test type	Functional testing (ensuring expected behavior) Cross-browser testing (compatibility in different web browsers) Regression testing (ensuring build after each commit in CI)	Nonfunctional testing (e.g., load, security, accessibility, or localization)
Test methodology	TLD (implementing tests when SUT is available)	BDD (defining user scenarios at early development stages)

In the next chapter, you discover how to set up a Java project using Maven or Gradle as build tools. This project will contain end-to-end tests for web applications using JUnit and TestNG as the unit testing frameworks and calls to the Selenium WebDriver API. In addition, you will learn how to control different web browsers (e.g., Chrome, Firefox, or Edge) with a basic test case (the Selenium WebDriver's version of the classic *hello world*).

CHAPTER 2

Preparing for Testing

This chapter aims to implement your first end-to-end test using Selenium WebDriver and the Java language. To do that, we first review the technical requirements in terms of previous knowledge, hardware, and software. Second, this chapter provides an overview for setting up a Java project that includes Selenium WebDriver tests. You can use a build tool like Maven or Gradle to ease the project setup. Finally, you will learn to implement a basic end-to-end test with Selenium WebDriver, i.e., a *hello world* test. We will implement this test in several flavors, using different web browsers (such as Chrome, Edge, or Firefox) and unit testing frameworks (JUnit and TestNG). Remember that every code example in this book is available in an open source GitHub repository (*https://github.com/bonigarcia/selenium-webdriver-java*). Thus, you can reuse the content and configuration of this repository as the foundation for your own tests.

Requirements

The first requirement to start using Selenium WebDriver with Java is comprehending the Java language and object-oriented programming. It is not necessary to be an expert, but basic knowledge about it is required. Then, you can use Selenium WebDriver in any mainstream operating system: Windows, Linux, or macOS. Therefore, you can select the computer type you prefer. In principle, there are no specific requirements about its hardware in terms of memory, CPU, hard disk, etc., so any mid-tier computer will do.

Java Virtual Machine

Next, you need a Java Virtual Machine (JVM) installed on your computer. There are two types of distributions for the JVM. The first option is the Java Runtime Environment (JRE), which includes the JVM and the Java standard API. The second option is the Java Development Kit (JDK), which is the JRE plus a Software Development Kit (SDK) for Java (such as the `javac` compiler and other tools). Since we are developing in Java, I recommend using JDK (although some IDEs also incorporate an SDK for Java). For the Java version, I recommend using at least JDK 8 since it is the long-term support version commonly supported in many Java projects at the time of this writing.

Text Editor or IDE

To code our Java tests, we need a text editor or IDE. IDEs provide an excellent experience for development because they have a full-fledged environment (for coding, running, debugging, autocompletion, etc.). Nevertheless, you can get similar practice using any text editor you like, used in conjunction with command-line tools (for running, debugging, etc.). Overall, it depends on your personal preferences to choose one or another. Some popular alternatives for text editors are Sublime Text (*https://www.sublimetext.com*), Atom (*https://atom.io*), Notepad++ (*https://notepad-plusplus.org*), or Vim (*https://www.vim.org*), among others. IDEs include Eclipse (*https://www.eclipse.org*), IntelliJ IDEA (*https://www.jetbrains.com/idea*), NetBeans (*https://netbeans.apache.org*), or Visual Studio Code (*https://code.visualstudio.com*).

Browsers and Drivers

An initial way to carry out automation with Selenium WebDriver is to use local browsers. I consider the following browsers for this book: Chrome, Edge, and Firefox. I refer to them as *main browsers* for several reasons. First, they are very popular worldwide, and because we are testing web applications with Selenium WebDriver, we want to use the same browser as our potential users. Second, these browsers are *evergreen* (i.e., they upgrade themselves automatically). Third, these browsers are available for the major operating systems: Windows, Linux, and macOS (unlike Safari, which is also a popular browser but is only available on macOS). Lastly, these browsers are available in the Continuous Integration (CI) environment used in the GitHub repository (i.e., GitHub Actions).

The last requirement for controlling web browsers with Selenium WebDriver is the driver binaries: chromedriver (for Chrome), msedgedriver (for Edge), and geckodriver (for Firefox). As discussed in Chapter 1, driver management involves three steps: download, setup, and maintenance. To avoid the potential problems explained in that chapter, I strongly recommend automating this process with WebDriverManager (*https://bonigarcia.dev/webdrivermanager*).

Appendix B provides fine-grained details about the automated driver management process performed by WebDriverManager. In addition, and just in case you need it for some reason, this appendix explains how to carry out the driver management manually.

Build Tools

Another important component is the *build tool*. Build tools are software utilities used to automate the creation of executable applications from source code. These tools ease project management in terms of dependencies management, compilation, packaging, test execution, and deployment. Overall, build tools are a convenient way to automate the development of software projects, both in build servers (e.g., GitHub Actions) and developer machines. Therefore, I highly recommend using a build tool to set up your project. The alternatives we cover in this book are:

Maven (https://maven.apache.org)
> An open source build automation tool maintained by the Apache Software Foundation. It is used primarily for Java projects, although it also supports other languages such as C#, Ruby, or Scala.

Gradle (https://gradle.org)
> Another open source build automation tool for software development. It supports Java and other languages such as Kotlin, Groovy, Scala, C/C++, or JavaScript.

The recommended versions are Maven 3+ and Gradle 6+. For completeness, I use both build tools in the example repository. Again, the final choice to use one or another depends on your preferences.

If you plan to use an IDE for developing and running your tests, a build tool is not strictly necessary. Nevertheless, I recommend installing at least one of these tools in your computer to replicate the environment typically used in build servers (e.g., Jenkins, GitHub Actions, etc.).

Optional Software

In addition to the software already explained, some other programs are convenient to make the most of this book. First, you can use Git (*https://git-scm.com*) for source code management. Since the test examples presented in this book are available on GitHub, you can use Git to fork (or clone) and update this repository.

The second optional tool is Docker (*https://www.docker.com*). In this book, I show you how to use Docker to execute containerized browsers (see Chapter 6). For this reason, I strongly recommend you install a *Docker Engine* on your computer (it is available for Linux, macOS, and Windows 10).

Finally, you can use different web browsers if you need them. In addition to the main browsers (Chrome, Edge, and Firefox), it is possible to use other browsers with Selenium WebDiver, such as Safari (*https://www.apple.com/safari*) in macOS, or Opera (*https://www.opera.com*), Chromium (*https://www.chromium.org*), and HtmlUnit (*https://htmlunit.sourceforge.io*) (a headless browser, i.e., GUI-less browser) in any operating system.

Legacy Browsers

In addition to the browsers already presented, you can use even more browsers with Selenium WebDriver. However, I do not recommend these browsers since they are deprecated and not maintained anymore. These browsers are:

Internet Explorer
> Microsoft's web browser for Windows systems, first released in 1995 and discontinued in 2022

PhantomJS
> Headless browser, first released in 2011 and discontinued in 2018

Project Setup

You can find all the code examples of this book in a GitHub repository (*https://github.com/bonigarcia/selenium-webdriver-java*). This repository is open source, released under the terms of the Apache 2.0 license. The repository has multiple aims. First, it is convenient to group all the examples in a single site. Second, you can use its setup (Maven or Gradle) as a skeleton for your projects.

 The following subsections describe the general requirements to create a Java project containing Selenium WebDriver tests. Appendix C provides low-level details about the configuration of the examples repositories.

Project Layout

The *project layout* is the directory structure used to store the different assets of a software project (e.g., source code, binary files, static resources, and so on). Maven and Gradle use an equivalent layout for Java projects. We can execute the examples repository with both build tools, thanks to this.

As illustrated in Figure 2-1, the following set of folders (labeled as *scaffolding folders*) are identical in both build tools:

src/main/java
    Application source code (i.e., Java files)

src/main/resources
    Application resources files (i.e., properties, configuration files, etc.)

src/test/java
    Test source code (i.e., Java files used for testing)

src/test/resources
    Test resources files (i.e., additional assets used for testing)

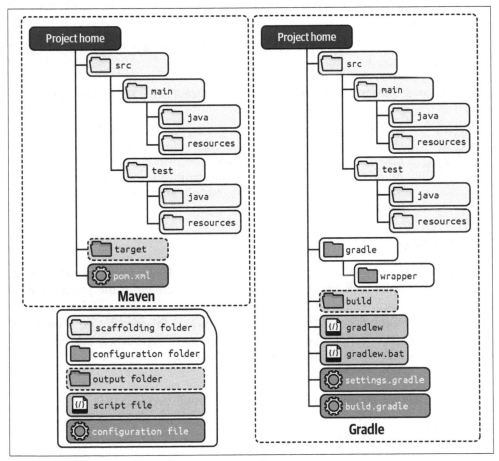

Figure 2-1. Project layout in Maven and Gradle

The rest of the project layout is different in both build tools. The first difference is the configuration file. On the one hand, this file is unique and called `pom.xml` (Project Object Model) in Maven. On the other hand, there are two files in Gradle for configuration, called `settings.gradle` and `build.gradle`. The second difference between Maven and Gradle is the output folder. In both cases, the build tools created this folder to save the resulting build (i.e., compiled classes, resulting packaged files, etc.). The name of this folder is `target` in Maven and `build` in Gradle. Finally, Gradle contains a set of folders and files for the so-called Gradle *wrapper*. This wrapper is a script file (called `gradlew` for Unix-like systems and `gradlew.bat` for Windows) that provides the following benefits:

- Build a project without installing Gradle on the local machine
- Require use of a given version (which can be different from the locally installed instance of Gradle)
- Upgrade to a new version easily by changing the wrapper artifacts (in folder `gradle/wrapper`)

As of version 4, Maven has adopted the wrapper concept using the `mvnw` script.

 It is beyond the scope of this book to explain all the features provided by Maven and Gradle. Nevertheless, you can find more information about their build lifecycle and typical commands in Appendix C. For further information, consider reading the official Maven (*https://maven.apache.org/guides*) and Gradle (*https://docs.gradle.org*) documentation.

Dependencies

The dependencies of a software project are the required libraries or plug-ins. Among other features, build tools enable the automated management of the project dependencies. To that aim, we need to specify the *coordinates* of such dependencies in the project configuration file (see the following subsections for specifics on Maven and Gradle). The coordinates of a Java project are a group of three labels that univocally identify this project (e.g., a library, plug-in, etc.), namely:

groupId
    Organization, company, person, etc., that created the project.

artifactId
    Unique name that identifies the project.

```
version
```
Particular release of the project. By default, I recommend you use the latest version of every release.

Semantic Versioning

A popular way to select a project version is Semantic Versioning (*https://semver.org*), also called *SemVer*. According to the SemVer manifesto, a release has three parts separated with dots, i.e., `MAJOR.MINOR.PATCH`. In a nutshell, `MAJOR` identifies incompatible changes, `MINOR` identifies backward-compatible changes, and `PATCH` identifies bug fixes.

This section explains the Java dependencies I use in the examples repository. First, of course, we need Selenium WebDriver to carry out browser automation. This dependency is the only one strictly mandatory. Then, I recommend using additional dependencies for automated driver management utility, unit testing framework, fluent assertions, and logging. The remainder of this section explains the motivation and basic use of each of these utilities.

Selenium WebDriver

One of the most relevant concepts of Selenium WebDriver is the `WebDriver` hierarchy, which is a collection of classes aimed at controlling different web browsers. As you can see in Figure 2-2, this hierarchy follows the object-oriented programming paradigm. On the top, we find the `WebDriver` interface, the parent of the whole structure. The lower part of the hierarchy corresponds to Java classes that drive single browsers. For instance, we need to use an instance of the class `ChromeDriver` to control a local Chrome browser. Table 2-1 shows a comprehensive summary of the main classes of the `WebDriver` hierarchy and their corresponding target browsers.

Table 2-1. Description of the `WebDriver` hierarchy

Package	Class	Browser
`org.openqa.selenium.chrome`	`ChromeDriver`	Chrome
`org.openqa.selenium.edge`	`EdgeDriver`	Edge
`org.openqa.selenium.firefox`	`FirefoxDriver`	Firefox
`org.openqa.selenium.safari`	`SafariDriver`	Safari
`org.openqa.selenium.opera`	`OperaDriver`	Opera
`org.openqa.selenium.ie`	`InternetExplorerDriver`	Internet Explorer
`org.openqa.selenium.remote`	`RemoteWebDriver`	Remote browsers (see Chapter 6)

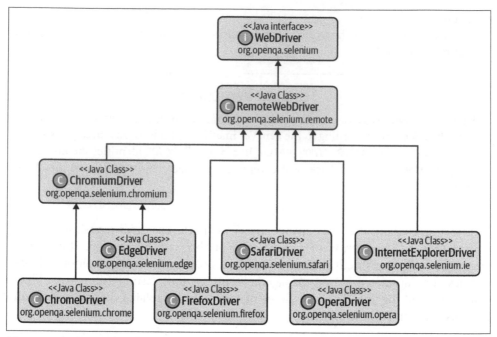

Figure 2-2. Hierarchy of the WebDriver *object*

Automated driver management

It is mandatory to resolve the corresponding driver before instantiating an object of the WebDriver hierarchy. For example, to control Chrome with ChromeDriver, we first need to have installed this browser on the local machine. Second, we need to manage chromedriver. To avoid the potential problems related to manual driver management (see Chapter 1), I recommend carrying out the whole driver management process (download, setup, and maintenance) in an automated manner. Concerning Java, the reference implementation is WebDriverManager (*https://bonigarcia.dev/webdrivermanager*), a Selenium WebDriver helper library that allows automated driver management. This section explains how to use WebDriverManager as a Java dependency.

Once the WebDriverManager dependency is resolved in our project (see Appendix C for the configuration details), we can use the WebDriverManager API to manage drivers. This API provides a set of singletons (called *managers*) to download, set up, and maintain drivers. These singletons are accessible through the WebDriverManager class. For instance, we need to invoke the method chromedriver() to manage the driver required by Chrome, i.e., chromedriver, as follows:

```
WebDriverManager.chromedriver().setup();
WebDriver driver = new ChromeDriver();
```

Table 2-2 summarizes the basic WebDriverManager calls for all the supported browsers. In addition to these basic calls (i.e., the method `setup()`), WebDriverManager exposes a fluent API for advanced configuration. See Appendix B for more details about the WebDriverManager methodology, configuration capabilities, and other uses, such as a command-line interface tool (from the shell), as a server (using a RESTlike [REpresentational State Transfer] API), as an agent (using Java instrumentation), or as a Docker container.

Table 2-2. WebDriverManager basic calls

WebDriverManager basic call	Browser	Driver
`WebDriverManager.chromedriver().setup();`	Chrome	chromedriver
`WebDriverManager.edgedriver().setup();`	Edge	msedgedriver
`WebDriverManager.firefoxdriver().setup();`	Firefox	geckodriver
`WebDriverManager.operadriver().setup();`	Opera	operadriver
`WebDriverManager.chromiumdriver().setup();`	Chromium	chromedriver
`WebDriverManager.iedriver().setup();`	Internet Explorer	IEDriverServer

Unit testing frameworks

As explained in Chapter 1, unit testing frameworks are the basis for creating different types of tests. This book will teach you how to implement end-to-end tests for web applications using Selenium WebDriver. Hence, I suggest embedding the Selenium WebDriver calls within tests created with a particular unit testing framework. The alternative I recommend is one of these options: JUnit 4, JUnit 5 (alone or in conjunction with Selenium-Jupiter, which is an extension for Selenium WebDriver), or TestNG. The following subsections provide more details about these alternatives. My advice is to focus on the unit testing framework and the build tool you prefer to continue practicing with the examples presented in the rest of the book.

JUnit 4. JUnit is a unit testing framework for Java created by Erich Gamma and Kent Beck in 1999. It is considered the de facto standard framework for developing tests in Java. In JUnit, a *test* is a method within a Java class used for testing. As of JUnit 4, Java annotations are the building blocks for developing JUnit tests. The fundamental annotation of JUnit 4 is `@Test` since it allows identifying the method(s) that contain the test logic (i.e., the code used to exercise and verify a piece of software). In addition, there are other annotations to identify the methods used for the setup (i.e., what happens before the tests) and the teardown (i.e., what happens after the tests).

- `@BeforeClass` is executed once before all tests.
- `@Before` is executed before each test.

- @After is executed after each test.
- @BeforeClass is executed once after all tests.

Figure 2-3 shows a graphical representation of the basic test lifecycle in JUnit 4.

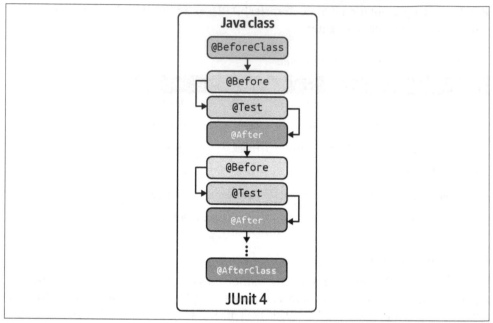

Figure 2-3. JUnit 4 test lifecycle

JUnit 5. Due to several limitations in JUnit 4 (such as monolithic architecture or impossible-to-compose JUnit runners), the JUnit team released a new major version (i.e., JUnit 5) in 2017. JUnit has been redesigned entirely in version 5, following a modular architecture consisting of three components (see Figure 2-4). The first component is the JUnit *Platform*, the foundation of the whole framework. The goal of the JUnit Platform is twofold:

- It allows the discovery and execution (sequential or parallel) of tests in the JVM through the *test launcher* API. This API is typically used by programmatic clients such as build tools and IDEs.
- It defines the *test engine* API for running tests on the JUnit Platform. This API is typically used by frameworks that provide programming models for testing.

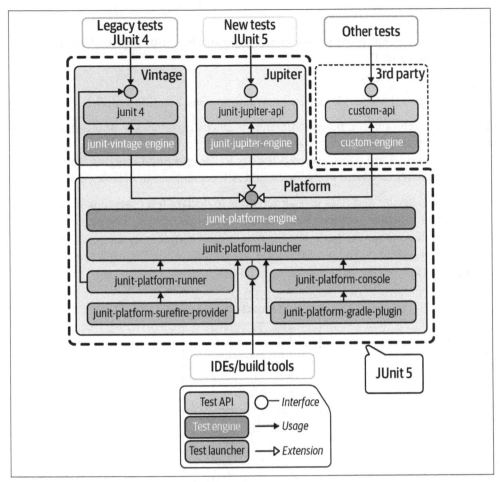

Figure 2-4. JUnit 5 architecture

Thanks to the test engine API, third-party test frameworks can execute tests on top of the JUnit Platform. Some examples of existing testing frameworks that have implemented test engines for JUnit 5 are TestNG (*https://github.com/junit-team/testng-engine*), Cucumber (*https://github.com/cucumber/cucumber-jvm*), or Spock (*https://github.com/spockframework/spock*). In addition, JUnit 5 provides two out-of-the-box implementations of the test engine API. These engines are the remaining components of the JUnit 5 architecture, namely:

Vintage

Test engine that provides backward compatibility with legacy JUnit tests (i.e., versions 3 and 4).

Jupiter

Test engine that provides a new programming and extension model

Jupiter is a relevant component of JUnit 5 since it provides a brand-new API to develop tests using a robust programming model. Some of the features of this programming model are parameterized tests, parallel execution, tagging and filtering, ordered tests, repeated and nested tests, and rich capabilities to disable (ignore) tests.

Like JUnit 4, Jupiter also uses Java annotations to declare test cases. For instance, the annotation to identify methods with testing logic is also @Test. The name of the rest of the annotations for the basic test lifecycle is a bit different in Jupiter: @BeforeAll, @BeforeEach, @AfterEach, and @AfterAll. As you can see in Figure 2-5, each of these annotations follows the same workflow of JUnit 4.

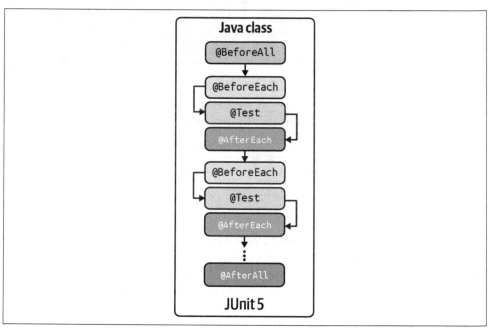

Figure 2-5. JUnit 5 test lifecycle

Thus, the structure of a Jupiter test using Selenium WebDriver and WebDriverManager is quite similar in JUnit 4 and JUnit 5. In addition to the change in the setup and teardown annotation names, the test methods (and their lifecycle) are not required to be `public` in the Jupiter programming model.

 This book will teach you the basics of Jupiter applied to end-to-end testing with Selenium WebDriver. See the *hello world* example in the next section for a complete test based on JUnit 5. Please check the JUnit 5 documentation (*https://junit.org/junit5/docs/current/user-guide*) for further details.

JUnit 5 with Selenium-Jupiter. The extension model of Jupiter allows adding custom features to the default programming model. To that aim, Jupiter provides an API that developers can extend (using interfaces called *extension points*) to provide custom functionality. The categories of these extension points are:

Test lifecycle callbacks
　　To include custom logic in different moments of the test lifecycle

Parameter resolution
　　To implement dependency injection (i.e., parameters injected in test methods or constructors)

Test templates
　　To repeat the tests based on a given context

Conditional test execution
　　To enable or disable tests depending on custom conditions

Exception handling
　　To manage Java exceptions during the test and its lifecycle

Test instance
　　To create and process test class instances

Intercepting invocations
　　To intercept calls to test code (and decide whether or not these calls proceed)

As a Jupiter developer, you can implement your custom extension or use the existing ones. Table 2-3 shows some examples of Jupiter extensions.

Table 2-3. Jupiter extensions

Name	Description	License	Maintainer	Website
JUnit Pioneer	Extension pack for Jupiter	EPL 2.0	JUnit Pioneer team	https://junit-pioneer.org
rerunner-jupiter	Extension for rerunning failed Jupiter tests	Apache 2.0	Artem Sokovets	https://github.com/artsok/rerunner-jupiter
MockitoExtension	Jupiter extension for initializing mocks and handling stubbings	MIT	Mockito team	https://github.com/mockito/mockito
QuickPerf	Library for evaluating some performance-related properties	Apache 2.0	QuickPerf team	https://github.com/quick-perf/quickperf
Selenium-Jupiter	Jupiter extension for Selenium WebDriver	Apache 2.0	Boni García	https://bonigarcia.dev/selenium-jupiter
SpringExtension	Jupiter extension for the Spring Framework	Apache 2.0	Pivotal Software	https://spring.io/projects/spring-framework

Selenium-Jupiter is an attractive option in the context of this book since it enables using Selenium WebDriver in Jupiter tests seamlessly. The bases of Selenium-Jupiter are as follows (see the next section for a *hello world* test based on Selenium-Jupiter):

Reduced boilerplate code in test cases
Thanks to the parameter resolution feature provided by the Jupiter programming model, Selenium-Jupiter allows declaring an object of the `WebDriver` hierarchy (e.g., `ChromeDriver`, `FirefoxDriver`, etc.) to control web browsers from tests as a constructor or test parameter.

Automated driver management through WebDriverManager
Thanks to the test lifecycle callbacks provided by the extension model, the use of WebDriverManager is entirely transparent for Selenium-Jupiter users.

Advanced capabilities for end-to-end testing
This includes, for instance, seamless integration with Docker, test templates (for cross-browser testing), or troubleshooting and monitoring capabilities (e.g., session recordings or configurable screenshots).

TestNG. The last unit testing framework I use in this book is TestNG. Some of the more significant features that TestNG provides are parallel test execution, test prioritization, data-driven testing using custom annotations, and the creation of detailed HTML reports.

In the same way as JUnit 4 and Jupiter, TestNG also uses Java annotations to declare tests and their lifecycle (i.e., what happens before and after each test). Again, the annotation `@Test` is used to designate test methods. Then, it provides the annotations `@BeforeClass` and `@BeforeMethod` to specify the test setup, and `@AfterMethod` and

@AfterClass for the teardown (see Figure 2-6). In addition, TestNG allows grouping the tests contained in Java classes using the following terminology:

- *Suite* consists of one or more *tests*.
- *Test* consists of one or more *classes*.
- *Class* is a Java class with testing method(s), e.g., annotated with @Test.

Following this notation, and as represented in Figure 2-6, TestNG provides additional annotations to execute custom logic before and after the suite and the test(s).

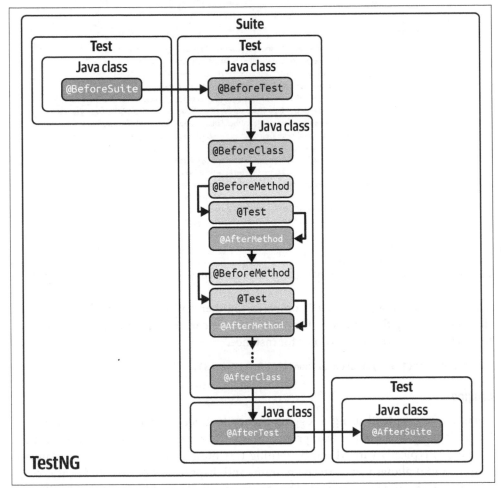

Figure 2-6. TestNG test lifecycle

Fluent assertions

As introduced in Chapter 1, there are different libraries for assertions. These libraries typically provide a rich set of fluent assertions and comprehensive error messages. Among these alternatives, I use the library AssertJ (*https://joel-costigliola.github.io/assertj*) in the examples repository. The reason is twofold. First, we can select the available methods for quickly asserting data using the autocompletion feature in IDEs (typically available using Ctrl + space after the static method `assertThat`). Figure 2-7 shows an example of the inspection of this method using an IDE (Eclipse in this example).

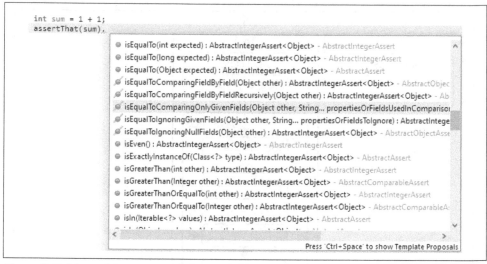

Figure 2-7. Manual inspection of the available assertion methods in AssertJ using Eclipse

The second advantage of AssertJ compared to other options is that it allows an assertions chain using dot notation. Thanks to this, we can concatenate several conditions to create more readable assertions, for instance:

```
assertThat(1 + 1).isGreaterThan(1).isLessThan(3);
```

Logging

Finally, I recommend using a logging library to trace your Java code. As you may know, logging is a simple way programmers track events when software executes. Logging is typically carried out by writing text messages into a file or the standard output, and it allows you to trace programs and diagnose problems. Today, it is common to use specific libraries to do logging effectively. These libraries provide different benefits, such as the level of granularity for messages (e.g., debug, warning, or error), timestamping, or configuration capabilities.

Hello World

We are ready to put all the pieces explained in this chapter together and implement our first end-to-end test. As you may know, a *hello world* program is a simple piece of code that many programming languages use to illustrate basic syntax. Example 2-1 shows the Selenium WebDriver's version of this classic *hello world*.

 The following example uses JUnit 5 as the unit testing framework to embed the call to Selenium WebDriver. Remember that you can find the other flavors (i.e., JUnit 4, JUnit 5 with Selenium-Jupiter, and TestNG) in the examples repository (*https://github.com/bonigar cia/selenium-webdriver-java*).

Example 2-1. Hello world using Chrome and JUnit 5

```
class HelloWorldChromeJupiterTest {

    static final Logger log = getLogger(lookup().lookupClass());

    private WebDriver driver; ❶

    @BeforeAll
    static void setupClass() {
        WebDriverManager.chromedriver().setup(); ❷
    }

    @BeforeEach
    void setup() {
        driver = new ChromeDriver(); ❸
    }

    @Test
    void test() {
        // Exercise
        String sutUrl = "https://bonigarcia.dev/selenium-webdriver-java/";
        driver.get(sutUrl); ❹
        String title = driver.getTitle(); ❺
        log.debug("The title of {} is {}", sutUrl, title); ❻

        // Verify
        assertThat(title).isEqualTo("Hands-On Selenium WebDriver with Java"); ❼
    }

    @AfterEach
    void teardown() {
        driver.quit(); ❽
    }

}
```

❶ We declare a Java attribute using the interface `WebDriver`. We use this variable in tests to control web browsers with Selenium WebDriver.

❷ In the setup for all tests within this class (i.e., executed once), we call WebDriver-Manager to manage the required driver. In this example, since we use Chrome as a browser, we need to resolve chromedriver.

❸ In the test setup (executed once per test method), we instantiate the `WebDriver` object to control Chrome. In other words, we create an object of the type `Chrome Driver`.

❹ The test logic uses the Selenium WebDriver API through the `driver` variable. First, the test exercises the System Under Test (SUT). To that aim, we open the practice site (*https://bonigarcia.dev/selenium-webdriver-java*) using the `get()` method of our `webdriver` variable (which represents a Chrome browser, in this case).

❺ We get the web page title using the method `getTitle()`.

❻ For debugging purposes, we log that title using the `DEBUG` level.

❼ The last part of the test contains an AssertJ assertion. In this case, we verify the web page title is as expected.

❽ At the end of each test, we need to close the browser. To that aim, we can invoke the method `quit()` of the `driver` object (see more info about how to close `Web Driver` objects in Chapter 3).

You can execute this test in different ways. I recommend getting a local copy of the examples repository. You can use the GitHub website to download a complete copy of the source code. Alternatively, you can use Git to clone the repo using the shell, as follows:

```
git clone https://github.com/bonigarcia/selenium-webdriver-java
```

Then, you can use Maven or Gradle (as explained in Appendix C) to run the tests from the shell. In addition, you can import the cloned Maven/Gradle projects into an IDE. IDEs provide built-in capabilities to execute the test from their GUI. For instance, Figure 2-8 shows a screenshot of the execution of the previous *hello world* test in Eclipse (in this case, using the command Run → Run As → JUnit Test). Notice that in the integrated console (at the bottom of the picture), the first traces correspond to the driver resolution by WebDriverManager. Then, the browser starts through chromedriver, and finally, we can see the test traces (concretely, the web page title).

Figure 2-8. Screenshot of the execution of the Selenium WebDriver's hello world in Eclipse

The *hello world* versions using JUnit 4 and TestNG are almost identical to JUnit 5 but use different annotations for the test lifecycle (e.g., JUnit 4's `@Before` instead of JUnit 5's `@BeforeEach`, etc.). Regarding JUnit 5 plus Selenium-Jupiter, the code is a bit more compact. Example 2-2 shows this *hello world* version. As you can see, there is no need to declare the setup and teardown. We simply need to declare the `WebDriver` object we want as a test parameter (`FirefoxDriver` in this case), and Selenium-Jupiter takes care of the driver management (also with WebDriverManager), object instantiation, and browser disposal.

Example 2-2. Hello world using Firefox and Selenium-Jupiter

```
@ExtendWith(SeleniumJupiter.class)
class HelloWorldFirefoxSelJupTest {

    @Test
    void test(FirefoxDriver driver) {
        // Same test logic than other "hello world" tests
    }

}
```

Using Additional Browsers

In addition to what I am calling *main* browsers in this book (i.e., Chrome, Edge, and Firefox), the example repository contains the *hello world* test using other browsers: Opera, Chromium, Safari, and HtmlUnitDriver (a Selenium WebDriver–compatible driver for the HtmlUnit headless browser). These tests, contained in the package `helloworld_otherbrowsers` of this repository, are slightly different from the raw *hello world* versions. For instance, Example 2-3 shows the JUnit 5 class setup of the *hello world* test using Opera. Since this browser might not be available in the machine running the test (e.g., Opera is not available in GitHub Actions), I use *assumptions* to disable the test in runtime conditionally.

Example 2-3. Class setup using Opera and JUnit 5

```
@BeforeAll
static void setupClass() {
    Optional<Path> browserPath = WebDriverManager.operadriver()
            .getBrowserPath(); ❶
    assumeThat(browserPath).isPresent(); ❷
    WebDriverManager.operadriver().setup();
}
```

❶ We use WebDriverManager to locate the browser path.

❷ If this path does not exist, we assume the browser is not installed in the system, so the test is skipped (using an AssertJ assumption).

As usual, you can find this test using other unit testing frameworks in the examples repository. The JUnit 5 and TestNG versions use the equivalent test setup to the previous snippet. Nevertheless, there is a difference when using JUnit 5 plus Selenium-Jupiter. As you can see in Example 2-4, Selenium-Jupiter simplifies the assumption logic by using a custom annotation (called `EnabledIfBrowserAvailable`) to disable tests depending on the browser availability (Safari in this example).

Example 2-4. Hello world using Safari and JUnit 5 plus Selenium-Jupiter

```
@EnabledIfBrowserAvailable(SAFARI)
@ExtendWith(SeleniumJupiter.class)
class HelloWorldSafariSelJupTest {

    @Test
    void test(SafariDriver driver) {
        // Same test logic than other "hello world" tests
    }

}
```

To control Safari with Selenium WebDriver, we need to configure Safari manually to authorize remote automation. To that aim, first, we show the develop menu by clicking on the menu option Safari → Preferences → Advanced tab. Then, we enable the "Show Develop Menu" checkbox. After that, the "Develop" menu should appear. Finally, we click on the option "Allow Remote Automation" (see Figure 2-9).

Figure 2-9. Enable Safari remote automation on macOS

Summary and Outlook

This chapter provides the foundations for developing end-to-end tests for web applications using Selenium WebDriver and Java. The first important decision you need to make is to decide in which unit testing framework to embed the Selenium WebDriver calls to implement these tests. For the sake of diversity and completeness, I propose four options in this book: JUnit 4, JUnit 5, JUnit 5 plus Selenium-Jupiter, and TestNG. They are all equivalent for basic Selenium WebDriver tests. For more advanced uses, Chapter 8 will cover the specific features of each testing framework that could be relevant to WebDriver tests (e.g., parameterized tests for cross-browser testing). Another decision you should make is to choose a build tool. In this book, I propose two options: Maven and Gradle. Once again, both are similar for standard development practices.

The second part of this book is focused on the Selenium WebDriver API and begins next. To get started, Chapter 3 covers the fundamental notions of the Selenium WebDriver API in terms of WebDriver objects, web elements location, user impersonation (keyboard and mouse actions), and waiting strategies. As usual, this chapter is guided by code examples available on the repository hosted in GitHub.

The Selenium WebDriver API

Selenium WebDriver is an open source library that allows controlling web browsers (e.g., Chrome, Edge, or Firefox, to name a few) programmatically as a real user would do. It provides a cross-browser API that you can use to implement end-to-end tests for web applications. This part of the book presents an in-depth summary of the Selenium WebDriver API. The following chapters aim to be very practical. For this reason, I explain each feature of the Selenium WebDriver API using ready-to-use tests available on the examples repository in GitHub.

CHAPTER 3

WebDriver Fundamentals

This chapter presents the elementary aspects of the Selenium WebDriver API. To that aim, we review first the different ways to create instances of the WebDriver hierarchy (e.g., ChromeDriver, EdgeDriver, FirefoxDriver, etc.). Also, we explore the main methods available in these objects. Among them, locating the different elements in a web page is essential. Thus, you will discover the possible locators, i.e., strategies to find the elements within a web page (called WebElement in the Selenium WebDriver API), such as by tag name, link text, HTML attribute (identifier, name, or class), CSS selector, or XPath. Another critical aspect of the Selenium WebDriver API covered in this chapter is the impersonation of user actions (i.e., automated interactions with web pages using the keyboard and mouse). The last part of this chapter presents the ability to wait for web elements. This feature is critical due to the dynamic and asynchronous nature of web applications.

Basic WebDriver Usage

This section covers three fundamental aspects related to WebDriver objects. First, we review the different ways to create them. Second, we study their basic operations. Finally, we analyze the different ways to dispose of these objects (typically at the end of a test, for closing the browser).

WebDriver Creation

As introduced in Chapter 2, to control browsers with Selenium WebDriver in Java, the first step is to create WebDriver instances. Thus, we need to create a Chrome Driver object when using Chrome, EdgeDriver for Edge, FirefoxDriver for Firefox, and so on. The basic way to create instances of these types is to use the new operator in Java. For example, we create a ChromeDriver object as follows:

```
WebDriver driver = new ChromeDriver();
```

The use of the operator new for creating WebDriver instances is perfectly correct, and you can use it in your tests. Nevertheless, it is worth reviewing other possibilities that can provide additional benefits depending on specific use cases for creating these objects. These alternatives are the WebDriver and the WebDriverManager builders.

WebDriver builder

The Selenium WebDriver API provides a built-in method following the *builder pattern* to create WebDriver instances. This feature is accessible through the static method builder() of the RemoteWebDriver class and provides a fluent API for creating WebDriver objects. Table 3-1 presents the available methods for this builder. Example 3-1 shows a test skeleton using the WebDriver builder.

Table 3-1. WebDriver builder methods

Method	Description
oneOf(Capabilities options)	Browser-specific capabilities
addAlternative(Capabilities options)	Alternative browser-specific capabilities (see Chapter 5)
addMetadata(String key, Object value)	Add custom metadata, typically used for requesting additional features in cloud providers (see Chapter 6)
setCapability(String capabilityName, Object value)	Individual browser-specific capabilities (see Chapter 5)
address(String uri) address(URL url) address(URI uri)	Set the address of the remote server (see Chapter 6)
config(ClientConfig config)	Specific configuration when using a remote server, such as the connection timeout or proxy settings
withDriverService(DriverService service)	Specific configuration for the local driver (e.g., chromedriver), such as its file location, used port, timeout, or arguments
build()	Last method in the builder pattern, devoted to creating a Web Driver instance

 Chapter 5 explains the details about *browser-specific capabilities* (such as ChromeOptions). At this point, we use these classes just to select a browser type (e.g., ChromeOptions for Chrome, Edge Options for Edge, or FirefoxOptions for Firefox).

Example 3-1. Test skeleton using the WebDriver builder

```
class WebDriverBuilderJupiterTest {

    WebDriver driver;

    @BeforeAll
    static void setupClass() {
        WebDriverManager.chromedriver().setup(); ❶
    }

    @BeforeEach
    void setup() {
        driver = RemoteWebDriver.builder().oneOf(new ChromeOptions()).build(); ❷
    }

    @AfterEach
    void teardown() {
        driver.quit();
    }

    @Test
    void test() {
        // TODO: use variable "driver" to call the Selenium WebDriver API
    }

}
```

❶ As usual, before the actual `WebDriver` instantiation, we resolve the required driver (chromedriver in this example) using WebDriverManager.

❷ We create the `WebDriver` instance using the WebDriver builder. Since we want to use Chrome in this test, we use a `ChromeOptions` object as the capabilities argument (using the method `oneOf()`).

From a functional point of view, this example works in the same way as the regular *hello world* tests presented in Chapter 2. Nevertheless, the WebDriver builder API easily allows specifying a different behavior. Consider the following snippet as an example. This code changes the setup method and creates a `SafariDriver` instance. Suppose the instantiation of this object is not possible (typically, when the test is not executed on macOS, and therefore, Safari is not available in the system). In that case, we use Chrome as an alternative browser.

```
    @BeforeEach
    void setup() {
        driver = RemoteWebDriver.builder().oneOf(new SafariOptions())
                .addAlternative(new ChromeOptions()).build();
    }
```

WebDriverManager builder

Another possibility to create `WebDriver` objects is using WebDriverManager. In addition to resolving drivers, as of version 5, WebDriverManager provides a `WebDriver` builder utility. Example 3-2 shows a test skeleton using this builder.

Example 3-2. Test skeleton using the WebDriverManager builder

```
class WdmBuilderJupiterTest {

    WebDriver driver;

    @BeforeEach
    void setup() {
        driver = WebDriverManager.chromedriver().create(); ❶
    }

    @AfterEach
    void teardown() {
        driver.quit();
    }

    @Test
    void test() {
        // TODO: use variable "driver" to call the Selenium WebDriver API
    }

}
```

❶ WebDriverManager resolves the required driver (chromedriver in this case) and creates an instance of the proper `WebDriver` type (`ChromeDriver` in this case) in a single line.

This approach has different benefits. First, it enables less verbose tests since the driver resolution and `WebDriver` instantiation are simultaneous. Second, it allows specifying the browser type (i.e., Chrome, Firefox, etc.) simply by selecting a specific manager (i.e., `chromedriver()`, `firefoxdriver()`, etc.). Moreover, we can easily parameterize the selection of a manager to create cross-browser tests (see Chapter 8). Finally, the WebDriverManager allows you to specify browser-specific capabilities (see Chapter 5) and effortlessly use browsers in a Docker container (see Chapter 6).

WebDriverManager keeps a reference to `WebDriver` objects created using this approach. In addition, it launches a shutdown hook to watch the correct disposal of `WebDriver` instances. If `WebDriver` sessions are live when the JVM is shutting down, WebDriverManager quits these browser(s). You can play with this feature by removing the `teardown()` method of the example before.

Although WebDriverManager quits the `WebDriver` objects automatically, I recommend you do it explicitly in each test. Otherwise, in the typical case of executing a test suite, all browsers remain open until the end of the test suite execution.

WebDriver Methods

The `WebDriver` interface provides a group of methods that are the basis of the Selenium WebDriver API. Table 3-2 presents a summary of these methods. Example 3-3 shows a basic test using several of these methods.

Table 3-2. WebDriver methods

Method	Return	Description
get(String url)	void	Load a web page in the current browser.
getCurrentUrl()	String	Get the URL currently loaded in the browser.
getTitle()	String	Get the title (`<title>` HTML tag) of the current web page.
findElement(By by)	WebElement	Find the first `WebElement` using a given locator in the current web page. In other words, if several elements match the locator, the first one (in the Document Object Model [DOM]) is returned (see "Locating WebElements" on page 59 for further details).
findElements(By by)	List<WebElement>	Find every `WebElement` using a given locator in the current web page (see also "Locating WebElements" on page 59).
getPageSource()	String	Get the HTML source code of the current web page.
navigate()	Navigation	Access the browser history and navigate to a given URL (see Chapter 4).
getWindowHandle()	String	Get the *window handle*, i.e., a unique identifier for the open window in the current browser (see Chapter 4).
getWindowHandles()	Set<String>	Get the set of window handles currently open in the current browser (see also Chapter 4).
switchTo()	TargetLocator	Select a frame or window in the current browser (see Chapter 4).
manage()	Options	Generic utility for managing different aspects of the browser (e.g., browser size and position, cookies, timeouts, or logs).
close()	void	Close the current window, quitting the browser if there are no more windows opened.
quit()	void	Close all windows and quit the browser.

From now on, I illustrate the examples showing only the test logic. These tests use a `WebDriver` object created before the test (in the setup method) and closed after the test (in the teardown method). As a convention, I show the JUnit 5 tests in the book (although you can find them also for JUnit 4, Selenium-Jupiter, and TestNG in the examples repository).

Example 3-3. Test using several basic methods of the Selenium WebDriver API

```
@Test
void testBasicMethods() {
    String sutUrl = "https://bonigarcia.dev/selenium-webdriver-java/";
    driver.get(sutUrl); ❶

    assertThat(driver.getTitle())
            .isEqualTo("Hands-On Selenium WebDriver with Java"); ❷
    assertThat(driver.getCurrentUrl()).isEqualTo(sutUrl); ❸
    assertThat(driver.getPageSource()).containsIgnoringCase("</html>"); ❹
}
```

❶ We open the practice website.

❷ We verify the page title is as expected.

❸ We confirm the current URL is still the same.

❹ We check that the source HTML of the page contains a given tag.

Convention for Test Names and Classes in the Examples Repository

For ease of locating tests in the examples repository, I follow a naming convention. The name of each presented test always starts with the word test followed by a descriptive label. Then, I use this label as the prefix of the Java class containing the test. For instance, you can find the previous test (called testBasicMethods) in the classes BasicMethodsJUnit4Test (using JUnit 4), BasicMethodsJupiterTest (using JUnit 5), BasicMethodsSelJupTest (using JUnit 5 plus Selenium-Jupiter), and Basic MethodsNGTest (using TestNG).

Session Identifier

Each time we instantiate a WebDriver object, the underlying driver (e.g., chrome-driver, geckodriver, etc.) creates a unique identifier called *sessionId* to track the browser session. We can use this value in our test to univocally identify a browser session. For that, we need to invoke the method getSessionId() in our driver object. Notice this method is not available in Table 3-2, because it belongs to the RemoteWeb Driver class. In practice, the types we use to control browsers (e.g., ChromeDriver, FirefoxDriver, etc.) inherit from that class. Therefore, we simply need to cast the WebDriver object to RemoteWebDriver to invoke the getSessionId() method. Example 3-4 shows a basic test using it.

Example 3-4. Test reading the sessionId

```
@Test
void testSessionId() {
    driver.get("https://bonigarcia.dev/selenium-webdriver-java/");

    SessionId sessionId = ((RemoteWebDriver) driver).getSessionId(); ❶
    assertThat(sessionId).isNotNull(); ❷
    log.debug("The sessionId is {}", sessionId.toString()); ❸
}
```

❶ We cast the driver object to `RemoteWebDriver` and read its sessionId.

❷ We verify the sessionId has some value.

❸ We log the sessionId on the standard output.

WebDriver Disposal

As you can see in Table 3-2, there are two methods to dispose of the `WebDriver` objects, called `close()` and `quit()`. As a general rule, I use `quit()` in the examples since this method closes the browser and every associated window. On the other hand, the method `close()` terminates only the current window. Therefore, I only use `close()` in the case of handling different windows (or tabs) in the same browser, and I want to finish some of the windows (or tabs) and still use the rest.

Locating WebElements

One of the most relevant aspects of the Selenium WebDriver API is the ability to interact with the different elements of a web page. These elements are handled by Selenium WebDriver using the interface `WebElement`, an abstraction for HTML elements. As introduced in Table 3-2, there are two methods to locate `WebElement` in a given web page. First, the method `findElement()` returns the first occurrence (if any) of a given node in the Document Object Model (DOM). Second, the method `find Elements()` returns a list of DOM nodes. Both methods accept a parameter By, which specifies the location strategy.

The Document Object Model (DOM)

The DOM is a cross-platform interface that allows representing XML-like documents (e.g., web pages, based on HTML) in a tree structure. Example 3-5 shows an small web page; the associated DOM tree structure in memory is represented in Figure 3-1. As you can see, each HTML tag (e.g., <html>, <head>, <body>, <a>, etc.) produces a node (or element) in the tree. Then, each standard HTML attribute (e.g., charset, href, etc.) produces an equivalent DOM *property*. Also, the text content of the HTML tags is available in the resulting tree. Languages like JavaScript use DOM methods to access and modify the tree structure. Thanks to this, web pages are dynamic and can change their layout and content in response to user events.

Example 3-5. Basic web page

```
<!DOCTYPE html>
<html>
<head>
  <meta charset="utf-8">
  <title>DOM example</title>
</head>
<body>
  <h1>Heading text</h1>
  <a href="#">Link text</a>
</body>
</html>
```

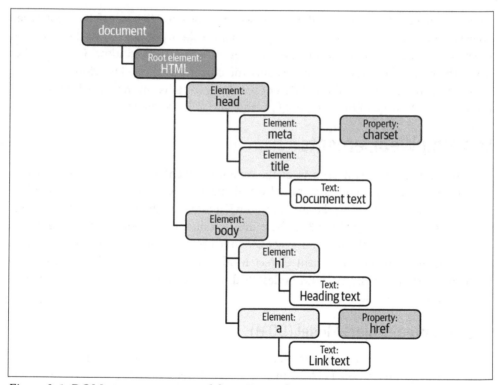

Figure 3-1. DOM structure generated from Example 3-5

WebElement Methods

Table 3-3 contains a summary of the available methods in the WebElement class. You will find examples of each method in the following parts of this section.

Table 3-3. WebElement methods

Method	Return	Description
click()	void	Perform a mouse click (i.e., a left-click) in the current element.
submit()	void	Send a web form (when the current element is a form).
sendKeys(CharSequence... keys)	void	Simulate typing with the keyboard (e.g., in input text elements).
clear()	void	Reset the value of an input text element.
getTagName()	String	Get the tag name of the element.
getDomProperty(String name)	String	Get the value of a DOM property.
getDomAttribute(String name)	String	Get the value of the element attribute as declared in its HTML markup.
getAttribute(String name)	String	Get the value of the given HTML attribute (e.g., class) as a String. More precisely, this method attempts to get a meaningful value of the DOM property with the given name if it exists. For instance, for boolean attributes (e.g., readonly), it returns true if it exists or null if not.
getAriaRole()	String	Get element role as defined on the W3C WAI-ARIA (*https://www.w3.org/TR/wai-aria*) specification.
getAccessibleName()	String	Get element accessible name as defined by WAI-ARIA.
isSelected()	boolean	Determine if a checkbox, option in a select, or radio button is selected.
isEnabled()	boolean	Determine if an element is enabled or not (e.g., a form field).
isDisplayed()	boolean	Determine if an element is visible or not.
getText()	String	Get the visible text of the element, including its sub-elements (if any).
getLocation()	Point	Get the position (*x* and *y* coordinates) from the top-left corner of the rendered element.
getSize()	Dimension	Get the width and height of the rendered element.
getRect()	Rectangle	Get the location and size of the rendered element.
getCssValue(String propName)	String	Get the value of a CSS property of the element.
getShadowRoot()	SearchContext	Get the shadow root to search in a shadow tree (see "The Shadow DOM" on page 118).

Method	Return	Description
findElements(By by)	List<WebElement>	Find all subelements that match the locator within the current element.
findElement(By by)	WebElement	Find the first subelement that matches the locator within the current element.

Location Strategies

Selenium WebDriver provides eight basic location strategies, summarized in Table 3-4. In addition, as explained in the next subsections, there are other advanced location strategies, namely, compound and relative locators.

We specify the basic locators using the class By in the Selenium WebDriver API. The following subsections show examples of all these strategies. We use the practice web form (*https://bonigarcia.dev/selenium-webdriver-java/web-form.html*) to that aim. Figure 3-2 shows a screenshot of this form.

Table 3-4. Summary of the location strategies in Selenium WebDriver

Locator	Finds elements based on
Tag name	The name of HTML tag (e.g., a, p, div, img, etc.).
Link text	The exact text value displayed by a link (i.e., a HTML tag).
Partial link text	The text contained in a link (i.e., a HTML tag).
Name	The value of the attribute name.
Id	The value of the attribute id.
Class name	The value of the attribute class.
CSS selector	Patterns that follow the W3C Selectors (*https://www.w3.org/TR/selectors*) recommendation. The original aim of CSS patterns is to select element(s) in a web page to apply CSS styles. Selenium WebDriver allows reusing these CSS selectors to find web elements and interact with them.
XPath	Queries that follow the XPath (*https://www.w3.org/TR/xpath*) (XML Path Language) language. XPath is a W3C standard query language for selecting nodes from an XML-like document (e.g., web pages).

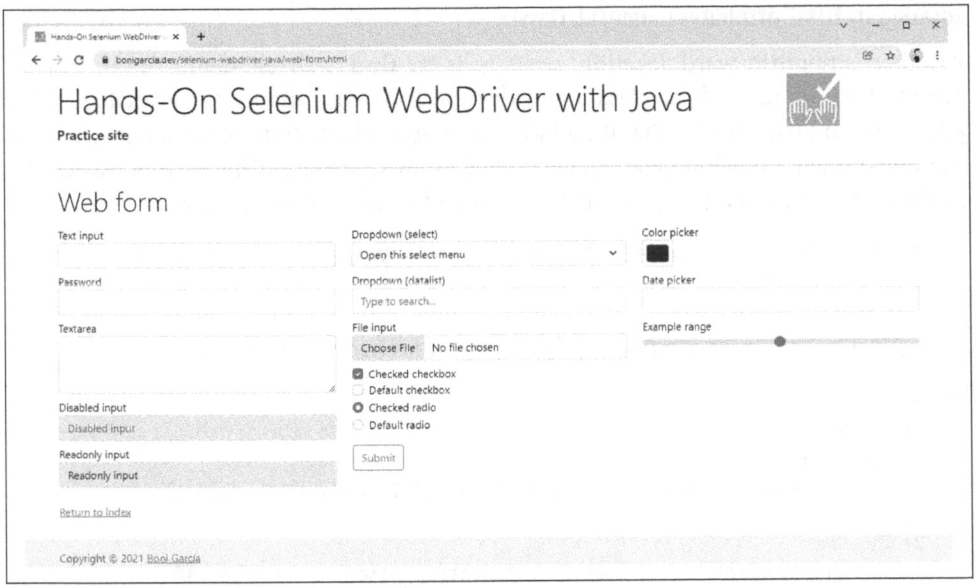

Figure 3-2. Practice web form used in the locator examples

Locating by HTML tag name

One of the most basic strategies for finding web elements is by tag name. Example 3-6 shows a test using this strategy. This test locates the text area available in the practice web form, whose HTML markup is the following:

```
<textarea class="form-control" id="my-textarea" rows="3"></textarea>
```

Example 3-6. Test using a locator strategy by tag name

```java
@Test
void testByTagName() {
    driver.get(
            "https://bonigarcia.dev/selenium-webdriver-java/web-form.html");

    WebElement textarea = driver.findElement(By.tagName("textarea")); ❶
    assertThat(textarea.getDomAttribute("rows")).isEqualTo("3"); ❷
}
```

❶ We use the locator `By.tagName("textarea")` to find this element. In this case, since this is the only text area declared on the web page, we can be sure that the method `findElement()` will locate this element.

❷ We ensure the attribute `rows` value is the same as defined in the HTML markup.

Locating by HTML attributes (name, id, class)

Another straightforward location strategy is to find web elements by an HTML attribute, i.e., name, id, or class. Consider the following input text available in the practice web form. Notice that it includes the standard attributes class, name, id, and the nonstandard attribute myprop (included to illustrate the difference between several WebDriver methods). Example 3-7 shows a test using this strategy.

```
<input type="text" class="form-control" name="my-text" id="my-text-id"
    myprop="myvalue">
```

Example 3-7. Test using locators by HTML attributes (name, id, and class)

```
@Test
void testByHtmlAttributes() {
    driver.get(
            "https://bonigarcia.dev/selenium-webdriver-java/web-form.html");

    // By name
    WebElement textByName = driver.findElement(By.name("my-text"));  ❶
    assertThat(textByName.isEnabled()).isTrue();  ❷

    // By id
    WebElement textById = driver.findElement(By.id("my-text-id"));  ❸
    assertThat(textById.getAttribute("type")).isEqualTo("text");  ❹
    assertThat(textById.getDomAttribute("type")).isEqualTo("text");
    assertThat(textById.getDomProperty("type")).isEqualTo("text");

    assertThat(textById.getAttribute("myprop")).isEqualTo("myvalue");  ❺
    assertThat(textById.getDomAttribute("myprop")).isEqualTo("myvalue");
    assertThat(textById.getDomProperty("myprop")).isNull();

    // By class name
    List<WebElement> byClassName = driver
            .findElements(By.className("form-control"));  ❻
    assertThat(byClassName.size()).isPositive();  ❼
    assertThat(byClassName.get(0).getAttribute("name")).isEqualTo("my-text");  ❽
}
```

❶ We locate the text input by name.

❷ We assert that the element is enabled (i.e., the user can type in it).

❸ We find the same text input element by id.

❹ This assertion (and the next two) returns the same value since the attribute type is standard, and as previously explained, it becomes a *property* in the DOM.

❺ This assertion (and the next two) return different values since the attribute myprop is not standard, and for this reason, it is not available as a DOM property.

❻ We locate a list of elements by class.

❼ We verify the list has more than one element.

❽ We check that the first element found by class is the same as the input text located before.

Locating by link text

The last basic locator is by link text. This strategy is twofold: locate by exact and by partial text occurrence. We use a link in the practice web form to illustrate this locator in the following HTML markup. Then, Example 3-8 shows a test using these locators.

```
<a href="./index.html">Return to index</a>
```

Example 3-8. Test using locators by text link

```
@Test
void testByLinkText() {
    driver.get(
            "https://bonigarcia.dev/selenium-webdriver-java/web-form.html");

    WebElement linkByText = driver
            .findElement(By.linkText("Return to index")); ❶
    assertThat(linkByText.getTagName()).isEqualTo("a"); ❷
    assertThat(linkByText.getCssValue("cursor")).isEqualTo("pointer"); ❸

    WebElement linkByPartialText = driver
            .findElement(By.partialLinkText("index")); ❹
    assertThat(linkByPartialText.getLocation())
            .isEqualTo(linkByText.getLocation()); ❺
    assertThat(linkByPartialText.getRect()).isEqualTo(linkByText.getRect());
}
```

❶ We locate an element by its full link text.

❷ We check its tag name is a.

❸ We check its CSS property cursor is pointer (i.e., the style typically used for clickable elements).

❹ We find an element by partial link text. This link will be the same as in step 1.

❺ We verify both elements share the same position and size.

Locating by CSS selectors

The strategies we have seen so far are easy to apply but also have some limitations. First, locating by tag name can be tricky since it is likely that the same tag will occur many times on a web page. Next, finding elements by HTML attributes (name, id, or class) is a limited approach since these attributes are not always available. In addition, ids can be autogenerated and volatile between different sessions. Lastly, the location by link text is limited only to links. To overcome these limitations, Selenium Web-Driver provides two powerful location strategies: CSS selector and XPath.

There are many possibilities for creating CSS selectors. Table 3-5 shows a comprehensive summary with the basic CSS selectors.

Table 3-5. Basic CSS selectors

Category	Syntax	Description	Example	Example explanation
Universal	`*`	Select all elements	`*`	Match all elements
Type	`elementName`	Select all elements with a given tag name	`input`	Match all `<input>` elements
Class	`.classname`	Select elements with a given `class` attribute	`.form-control`	Match all elements with class of `form-control`
Id	`#id`	Select elements with a given `id` attribute	`#my-text-id`	Match all elements with id `my-text-id`
Attribute	`[attr]`	Select elements with a given attribute	`[target]`	Match all elements with a `target` attribute
	`[attr=value]`	Select elements with a given attribute and value	`[target=_blank]`	Match all elements with a `target="_blank"` attribute
	`[attr~=value]`	Select elements with a given attribute containing some text value	`[title~=hands]`	Match all elements with a title attribute containing the word `hands`
	`[attr|=value]`	Select elements with a given attribute equal to or starting by some value	`[lang|=en]`	Match all elements equal to or starting with `en`
	`[attr^=value]`	Select elements with a given attribute starting by some value	`a[href^="https"]`	Match all links whose `href` attribute starts with `https`
	`[attr$=value]`	Select elements with a given attribute ending by some value	`a[href$=".pdf"]`	Match all links whose `href` attribute ends with `.pdf`
	`[attr*=value]`	Select elements with a given attribute value containing some string	`a[href*="github"]`	Match all links whose `href` attribute contains `github`

The following HTML excerpt shows the hidden input text available in the practice web form. Then, Example 3-9 illustrates a possible way to locate this element using a

CSS selector. One advantage of this locator is that the selector will still work even when changing the attribute name in HTML markup.

```
<input type="hidden" name="my-hidden">
```

Example 3-9. Test using a basic locator with CSS selector

```
@Test
void testByCssSelectorBasic() {
    driver.get(
            "https://bonigarcia.dev/selenium-webdriver-java/web-form.html");

    WebElement hidden = driver
            .findElement(By.cssSelector("input[type=hidden]")); ❶
    assertThat(hidden.isDisplayed()).isFalse(); ❷
}
```

❶ We use a CSS selector to locate the hidden input.

❷ We check the hidden field is not visible.

There are plenty of possibilities to create advanced CSS selectors. Table 3-6 shows a summary with some of them. The complete reference of CSS selectors is available in the official W3C recommendation (*https://www.w3.org/TR/selectors*).

Table 3-6. Advanced CSS selectors

Category	Syntax	Description	Example	Example explanation
Grouping	,	Group two (or more) selectors	div, span	Match both <span> and <div> elements
Combinators	(space)	Select elements that are descendants	div span	Match all <span> that are inside a <div>
	A > B	Select elements that are direct children of another element	ul > li	Match all <li> elements nested directly inside to <ul>
	A ~ B	Select elements sharing the same parent (i.e., *siblings*), and the second element follows the first (not necessarily immediately)	p ~ span	Match all <span> that follow a <p> (immediately or not)
	A + B	Sibling elements, and the second element immediately follows the first	h2 + p	Match all <p> that immediately follows <h2>
Pseudo	:	Select a CSS *pseudoclass* (i.e., a special state of the selected element)	a:visited	Match all already visited links
	:nth-child(n)	Select elements based on their position in a group (starting from the beginning)	p:nth-child(2)	Match every second <p> child

Category	Syntax	Description	Example	Example explanation
	:not(selector)	Select elements not matching a given selector	:not(p)	Match every element different from <p>
	:nth-last-child(n)	Select elements based on their position in a group (starting from the end)	p:nth-last-child(2)	Match every second <p> child (counting from the last child)
	::	Select a CSS *pseudoelement* (i.e., a specific part of the selected element)	p::first-line	Match the first line of all <p> elements

Consider the following piece of HTML (as usual, contained in the practice web form). As you can see, there are a couple of checkboxes: one of them is checked, and the other is not. We can determine which element is checked using the Selenium WebDriver API and CSS selectors. To that aim, Example 3-10 uses CSS pseudoclass.

```
<input class="form-check-input" type="checkbox" name="my-check" id="my-check-1"
        checked>
<input class="form-check-input" type="checkbox" name="my-check" id="my-check-2">
```

Example 3-10. Test using advanced locators with CSS selectors

```
@Test
void testByCssSelectorAdvanced() {
    driver.get(
            "https://bonigarcia.dev/selenium-webdriver-java/web-form.html");

    WebElement checkbox1 = driver
            .findElement(By.cssSelector("[type=checkbox]:checked")); ❶
    assertThat(checkbox1.getAttribute("id")).isEqualTo("my-checkbox-1"); ❷
    assertThat(checkbox1.isSelected()).isTrue(); ❸

    WebElement checkbox2 = driver
            .findElement(By.cssSelector("[type=checkbox]:not(:checked)")); ❹
    assertThat(checkbox2.getAttribute("id")).isEqualTo("my-checkbox-2"); ❺
    assertThat(checkbox2.isSelected()).isFalse(); ❻
}
```

❶ We use the pseudoclass *checked* to locate clicked checkboxes.

❷ We check the element id is as expected.

❸ We confirm the selected is checked.

❹ We use the pseudoclass *checked* and the operator *not* to locate default checkboxes.

❺ We check the element id is as expected.

❻ We confirm the selected is unchecked.

Locating by XPath

XPath (XML Path Language) is a powerful way of navigating to the DOM of XML-like documents, such as HTML pages. It includes over two hundred built-in functions to create advanced queries to select nodes. There are two types of XPath queries. First, *absolute* queries use the symbol slash (/) to traverse the DOM from the root node. For example, considering the basic HTML page in Example 3-5, to select the link element present in this page using this approach, we need the following XPath query:

```
/html/body/a
```

Absolute XPath queries are easy to create, but they have a relevant inconvenience: any minimal change in the page layout would make a locator built with this strategy fail. For this reason, as a general rule, the usage of absolute XPaths is discouraged. Instead, *relative* queries are more convenient.

The general syntax for relative XPath queries is as follows:

```
//tagname[@attribute='value']
```

Example 3-11 shows a test with an XPath locator to select the hidden field in the practice web.

Example 3-11. Test using a basic locator with XPath

```java
@Test
void testByXPathBasic() {
    driver.get(
            "https://bonigarcia.dev/selenium-webdriver-java/web-form.html");

    WebElement hidden = driver
            .findElement(By.xpath("//input[@type='hidden']")); ❶
    assertThat(hidden.isDisplayed()).isFalse(); ❷
}
```

❶ We locate the hidden field in the practice web.

❷ We verify this element is not visible to the user.

The real power of XPath comes from its built-in functions. Table 3-7 contains some of the most relevant XPath functions. You can find the complete XPath reference in the W3C XPath Recommendations (*https://www.w3.org/TR/xpath*).

Table 3-7. Summary of relevant XPath built-in functions

Category	Syntax	Description	Example	Example explanation
Attributes	`contains(@attr, 'string')`	Check if an attribute contains a string	`//a[contains(@href, 'github')]`	Match links with `href` containing `github`
	`starts-with(@attr, 'string')`	Check if an attribute starts with a string	`//a[starts-with(@href, 'https')]`	Match all links using HTTPS
	`ends-with(@attr, 'string')`	Check if an attribute end with a string	`//a[ends-with(@href, https)]`	Match all links to PDF documents
Text	`text()='string'`	Locate elements based on text content	`//*[text()=click]`	Match all elements with the text `click`
Child nodes	`[index]`	Locate children elements	`//div/*[0]`	First child of a `<div>`
Boolean	`or`	Logic operator *or*	`//@type='submit' or @type='reset']`	Match buttons to submit and clear forms
	`and`	Logic operator *and*	`//@type='submit' and @id ='my-button']`	Match submit buttons with a given id
	`not()`	Logic operator *not*	`//@type='submit' and not(@id ='my-button')]`	Match submit buttons different to a given id
Axes (used to locate relative nodes)	`following::item`	Nodes that come after the current one	`//*[@type='text']// following::input`	Match all input fields after the first text input
	`descendant::item`	Select descendant elements (child, etc.) of current node	`//*[@id='my-id']// descendant::a`	Match all descendant links from a given parent node
	`ancestor::item`	Select ancestor elements (parent, etc.) of current node	`//input[@id='my-id']//ances tor::label`	Match all antecedent labels from a given input text
	`child::item`	Select children elements of current node	`//*[@id='my-id']// child::li`	Match all list element under a given node
	`preceding::item`	Select all nodes that come before the current one	`//*[@id='my-id']// preceding::input`	Match all `input` before a given node
	`following-sibling::item`	Select following nodes that come before the current one	`//*[@id='my-id']// following-sibling::input`	Match the next input before a given node
	`parent::item`	Select parent of the current node	`//*[@id='my-id']// parent::div`	Match the parent `div` element of a given node

Example 3-12 shows how to use XPath locators for the radio buttons available in the practice web form. The HTML markup for these radio buttons is:

```
<input class="form-check-input" type="radio" name="my-radio" id="my-radio-1"
        checked>
<input class="form-check-input" type="radio" name="my-radio" id="my-radio-2">
```

Example 3-12. Test using advanced locators with XPath

```
@Test
void testByXPathAdvanced() {
    driver.get(
            "https://bonigarcia.dev/selenium-webdriver-java/web-form.html");

    WebElement radio1 = driver
            .findElement(By.xpath("//*[@type='radio' and @checked]")); ❶
    assertThat(radio1.getAttribute("id")).isEqualTo("my-radio-1"); ❷
    assertThat(radio1.isSelected()).isTrue(); ❸

    WebElement radio2 = driver
            .findElement(By.xpath("//*[@type='radio' and not(@checked)]")); ❹
    assertThat(radio2.getAttribute("id")).isEqualTo("my-radio-2"); ❺
    assertThat(radio2.isSelected()).isFalse(); ❻
}
```

❶ We use XPath to locate the checked radio buttons.

❷ We check the element id is as expected.

❸ We confirm the selected is checked.

❹ We use XPath to locate the unchecked radio buttons.

❺ We check the element id is as expected.

❻ We confirm the selected is unchecked.

 "What Strategy Should You Use?" on page 80 provides a comparison between CSS selectors and XPath and gives some hints for selecting one or another locator strategies.

Finding Locators on a Web Page

As introduced in Table 1-4 in Chapter 1, there are different tools we can use to help generate locators for our WebDriver tests. This section shows how to use the main features of the built-in developer tools in major browsers, i.e., Chrome DevTools (*https://developer.chrome.com/docs/devtools*) for Chromium-based browsers (e.g., Chrome and Edge) and Firefox Developer Tools (*https://developer.mozilla.org/en-US/docs/Tools*) (for Firefox).

You can open both of these developer tools by right-clicking on the portion of the web page UI that you want to test and then selecting the option menu *Inspect*. Figure 3-3 shows a screenshot of Chrome DevTools placed at the bottom of the browser (you can move it if you want).

Developer tools provide different ways to locate elements in a web page. First, we use the element selector by clicking on the icon (an arrow over a box) in the upper left corner of the developer tools pane. Then, we can move the mouse over the page to highlight each web element and inspect the elements panel to check their markup, attributes, etc.

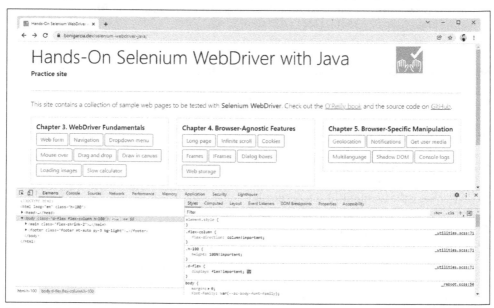

Figure 3-3. Use of Chrome DevTools while navigating the practice site

In the same view, we can use the tool to copy its CSS or XPath selector by right-clicking on the element and then selecting the menu option "Copy." This mechanism allows getting the full CSS or XPath selector. It can be the first approach to generate a locator quickly, although I do not recommend using these locators directly since they tend to be brittle (i.e., linked to the current page layout) and are hard to read.

To create robust CSS or XPath locators, we need to think about the specific character-istics of the web pages we are working with and create a custom selector based on that knowledge. Again, the developer tools can help us in this task. We can press the key combination Ctrl + F to search by string, CSS selector, or XPath in Chrome DevTools. Figure 3-4 shows an example of this feature in action.

Notice we are using the practice web form, and we type the string `#my-text-id`, which corresponds to the element with a given id using a CSS selector. DevTools found the web element on the page and highlighted it.

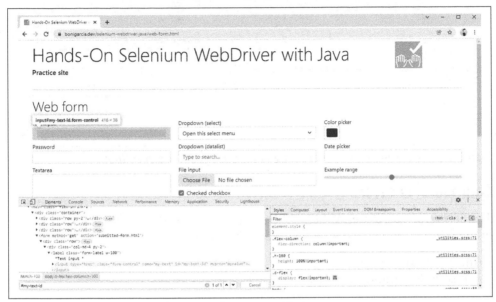

Figure 3-4. Searching CSS selector in Chrome DevTools

We can use a similar approach in Firefox. We need to use the console panel and type `$$("css-selector")` for searching by CSS selector or `$x("xpath-query")` for XPath queries. Figure 3-5 shows how to locate the first input text element of the practice web form by id, using a CSS selector and an XPath query.

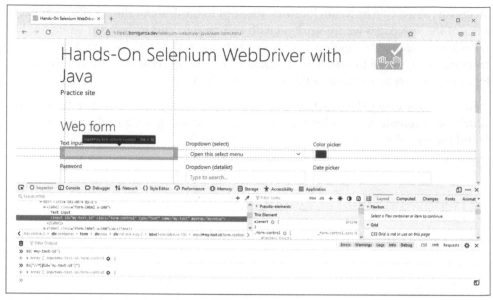

Figure 3-5. Searching CSS selector and XPath in Firefox Developer Tools

Compound Locators

The Selenium WebDriver API has several support classes that enable the composition of the different locator types we have seen. These classes are:

ByIdOrName(String idOrName)
> It seeks by id, and if that is not available, it seeks by name.

ByChained(By... bys)
> It seeks elements in a sequence (i.e., the second one should appear inside the first one, and so on).

ByAll(By... bys)
> It seeks elements that match a number of location strategies (following an *and* logic condition for these locators).

Example 3-13 shows a test using ByIdOrName. This test looks for the following file-select field available in the practice web form. Notice that this field specifies the attribute name (but not id).

```
<input class="form-control" type="file" name="my-file">
```

Example 3-13. Test using by id or name compound locator

```
@Test
void testByIdOrName() {
    driver.get(
            "https://bonigarcia.dev/selenium-webdriver-java/web-form.html");

    WebElement fileElement = driver.findElement(new ByIdOrName("my-file")); ❶
    assertThat(fileElement.getAttribute("id")).isBlank(); ❷
    assertThat(fileElement.getAttribute("name")).isNotBlank(); ❸
}
```

❶ We use a locator by id or name.

❷ We check the element has the attribute name.

❸ We verify the absence of the attribute name in the same element.

Example 3-14 shows two tests illustrating the difference between ByChained and ByAll. Both locators use the practice web form again. If you inspect its source code, you will notice that there are three single <div class="row"> inside the <form>.

Example 3-14. Test using by chained and by all compound locators

```
@Test
void testByChained() {
    driver.get(
            "https://bonigarcia.dev/selenium-webdriver-java/web-form.html");

    List<WebElement> rowsInForm = driver.findElements(
            new ByChained(By.tagName("form"), By.className("row"))); ❶
    assertThat(rowsInForm.size()).isEqualTo(1); ❷
}

@Test
void testByAll() {
    driver.get(
            "https://bonigarcia.dev/selenium-webdriver-java/web-form.html");

    List<WebElement> rowsInForm = driver.findElements(
            new ByAll(By.tagName("form"), By.className("row"))); ❸
    assertThat(rowsInForm.size()).isEqualTo(5); ❹
}
```

❶ We use the locator using ByChained.

❷ We find one element since only one row element is within the form.

❸   We use the locator using `ByAll`.

❹   We find five elements, since the locator matches a `<form>` element plus four `<div class="row">` available on the page.

Relative Locators

Selenium WebDriver version 4 incorporates a new way to find elements in a web page: *relative locators*. These new locators aim to find web elements relative to another known element. This feature is based on the CSS *box model*. The model determines that each element of a web document is rendered using a rectangular box. Figure 3-6 shows an example of this box model for a given web element in the practice form.

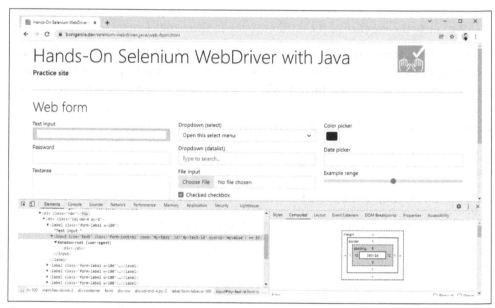

Figure 3-6. Practice form showing the box model of a web element

Using this box model, the relative locators available in the Selenium WebDriver API allow finding elements in relation to the position of another web element. To this aim, first, we need to locate that web element using the standard location strategies (e.g., by id, name, attribute, etc.). Then, we need to specify the locator type obtained by proximity to the original web element using the static method `with` of the class `RelativeLocator`. As a result, we get a `RelativeBy` object, which extends the abstract class `By`, used in the standard locator strategies. A `RelativeBy` object provides the following methods to carry out relative location:

`above()`
>Finds element(s) located on the top of the original element.

`below()`
>Finds element(s) located under the original element.

`near()`
>Finds element(s) located close to the original element. The default distance to consider an element near to some other is one hundred pixels. This locator is overloaded to specify another distance.

`toLeftOf()`
>Finds element(s) located at the left side of the original element.

`toRightOf()`
>Finds element(s) located at the right side of the original element.

Example 3-15 shows a basic test using relative locators. Once again, we use the practice web form to illustrate this feature.

Example 3-15. Test using relative locators

```
@Test
void testRelativeLocators() {
    driver.get(
            "https://bonigarcia.dev/selenium-webdriver-java/web-form.html");

    WebElement link = driver.findElement(By.linkText("Return to index")); ❶
    RelativeBy relativeBy = RelativeLocator.with(By.tagName("input")); ❷
    WebElement readOnly = driver.findElement(relativeBy.above(link)); ❸
    assertThat(readOnly.getAttribute("name")).isEqualTo("my-readonly"); ❹
}
```

❶ We locate the link whose text is `Return to index`.

❷ We specify the relative locator type, which will be by tag name the `input`.

❸ We use a relative locator to find a web element (which should be an `input` filed) above the original web element (i.e., a link).

❹ We verify the element above the reference link is a read-only field (see Figure 3-2 to double-check it).

Relative locators can be helpful for finding elements based on the relative position of other elements. On the other hand, this strategy can be very sensitive to page layout. For example, you need to be careful when using relative locators in responsive pages since the layout can vary depending on the viewport.

A challenging example

The examples we have seen so far are reasonably simple. Let's now look at a more complex use case. A nondefault element in the practice web is the *date picker*. As its name suggests, this element provides a handy way to select dates using a web GUI. Since the CSS framework used in the practice site is Bootstrap (*https://getbootstrap.com*), I implemented the date picker using bootstrap-datepicker (*https://github.com/uxsolutions/bootstrap-datepicker*). This date picker is attached to an input field. When the user clicks on this field, a calendar appears on the web page (see Figure 3-7). The user can select a given date by clicking the preferred date by navigating to the different days, months, and years.

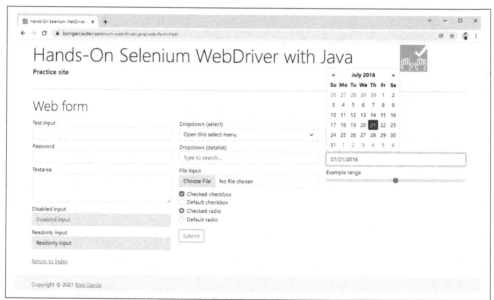

Figure 3-7. Date picker in the practice web form

We want to implement an automated test using Selenium WebDriver that selects the current day and month but the previous year by interacting with the date picker GUI. Example 3-16 shows the resulting implementation.

To follow this example, I recommend you open the practice web form (see URL in the code example) in your browser and use the developer tools to inspect the internal elements of the date picker selector, paying attention to the different selector strategies used.

Example 3-16. Test interacting with a date picker

```
@Test
void testDatePicker() {
    driver.get(
            "https://bonigarcia.dev/selenium-webdriver-java/web-form.html");

    // Get the current date from the system clock ❶
    LocalDate today = LocalDate.now();
    int currentYear = today.getYear();
    int currentDay = today.getDayOfMonth();

    // Click on the date picker to open the calendar ❷
    WebElement datePicker = driver.findElement(By.name("my-date"));
    datePicker.click();

    // Click on the current month by searching by text ❸
    WebElement monthElement = driver.findElement(By.xpath(
            String.format("//th[contains(text(),'%d')]", currentYear)));
    monthElement.click();

    // Click on the left arrow using relative locators ❹
    WebElement arrowLeft = driver.findElement(
            RelativeLocator.with(By.tagName("th")).toRightOf(monthElement));
    arrowLeft.click();

    // Click on the current month of that year ❺
    WebElement monthPastYear = driver.findElement(RelativeLocator
            .with(By.cssSelector("span[class$=focused]")).below(arrowLeft));
    monthPastYear.click();

    // Click on the present day in that month ❻
    WebElement dayElement = driver.findElement(By.xpath(String.format(
            "//td[@class='day' and contains(text(),'%d')]", currentDay)));
    dayElement.click();

    // Get the final date on the input text ❼
    String oneYearBack = datePicker.getAttribute("value");
    log.debug("Final date in date picker: {}", oneYearBack);

    // Assert that the expected date is equal to the one selected in the
    // date picker  ❽
    LocalDate previousYear = today.minusYears(1);
    DateTimeFormatter dateFormat = DateTimeFormatter
            .ofPattern("MM/dd/yyyy");
    String expectedDate = previousYear.format(dateFormat);
```

```
log.debug("Expected date: {}", expectedDate);

assertThat(oneYearBack).isEqualTo(expectedDate);
}
```

❶ Get the current date from the system clock. We use the standard `java.time` API for this.

❷ Click on the date picker to open the calendar. We use a locator by name (`By.name("my-date")`).

❸ Click on the current month by searching by text. We use an XPath query for this locator. After this step, the rest of the months of the year appear in the date picker GUI.

❹ Click on the left arrow using relative locators (i.e., right of the month element). After this step, the calendar moves to the previous year.

❺ Click on the current month of that year. We use a CSS selector here.

❻ Click on the present day in that month. We use an XPath query in this step. After the click, the date is selected, and the value appears in the input text.

❼ Get the final date on the input text. We use a basic locator by attribute here.

❽ Assert that the expected date is equal to the one selected in the date picker. We calculate the expected date using standard Java, and as usual, AssertJ for the assertion.

What Strategy Should You Use?

In this section, we review the different alternatives the Selenium WebDriver API allows for locating elements in a web page. This topic is one of the most fundamental routines for browser automation with Selenium WebDriver. Maybe you are asking yourself: *What is the best strategy I should use?* As Dr. Alfred Lanning (character in the novel and movie *I, Robot*) would say: "That, detective, is the right question." In my opinion, that is a difficult question, and it has no simple answer. In other words, the answer to this question could be "it depends." This section presents several hints for identifying a suitable locator strategy for common use cases. First, Table 3-8 compares the different locating strategies.

Table 3-8. Pros, cons, and typical use cases of the different locating strategies

Locator	Pros	Cons	Typical use case
By attribute (id, name, class)	Easy to use	These attributes are not always available	Elements that define these attributes immutably (i.e., it does not change dynamically)
By link text (total or partial)	Easy to use	Only available for links	For text links
By tag name	Easy to use	Hard to select one specific element when the tag repeatedly appears on the page	When the tag is unique, or the resulting DOM node has a fixed position
By CSS selector or by XPath	Very powerful	It is not easy to write robust selectors	For complex locators
Compound locators	Easy way to compose existing locators	Limited to specific situations	When looking for id or name (ByIdOrName), when looking for nested elements (ByChained), and when using several strategies at the same time (ByAll)
Relative locators	Human language approach	It needs to be combined with other locators	Find element based on the relative position (above, below, near, etc.) of a known element

As you can see in this table, CSS selectors and XPath share the same pros, cons, and use cases. Does it mean these strategies are the same? The answer is no. Both are very powerful and allow the creation of complex locators. Nevertheless, there are relevant distinctions between them. Table 3-9 summarizes these differences.

Table 3-9. Some differences between XPath and CSS selector

XPath	CSS selector
XPath allows bidirectional location, i.e., the traversal can be from parent to child and vice versa	CSS allows one-directional locations, i.e., the traversal is from parent to child only
XPath is slower in terms of performance	CSS has faster performance than XPath
XPath allows the identification of visible text on the screen using the text() function	CSS does not allow locating elements by its text content

To better illustrate the difference between XPath and CSS selectors, Table 3-10 compares specific locators using both strategies.

Table 3-10. Examples comparing XPath and CSS selector

Locator	XPath	CSS selector
All elements	//*	*
All <div> elements	//div	div
Element by id	//*[@id='my-id']	#my-id
Element by class	//*[contains(@class='my-class')]	.my-class
Element with attribute	//*[@attr]	*[attr]

Locator	XPath	CSS selector
Find by text in a <div>	//div[text()='search-string']	Not possible
First child of a <div>	//div/*[1]	div>*:first-child
All <div> with a link child	//div[a]	Not possible
Next element in a <div>	//div/following-sibling::*[1]	div + *
Previous element of a <div>	//div/preceding-sibling::*[1]	Not possible

In conclusion, we can see that XPath provides the most general strategy. Nevertheless, there are some cases in which the CSS selectors offer a friendlier syntax (e.g., locating by id or class) and better general performance.

Keyboard Actions

As introduced in Table 3-3, two main methods in WebDriver objects allow impersonating keyboard user actions: sendKeys() and clear(). Example 3-17 shows a test using these methods.

Example 3-17. Test impersonating keyboard events

```
@Test
void testSendKeys() {
    driver.get(
            "https://bonigarcia.dev/selenium-webdriver-java/web-form.html");

    WebElement inputText = driver.findElement(By.name("my-text")); ❶
    String textValue = "Hello World!";
    inputText.sendKeys(textValue); ❷
    assertThat(inputText.getAttribute("value")).isEqualTo(textValue); ❸

    inputText.clear(); ❹
    assertThat(inputText.getAttribute("value")).isEmpty(); ❺
}
```

❶ We use the practice web form to locate the input text named my-text.

❷ We simulate a keyboard typing on it using the method sendKeys().

❸ We assess the input value is as expected.

❹ We reset its content using clear().

❺ We assess the input value is empty.

File Uploading

There are several use cases in which we will need to impersonate keyboard actions when interacting with web pages through Selenium WebDriver. The first one is file uploading. The standard mechanism to upload files for web applications is using `<input>` elements with `type="file"`. For instance, the practice web form contains one of these elements:

```
<input class="form-control" type="file" name="my-file">
```

The Selenium WebDriver API does not provide a mechanism to handle file inputs. Instead, we should treat input elements for uploading files as regular text inputs, so we need to simulate the user typing them. In particular, we need to type the absolute file path to be uploaded. Example 3-18 illustrates how.

Example 3-18. Test uploading a file

```
@Test
void testUploadFile() throws IOException {
    String initUrl = "https://bonigarcia.dev/selenium-webdriver-java/web-form.html";
    driver.get(initUrl);

    WebElement inputFile = driver.findElement(By.name("my-file")); ❶

    Path tempFile = Files.createTempFile("tempfiles", ".tmp"); ❷
    String filename = tempFile.toAbsolutePath().toString();
    log.debug("Using temporal file {} in file uploading", filename);
    inputFile.sendKeys(filename); ❸

    driver.findElement(By.tagName("form")).submit(); ❹
    assertThat(driver.getCurrentUrl()).isNotEqualTo(initUrl); ❺
}
```

❶ We locate the input field using a by-name strategy.

❷ We create a temporal file using standard Java.

❸ We type its absolute path to the input field.

❹ We submit the form.

❺ We verify that the resulting page (defined in `action` form attribute) is different from the initial web page.

 The file path sent to the input file should correspond to an existing archive in the machine running the test. Otherwise, the test fails with an `InvalidArgumentException` exception. See "WebDriver Exceptions" on page 142 in Chapter 5 for further details about exceptions.

When uploading a file to a remote browser (as explained in Chapter 6), we need to load the file from the local file system explicitly. The following line shows how to specify a local file detector.

```
((RemoteWebDriver) driver).setFileDetector(new LocalFileDetector());
```

Range Sliders

A similar situation happens with `<input type="range">` form fields. These elements allow users to select a number in a range using a graphical slider. You can find an example in the practice web form:

```
<input type="range" class="form-range" name="my-range" min="0" max="10" step="1"
        value="5">
```

Again, the Selenium WebDriver API does not provide any particular utility to handle these fields. We can interact with them by impersonating keyboard actions with Selenium WebDriver. Example 3-19 shows a test interaction with these fields.

Example 3-19. Test selecting a number with a form slider

```
@Test
void testSlider() {
    driver.get(
            "https://bonigarcia.dev/selenium-webdriver-java/web-form.html");

    WebElement slider = driver.findElement(By.name("my-range"));
    String initValue = slider.getAttribute("value");
    log.debug("The initial value of the slider is {}", initValue);

    for (int i = 0; i < 5; i++) {
        slider.sendKeys(Keys.ARROW_RIGHT); ❶
    }
```

```
        String endValue = slider.getAttribute("value");
        log.debug("The final value of the slider is {}", endValue);
        assertThat(initValue).isNotEqualTo(endValue); ❷
}
```

❶ We send a keyboard key to the range field available in the practice web form. We
    use the class `Keys` available in the Selenium WebDriver API to handle special
    keyboard characters. In particular, we send the right arrow key to the slider, and
    as a result, it moves to the right (i.e., it increases the selected number within the
    range).

❷ We assert the resulting selected value is different from the one in the original
    position.

Mouse Actions

In addition to the keyboard, the other primary input device for interacting with web
applications is the computer mouse. First of all, the single-click (also known as left-
click or simply *click*) is impersonated by the Selenium WebDriver API using the
method `click()`, which is one of the methods available per `WebElement` in Selenium
WebDriver. This section shows examples of two typical use cases using this feature:
web navigation and interaction with checkboxes and radio buttons in web forms.

Other common mouse actions are right-clicking (also known as *context-click*),
double-clicking, cursor movement, drag and drop, or mouseover. Selenium Web-
Driver allows impersonating these actions using a helper class called `Actions`. See the
next section for further details. Finally, scrolling is possible in WebDriver by executing JavaScript. I explain this feature in "Executing JavaScript" on page 101.

Web Navigation

Example 3-20 shows a test implementing automated web navigation with Selenium
WebDriver. This test locates links using XPath and clicks on them, invoking the
method `click()`. In the end, it reads the text content of the web page body and verifies it contains an expected string.

Example 3-20. Test navigating by clicking on links

```
@Test
void testNavigation() {
    driver.get("https://bonigarcia.dev/selenium-webdriver-java/");

    driver.findElement(By.xpath("//a[text()='Navigation']")).click();
    driver.findElement(By.xpath("//a[text()='Next']")).click();
    driver.findElement(By.xpath("//a[text()='3']")).click();
```

```
driver.findElement(By.xpath("//a[text()='2']")).click();
driver.findElement(By.xpath("//a[text()='Previous']")).click();

String bodyText = driver.findElement(By.tagName("body")).getText();
assertThat(bodyText).contains("Lorem ipsum");
}
```

Checkboxes and Radio Buttons

Example 3-21 shows another basic use of the click() method for manipulating checkboxes and radio buttons. To verify the expected state of these elements after the click action, we use an assertion based on the result of the isSelected() method.

Example 3-21. Test interacting with checkboxes and radio buttons

```
@Test
void testNavigation() {
    driver.get(
            "https://bonigarcia.dev/selenium-webdriver-java/web-form.html");

    WebElement checkbox2 = driver.findElement(By.id("my-checkbox-2"));
    checkbox2.click();
    assertThat(checkbox2.isSelected()).isTrue();

    WebElement radio2 = driver.findElement(By.id("my-radio-2"));
    radio2.click();
    assertThat(radio2.isSelected()).isTrue();
}
```

User Gestures

Selenium WebDriver provides the class Actions, a powerful asset to automate different user actions, both for keyboard and mouse. This class follows the *builder* pattern. This way, you can chain several methods (i.e., different actions) and perform all of them at the end by calling build(). Table 3-11 summarizes the public methods available in this class. We review these methods through examples in the following subsections.

Table 3-11. Actions methods

Method	Description
keyDown(CharSequence key) keyDown(WebElement target, CharSequence key)	Send a single key (it could be a special character using the class Keys) in the current position (or a given element). The key remains pressed until calling to keyUp().
keyUp(CharSequence key) keyUp(WebElement target, CharSequence key)	Release a key previously pressed with keyDown().
sendKeys(CharSequence... keys) sendKeys(WebElement target, CharSequence... keys)	Send a key sequence in the current position (or a given element). This method is different from WebElement#sendKeys(CharSequence...) in two ways: 1) Modifier keys (e.g., Keys.CONTROL, Keys.SHIFT) are not released explicitly. 2) There is no refocus on the element, so Keys.TAB should work.
clickAndHold() clickAndHold(WebElement target)	Click without releasing the current position (or the middle of a given element).
release() release(WebElement target)	Release the left-click mouse button previously pressed with clickAndHold().
click() click(WebElement target)	Click on the current position (or a given element).
doubleClick() doubleClick(WebElement target)	Double-click on the current position (or element).
contextClick() contextClick(WebElement target)	Right-click on the current position (or element).
moveToElement(WebElement target) moveToElement(WebElement target, int xOffset, int yOffset)	Move mouse cursor to the middle (or shifted to a given offset) of a given element.
moveByOffset(int xOffset, int yOffset)	Move the mouse from its current position (0,0 by default) by the given offset.

dragAndDrop(WebElement source,
    WebElement target)
dragAndDropBy(WebElement source,
    int xOffset, int yOffset)
dragAndDropBy(WebElement source,
    int xOffset, int yOffset)
	This action consists of three steps: 1) Click and hold at the middle (or shifted by a given offset) of the source element location. 2) Move the mouse to the target element location. 3) Release the mouse click.

pause(long pause) pause(Duration duration)	Perform a pause in the actions chain (in milliseconds or using a Java Duration).
build()	Generate a composite action containing all previous actions.
perform()	Execute the composite action.

Right-Click and Double-Click

You can find a demo page using three dropdown menus on the practice site (see Figure 3-8). On this page, the first dropdown menu appears when clicking on its button, the second one uses the right-click, and the third one requires a double-click. Example 3-22 shows a test using this page to impersonate user gestures through the WebDriver class `Actions`.

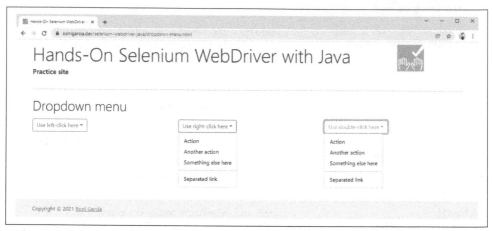

Figure 3-8. Practice web page with dropdown menus

Example 3-22. Test using context and double-click

```
@Test
void testContextAndDoubleClick() {
    driver.get(
            "https://bonigarcia.dev/selenium-webdriver-java/dropdown-menu.html");
    Actions actions = new Actions(driver);

    WebElement dropdown2 = driver.findElement(By.id("my-dropdown-2"));
    actions.contextClick(dropdown2).build().perform(); ❶
    WebElement contextMenu2 = driver.findElement(By.id("context-menu-2"));
    assertThat(contextMenu2.isDisplayed()).isTrue(); ❷

    WebElement dropdown3 = driver.findElement(By.id("my-dropdown-3"));
    actions.doubleClick(dropdown3).build().perform(); ❸
    WebElement contextMenu3 = driver.findElement(By.id("context-menu-3"));
    assertThat(contextMenu3.isDisplayed()).isTrue(); ❹
}
```

❶ We use `contextClick()` in the middle dropdown menu.

❷ We verify the middle menu is correctly displayed.

❸ We use doubleClick() in the right dropdown menu.

❹ We verify the right menu is correctly displayed.

Mouseover

The second example handling Actions uses a sample web page implementing a mouseover. This page displays four images. Each one shows a text label below the image when the mouse pointer is over. Example 3-23 contains a test that uses this page. Figure 3-9 shows this page when the mouse is over the first picture.

Example 3-23. Test using mouseover

```
@Test
void testMouseOver() {
    driver.get(
            "https://bonigarcia.dev/selenium-webdriver-java/mouse-over.html");
    Actions actions = new Actions(driver);

    List<String> imageList = Arrays.asList("compass", "calendar", "award",
            "landscape");
    for (String imageName : imageList) { ❶
        String xpath = String.format("//img[@src='img/%s.png']", imageName);
        WebElement image = driver.findElement(By.xpath(xpath)); ❷
        actions.moveToElement(image).build().perform(); ❸

        WebElement caption = driver.findElement(
                RelativeLocator.with(By.tagName("div")).near(image)); ❹

        assertThat(caption.getText()).containsIgnoringCase(imageName); ❺
    }
}
```

❶ We iterate a string list to locate the four images of the page.

❷ We use XPath to find each <img> web element.

❸ We use moveToElement() to move the mouse pointer to the middle of each image.

❹ We use relative locators to find the displayed label.

❺ We use assertions to verify that the text is as expected.

Figure 3-9. Practice web page with mouse-over images

Drag and Drop

Example 3-24 illustrates the use of drag and drop. This test uses the practice web shown in Figure 3-10.

Example 3-24. Test using drag and drop

```
@Test
void testDragAndDrop() {
    driver.get(
            "https://bonigarcia.dev/selenium-webdriver-java/drag-and-drop.html");
    Actions actions = new Actions(driver);

    WebElement draggable = driver.findElement(By.id("draggable"));  ❶
    int offset = 100;
    Point initLocation = draggable.getLocation();
    actions.dragAndDropBy(draggable, offset, 0)
            .dragAndDropBy(draggable, 0, offset)
            .dragAndDropBy(draggable, -offset, 0)
            .dragAndDropBy(draggable, 0, -offset).build().perform();  ❷
    assertThat(initLocation).isEqualTo(draggable.getLocation());  ❸

    WebElement target = driver.findElement(By.id("target"));  ❹
    actions.dragAndDrop(draggable, target).build().perform();  ❺
    assertThat(target.getLocation()).isEqualTo(draggable.getLocation());  ❻
}
```

❶ We locate the *draggable* element.

❷   We use `dragAndDropBy()` to move this element a fixed number of pixels (100) four times (right, bottom, left, and up).

❸   We assert the element position is the same as the beginning.

❹   We find a second element (not draggable this time).

❺   We use `dragAndDrop()` to move the draggable element to the second one.

❻   We assert the position of both elements is the same.

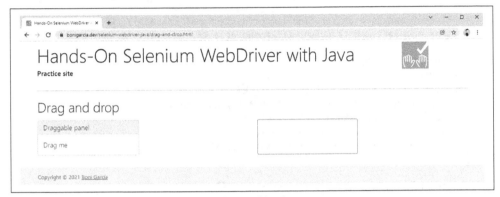

Figure 3-10. Practice web page with a draggable element

Click and Hold

The following example shows complex user gestures, including click and hold. To that aim, we practice with the web page in Figure 3-11.

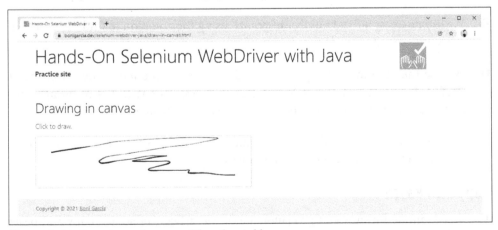

Figure 3-11. Practice web page with a drawable canvas

This page uses an open source JavaScript library called Signature Pad (*https://github.com/szimek/signature_pad*) to draw signatures in HTML canvas using the mouse. Example 3-25 shows a test using it.

Example 3-25. Test drawing a circumference on a canvas

```
@Test
void testClickAndHold() {
    driver.get(
            "https://bonigarcia.dev/selenium-webdriver-java/draw-in-canvas.html");
    Actions actions = new Actions(driver);

    WebElement canvas = driver.findElement(By.tagName("canvas")); ❶
    actions.moveToElement(canvas).clickAndHold(); ❷

    int numPoints = 10;
    int radius = 30;
    for (int i = 0; i <= numPoints; i++) { ❸
        double angle = Math.toRadians(360 * i / numPoints);
        double x = Math.sin(angle) * radius;
        double y = Math.cos(angle) * radius;
        actions.moveByOffset((int) x, (int) y); ❹
    }

    actions.release(canvas).build().perform(); ❺
}
```

❶ We locate the canvas by tag name.

❷ We move the mouse to this element with `moveToElement()` and then add the action `clickAndHold()` (for drawing into the canvas) to the actions pipeline.

❸ We iterate using a fixed number of points, using the equation to find the points in a circumference.

❹ We use the circumference points (x and y) to move the mouse by offset (`moveByOffset()`). Since the click is held from the previous step, the resulting compound action will move the mouse while the click button is pressed.

❺ We release the click, build the action, and carry out the whole chain. As a result, a circumference should appear on the canvas.

Copy and Paste

This last example for user gestures automates a pervasive user action: copy and paste using the keyboard. Here, we use the web form available on the practice website. Example 3-26 shows a test impersonating copy and paste.

Example 3-26. Test impersonating copy and paste

```
@Test
void testCopyAndPaste() {
    driver.get(
            "https://bonigarcia.dev/selenium-webdriver-java/web-form.html");
    Actions actions = new Actions(driver);

    WebElement inputText = driver.findElement(By.name("my-text"));   ❶
    WebElement textarea = driver.findElement(By.name("my-textarea"));

    Keys modifier = SystemUtils.IS_OS_MAC ? Keys.COMMAND : Keys.CONTROL;   ❷
    actions.sendKeys(inputText, "hello world").keyDown(modifier)
            .sendKeys(inputText, "a").sendKeys(inputText, "c")
            .sendKeys(textarea, "v").build().perform();   ❸

    assertThat(inputText.getAttribute("value"))
            .isEqualTo(textarea.getAttribute("value"));   ❹
}
```

❶ We locate two web elements: an input text and a text area.

❷ We use a modifier key for sending the combination Ctrl + C for copying (in Windows and Linux) or Cmd + C for copying (in macOS). To this aim, we use the class `SystemUtils`, available in the open source library Apache Commons IO (*https://commons.apache.org/proper/commons-io*) (this dependency is used transitively in the Maven/Gradle project).

❸ We implement the actions chain composed of the following steps:

1. Send the char sequence `hello world` to the input text.

2. Press the key modifier (Ctrl or Cmd, depending on the operating system). Remember that this key remains pressed until we explicitly release it.

3. We send the key `a` to the input text. Since the modifier is active, the resulting combination is Ctrl + A (or Cmd + A), and as a result, all the text present in the input text is selected.

4. We send the key `c` to the input text. Again, since the modifier is active, the combination is Ctrl + C (or Cmd + C), and the input text is copied to the clipboard.

5. We send the key `v` to the text area. This means sending Ctrl + V (or Cmd + V), and the clipboard content is pasted to the text area.

❹ We assert the content of both elements (input text and text area) is the same at the end of the text.

Waiting Strategies

Web applications are client-server distributed services in which the clients are the web browsers and the web servers are usually remote hosts. The intermediate network latency could affect the reliability of a WebDriver test. For instance, in the case of high-latency networks or overloaded servers, a slow response might negatively affect the expected conditions of WebDriver tests. In addition, modern web applications tend to be dynamic and asynchronous. Nowadays, JavaScript allows executing nonblocking (i.e., asynchronous) operations using different mechanisms, such as callbacks, promises, or async/await. In addition, we can retrieve data from other servers asynchronously, for example, using AJAX (Asynchronous JavaScript and XML) or REST (REpresentational State Transfer) services.

All in all, it is of paramount importance to have mechanisms pause and wait for certain conditions in our WebDriver tests. For this reason, the Selenium WebDriver API provides different waiting assets. The three principal waiting strategies are *implicit*, *explicit*, and *fluent* waits. The following subsections explain and show examples.

 For waiting in Java, you might think about including `Thread.sleep()` commands in your code. On the one hand, it is a simple solution, but on the other hand, it is considered a *bad smell* (i.e., a weak sign) that could lead to unreliable tests (since the delay conditions can change). As a general rule, I strongly discourage you from using it. Instead, consider using the aforementioned wait strategies.

Implicit Wait

The first waiting strategy provided by Selenium WebDriver is called *implicit*. This mechanism allows specifying an amount of time before throwing an exception when finding an element. By default, this wait has a value of zero seconds (i.e., it does not wait at all). But when we define an implicit wait value, Selenium WebDriver polls the DOM during the implicit wait value when trying to find an element. The poll time is specific to the driver implementation and is frequently less than five hundred ms. If the element is present in the elapsed time, the script continues. Otherwise, it throws an exception.

Example 3-27 illustrates this strategy. This test uses a practice page (see Figure 3-12) that dynamically loads several images into the DOM. Since these images are not available just before the page is loaded, we need to wait for these images to be available.

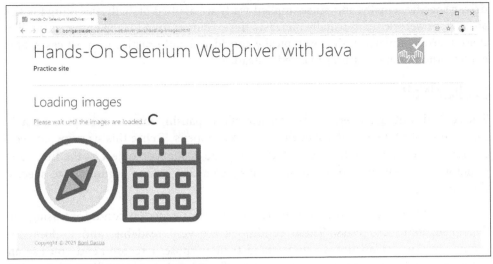

Figure 3-12. *Practice web page loading images*

Example 3-27. *Test using an implicit wait in the "loading images" page*

```
@Test
void testImplicitWait() {
    driver.get(
            "https://bonigarcia.dev/selenium-webdriver-java/loading-images.html");
    driver.manage().timeouts().implicitlyWait(Duration.ofSeconds(10)); ❶

    WebElement landscape = driver.findElement(By.id("landscape")); ❷
    assertThat(landscape.getAttribute("src"))
            .containsIgnoringCase("landscape");
}
```

❶ Before interacting with the elements, we specify an implicit wait strategy. In this case, we set up a timeout of 10 seconds.

❷ In the following calls, we use the Selenium WebDriver API as usual.

 You can play with this feature by dropping the implicit wait from the test (step 1). If you do that, you will notice that the test fails in step 2 due to a NoSuchElementException.

Although supported by the Selenium WebDriver API, implicit waits have different inconveniences you need to know. First, an implicit wait only works on finding elements. Second, we cannot customize its behavior since its implementation is driver-specific. Finally, and since implicit waits are applied globally, checking for the absence of web elements usually increases the execution time for the entire script. For these reasons, implicit waits are typically considered bad practice in most cases, and explicit and fluent waits are preferred instead.

Explicit Wait

The second waiting strategy, called *explicit*, allows pausing the test execution a maximum amount of time until a specific condition happens. To use this strategy, we need to create an instance of `WebDriverWait`, using the `WebDriver` object as the first constructor argument, and an instance of `Duration` as the second argument (to specify the timeout).

Selenium WebDriver provides a comprehensive set of expected conditions using the `ExpectedConditions` class. These conditions are very readable, and it does not require further explanation to understand their purpose. I recommend you use an autocomplete feature in your favorite IDE to discover all the possibilities. For example, Figure 3-13 shows this list in Eclipse.

Figure 3-13. Autocomplete in Eclipse for the ExpectedConditions class

Example 3-28 shows a test using an explicit wait. In the example, we use the `presenceofElementLocated` condition to wait until one of the images is available on the practice web page.

Example 3-28. Test using an explicit wait in the "loading images" page

```java
@Test
void testExplicitWait() {
    driver.get(
            "https://bonigarcia.dev/selenium-webdriver-java/loading-images.html");
    WebDriverWait wait = new WebDriverWait(driver, Duration.ofSeconds(10)); ❶

    WebElement landscape = wait.until(ExpectedConditions
            .presenceOfElementLocated(By.id("landscape"))); ❷
    assertThat(landscape.getAttribute("src"))
            .containsIgnoringCase("landscape");
}
```

❶ We create the `wait` instance. In this case, the selected timeout is 10 seconds.

❷ We explicitly wait for a given condition (in this case, the presence of a given element) by invoking the `until()` method in the `WebDriverWait` object. To achieve a more readable statement, you can also statically import this expected condition (`presenceOfElementLocated`). In this book, I decided to keep the class name (`ExpectedConditions`) in these conditions to ease the autocomplete feature in IDEs as described before.

Example 3-29 shows another test using explicit waits. This test uses another practice web page called "slow calculator," which contains a GUI of a basic calculator, tuned to wait a configurable time to get the result of basic arithmetic operations (by default, five seconds). Figure 3-14 shows a screenshot of this page.

Example 3-29. Test using an explicit wait in the "slow calculator" page

```java
@Test
void testSlowCalculator() {
    driver.get(
            "https://bonigarcia.dev/selenium-webdriver-java/slow-calculator.html");

    // 1 + 3
    driver.findElement(By.xpath("//span[text()='1']")).click(); ❶
    driver.findElement(By.xpath("//span[text()='+']")).click();
    driver.findElement(By.xpath("//span[text()='3']")).click();
    driver.findElement(By.xpath("//span[text()='=']")).click();

    // ... should be 4, wait for it
    WebDriverWait wait = new WebDriverWait(driver, Duration.ofSeconds(10));
    wait.until(ExpectedConditions.textToBe(By.className("screen"), "4")); ❷
}
```

❶ We use XPath locators to click the buttons corresponding to operation 1 + 3.

❷ Since the test should wait until the result is ready, we explicitly wait for that. In this case, the condition is the text of the element with a class name screen is equal to 4.

Figure 3-14. Practice web page with the "slow calculator" demo

Fluent Wait

The last strategy is a *fluent* wait. This mechanism is a generalization of explicit waits. In other words, we use fluent waits for pausing the test until certain conditions, but in addition, fluent waits provide fine-grained configuration capabilities. Table 3-12 summarizes the methods available in FluentWait. As its name suggests, this class provides a fluent API, and therefore, we can chain several invocations in the same line. Example 3-30 shows a test using fluent wait.

Table 3-12. Fluent wait methods

Method	Description
withTimeout(Duration timeout)	Timeout using Java Duration
pollingEvery(Duration interval)	How often the condition is evaluated (five hundred ms by default)
withMessage(String message) withMessage(Supplier<String> messageSupplier)	Custom error message

ignoring(Class<? extends Throwable> exceptionType)
ignoring(Class<? extends Throwable> firstType,
    Class<? extends Throwable> secondType)
ignoreAll(Collection<Class<? extends Throwable>>
    types)
	Ignore specific exceptions while waiting for a condition

Method	Description
until(Function<? super T, V> isTrue)	Expected condition

Example 3-30. Test using a fluent wait

```
@Test
void testFluentWait() {
    driver.get(
            "https://bonigarcia.dev/selenium-webdriver-java/loading-images.html");
    Wait<WebDriver> wait = new FluentWait<>(driver)
            .withTimeout(Duration.ofSeconds(10))
            .pollingEvery(Duration.ofSeconds(1))
            .ignoring(NoSuchElementException.class); ❶

    WebElement landscape = wait.until(ExpectedConditions
            .presenceOfElementLocated(By.id("landscape")));
    assertThat(landscape.getAttribute("src"))
            .containsIgnoringCase("landscape");
}
```

❶ As you can see, this test is very similar to Example 3-28, although using a `Fluent Wait` instance, we can specify additional characteristics. In this case, we change the poll time to one second.

  The class `WebDriverWait` (presented in the previous subsection) extends the generic class `FluentWait`. Thus, you can use all the methods shown in Table 3-12 for explicit waits too.

Related Features in Selenium WebDriver

In addition to the previously introduced waiting strategies, there are other complementary characteristics in Selenium WebDriver you should be aware of:

Loading strategies
> Selenium WebDriver allows specifying different approaches for page loading. This feature is accessible through browser-specific capabilities (e.g., using `ChromeOptions`, `FirefoxOptions`, etc.). For this reason, I explain this feature in "Page Loading Strategies" on page 151.

Timeouts
> Selenium WebDriver allows specifying the maximum elapsed time for page and script loading. I explain this feature in "Timeouts" on page 110.

Summary and Outlook

This chapter presented the foundations of the Selenium WebDriver API. First, you learned how to create and shut down `WebDriver` instances. These objects represent a browser controlled with Selenium WebDriver. This way, we use an instance of `Chrome Driver` for Chrome, `FirefoxDriver` for Firefox, etc. Second, you looked at `Web Element`, a class representing different web page elements (e.g., links, images, form fields, etc.). Selenium WebDriver provides several strategies to locate web elements: by HTML attribute (id, name, or class), tag name, link text (complete or partial), CSS selector, and XPath. We also looked at a brand-new strategy of Selenium WebDriver 4 called relative locators. Then, we covered user actions' impersonation, using the keyboard and the mouse. You can use these actions from simple actions (e.g., clicking a link, filling a text input, etc.) to complex user gestures (e.g., drag and drop, click and hover, etc.). Finally, we examined the ability to wait in Selenium WebDriver tests. This feature is critical due to the current distributed, dynamic, and asynchronous nature of web applications. There are three main wait strategies in Selenium WebDriver: implicit (specify a general timeout to wait for elements), explicit (pause test execution until a given condition), and fluent (extension of an explicit wait with some fine-grained setup).

The next chapter continues digging into the Selenium WebDriver API. In particular, Chapter 4 reviews those interoperable features in different browsers (Chrome, Edge, Firefox, etc.). Among these features, you will discover how to execute JavaScript, specify event listeners, configure timeouts for page and script loading, manage the browser history, make screenshots, manipulate cookies, manipulate dropdown lists (i.e., selects and data lists), handle window targets (i.e., tabs, frames, and iframes) and dialog boxes (i.e., alerts, prompts, confirmation, and modal pop-ups), use web storage, and understand the WebDriver exceptions.

CHAPTER 4

Browser-Agnostic Features

This chapter reviews those features of Selenium WebDriver that are interoperable in different web browsers. In this group, a relevant multipurpose characteristic is executing JavaScript. Also, the Selenium WebDriver API allows configuring timeouts for page and script loading. Another convenient feature is making screenshots of the browser screen, or only the portion corresponding to a given element. Then, we can manage different aspects of the controlled browser using WebDriver, such as browser size and position, history, or cookies. Then, WebDriver provides various assets for controlling specific web elements, such as dropdown lists (i.e., HTML select fields and data lists), navigation targets (i.e., windows, tabs, frames, and iframes), or dialog boxes (i.e., alerts, prompts, confirmations, and modal dialogs). Finally, we discover how to handle local and session data using web storage, implement event listeners, and use the exceptions provided by the Selenium WebDriver API.

Executing JavaScript

JavaScript is a high-level programming language supported by all major browsers. We can use JavaScript in the client side of web applications for a wide variety of operations, such as DOM manipulation, user interaction, handling requests-responses from remote servers, or working with regular expressions, among many other functions. Luckily for test automation, Selenium WebDriver allows injecting and executing arbitrary pieces of JavaScript. To that aim, Selenium WebDriver API provides the interface `JavascriptExecutor`. Table 4-1 introduces the available public methods in this interface grouped into three categories: synchronous, pinned, and asynchronous scripts. The subsections following provide more details and illustrate their use through different examples.

Table 4-1. JavascriptExecutor methods

Category	Method	Return	Description
Synchronous scripts	executeScript(String script, Object... args)	Object	Execute JavaScript code on the current page.
Pinned scripts	pin(String script)	ScriptKey	Attach a piece of JavaScript to a WebDriver session. The *pinned* scripts can be used multiple times while the WebDriver session is alive.
	unpin(ScriptKey key)	void	Detach a previously pinned script to the WebDriver session.
	getPinnedScripts()	Set<ScriptKey>	Collect all pinned scripts (each one identified by a unique ScriptKey).
	executeScript(ScriptKey key, Object... args)	Object	Call previously pinned script (identified with its ScriptKey).
Asynchronous scripts	executeAsyncScript(String script, Object... args)	Object	Execute JavaScript code (typically an asynchronous operation) on the current page. The difference with executeScript() is that scripts executed with executeAsyncScript() must explicitly signal their termination by invoking a callback function. By convention, this callback is injected into the script as its last argument.

Any driver object that inherits from the class RemoteWebDriver also implements the JavascriptExecutor interface. Therefore, when using a major browser (e.g., Chrome Driver, FirefoxDriver, etc.) declared using the generic WebDriver interface, we can cast it to JavascriptExecutor as shown in the following snippet. Then, we can use the executor (using variable js in the example) to invoke the methods presented in Table 4-1.

```
WebDriver driver = new ChromeDriver();
JavascriptExecutor js = (JavascriptExecutor) driver;
```

Synchronous Scripts

The method executeScript() of a JavascriptExecutor object allows executing a piece of JavaScript in the context of the current web page in a WebDriver session. The invocation of this method (in Java) blocks the control flow until the script terminates. Therefore, we typically use this method for executing synchronous scripts in a web page under test. The method executeScript() allows two arguments:

String script
> Mandatory JavaScript fragment to be executed. This code is executed in the body of the current page as an anonymous function (i.e., a JavaScript function without a name).

`Object... args`
> Optional arguments script. These arguments must be one of the following types: number, boolean, string, `WebElement`, or a `List` of these types (otherwise, WebDriver throws an exception). These arguments are available in the injected script using the `arguments` built-in JavaScript variable.

When the script returns some value (i.e., the code contains a `return` statement), the Selenium WebDriver `executeScript()` method also returns a value in Java (otherwise, `executeScript()` returns `null`). The possible returned types are:

`WebElement`
> When returning an HTML element

`Double`
> For decimals

`Long`
> For nondecimal numbers

`Boolean`
> For boolean values

`List<Object>`
> For arrays

`Map<String, Object>`
> For key-value collections

`String`
> For all other cases

The situations that require executing JavaScript with Selenium WebDriver are very heterogeneous. The following subsections review two cases where the Selenium Web-Driver does not provide built-in features, and instead, we need to use JavaScript to automate them: scrolling a web page and handling a color picker in a web form.

Scrolling

As explained in Chapter 3, Selenium WebDriver allows impersonating different mouse actions, including click, right-click, or double-click, among others. Nevertheless, scrolling down or up a web page is not possible using the Selenium WebDriver API. Instead, we can achieve this automation easily by executing a simple JavaScript line. Example 4-1 shows a basic example using a practice web page (see the URL of this page in the first line of the test method).

Example 4-1. Test executing JavaScript to scroll down a pixels amount

```
@Test
void testScrollBy() {
    driver.get(
            "https://bonigarcia.dev/selenium-webdriver-java/long-page.html"); ❶
    JavascriptExecutor js = (JavascriptExecutor) driver; ❷

    String script = "window.scrollBy(0, 1000);";
    js.executeScript(script); ❸
}
```

❶ Open a practice web page containing very long text (see Figure 4-1).

❷ Cast the `driver` object to `JavascriptExecutor`. We will use the variable `js` to execute JavaScript in the browser.

❸ Execute a piece of JavaScript code. In this case, we call the JavaScript function `scrollBy()` to scroll the document by a given amount (in this case, 1,000 px down). Notice that this fragment does not use `return`, and therefore, we do not receive any returned object in the Java logic. In addition, we are not passing any argument to the script.

Figure 4-1. Practice web page with long content

Example 4-2 shows another test using scrolling and the same example web page as before. This time, instead of moving a fixed number of pixels, we move the document scroll until the last paragraph in the web page.

Example 4-2. Test executing JavaScript to scroll down to a given element

```
@Test
void testScrollIntoView() {
    driver.get(
            "https://bonigarcia.dev/selenium-webdriver-java/long-page.html");
    JavascriptExecutor js = (JavascriptExecutor) driver;
    driver.manage().timeouts().implicitlyWait(Duration.ofSeconds(10)); ❶

    WebElement lastElememt = driver
            .findElement(By.cssSelector("p:last-child")); ❷
    String script = "arguments[0].scrollIntoView();"; ❸
    js.executeScript(script, lastElememt); ❹
}
```

❶ To make this test robust, we specify an implicit timeout. Otherwise, the test might fail if the page is not entirely loaded when executing the subsequent commands.

❷ We locate the last paragraph in the web page using a CSS selector.

❸ We define the script to be injected into the page. Notice the script does not return any value, but as a novelty, it uses the first function argument to invoke the Java-Script function `scrollIntoView()`.

❹ We execute the previous script, passing the located `WebElement` as an argument. This element will be the first argument for the script (i.e., `arguments[0]`).

The last example of scrolling is *infinite scroll*. This technique enables the dynamic loading of more content when the user reaches the end of the web page. Automating this kind of web page is an instructive use case since it involves different aspects of the Selenium WebDriver API. For example, you can use a similar approach to crawl web pages using Selenium WebDriver. Example 4-3 shows a test using an infinite scroll page.

Example 4-3. Test executing JavaScript in an infinite scroll page

```
@Test
void testInfiniteScroll() {
    driver.get(
            "https://bonigarcia.dev/selenium-webdriver-java/infinite-scroll.html");
    JavascriptExecutor js = (JavascriptExecutor) driver;
    WebDriverWait wait = new WebDriverWait(driver, Duration.ofSeconds(10)); ❶

    By pLocator = By.tagName("p");
    List<WebElement> paragraphs = wait.until(
            ExpectedConditions.numberOfElementsToBeMoreThan(pLocator, 0));
    int initParagraphsNumber = paragraphs.size(); ❷
```

```
WebElement lastParagraph = driver.findElement(
        By.xpath(String.format("//p[%d]", initParagraphsNumber))); ❸
String script = "arguments[0].scrollIntoView();";
js.executeScript(script, lastParagraph); ❹

wait.until(ExpectedConditions.numberOfElementsToBeMoreThan(pLocator,
        initParagraphsNumber)); ❺
}
```

❶ We define an explicit wait since we need to pause the test until the new content is loaded.

❷ We find the initial number of paragraphs on the page.

❸ We locate the last paragraph of the page.

❹ We scroll down into this element.

❺ We wait until more paragraphs are available on the page.

Color picker

A *color picker* in HTML is an input type that allows users to select a color by clicking and dragging the cursor using a graphical area. The practice web form contains one of these elements (see Figure 4-2).

Figure 4-2. Color picker in the practice web form

The following code shows the HTML markup for the color picker. Notice that it sets an initial color value (otherwise, the default color is black).

```
<input type="color" class="form-control form-control-color" name="my-colors"
        value="#563d7c">
```

Example 4-4 illustrates how to interact with this color picker. Because the Selenium WebDriver API does not provide any asset to control color pickers, we use JavaScript. In addition, this test also illustrates the use of Color, a support class available in the Selenium WebDriver API for working with colors.

Example 4-4. Test executing JavaScript to interact with a color picker

```
@Test
void testColorPicker() {
    driver.get(
            "https://bonigarcia.dev/selenium-webdriver-java/web-form.html");
    JavascriptExecutor js = (JavascriptExecutor) driver;

    WebElement colorPicker = driver.findElement(By.name("my-colors")); ❶
    String initColor = colorPicker.getAttribute("value"); ❷
    log.debug("The initial color is {}", initColor);

    Color red = new Color(255, 0, 0, 1); ❸
    String script = String.format(
            "arguments[0].setAttribute('value', '%s');", red.asHex());
    js.executeScript(script, colorPicker); ❹

    String finalColor = colorPicker.getAttribute("value"); ❺
    log.debug("The final color is {}", finalColor);
    assertThat(finalColor).isNotEqualTo(initColor); ❻
    assertThat(Color.fromString(finalColor)).isEqualTo(red);
}
```

❶ We locate the color picker by name.

❷ We read the initial value of the color picker (it should be #563d7c).

❸ We define a color to work with using the following RGBA components: red=255 (maximum value), green=0 (minimum value), blue=0 (minimum value), and alpha=1 (maximum value, i.e., fully opaque).

❹ We use JavaScript to change the value selected in the color picker. Alternatively, we can change the selected color invoking the statement colorPicker.send Keys(red.asHex());.

❺ We read the resulting value of the color picker (it should be #ff0000).

❻ We assert that the color is different from the initial value, but as expected.

Pinned Scripts

The Selenium WebDriver API allows you to *pin* scripts in Selenium WebDriver 4. This feature enables attaching JavaScript fragments to a WebDriver session, assigning a unique key to each snippet, and executing these snippets on demand (even on different web pages). Example 4-5 shows a test using *pinned* scripts.

Example 4-5. Test executing JavaScript as pinned scripts

```
@Test
void testPinnedScripts() {
    String initPage = "https://bonigarcia.dev/selenium-webdriver-java/";
    driver.get(initPage);
    JavascriptExecutor js = (JavascriptExecutor) driver;

    ScriptKey linkKey = js
            .pin("return document.getElementsByTagName('a')[2];"); ❶
    ScriptKey firstArgKey = js.pin("return arguments[0];"); ❷

    Set<ScriptKey> pinnedScripts = js.getPinnedScripts(); ❸
    assertThat(pinnedScripts).hasSize(2); ❹

    WebElement formLink = (WebElement) js.executeScript(linkKey); ❺
    formLink.click(); ❻
    assertThat(driver.getCurrentUrl()).isNotEqualTo(initPage); ❼

    String message = "Hello world!";
    String executeScript = (String) js.executeScript(firstArgKey, message); ❽
    assertThat(executeScript).isEqualTo(message); ❾

    js.unpin(linkKey); ❿
    assertThat(js.getPinnedScripts()).hasSize(1); ⓫
}
```

❶ We attach a JavaScript fragment to locate an element in the web page. Notice that we could do the same with the standard WebDriver API. Nevertheless, we use this approach for demo purposes.

❷ We attach another piece of JavaScript that returns whatever we pass to it as a first parameter.

❸ We read the set of pinned scripts.

❹ We assert the number of pinned scripts is as expected (i.e., 2).

❺ We execute the first pinned script. As a result, we get the third link in the web page as a `WebElement` in Java.

❻ We click on this link, which should correspond to the practice web link. As a result, the browser should navigate to that page.

❼ We assert the current URL is different from the initial one.

❽ We execute the second pinned script. Notice that it is possible to run the pinned script even though the page has changed in the browser (since the script is attached to the session and not to a single page).

❾ We assert the returned message is as expected.

❿ We unpin one of the scripts.

⓫ We verify the number of pinned scripts is as expected (i.e., 1 at this point).

Asynchronous Scripts

The method `executeAsyncScript()` of the `JavascriptExecutor` interface allows executing JavaScript scripts in the context of a web page using Selenium WebDriver. In the same way that `executeScript()` explained previously, `executeAsyncScript()` executes an anonymous function with the provided JavaScript code in the body of the current page. The execution of this function blocks the Selenium WebDriver control flow. The difference is that in `executeAsyncScript()`, we must explicitly signal the script termination by invoking a *done* callback. This callback is injected into the executed script as the last argument (i.e., `arguments[arguments.length - 1]`) in the corresponding anonymous function. Example 4-6 shows a test using this mechanism.

Example 4-6. Test executing asynchronous JavaScript

```
@Test
void testAsyncScript() {
    driver.get("https://bonigarcia.dev/selenium-webdriver-java/");
    JavascriptExecutor js = (JavascriptExecutor) driver;

    Duration pause = Duration.ofSeconds(2); ❶
    String script = "const callback = arguments[arguments.length - 1];"
            + "window.setTimeout(callback, " + pause.toMillis() + ");"; ❷

    long initMillis = System.currentTimeMillis(); ❸
    js.executeAsyncScript(script); ❹
    Duration elapsed = Duration
            .ofMillis(System.currentTimeMillis() - initMillis); ❺
```

```
    log.debug("The script took {} ms to be executed", elapsed.toMillis());
    assertThat(elapsed).isGreaterThanOrEqualTo(pause); ❻
}
```

❶ We define a pause time of 2 seconds.

❷ We define the script to be executed. In the first line, we define a constant for the callback (i.e., the last script argument). After that, we use the JavaScript function `window.setTimeout()` to pause the script execution for a given amount of time.

❸ We get the current system time (in milliseconds).

❹ We execute the script. If everything works as expected, the test execution blocks in this line for second seconds (as defined in step 1).

❺ We calculate the time required to execute the previous line.

❻ We assert the elapsed time is as expected (typically, some milliseconds above the defined pause time).

 You can find an additional example that executes an asynchronous script on "Notifications" on page 162.

Timeouts

Selenium WebDriver allows specifying three types of timeouts. We can use them by invoking the method `manage().timeouts()` in the Selenium WebDriver API. The first timeout is the implicit wait, already explained in "Implicit Wait" on page 94 (as part of waiting strategies). The other options are page loading and script loading timeouts, explained next.

Page Loading Timeout

The *page loading timeout* provides a time limit to interrupt a navigation attempt. In other words, this timeout limits the time in which a web page is loaded. When this timeout (which has a default value of 30 seconds) is exceeded, an exception is thrown. Example 4-7 shows an example of this timeout. As you can see, this piece of code is a dummy implementation of a *negative* test. In other words, it checks unexpected conditions in the SUT.

Example 4-7. Test using a page loading timeout

```
@Test
void testPageLoadTimeout() {
    driver.manage().timeouts().pageLoadTimeout(Duration.ofMillis(1)); ❶

    assertThatThrownBy(() -> driver
            .get("https://bonigarcia.dev/selenium-webdriver-java/"))
                .isInstanceOf(TimeoutException.class); ❷
}
```

❶ We specify the minimum possible page loading timeout, which is one millisecond.

❷ We load a web page. This invocation (implemented as Java lambda) will fail since it is impossible to load that web page in less than one millisecond. For this reason, the exception `TimeoutException` is expected to be thrown in the lambda, using the AssertJ method `assertThatThrownBy`.

 You can play with this test by removing the timeout declaration (i.e., step 1). If you do that, the test will fail since an exception is expected but not thrown.

Script Loading Timeout

The *script loading timeout* provides a time limit to interrupt a script that is being evaluated. This timeout has a default value of three hundred seconds. Example 4-8 shows a test using a script loading timeout.

Example 4-8. Test using a script loading timeout

```
@Test
void testScriptTimeout() {
    driver.get("https://bonigarcia.dev/selenium-webdriver-java/");
    JavascriptExecutor js = (JavascriptExecutor) driver;
    driver.manage().timeouts().scriptTimeout(Duration.ofSeconds(3)); ❶

    assertThatThrownBy(() -> {
        long waitMillis = Duration.ofSeconds(5).toMillis();
        String script = "const callback = arguments[arguments.length - 1];"
                + "window.setTimeout(callback, " + waitMillis + ");"; ❷
        js.executeAsyncScript(script);
    }).isInstanceOf(ScriptTimeoutException.class); ❸
}
```

❶ We define a script timeout of three seconds. This means that a script lasting for more than that time will throw an exception.

❷ We execute an asynchronous script that pauses the execution of five seconds.

❸ The script execution time is greater than the configured script timeout, resulting in a `ScriptTimeoutException`. Again, this example is a negative test, i.e., designed to expect this exception.

Screenshots

Selenium WebDriver is used mainly to carry out end-to-end functional testing of web applications. In other words, we use it to verify that web applications behave as expected by interacting with their user interface (i.e., using a web browser). This approach is very convenient to automate high-level user scenarios, but it also presents different difficulties. One of the main challenges in end-to-end testing is to diagnose the underlying cause of a failed test. Supposing the failure is legitimate (i.e., not induced by a poorly implemented test), the root cause might be diverse: the client side (e.g., incorrect JavaScript logic), the server side (e.g., internal exception), or the integration with other components (e.g., inadequate access to the database), among other reasons. One of the most pervasive mechanisms used in Selenium WebDriver for failure analysis is making browser screenshots. This section presents the mechanisms provided by the Selenium WebDriver API.

 "Failure Analysis" on page 265 reviews the framework-specific techniques to determine when a test has failed to carry out different failure analysis techniques, such as screenshots, recordings, and log gathering.

Selenium WebDriver provides the interface `TakesScreenshot` for making browser screenshots. Any driver object inheriting from `RemoteWebDriver` (see Figure 2-2) also implements this interface. Thus, we can cast a `WebDriver` object that instantiates one of the major browsers (e.g., `ChromeDriver`, `FirefoxDriver`, etc.) as follows:

```
WebDriver driver = new ChromeDriver();
TakesScreenshot ts = (TakesScreenshot) driver;
```

The interface `TakesScreenshot` only provides a method called `getScreenshotAs(Out putType<X> target)` to make screenshots. The parameter `OutputType<X> target` determines the screenshot type and the returned value. Table 4-2 shows the available alternatives for this parameter.

Table 4-2. OutputType parameters

Parameter	Description	Return	Example
OutputType.FILE	Make screenshot as a PNG file (located in a temporary system directory)	File	`File screenshot = ts.getScreenshotAs( OutputType.FILE);`
OutputType.BASE64	Make a screenshot in Base64 format (i.e., encoded as an ASCII string)	String	`String screenshot = ts.getScreenshotAs( OutputType.BASE64);`
OutputType.BYTES	Make a screenshot as a raw byte array	byte[]	`byte[] screenshot = ts.getScreenshotAs( OutputType.BYTES);`

 The method `getScreenshotAs()` allows making screenshots of the browser viewport. In addition, Selenium WebDriver 4 allows creating full-page screenshots using different mechanisms (see "Full-page screenshot" on page 183).

Example 4-9 shows a test for taking a browser screenshot in PNG format. Example 4-10 shows another test for creating a screenshot as a Base64 string. The resulting screenshot is shown in Figure 4-3.

Example 4-9. Test making a screenshot as a PNG file

```
@Test
void testScreenshotPng() throws IOException {
    driver.get("https://bonigarcia.dev/selenium-webdriver-java/");
    TakesScreenshot ts = (TakesScreenshot) driver;

    File screenshot = ts.getScreenshotAs(OutputType.FILE); ❶
    log.debug("Screenshot created on {}", screenshot);

    Path destination = Paths.get("screenshot.png"); ❷
    Files.move(screenshot.toPath(), destination, REPLACE_EXISTING); ❸
    log.debug("Screenshot moved to {}", destination);

    assertThat(destination).exists(); ❹
}
```

❶ We make the browser screen a PNG file.

❷ This file is located in a temporary folder by default, so we move it to a new file called `screenshot.png` (in the root project folder).

❸ We use standard Java to move the screenshot file to the new location.

❹ We use assertions to verify that the target file exists.

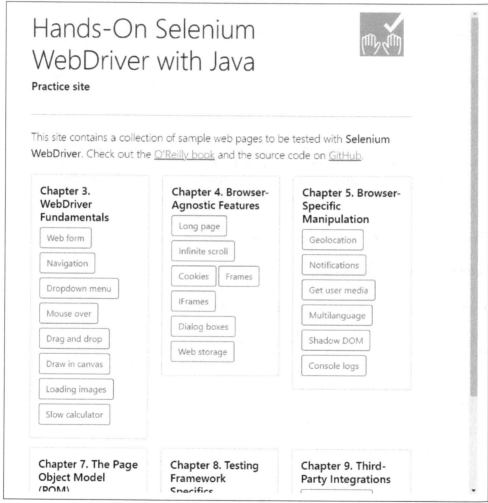

Figure 4-3. Browser screenshot of the practice site index page

Example 4-10. Test making a screenshot as Base64

```
@Test
void testScreenshotBase64() {
    driver.get("https://bonigarcia.dev/selenium-webdriver-java/");
    TakesScreenshot ts = (TakesScreenshot) driver;

    String screenshot = ts.getScreenshotAs(OutputType.BASE64); ❶
    log.debug("Screenshot in base64 "
            + "(you can copy and paste it into a browser navigation bar to watch it)\n"
            + "data:image/png;base64,{}", screenshot); ❷
    assertThat(screenshot).isNotEmpty(); ❸
}
```

❶ We make the browser screen in Base64 format.

❷ We append the prefix `data:image/png;base64,` to the Base64 string and log it in the standard output. You can copy and paste this resulting string in a browser navigation bar to display the picture.

❸ We assert that the screenshot string has content.

> Logging the screenshot in Base64 as presented in the previous example could be very useful for diagnosing failures when running tests in CI servers in which we do not have access to the file system (e.g., GitHub Actions).

WebElement Screenshots

The `WebElement` interface extends the `TakesScreenshot` interface. This way, it is possible to make partial screenshots of the visible content of a given web element. (See Example 4-11.) Notice that this test is very similar to the previous one using PNG files, but in this case, we invoke the method `getScreenshotAs()` directly using a web element. Figure 4-4 shows the resulting screenshot.

Example 4-11. Test making a partial screenshot as a PNG file

```
@Test
void testWebElementScreenshot() throws IOException {
    driver.get(
            "https://bonigarcia.dev/selenium-webdriver-java/web-form.html");

    WebElement form = driver.findElement(By.tagName("form"));
    File screenshot = form.getScreenshotAs(OutputType.FILE);
    Path destination = Paths.get("webelement-screenshot.png");
    Files.move(screenshot.toPath(), destination, REPLACE_EXISTING);
```

```
    assertThat(destination).exists();
}
```

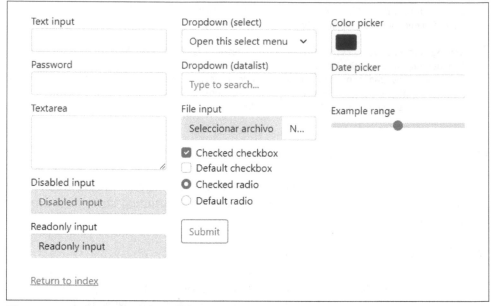

Figure 4-4. Partial screenshot of the practice web form

Window Size and Position

The Selenium WebDriver API allows manipulating browser size and position very easily using the `Window` interface. This type is accessible from a driver object using the following statement. Table 4-3 shows the available methods in this interface. Then, Example 4-12 shows a basic test about this feature.

```
Window window = driver.manage().window();
```

Table 4-3. Window methods

Method	Return	Description
getSize()	Dimension	Get the current window size. It returns the outer window dimension, not just the *viewport* (i.e., the visible area of a web page for end users).
setSize(Dimension targetSize)	void	Change the current window size (again, its outer dimension, and not the viewport).
getPosition()	Point	Get current window position (relative to the upper left corner of the screen).
setPosition(Point targetPosition)	void	Change the current window position (again, relative to the screen's upper left corner).
maximize()	void	Maximize the current window.

Method	Return	Description
minimize()	void	Minimize the current window.
fullscreen()	void	Fullscreen the current window.

Example 4-12. Test reading and changing the browser size and position

```
@Test
void testWindow() {
    driver.get("https://bonigarcia.dev/selenium-webdriver-java/");
    Window window = driver.manage().window();

    Point initialPosition = window.getPosition();     ❶
    Dimension initialSize = window.getSize();     ❷
    log.debug("Initial window: position {} -- size {}", initialPosition,
            initialSize);

    window.maximize();     ❸

    Point maximizedPosition = window.getPosition();
    Dimension maximizedSize = window.getSize();
    log.debug("Maximized window: position {} -- size {}", maximizedPosition,
            maximizedSize);

    assertThat(initialPosition).isNotEqualTo(maximizedPosition);     ❹
    assertThat(initialSize).isNotEqualTo(maximizedSize);
}
```

❶ We read the window position.

❷ We read the window size.

❸ We maximize the browser window.

❹ We verify that the maximized position (and size, in the following line) is different from the original window.

Browser History

Selenium WebDriver allows manipulating the browser history through the Naviga
tion interface. The following statement illustrates how to access this interface from a
WebDriver object. Using this interface is quite simple. Table 4-4 shows its public
methods, and Example 4-13 shows a basic example. Notice that this test navigates
into different web pages using these methods, and at the end of the test, it verifies the
web page URL is as expected.

```
Navigation navigation = driver.navigate();
```

Table 4-4. Navigation methods

Method	Return	Description
back()	void	Go back in the browser history
forward()	void	Go forward in the browser history
to(String url) to(URL url)	void	Load a new web page in the current window
refresh()	void	Refresh the current page

Example 4-13. Test using navigation methods

```
@Test
void testHistory() {
    String baseUrl = "https://bonigarcia.dev/selenium-webdriver-java/";
    String firstPage = baseUrl + "navigation1.html";
    String secondPage = baseUrl + "navigation2.html";
    String thirdPage = baseUrl + "navigation3.html";

    driver.get(firstPage);

    driver.navigate().to(secondPage);
    driver.navigate().to(thirdPage);
    driver.navigate().back();
    driver.navigate().forward();
    driver.navigate().refresh();

    assertThat(driver.getCurrentUrl()).isEqualTo(thirdPage);
}
```

The Shadow DOM

As introduced in "The Document Object Model (DOM)" on page 59, the DOM is a programming interface that allows us to represent and manipulate a web page using a tree structure. The *shadow DOM* is a feature of this programming interface that enables the creation of scoped subtrees inside the regular DOM tree. The shadow DOM allows the encapsulation of a group of a DOM subtree (called *shadow tree*, as represented in Figure 4-5) that can specify different CSS styles from the original DOM. The node in the regular DOM in which the shadow tree is attached is called the *shadow host*. The root node of the shadow tree is called the *shadow root*. As represented in Figure 4-5, the shadow tree is flattened into the original DOM in a single composed tree to be rendered in the browser.

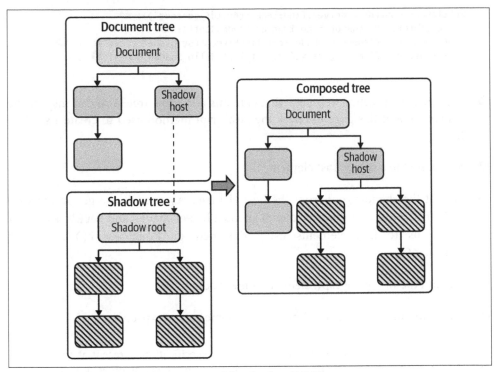

Figure 4-5. Schematic representation of the shadow DOM

The shadow DOM is part of the standard suite (together with HTML templates or custom elements) that allows the implementation of web components (*https://github.com/WICG/webcompo nents*) (i.e., reusable custom elements for web applications).

The shadow DOM allows the creation of self-contained components. In other words, the shadow tree is isolated from the original DOM. This feature is useful for web design and composition, but it can be challenging for automated testing with Selenium WebDriver (since the regular location strategies cannot find web elements within the shadow tree). Luckily, Selenium WebDriver 4 provides a `WebElement` method that allows access to the shadow DOM. Example 4-14 demonstrates this use.

Example 4-14. Test reading the shadow DOM

```
@Test
void testShadowDom() {
    driver.get(
            "https://bonigarcia.dev/selenium-webdriver-java/shadow-dom.html"); ❶
```

```
    WebElement content = driver.findElement(By.id("content")); ❷
    SearchContext shadowRoot = content.getShadowRoot(); ❸
    WebElement textElement = shadowRoot.findElement(By.cssSelector("p")); ❹
    assertThat(textElement.getText()).contains("Hello Shadow DOM"); ❺
}
```

❶ We open the practice web page that contains a shadow tree. You can inspect the source code of this page to check the JavaScript method used to create a shadow tree.

❷ We locate the shadow host element.

❸ We get the shadow root from the host element. As a result, we get an instance of SearchContext, an interface implemented by WebDriver and WebElement, that allows us to find elements using the methods findElement() and find Elements().

❹ We find the first paragraph element in the shadow tree.

❺ We verify the text content of the shadow element is as expected.

 This feature of the W3C WebDriver specification is recent at the time of this writing, and therefore might not be implemented in all drivers (e.g., chromedriver, geckodriver). For instance, it is available starting with version 96 of both Chrome and Edge.

Cookies

HTTP 1.x is a stateless protocol, meaning that the server does not track the user state. In other words, web servers do not remember users across different requests. The cookies mechanism is an extension to HTTP that allows tracking users by sending small pieces of text called *cookies* from server to client. These cookies must be sent back by clients, and this way, servers remember their clients. Cookies allow you to maintain web sessions or personalize the user experience on the website, among other functions.

Web browsers allow managing the browser cookies manually. Selenium WebDriver enables an equivalent manipulation, but programmatically. The Selenium WebDriver API provides the methods shown in Table 4-5 to accomplish this. They are accessible through the manage() function of a WebDriver object.

Table 4-5. Cookies management methods

Method	Return	Description
`addCookie(Cookie cookie)`	`void`	Add a new cookie
`deleteCookieNamed(String name)`	`void`	Delete an existing cookie by name
`deleteCookie(Cookie cookie)`	`void`	Delete an existing cookie by instance
`deleteAllCookies()`	`void`	Delete all cookies
`getCookies()`	`Set<Cookie>`	Get all cookies
`getCookieNamed(String name)`	`Cookie`	Get a cookie by name

As this table shows, the `Cookie` class provides an abstraction to a single cookie in Java. Table 4-6 summarizes the methods available in this class. In addition, this class has several constructors, which positionally accept the following parameters:

`String name`
Cookie name (mandatory)

`String value`
Cookie value (mandatory)

`String domain`
Domain in which the cookie is visible (optional)

`String path`
Path in which the cookie is visible (optional)

`Date expiry`
Cookie expiration date (optional)

`boolean isSecure`
Whether the cookie requires a secure connection (optional)

`boolean isHttpOnly`
Whether this cookie is an HTTP-only cookie, i.e., the cookie is not accessible through a client-side script (optional)

`String sameSite`
Whether this cookie is a same-site cookie, i.e., the cookie is restricted to a first-party or same-site context (optional)

Table 4-6. Cookie methods

Method	Return	Description
getName()	String	Read cookie name
getValue()	String	Read cookie value
getDomain()	String	Read cookie domain
getPath()	String	Read cookie path
isSecure()	boolean	Read if cookie requires a secure connection
isHttpOnly()	boolean	Read if cookie is HTTP-only
getExpiry()	Date	Read cookie expiry date
getSameSite()	String	Read cookie same-site context
validate()	void	Check the different fields of the cookie and throw an `IllegalArgument Exception` if it encounters any problem
toJson()	Map<String, Object>	Map cookie values as a key-value map

The following examples show different tests managing web cookies with the Selenium WebDriver API. These examples use a practice web page that shows the site cookies on the GUI (see Figure 4-6):

- Example 4-15 illustrates how to read the existing cookies of a website.
- Example 4-16 shows how to add new cookies.
- Example 4-17 explains how to edit existing cookies.
- Example 4-18 demonstrates how to delete cookies.

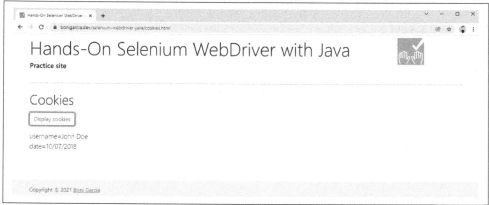

Figure 4-6. Practice web page for web cookies

Example 4-15. Test reading existing cookies

```
@Test
void testReadCookies() {
    driver.get(
            "https://bonigarcia.dev/selenium-webdriver-java/cookies.html");

    Options options = driver.manage(); ❶
    Set<Cookie> cookies = options.getCookies(); ❷
    assertThat(cookies).hasSize(2);

    Cookie username = options.getCookieNamed("username"); ❸
    assertThat(username.getValue()).isEqualTo("John Doe"); ❹
    assertThat(username.getPath()).isEqualTo("/");

    driver.findElement(By.id("refresh-cookies")).click(); ❺
}
```

❶ We get the Options object used to manage cookies.

❷ We read all the cookies available on this page. It should contain two cookies.

❸ We read the cookie with the name username.

❹ The value of the previous cookie should be John Doe.

❺ The last statement does not affect the test. We invoke this command to check the cookies in the browser GUI.

Example 4-16. Test adding new cookies

```
@Test
void testAddCookies() {
    driver.get(
            "https://bonigarcia.dev/selenium-webdriver-java/cookies.html");

    Options options = driver.manage();
    Cookie newCookie = new Cookie("new-cookie-key", "new-cookie-value"); ❶
    options.addCookie(newCookie); ❷
    String readValue = options.getCookieNamed(newCookie.getName())
            .getValue(); ❸
    assertThat(newCookie.getValue()).isEqualTo(readValue); ❹

    driver.findElement(By.id("refresh-cookies")).click();
}
```

❶ We create a new cookie.

❷   We add the cookie to the current page.

❸   We read the value of the cookie just added.

❹   We verify this value is as expected.

Example 4-17. Test editing existing cookies

```
@Test
void testEditCookie() {
    driver.get(
            "https://bonigarcia.dev/selenium-webdriver-java/cookies.html");

    Options options = driver.manage();
    Cookie username = options.getCookieNamed("username"); ❶
    Cookie editedCookie = new Cookie(username.getName(), "new-value"); ❷
    options.addCookie(editedCookie); ❸

    Cookie readCookie = options.getCookieNamed(username.getName()); ❹
    assertThat(editedCookie).isEqualTo(readCookie); ❺

    driver.findElement(By.id("refresh-cookies")).click();
}
```

❶   We read an existing cookie.

❷   We create a new cookie reusing the previous cookie name.

❸   We add the new cookie to the web page.

❹   We read the cookie just added.

❺   We verify the cookie has been correctly edited.

Example 4-18. Test deleting existing cookies

```
@Test
void testDeleteCookies() {
    driver.get(
            "https://bonigarcia.dev/selenium-webdriver-java/cookies.html");

    Options options = driver.manage();
    Set<Cookie> cookies = options.getCookies(); ❶
    Cookie username = options.getCookieNamed("username"); ❷
    options.deleteCookie(username); ❸

    assertThat(options.getCookies()).hasSize(cookies.size() - 1); ❹
```

```
    driver.findElement(By.id("refresh-cookies")).click();
}
```

❶　We read all cookies.

❷　We read the cookie with the name username.

❸　We delete the previous cookie.

❹　We verify the size of the cookies is as expected.

Dropdown Lists

A typical element in web forms is dropdown lists. These fields allow users to select one or more elements within an option list. The classical HTML tags used to render these fields are <select> and <options>. As usual, the practice web form contains one of these elements (see Figure 4-7), defined in HTML as follows:

```
<select class="form-select" name="my-select">
  <option selected>Open this select menu</option>
  <option value="1">One</option>
  <option value="2">Two</option>
  <option value="3">Three</option>
</select>
```

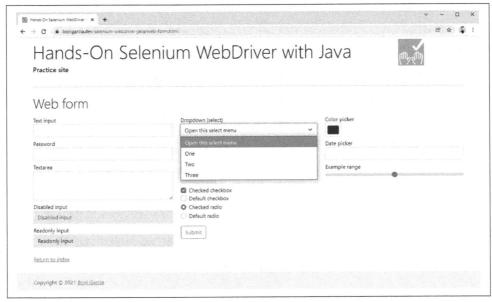

Figure 4-7. Select field in the practice web form

These elements are very spread out in web forms. For this reason, Selenium Web-Driver provides a helper class called `Select` to simplify their manipulation. This class wraps a select `WebElement` and provides a wide variety of features. Table 4-7 summarizes the public methods available in the `Select` class. After that, Example 4-19 shows a basic test using this class.

Table 4-7. Select methods

Method	Return	Description
`Select(WebElement element)`	Select	Constructor using a `WebElement` as parameter (it must be a `<select>` element); otherwise it throws an `UnexpectedTagNameException`
`getWrappedElement()`	WebElement	Get wrapped `WebElement` (i.e., the one used in the constructor)
`isMultiple()`	boolean	Whether the select element supports selecting multiple options
`getOptions()`	List<WebElement>	Read all options that belong to the select element
`getAllSelectedOptions()`	List<WebElement>	Read all selected options
`getFirstSelectedOption()`	WebElement	Read first selected option
`selectByVisibleText(String text)`	void	Select all options that match a given displayed text
`selectByIndex(int index)`	void	Select an option by index number
`selectByValue(String value)`	void	Select option(s) by value attribute
`deselectAll()`	void	Deselect all options
`deselectByValue(String value)`	void	Deselect option(s) by value attribute
`deselectByIndex(int index)`	void	Deselect by index number
`deselectByVisibleText(String text)`	void	Deselect options that match a given displayed text

Example 4-19. Test interacting with a select field

```
@Test
void test() {
    driver.get(
            "https://bonigarcia.dev/selenium-webdriver-java/web-form.html");

    Select select = new Select(driver.findElement(By.name("my-select"))); ❶
    String optionLabel = "Three";
    select.selectByVisibleText(optionLabel); ❷

    assertThat(select.getFirstSelectedOption().getText())
            .isEqualTo(optionLabel); ❸
}
```

❶ We find the select element by name and use the resulting `WebElement` to instantiate a `Select` object.

❷ We select one of the options available in this select, using a by-text strategy.

❸ We verify the selected option text is as expected.

Data List Elements

Another way to implement dropdown lists in HTML is using *data lists*. Although data lists are very similar to select elements from a graphical point of view, there is a clear distinction between them. On the one hand, select fields display an options list, and users choose one (or several) of the available options. On the other hand, data lists show a list of suggested options associated with an input form (text) field, and users are free to select one of those suggested values or type a custom value. The practice web form contains one of these data lists. You can find its markup in the following snippet and a screenshot in Figure 4-8.

```
<input class="form-control" list="my-options" name="my-datalist"
        placeholder="Type to search...">
<datalist id="my-options">
  <option value="San Francisco">
  <option value="New York">
  <option value="Seattle">
  <option value="Los Angeles">
  <option value="Chicago">
</datalist>
```

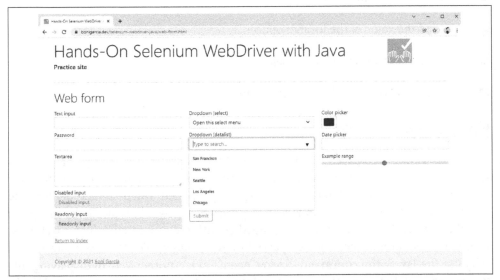

Figure 4-8. Data list field in the practice web form

Selenium WebDriver does not provide a custom helper class to manipulate data lists. Instead, we need to interact with them as standard input texts, with the distinction that their options are displayed when clicking on the input field. Example 4-20 shows a test illustrating this.

Example 4-20. Test interacting with a data list field

```java
@Test
void testDatalist() {
    driver.get(
            "https://bonigarcia.dev/selenium-webdriver-java/web-form.html");

    WebElement datalist = driver.findElement(By.name("my-datalist")); ❶
    datalist.click(); ❷

    WebElement option = driver
            .findElement(By.xpath("//datalist/option[2]")); ❸
    String optionValue = option.getAttribute("value"); ❹
    datalist.sendKeys(optionValue); ❺

    assertThat(optionValue).isEqualTo("New York"); ❻
}
```

❶ We locate the input field used for the data list.

❷ We click on it to display its options.

❸ We find the second option.

❹ We read the value of the located option.

❺ We type that value in the input field.

❻ We assert the option value is as expected.

Navigation Targets

When navigating web pages using a browser, by default, we use a single page corresponding to the URL in the navigation bar. Then, we can open another page in a new browser tab. This second tab can be explicitly opened when a link defines the attribute `target`, or the user can force navigation to a new tab, typically by using the modifier key Ctrl (or Cmd in macOS) together with the mouse click into a web link. Another possibility is opening web pages in new windows. For this, web pages typically use the JavaScript command `window.open(url)`. Another way of displaying different pages at the same time is using *frames* and *iframes*. A frame is an HTML element type that defines a particular area (into a set called *frameset*) where a web page can be displayed. An iframe is another HTML element that allows embedding an HTML page into the current one.

 Using frames is not encouraged since these elements have many drawbacks, such as performance and accessibility problems. I explain how to use them through Selenium WebDriver for compatibility reasons. Nevertheless, I strongly recommend avoiding frames on brand-new web applications.

The Selenium WebDriver API provides the interface `TargetLocator` to deal with the previously mentioned targets (i.e., tabs, windows, frames, and iframes). This interface allows changing the focus of the future commands of a `WebDriver` object (to a new tab, windows, etc.). This interface is accessible by invoking the method `switchTo()` in a `WebDriver` object. Table 4-8 describes its public methods.

Table 4-8. TargetLocator methods

Method	Return	Description
frame(int index)	WebDriver	Change focus to a frame (or iframe) by index number.
frame(String nameOrId)	WebDriver	Change focus to a frame (or iframe) by name or id.
frame(WebElement frameElement)	WebDriver	Change focus to a frame (or iframe) previously located as a WebElement.
parentFrame()	WebDriver	Change focus to the parent context.
window(String nameOrHandle)	WebDriver	Switch the focus to another window, by name or *handle*. A window handle is a hexadecimal string that univocally identifies a window or tab.
newWindow(WindowType typeHint)	WebDriver	Creates a new browser window (using WindowType.WINDOW) or tab (WindowType.TAB) and switches the focus to it.
defaultContent()	WebDriver	Select the main document (when using iframes) or the first frame on the page (when using a frameset).
activeElement()	WebElement	Get the element currently selected.
alert()	Alert	Change focus to a window alert (see "Dialog Boxes" on page 133 for further details).

Tabs and Windows

Example 4-21 shows a test where we open a new tab for navigating a second web page. Example 4-22 shows an equivalent case but for opening a new window for the second web page. Notice that the difference between these examples is only the parameter `WindowType.TAB` and `WindowType.WINDOW`.

Example 4-21. Test opening a new tab

```
@Test
void testNewTab() {
    driver.get("https://bonigarcia.dev/selenium-webdriver-java/"); ❶
    String initHandle = driver.getWindowHandle(); ❷

    driver.switchTo().newWindow(WindowType.TAB); ❸
    driver.get(
            "https://bonigarcia.dev/selenium-webdriver-java/web-form.html"); ❹
    assertThat(driver.getWindowHandles().size()).isEqualTo(2); ❺

    driver.switchTo().window(initHandle); ❻
    driver.close(); ❼
    assertThat(driver.getWindowHandles().size()).isEqualTo(1); ❽
}
```

❶   We navigate to a web page.

❷   We get the current window handle.

❸   We open a new tab and change the focus to it.

❹   We open another web page (since the focus is in the second tab, the page is opened in the second tab).

❺   We verify that the number of window handles at this point is 2.

❻   We change the focus to the initial window (using its handle).

❼   We close only the current window. The second tab remains open.

❽   We verify that the number of window handles now is 1.

Example 4-22. Test opening a new window

```
@Test
void testNewWindow() {
    driver.get("https://bonigarcia.dev/selenium-webdriver-java/");
    String initHandle = driver.getWindowHandle();

    driver.switchTo().newWindow(WindowType.WINDOW); ❶
    driver.get(
            "https://bonigarcia.dev/selenium-webdriver-java/web-form.html");
    assertThat(driver.getWindowHandles().size()).isEqualTo(2);

    driver.switchTo().window(initHandle);
    driver.close();
```

```
    assertThat(driver.getWindowHandles().size()).isEqualTo(1);
}
```

❶ This line is different in the examples. In this case, we open a new window (instead of a tab) and focus on it.

Frames and Iframes

Example 4-23 shows a test in which the web page under test contains an iframe. Example 4-24 shows the equivalent case but using a frameset.

Example 4-23. Test handling iframes

```
@Test
void testIFrames() {
    driver.get(
            "https://bonigarcia.dev/selenium-webdriver-java/iframes.html"); ❶

    WebDriverWait wait = new WebDriverWait(driver, Duration.ofSeconds(10));
    wait.until(ExpectedConditions
            .frameToBeAvailableAndSwitchToIt("my-iframe")); ❷

    By pName = By.tagName("p");
    wait.until(ExpectedConditions.numberOfElementsToBeMoreThan(pName, 0)); ❸
    List<WebElement> paragraphs = driver.findElements(pName);
    assertThat(paragraphs).hasSize(20); ❹
}
```

❶ We open a web page that contains an iframe (see Figure 4-9).

❷ We use an explicit wait for waiting for the frame and switching to it.

❸ We use another explicit wait to pause until the paragraphs contained in the iframe are available.

❹ We assert the number of paragraphs is as expected.

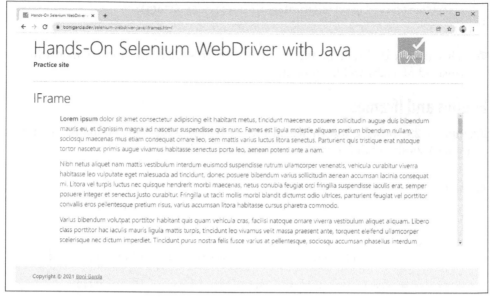

Figure 4-9. Practice web page using an iframe

Example 4-24. Test handling frames

```
@Test
void testFrames() {
    driver.get(
            "https://bonigarcia.dev/selenium-webdriver-java/frames.html"); ❶

    WebDriverWait wait = new WebDriverWait(driver, Duration.ofSeconds(10));
    String frameName = "frame-body";
    wait.until(ExpectedConditions
            .presenceOfElementLocated(By.name(frameName))); ❷
    driver.switchTo().frame(frameName); ❸

    By pName = By.tagName("p");
    wait.until(ExpectedConditions.numberOfElementsToBeMoreThan(pName, 0));
    List<WebElement> paragraphs = driver.findElements(pName);
    assertThat(paragraphs).hasSize(20);
}
```

❶ We open a web page that contains a frameset (see Figure 4-10).

❷ We wait for the frame to be available. Note that steps 2 and 3 in Example 4-23 are equivalent to this step.

❸ We change the focus to this frame.

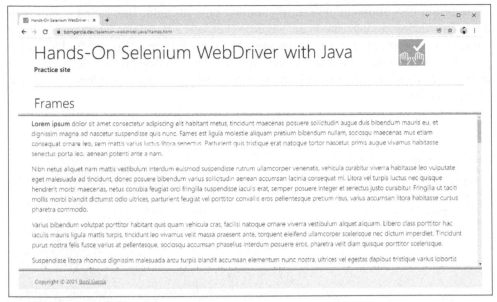

Figure 4-10. Practice web page using frames

Dialog Boxes

JavaScript provides different dialog boxes (sometimes called *pop-ups*) to interact with the user, namely:

Alert
To show a message and wait for the user to press the button OK (only choice in the dialog). For instance, the following code will open a dialog that displays "Hello world!" and waits for the user to press the OK button.

```
alert("Hello world!");
```

Confirm
To show a dialog box with a question and two buttons: OK and Cancel. For instance, the following code will open a dialog showing the message "Is this correct?" and prompting the user to click on OK or Cancel.

```
let correct = confirm("Is this correct?");
```

Prompt
To show a dialog box with a text message, an input text field, and the buttons OK and Cancel. For example, the following code shows a pop-up displaying "Please enter your name," a dialog box in which the user can type, and two buttons (OK and Cancel).

```
let username = prompt("Please enter your name");
```

In addition, CSS allows implementing another type of dialog box called *modal window*. This dialog disables the main window (but keeps it visible) while overlaying a child pop-up, typically showing a message and some buttons. You can find a sample page on the practice web page containing all these dialog boxes (alert, confirm, prompt, and modal). Figure 4-11 shows a screenshot of this page when the modal dialog is active.

Figure 4-11. Practice web page with dialog boxes (alert, confirm, prompt, and modal)

Alerts, Confirms, and Prompts

The Selenium WebDriver API provides the interface `Alert` to manipulate JavaScript dialogs (i.e., alerts, confirms, and prompts). Table 4-9 describes the methods provided by this interface. Then, Example 4-25 shows a basic test interacting with an alert.

Table 4-9. Alert methods

Method	Return	Description
`accept()`	void	To click OK
`getText()`	String	To read the dialog message
`dismiss()`	void	To click Cancel (not available in alerts)
`sendKeys(String text)`	void	To type some string in the input text (only available in prompts)

Example 4-25. Test handling an alert dialog

```
@Test
void testAlert() {
    driver.get(
            "https://bonigarcia.dev/selenium-webdriver-java/dialog-boxes.html"); ❶
    WebDriverWait wait = new WebDriverWait(driver, Duration.ofSeconds(5));

    driver.findElement(By.id("my-alert")).click(); ❷
    wait.until(ExpectedConditions.alertIsPresent()); ❸
    Alert alert = driver.switchTo().alert(); ❹
    assertThat(alert.getText()).isEqualTo("Hello world!"); ❺
    alert.accept(); ❻
}
```

❶ We open the practice web page that launches dialog boxes.

❷ We click on the left button to launch a JavaScript alert.

❸ We wait until the alert dialog is displayed on the screen.

❹ We change the focus to the alert pop-up.

❺ We verify that the alert text is as expected.

❻ We click on the OK button of the alert dialog.

We can replace steps 3 and 4 with a single explicit wait statement, as follows (you can find it in a second test in the same class in the examples repository):

```
Alert alert = wait.until(ExpectedConditions.alertIsPresent());
```

The next test (Example 4-26) illustrates how to deal with a confirm dialog. Notice this example is quite similar to the previous one, but in this case, we can invoke the method dismiss() to click on the Cancel button available on the confirm dialog. Finally, Example 4-27 shows how to manage a prompt dialog. In this case, we can type a string into the input text.

Example 4-26. Test handling a confirm dialog

```
@Test
void testConfirm() {
    driver.get(
            "https://bonigarcia.dev/selenium-webdriver-java/dialog-boxes.html");
    WebDriverWait wait = new WebDriverWait(driver, Duration.ofSeconds(5));

    driver.findElement(By.id("my-confirm")).click();
    wait.until(ExpectedConditions.alertIsPresent());
    Alert confirm = driver.switchTo().alert();
```

```
    assertThat(confirm.getText()).isEqualTo("Is this correct?");
    confirm.dismiss();
}
```

Example 4-27. Test handling a prompt dialog

```
@Test
void testPrompt() {
    driver.get(
            "https://bonigarcia.dev/selenium-webdriver-java/dialog-boxes.html");
    WebDriverWait wait = new WebDriverWait(driver, Duration.ofSeconds(5));

    driver.findElement(By.id("my-prompt")).click();
    wait.until(ExpectedConditions.alertIsPresent());
    Alert prompt = driver.switchTo().alert();
    prompt.sendKeys("John Doe");
    assertThat(prompt.getText()).isEqualTo("Please enter your name");
    prompt.accept();
}
```

Modal Windows

Modal windows are dialog boxes built with basic CSS and HTML. For this reason, Selenium WebDriver does not provide any specific utility for manipulating them. Instead, we use the standard WebDriver API (locators, waits, etc.) to interact with modal windows. Example 4-28 shows a basic test using the practice web page that contains dialog boxes.

Example 4-28. Test handling a modal dialog

```
@Test
void testModal() {
    driver.get(
            "https://bonigarcia.dev/selenium-webdriver-java/dialog-boxes.html");
    WebDriverWait wait = new WebDriverWait(driver, Duration.ofSeconds(5));

    driver.findElement(By.id("my-modal")).click();
    WebElement close = driver
            .findElement(By.xpath("//button[text() = 'Close']"));
    assertThat(close.getTagName()).isEqualTo("button");
    wait.until(ExpectedConditions.elementToBeClickable(close));
    close.click();
}
```

Web Storage

The Web Storage API (*https://html.spec.whatwg.org/multipage/webstorage.html*) allows web applications to store data locally in the client file system. This API provides two JavaScript objects:

`window.localStorage`
> To store data permanently

`window.sessionStorage`
> To store data during the session time (data is deleted when the browser tab is closed)

Selenium WebDriver provides the interface `WebStorage` for manipulating the Web Storage API. Most of the `WebDriver` types supported by Selenium WebDriver inherit this interface: `ChromeDriver`, `EdgeDriver`, `FirefoxDriver`, `OperaDriver`, and `Safari Driver`. This way, we can use this feature of these browsers. Example 4-29 demonstrates this use in Chrome. This test uses both types of web storage (local and session).

Example 4-29. Test using web storage

```
@Test
void testWebStorage() {
    driver.get(
            "https://bonigarcia.dev/selenium-webdriver-java/web-storage.html");
    WebStorage webStorage = (WebStorage) driver; ❶

    LocalStorage localStorage = webStorage.getLocalStorage();
    log.debug("Local storage elements: {}", localStorage.size()); ❷

    SessionStorage sessionStorage = webStorage.getSessionStorage();
    sessionStorage.keySet()
            .forEach(key -> log.debug("Session storage: {}={}", key,
                    sessionStorage.getItem(key))); ❸
    assertThat(sessionStorage.size()).isEqualTo(2);

    sessionStorage.setItem("new element", "new value");
    assertThat(sessionStorage.size()).isEqualTo(3); ❹

    driver.findElement(By.id("display-session")).click();
}
```

❶ We cast the driver object to `WebStorage`.

❷ We log the number of elements of local storage.

❸ We log the session storage (it should contain two elements).

❹ After adding a new element, there should be three elements in the session storage.

Event Listeners

The Selenium WebDriver API allows creating *listeners* that notify events happening in WebDriver and derived objects. In former versions of Selenium WebDriver, this feature was accessible through the class EventFiringWebDriver. This class is deprecated as of Selenium WebDriver 4, and instead, we should use the following:

EventFiringDecorator
> Wrapper class for WebDriver and derived objects (e.g., WebElement, TargetLoca tor, etc.). It allows registering one or more listeners (i.e., WebDriverListener instances).

WebDriverListener
> Interface that should implement the listeners registered in the decorator. It supports three types of events:

> *Before events*
>> Logic inserted just before some event starts

> *After events*
>> Logic inserted just after some event terminates

> *Error events*
>> Logic inserted before an exception is thrown

To implement an event listener, first, we should create a listener class. In other words, we need to create a class that implements the WebDriverListener. This interface defines all its methods using the default keyword, and therefore, it is optional to override their methods. Thanks to that feature (available as of Java 8), our class should only implement the method we need. There are plenty of listener methods available, for instance, afterGet() (executed *after* calling to the method get() in a WebDriver instance), or beforeQuit() (executed *before* calling to the quit() method in a WebDriver instance), to name a few. My recommendation for checking all these listeners is to use your favorite IDE to discover the possible methods to be overridden/implemented. Figure 4-12 shows the wizard for doing this in Eclipse.

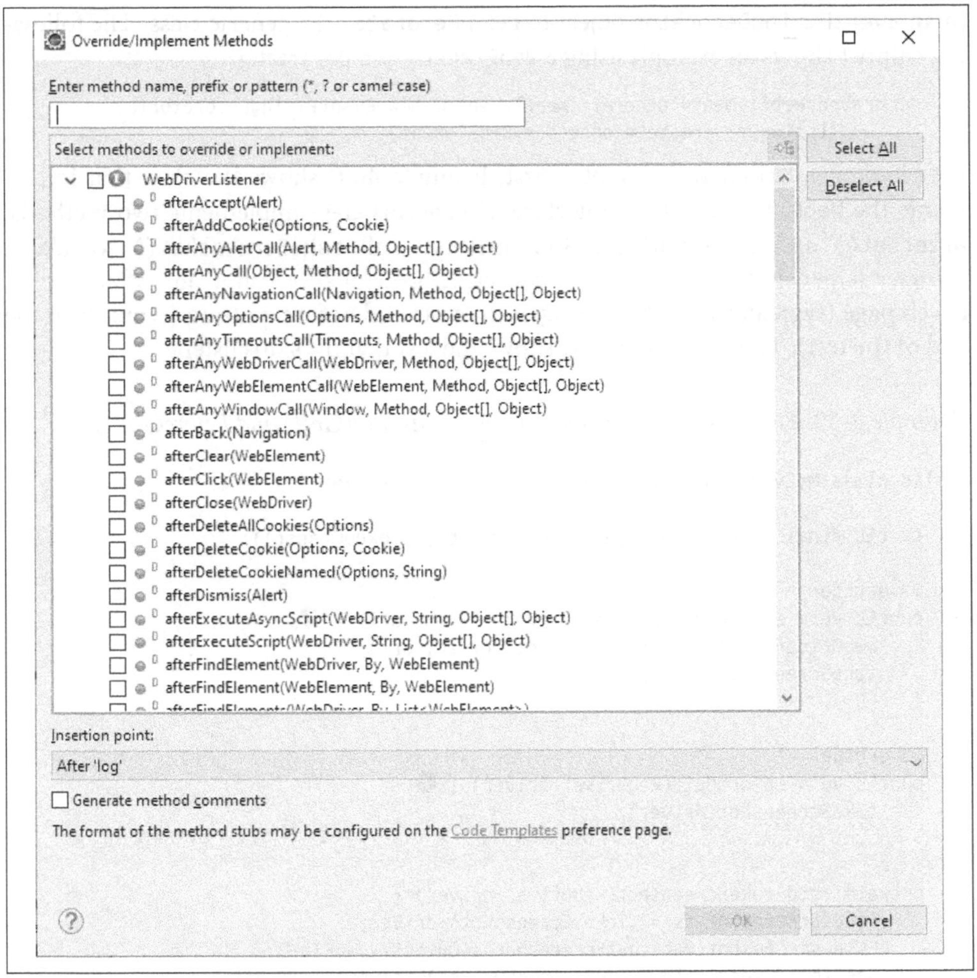

Figure 4-12. WebDriverListener methods in Eclipse

Once we have implemented our listener, we need to create the decorator class. There are two ways to do that. If we want to decorate a WebDriver object, we can create an instance of EventFiringDecorator (passing the listener as the argument to the constructor) and then invoke the method decorate() to pass the WebDriver object. For instance:

```
WebDriver decoratedDriver = new EventFiringDecorator(myListener)
        .decorate(originalDriver);
```

The second way is to decorate other objects of the Selenium WebDriver API, namely WebElement, TargetLocator, Navigation, Options, Timeouts, Window, Alert, or VirtualAuthenticator. In this case, we need to invoke the method createDecorated()

in an `EventFiringDecorator` object to get a `Decorated<T>` generic class. The following snippet shows an example using a `WebElement` as a parameter:

```
Decorated<WebElement> decoratedWebElement = new EventFiringDecorator(
        listener).createDecorated(myWebElement);
```

Let's look at a completed example. First, Example 4-30 shows the class that implements the `WebDriverListener` interface. Notice this class implements two methods: `afterGet()` and `beforeQuit()`. Both methods call `takeScreenshot()` to take a browser screenshot. All in all, we are collecting browser screenshots just after loading a web page (typically at the beginning of the test) and before quitting (typically at the end of the test). Then, Example 4-31 shows the test that uses this listener.

Example 4-30. Event listener implementing methods afterGet() and beforeQuit()

```
public class MyEventListener implements WebDriverListener {

    static final Logger log = getLogger(lookup().lookupClass());

    @Override
    public void afterGet(WebDriver driver, String url) { ❶
        WebDriverListener.super.afterGet(driver, url);
        takeScreenshot(driver);
    }

    @Override
    public void beforeQuit(WebDriver driver) { ❷
        takeScreenshot(driver);
    }

    private void takeScreenshot(WebDriver driver) {
        TakesScreenshot ts = (TakesScreenshot) driver;
        File screenshot = ts.getScreenshotAs(OutputType.FILE);
        SessionId sessionId = ((RemoteWebDriver) driver).getSessionId();
        Date today = new Date();
        SimpleDateFormat dateFormat = new SimpleDateFormat(
                "yyyy.MM.dd_HH.mm.ss.SSS");
        String screenshotFileName = String.format("%s-%s.png",
                dateFormat.format(today), sessionId.toString());
        Path destination = Paths.get(screenshotFileName); ❸

        try {
            Files.move(screenshot.toPath(), destination);
        } catch (IOException e) {
            log.error("Exception moving screenshot from {} to {}", screenshot,
                    destination, e);
        }
    }

}
```

❶ We override this method to execute custom logic *after* loading web pages with the WebDriver object.

❷ We override this method to execute custom logic *before* quitting the WebDriver object.

❸ We use a unique name for the PNG screenshots. For that, we get the system date (date and time) plus the session identifier.

Example 4-31. Test using EventFiringDecorator and the previous listener

```java
class EventListenerJupiterTest {

    WebDriver driver;

    @BeforeEach
    void setup() {
        MyEventListener listener = new MyEventListener();
        WebDriver originalDriver = WebDriverManager.chromedriver().create();
        driver = new EventFiringDecorator(listener).decorate(originalDriver); ❶
    }

    @AfterEach
    void teardown() {
        driver.quit();
    }

    @Test
    void testEventListener() {
        driver.get("https://bonigarcia.dev/selenium-webdriver-java/");
        assertThat(driver.getTitle())
                .isEqualTo("Hands-On Selenium WebDriver with Java");
        driver.findElement(By.linkText("Web form")).click(); ❷
    }

}
```

❶ We create a decorated WebDriver object using an instance on MyEventListener. We use the resulting driver to control the browser in the @Test logic.

❷ We click on a web link to change the page. The resulting two screenshots taken in the listener should be different.

WebDriver Exceptions

All the exceptions provided by the WebDriver API inherit from the class WebDriver Exception and are *unchecked* (see the following sidebar if you are unfamiliar with this terminology). Figure 4-13 shows these exceptions in Selenium WebDriver 4. As this image shows, there are many different exception types. Table 4-10 summarizes some of the most common causes.

Figure 4-13. Selenium WebDriver exceptions

Exceptions in Java

In Java, an exception is an event that disrupts the execution of a program. A class hierarchy is used to model different exception types in the standard Java API. The root of this hierarchy is the `Throwable` class. It has two subtypes:

`Error`
Irrecoverable problems. As a general rule, applications crash rather than handle these severe errors. Some examples are `OutOfMemoryError` or `StackOverflow Error`.

`Exception`
Recoverable problems. Applications can handle these exceptions by using `try-catch` blocks. There are two types of `Exception` classes:

Checked exceptions
Classes that directly inherit the `Throwable` class (except *RuntimeException* and *Error*). These exceptions are validated at compile time, and therefore we must handle them with `try-catch` blocks or rethrow using `throws`. Examples of check exceptions are `IOException` or `MalformedURLException`.

Unchecked exceptions
Classes that inherit from the `RuntimeException` class, which is a subtype of `Exception`. These exceptions do not require being handled with `try-catch` or rethrowing with `throws`. Some examples of unchecked exceptions are `NullPointerException` or `ArrayIndexOutOfBoundException`.

Table 4-10. Usual WebDriver exceptions and common causes

Exception	Description	Common causes
NoSuchElementException	Web element not available	• Invalid locator strategy • The element has not been rendered (maybe you need to wait for it)
NoAlertPresentException	Dialog (alert, prompt, or confirm) not available	Trying to perform an action (e.g., `accept()` or `dismiss()`) into an unavailable dialog
NoSuchWindowException	Window or tab not available	Trying to switch into an unavailable window or tab
NoSuchFrameException	Frame or iframe not available	Trying to switch into an unavailable frame or iframe
InvalidArgumentException	Incorrect argument when calling some method of the Selenium WebDriver API	• Bad URL in navigation methods • Nonexistent path when uploading files • Bad argument type in a JavaScript script

Exception	Description	Common causes
`StaleElementReferenceException`	The element is *stale*, i.e., it no longer appears on the page	The DOM gets updated when trying to interact with a previously located element
`UnreachableBrowserException`	Problem communicating with the browser	• The connection with the remote browser could not be established • The browser died in the middle of a WebDriver session
`TimeoutException`	Page loading timeout	Some web page takes longer than expected to load
`ScriptTimeoutException`	Script loading timeout	Some script takes longer than expected to execute

`ElementNotVisibleException`
`ElementNotSelectableException`
`ElementClickInterceptedException`
	The element is on the DOM but is not visible/selectable/clickable	• Insufficient (or nonexistent) wait until the element is displayed/selectable/clickable
		• The page layout (perhaps caused by viewport change) makes that element overlay on the element we try to interact with

Summary and Outlook

This chapter provided a comprehensive review of those WebDriver API features interoperable in different web browsers. Among them, you discovered how to execute JavaScript with Selenium WebDriver, with synchronous, pinned (i.e., attached to a WebDriver session), and asynchronous scripts. Then, you learned about timeouts, used to specify a time limit interval for page loading and script execution. Also, you saw how to manage several browser aspects, such as size and position, navigation history, the shadow DOM, and cookies. Next, you discovered how to interact with specific web elements, such as dropdown lists (select and data lists), navigation targets (windows, tabs, frames, and iframes), and dialog boxes (alerts, prompts, confirms, and modals). Finally, we reviewed the mechanism for implementing web storage and event listeners in Selenium WebDriver 4 and the most relevant WebDriver exceptions (and their common causes).

The next chapter continues to expose the features of the Selenium WebDriver API. The chapter explains those aspects specific to a given browser (e.g., Chrome, Firefox, etc.), including browser capabilities (e.g., `ChromeOptions`, `FirefoxOptions`, etc.), the Chrome DevTools Protocol (CDP), network interception, mocking geolocation coordinates, the WebDriver BiDirectional (BiDi) protocol, authentication mechanisms, or printing web pages to PDF, among other features.

CHAPTER 5

Browser-Specific Manipulation

As you have seen so far, many features of the Selenium WebDriver API are compatible across browsers, i.e., we can use Selenium WebDriver to control different types of browsers programmatically. Other parts of the Selenium WebDriver API are not interoperable among browsers. In other words, there are some WebDriver characteristics available for some browsers (e.g., Chrome or Edge) that are unavailable (or different) for others (e.g., Firefox). This chapter reviews these browser-specific features.

Browser Capabilities

Selenium WebDriver allows specifying browser-specific aspects by using *capabilities*. Examples of capabilities are headless mode, page loading strategies, use of web extensions, or push notifications management, among many others. As Figure 5-1 shows, the Selenium WebDriver API provides a set of Java classes to define these capabilities. The `Capabilities` interface is at the top of this hierarchy. Internally, the capabilities interface handles data using key-value pairs that encapsulate specific aspects of a browser. Then, different Java classes implement this interface to specify capabilities for web browsers (Chrome, Edge, Firefox, etc.). Table 5-1 summarizes the main classes of the `Capabilities` hierarchy and their corresponding target browsers.

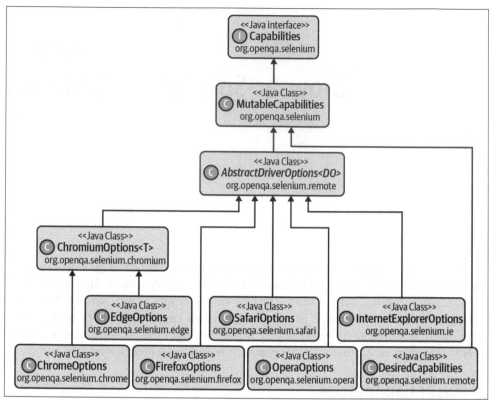

Figure 5-1. Capabilities hierarchy

Table 5-1. Description of the Capabilities hierarchy

Package	Class	Browser
org.openqa.selenium	MutableCapabilities	Generic (cross-browser)
org.openqa.selenium.chrome	ChromeOptions	Chrome
org.openqa.selenium.edge	EdgeOptions	Edge
org.openqa.selenium.firefox	FirefoxOptions	Firefox
org.openqa.selenium.safari	SafariOptions	Safari
org.openqa.selenium.opera	OperaOptions	Opera
org.openqa.selenium.ie	InternetExplorerOptions	Internet Explorer
org.openqa.selenium.remote	DesiredCapabilities	Remote browsers (see Chapter 6)

The following subsections review the most relevant capabilities for the major web browsers discussed in this book, i.e., Chrome, Edge, and Firefox. As Chrome and Edge are both Chromium-based browsers, the capabilities available for both browsers are equivalent. This fact is reflected in Figure 5-1, showing that capability classes `ChromeOptions` and `EdgeOptions` both inherit from the same parent (called `ChromiumOptions`).

Headless Browser

Browsers that do not require a GUI to interact with web applications are known as *headless* browsers. One of the primary uses of these browsers is end-to-end testing, i.e., automated interaction with web applications. Current web browsers such as Chrome, Edge, or Firefox can operate as headless browsers. The Selenium WebDriver API allows starting these browsers in headless mode using capabilities. To that aim, first, you need to create an instance of the browser capabilities. In the major browsers, these objects are instances of `ChromeOptions`, `EdgeOptions`, or `FirefoxOptions`, respectively. Then, you need to enable the headless mode by invoking the method `setHeadless(true)` in the browser capabilities object. Finally, you need to set these capabilities when creating a `WebDriver` object.

As "WebDriver Creation" on page 53 explained, we have different ways to create `WebDriver` objects. First, we can use a `WebDriver` constructor (e.g., `new Chrome Driver()`). Also, we can use a builder provided by the Selenium WebDriver API (i.e., `RemoteWebDriver.builder()`). Finally, we can use the WebDriverManager builder to resolve the driver and create the `WebDriver` instance in a single line of code. The following examples show these alternatives, used in conjunction with browser capabilities to enable the headless browser mode, namely:

- Example 5-1 uses Chrome in headless mode. This example creates a `WebDriver` instance using the required constructor (`ChromeDriver` in this case).

- Example 5-2 uses Edge in headless mode. This example creates a `WebDriver` instance using the builder available in the Selenium WebDriver API.

- Example 5-3 uses Firefox in headless mode. This example creates a `WebDriver` instance using WebDriverManager. Notice that the setup method is not required in this case since WebDriverManager resolves the driver in the same line as the WebDriver instantiation.

- Example 5-4 uses Chrome in headless mode through Selenium-Jupiter. This example uses the parameter resolution mechanism provided by Selenium-Jupiter, and so we simply declare a `ChromeDriver` parameter in the test method. Then, we decorate this parameter using the annotation `@Arguments` to specify the headless mode for this browser.

Example 5-1. Test using Chrome in headless mode

```
class HeadlessChromeJupiterTest {

    WebDriver driver;

    @BeforeAll
    static void setupClass() {
        WebDriverManager.chromedriver().setup(); ❶
    }

    @BeforeEach
    void setup() {
        ChromeOptions options = new ChromeOptions(); ❷
        options.setHeadless(true); ❸

        driver = new ChromeDriver(options); ❹
    }

    @AfterEach
    void teardown() {
        driver.quit();
    }

    @Test
    void testHeadless() {
        driver.get("https://bonigarcia.dev/selenium-webdriver-java/");
        assertThat(driver.getTitle()).contains("Selenium WebDriver");
    }

}
```

❶ We resolve the required driver (chromedriver in this case).

❷ We create the browser capabilities using the `ChromeOptions` constructor.

❸ We enable the headless mode. This line is equivalent to `options.add Arguments("--headless");`.

❹ We set up the browser capabilities by passing the options as a constructor parameter in the `ChromeDriver` constructor.

Example 5-2. Test using Edge in headless mode

```
class HeadlessEdgeJupiterTest {

    WebDriver driver;

    @BeforeAll
```

```
    static void setupClass() {
        WebDriverManager.edgedriver().setup(); ❶
    }

    @BeforeEach
    void setup() {
        EdgeOptions options = new EdgeOptions(); ❷
        options.setHeadless(true); ❸

        driver = RemoteWebDriver.builder().oneOf(options).build(); ❹
    }

    @AfterEach
    void teardown() {
        driver.quit();
    }

    @Test
    void testHeadless() {
        driver.get("https://bonigarcia.dev/selenium-webdriver-java/");
        assertThat(driver.getTitle()).contains("Selenium WebDriver");
    }

}
```

❶ As usual, we need to resolve the required driver (msedgedriver in this case).

❷ Since we aim to use Edge, we need to create an `EdgeOptions` instance to specify capabilities.

❸ We enable the headless mode. Again, this line is equivalent to `options.add Arguments("--headless");`.

❹ We use the WebDriver builder to create the `WebDriver` object, passing the options as a parameter.

Example 5-3. Test using Firefox in headless mode

```
class HeadlessFirefoxJupiterTest {

    WebDriver driver;

    @BeforeEach
    void setup() {
        FirefoxOptions options = new FirefoxOptions(); ❶
        options.setHeadless(true); ❷

        driver = WebDriverManager.firefoxdriver().capabilities(options)
                .create(); ❸
```

```
    }

    @AfterEach
    void teardown() {
        driver.quit();
    }

    @Test
    void testHeadless() {
        driver.get("https://bonigarcia.dev/selenium-webdriver-java/");
        assertThat(driver.getTitle()).contains("Selenium WebDriver");
    }

}
```

❶ We use Firefox in this test, and therefore, we create a `FirefoxOptions` object to specify capabilities.

❷ In the same way as in the previous examples, we enable the headless mode.

❸ In this example, we use WebDriverManager to resolve the required driver and create the `WebDriver` object while specifying the previously created browser capabilities.

 The strategy used to create the `WebDriver` objects in these examples is interchangeable. In other words, for example, we can also use the WebDriverManager builder for each browser in headless mode.

Example 5-4. Test using Chrome in headless mode with Selenium-Jupiter

```
@ExtendWith(SeleniumJupiter.class)
class HeadlessChromeSelJupTest {

    @Test
    void testHeadless(@Arguments("--headless") ChromeDriver driver) { ❶
        driver.get("https://bonigarcia.dev/selenium-webdriver-java/");
        assertThat(driver.getTitle()).contains("Selenium WebDriver");
    }

}
```

❶ We use the annotation `@Arguments` to specify the headless mode in the browser (Chrome in this case).

Page Loading Strategies

Selenium WebDriver allows configuring different approaches for loading web pages. For that, the Selenium WebDriver API provides the `PageLoadStrategy` enumeration. Table 5-2 describes the possible values of this enumeration and their purposes. Selenium WebDriver internally uses the property `document.readyState` of the DOM API to check the web page loading state.

Table 5-2. PageLoadStrategy values

Loading strategy	Description	Readiness state
PageLoadStrategy.NORMAL	Default mode. Selenium WebDriver waits until the entire page is loaded (i.e., the HTML content and subresources, such as stylesheets, images, JavaScript files, etc.).	"complete"
PageLoadStrategy.EAGER	Selenium WebDriver waits until the HTML document has finished loading and parsing, but subresources (scripts, images, stylesheets, etc.) are still loading.	"interactive"
PageLoadStrategy.NONE	Selenium WebDriver waits only until the HTML document is downloaded.	"loading"

We need to invoke the method `setPageLoadStrategy()` of the browser capabilities (e.g., `ChromeOptions`, `FirefoxOptions`, etc.) to set up these strategies (NORMAL, EAGER, or NONE). Example 5-5 shows a test using Chrome and the NORMAL strategy. In the examples repository, you can find equivalent examples for Edge and Firefox using the other strategies (EAGER and NONE). In these examples, in addition to specifying a loading strategy in the test setup, the test logic calculates the required time to load the page, displaying this value in the standard output.

Example 5-5. Test using a normal page loading strategy in Chrome

```
class PageLoadChromeJupiterTest {

    static final Logger log = getLogger(lookup().lookupClass());

    WebDriver driver;

    PageLoadStrategy pageLoadStrategy;

    @BeforeEach
    void setup() {
        ChromeOptions options = new ChromeOptions(); ❶
        pageLoadStrategy = PageLoadStrategy.NORMAL;
        options.setPageLoadStrategy(pageLoadStrategy); ❷

        driver = WebDriverManager.chromedriver().capabilities(options).create(); ❸
    }
```

```
@AfterEach
void teardown() {
    driver.quit();
}

@Test
void testPageLoad() {
    long initMillis = System.currentTimeMillis(); ❹
    driver.get("https://bonigarcia.dev/selenium-webdriver-java/");
    Duration elapsed = Duration
            .ofMillis(System.currentTimeMillis() - initMillis); ❺

    Capabilities capabilities = ((RemoteWebDriver) driver)
            .getCapabilities(); ❻
    Object pageLoad = capabilities
            .getCapability(CapabilityType.PAGE_LOAD_STRATEGY); ❼
    String browserName = capabilities.getBrowserName();
    log.debug(
            "The page took {} ms to be loaded using a '{}' strategy in {}",
            elapsed.toMillis(), pageLoad, browserName); ❽

    assertThat(pageLoad).isEqualTo(pageLoadStrategy.toString()); ❾
}

}
```

❶ Since we use Chrome in this test, we instantiate `ChromeOptions` to specify capabilities.

❷ We set up the page loading strategy to `NORMAL`.

❸ We use WebDriverManager to resolve the driver, create the `WebDriver` instance, and specify the capabilities.

❹ We get the system timestamp before loading the page.

❺ We get the system timestamp after loading the page.

❻ We read the `WebDriver` object capabilities.

❼ We read the used page loading strategy.

❽ We trace the time required to load the web page.

❾ We verify that the loading strategy is as initially configured.

Device Emulation

Major web browsers use development tools (i.e., DevTools in Chromium-based browsers and Developer Tools in Firefox) to simulate mobile devices in these ways:

Simulating a mobile viewport
> To reduce user visible area of a web page using the width and height of a given mobile device

Throttling the network
> To slow the connectivity speed to simulate mobile networks (e.g., 3G)

Throttling the CPU
> To slow processing performance

Simulating geolocation
> To set custom Global Positioning System (GPS) coordinates

Setting orientation
> To rotate the screen

Figure 5-2 shows a screenshot of Chrome using mobile emulation through DevTools.

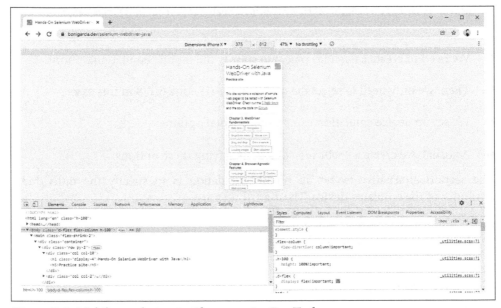

Figure 5-2. Mobile emulation in Chrome using DevTools

At the time of this writing, this mobile device emulation can be automated through the Selenium WebDriver API in Chromium-based browsers (Chrome and Edge) but not Firefox (since it is not implemented in geckodriver). For that, we need to set the experimental option `mobileEmulation` in `ChromeOptions` or `EdgeOptions`.

Then, there are two alternatives to specify the mobile device to be emulated. First, we can specify a particular mobile device (e.g., Pixel 2, iPad Pro, or Galaxy Fold, to name a few). Since this list is updated in each Chromium release, the best way to check the possibilities is to inspect the available devices in DevTools (e.g., iPhone X is selected in Figure 5-2). Example 5-6 shows a test setup in which we specify a given mobile device using the label `iPhone 6/7/8`.

Example 5-6. Test setup using mobile emulation by specifying a device

```
@BeforeEach
void setup() {
    ChromeOptions options = new ChromeOptions();
    Map<String, Object> mobileEmulation = new HashMap<>(); ❶
    mobileEmulation.put("deviceName", "iPhone 6/7/8"); ❷
    options.setExperimentalOption("mobileEmulation", mobileEmulation); ❸

    driver = WebDriverManager.chromedriver().capabilities(options).create(); ❹
}
```

❶ We need to create a `HashMap` object to specify the mobile emulation options.

❷ Then, we only need to select the device name (iPhone 6/7/8 in this case).

❸ We set up device emulation using experimental options.

❹ As usual, we create a `WebDriver` object specifying these options.

The second alternative to set up mobile emulation is to specify the individual attributes of the emulated device. These attributes are:

width
Device screen width (in pixels)

height
Device screen height (in pixels)

pixelRatio
Ratio between physical pixels and logical pixels

touch
Whether to emulate touch events; the default value is `true`

In addition to these attributes, we can specify the *user agent* of the emulated device. In HTTP, the user agent is a string specified in request headers that univocally identifies the type of web browser. It contains the development code name, version, platform, and other information. Example 5-7 shows a test setup illustrating the use of this feature.

Example 5-7. Test setup using device emulation by specifying individual attributes

```
@BeforeEach
void setup() {
    EdgeOptions options = new EdgeOptions();
    Map<String, Object> mobileEmulation = new HashMap<>();
    Map<String, Object> deviceMetrics = new HashMap<>();  ❶
    deviceMetrics.put("width", 360);
    deviceMetrics.put("height", 640);
    deviceMetrics.put("pixelRatio", 3.0);
    deviceMetrics.put("touch", true);
    mobileEmulation.put("deviceMetrics", deviceMetrics);  ❷
    mobileEmulation.put("userAgent",
            "Mozilla/5.0 (Linux; Android 4.2.1; en-us; Nexus 5 Build/JOP40D) "
                    + "AppleWebKit/535.19 (KHTML, like Gecko) "
                    + "Chrome/18.0.1025.166 Mobile Safari/535.19");  ❸
    options.setExperimentalOption("mobileEmulation", mobileEmulation);

    driver = WebDriverManager.edgedriver().capabilities(options).create();
}
```

❶ We create a hashmap to store the individual attributes of an emulated mobile, namely, `width`, `height`, `pixelRatio`, and `touch`.

❷ We set these attributes by setting the label `deviceMetrics` in the mobile emulation map.

❸ We set a custom user agent for a Chrome Mobile 18 in a Nexus 5 device.

Web Extensions

Web extensions (also called *add-ons* or *plug-ins*) are programs that can modify or enhance the default operation of a web browser. Users typically install web extensions using web stores. These stores are web applications supported by browser maintainers for hosting public web extensions. Table 5-3 summarizes the web stores for Chrome, Edge, and Firefox.

Table 5-3. Web stores for the major browsers

Web Store	Browser	URL
Chrome web store	Chrome	*https://chrome.google.com/webstore/category/extensions*
Edge add-ons	Edge	*https://microsoftedge.microsoft.com/addons/Microsoft-Edge-Extensions-Home*
Firefox browser add-ons	Firefox	*https://addons.mozilla.org/en-US/firefox*

We can install web extensions in a WebDriver session using capabilities. For that, in Chromium-based browsers, like Chrome and Edge, we use the method `addExten sions()` of a `ChromeOptions` or `EdgeOptions` object. Example 5-8 shows a test setup to install a local extension in Chrome.

Example 5-8. Test setup installing a web extension in Chrome

```
@BeforeEach
void setup() throws URISyntaxException {
    Path extension = Paths
            .get(ClassLoader.getSystemResource("dark-bg.crx").toURI()); ❶
    ChromeOptions options = new ChromeOptions();
    options.addExtensions(extension.toFile()); ❷

    driver = WebDriverManager.chromedriver().capabilities(options).create();
}
```

❶ We install a web extension packed as a Chrome Extension (CRX) file. This file is a test resource (located in the folder `src\test\resources` of the Java project). This extension changes the website look and feel to use light text on a dark background. Figure 5-3 shows a screenshot of the practice website when loaded by a WebDriver test using this extension.

❷ We add the extension in the Chrome options, passing the extension as a Java `File`.

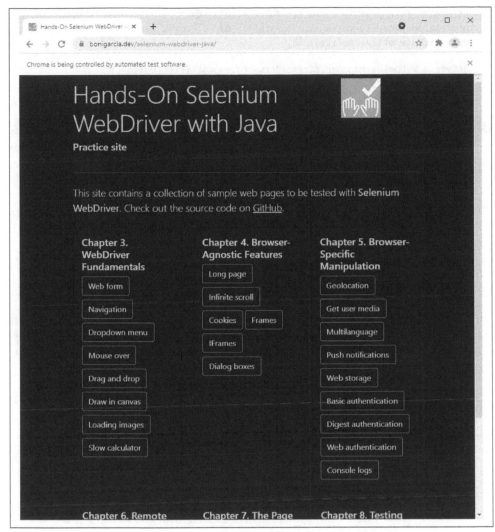

Figure 5-3. Practice site when it is loaded using the dark-bg.crx extension

Firefox also allows loading web extensions when it is controlled with WebDriver. Nevertheless, the syntax is different. Example 5-9 illustrates this.

Example 5-9. Test setup installing a web extension in Firefox

```
@BeforeEach
void setup() throws URISyntaxException {
    Path extension = Paths
            .get(ClassLoader.getSystemResource("dark-bg.xpi").toURI()); ❶
    FirefoxOptions options = new FirefoxOptions();
```

```
FirefoxProfile profile = new FirefoxProfile(); ❷
profile.addExtension(extension.toFile()); ❸
options.setProfile(profile); ❹

driver = WebDriverManager.firefoxdriver().capabilities(options)
        .create();
}
```

❶ We use the same extension as in Chrome/Edge, but in this case, the packaging is specific for Firefox. Notice that the file is different. This time, it is packaged as an *XPInstall* file, i.e., a zipped archive containing the web extension source code, resources (e.g., images), and metadata.

❷ We need to create a custom Firefox profile (i.e., the store where custom settings are configured).

❸ We add the extension as a Java `File` to the Firefox profile.

❹ We set the profile in the Firefox options.

Chromium-based browsers (e.g., Chrome, Edge) also allow loading an extension from its source code (i.e., not packaged as a CRX file). This feature can be very convenient for automated testing of web extensions during their development. Example 5-10 shows a test setup that illustrates this feature.

Example 5-10. Test setup installing a web extension from its source code in Edge

```
@BeforeEach
void setup() throws URISyntaxException {
    Path extension = Paths
            .get(ClassLoader.getSystemResource("web-extension").toURI()); ❶
    EdgeOptions options = new EdgeOptions();
    options.addArguments(
            "--load-extension=" + extension.toAbsolutePath().toString()); ❷

    driver = WebDriverManager.edgedriver().capabilities(options).create();
}
```

❶ The extension used in this example is located in the folder `web-extension`; it is a test resource folder (stored in `src\test\resources` of the Java project). This extension follows the Browser Extensions API (*https://developer.mozilla.org/en-US/docs/Mozilla/Add-ons/WebExtensions*). It uses JavaScript to change the content of first-level headers (`h1` tags) with a custom message. Figure 5-4 shows a screenshot of the practice website when using this extension.

❷ We specify the extension path using the `--load-extension` argument.

Selenium WebDriver creates a new browser profile in each execution. For this reason, the installation of web extensions through Selenium WebDriver is not permanent in the target browsers.

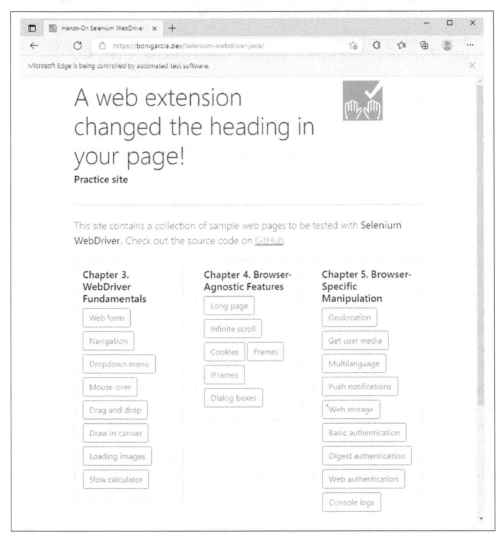

Figure 5-4. Practice site when it is loaded using the local extension

As of Selenium 4.1, Firefox also allows installing web extensions from its source code. To that aim, `FirefoxDriver` extends the interface `HasExtensions`, providing the method `installExtension`. Example 5-11 shows a test setup using this feature.

Example 5-11. Test setup installing a web extension from its source code in Firefox

```
@BeforeEach
void setup() throws URISyntaxException {
    Path extensionFolder = Paths
            .get(ClassLoader.getSystemResource("web-extension").toURI()); ❶
    zippedExtension = zipFolder(extensionFolder); ❷

    driver = WebDriverManager.firefoxdriver().create();
    ((FirefoxDriver) driver).installExtension(zippedExtension, true); ❸
}
```

❶ We use the source code (located in the project classpath) of a web extension.

❷ The method `installExtension` requires that the extension installed from its source code is zipped. WebDriverManager provides the static helper method called `zipFolder(Path)` to ease this process.

❸ We install the zipped extension as a temporal add-on in Firefox.

Geolocation

The Geolocation API (*https://www.w3.org/TR/geolocation*) is a W3C specification that allows access to the geographical location information associated with the hosting device (e.g., laptop or mobile) of the web browser. Usual geolocation data sources include GPS data and the location inferred from the network, such as the IP address. The Geolocation API is available in a web browser calling the JavaScript object `navigator.geolocation`. When using this statement, and for privacy reasons, a pop-up prompts the user for permission to report location data.

The practice site contains a web page using geolocation. Figure 5-5 shows a screenshot of this page. This figure shows the permission pop-up shown to the user when clicking the button "Get coordinates." To handle this dialog using the Selenium WebDriver API, we use capabilities. Like other occasions, the required capabilities to grant access to the geolocation data are different in Chrome/Edge than in Firefox. The following code snippets show the difference. First, Example 5-12 shows a test setup where geolocation access is granted in Chrome. The same experimental preference (`profile.default_content_setting_values.geolocation`) would be used in Edge (as usual, you can find the complete test in the examples repository). Then, Example 5-13 shows the equivalent test setup, but using Firefox.

Figure 5-5. Practice site showing the geolocation permission pop-up

Example 5-12. Test setup to allow geolocation in Chrome

```
@BeforeEach
void setup() {
    ChromeOptions options = new ChromeOptions();
    Map<String, Object> prefs = new HashMap<>(); ❶
    prefs.put("profile.default_content_setting_values.geolocation", 1); ❷
    options.setExperimentalOption("prefs", prefs); ❸

    driver = WebDriverManager.chromedriver().capabilities(options).create();
}
```

❶ We create a hashmap for experimental options.

❷ We set to 1 the experimental option `profile.default_content_setting_values.geolocation` to allow accessing the geolocation position. The other possible values are: 0 for the default behavior and 2 for blocking access to the geolocation data.

❸ We set the experimental options using the label `prefs` in the Chrome options.

 Suppose you need to access the geolocation coordinates using Chrome or Edge in a macOS machine. In that case, you will also need to enable the location services for these browsers in the macOS preferences (System Preferences → Security & Privacy → Location Services). Figure 5-6 shows this configuration.

Figure 5-6. Enabling location services for Chrome and Edge in macOS

Example 5-13. Test setup to allow geolocation in Firefox

```
@BeforeEach
void setup() {
    FirefoxOptions options = new FirefoxOptions();
    options.addPreference("geo.enabled", true); ❶
    options.addPreference("geo.prompt.testing", true); ❷
    options.addPreference("geo.provider.use_corelocation", true); ❸

    driver = WebDriverManager.firefoxdriver().capabilities(options)
            .create();
}
```

❶ To enable the Geolocation API

❷ To grant access to the geolocation data (i.e., click on allow in the access pop-up)

❸ To gather data using all the available components in the device, such as GPS, WiFi, or Bluetooth

Notifications

The Notifications API (*https://notifications.spec.whatwg.org*) is a standard web API that allows websites to send notifications displayed at the operating system desktop. This API is available through the JavaScript object Notification. Before a website can send notifications, the user must grant permission. This consent is prompted to the user in a dialog pop-up similar to geolocation data. The practice site contains a web page using the Notification API. Figure 5-7 shows a screenshot of the notification permission pop-up for this page. Figure 5-8 shows the message sent by this web page on a Linux host.

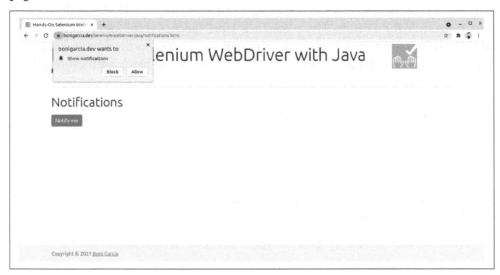

Figure 5-7. Practice site showing the notification permission pop-up

Figure 5-8. Practice site showing a notification in a Linux desktop

The Selenium WebDriver API allows granting notifications by using capabilities. Like in other features, the syntax of these capabilities is different in Chrome/Edge and Firefox. Example 5-14 shows the test setup to enable notifications as Chrome options. We use the same preference (`profile.default_content_setting_val ues.notifications`) to allow notifications in Edge. Example 5-15 shows the equivalent test setup for Firefox. The preference label (`permissions.default.desktop-notification`) is different in this case, although its value (1) is the same for allowing notifications. The other possible value is 2, which is used to block notifications (both in Chrome/Edge and Firefox).

Example 5-14. Test setup to allow notifications in Chrome

```
@BeforeEach
void setup() {
    ChromeOptions options = new ChromeOptions();
    Map<String, Object> prefs = new HashMap<>();
    prefs.put("profile.default_content_setting_values.notifications", 1);
    options.setExperimentalOption("prefs", prefs);

    driver = WebDriverManager.chromedriver().capabilities(options).create();
}
```

Example 5-15. Test setup to allow notifications in Firefox

```
@BeforeEach
void setup() {
    FirefoxOptions options = new FirefoxOptions();
    options.addPreference("permissions.default.desktop-notification", 1);

    driver = WebDriverManager.firefoxdriver().capabilities(options)
            .create();
}
```

Example 5-16 shows the test logic used with the previous setup. As usual, you can find the complete test case in the examples repository. This test is an example of asynchronous script execution. This script overrides the original Notification JavaScript object. The new implementation of this object gets the title of the notification message, which is returned in the script callback to the WebDriver test.

Example 5-16. Test handling notifications

```
@Test
void testNotifications() {
    driver.get(
            "https://bonigarcia.dev/selenium-webdriver-java/notifications.html");
    JavascriptExecutor js = (JavascriptExecutor) driver;
```

```
        String script = String.join("\n",
                "const callback = arguments[arguments.length - 1];", ❶
                "const OldNotify = window.Notification;", ❷
                "function newNotification(title, options) {", ❸
                "    callback(title);", ❹
                "    return new OldNotify(title, options);", ❺
                "}",
                "newNotification.requestPermission = " +
                        "OldNotify.requestPermission.bind(OldNotify);",
                "Object.defineProperty(newNotification, 'permission', {",
                "    get: function() {",
                "        return OldNotify.permission;",
                "    }",
                "});",
                "window.Notification = newNotification;",
                "document.getElementById('notify-me').click();"); ❻
        log.debug("Executing the following script asynchronously:\n{}", script);

        Object notificationTitle = js.executeAsyncScript(script); ❼
        assertThat(notificationTitle).isEqualTo("This is a notification"); ❽
}
```

❶ As usual in asynchronous script execution, the last argument is the callback function used to signal the script termination.

❷ We store a copy of the original Notification constructor.

❸ We create a new constructor for notifications.

❹ We pass the message title as an argument in the callback. As a result, the title is
   returned to the WebDriver call (Java in this case).

❺ We use the old constructor to create an original Notification object.

❻ We click on the button that triggers the notification on the web page.

❼ We get the returned object after the script execution.

❽ We verify the notification title is as expected.

Browser Binary

Selenium WebDriver detects the path of controlled web browsers (Chrome, Firefox,
etc.) out of the box. Nevertheless, we can specify a custom path for the browser executable file using capabilities. This feature can be helpful when the installation path of
the browser is not standard (for instance, in the case of beta/development/canary
browsers).

We use the same capabilities syntax to specify the binary path for Chrome, Edge, and Firefox. Example 5-17 shows a test setup using Chrome beta.

Example 5-17. Test setup setting a custom binary path for Chrome

```
@BeforeEach
void setup() {
    Path browserBinary = Paths.get("/usr/bin/google-chrome-beta"); ❶
    assumeThat(browserBinary).exists(); ❷

    ChromeOptions options = new ChromeOptions();
    options.setBinary(browserBinary.toFile()); ❸
    driver = WebDriverManager.chromedriver().capabilities(options).create();
}
```

❶ We use a Java `Path` to get the browser binary path (in this case, Chrome beta in Linux).

❷ We use assumptions to conditionally skip this test when the previous path does not exist (e.g., in the CI server).

❸ We use the method `setBinary` of the Chrome options to set the binary path (as a Java `File`).

Web Proxies

In computer networking, a *proxy* is a server that acts as an intermediary between a client and a server. A web proxy is a proxy between a browser and a web server, and it can serve multiple purposes, such as:

Access region-specific information
The proxy is typically located in a different region than the client, and the server consequently replies to that region.

Avoiding restrictions
A proxy can help access blocked websites, for example, by an intermediate firewall.

Capture network traffic
A proxy can gather HTTP requests and responses.

Caching
A proxy can allow faster website retrieval.

Figure 5-9 represents the location of a web proxy in the Selenium WebDriver architecture compared to the typical scenario in which a web proxy is not used. As you can see, the web proxy is placed in the middle of the browser and the web application under test, and it works at the HTTP level. This way, the web proxy allows implementing the previously mentioned purposes (e.g., capturing HTTP network traffic) in Selenium WebDriver tests.

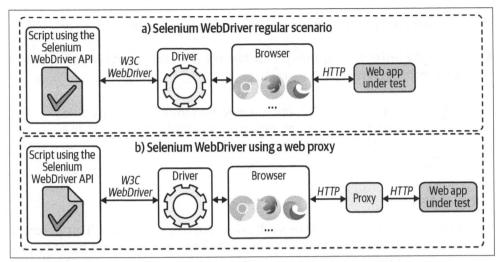

Figure 5-9. Selenium WebDriver architecture with and without a web proxy

The Selenium WebDriver API provides a `Proxy` class to configure a web proxy. This class is configured into a `WebDriver` object using capabilities. Example 5-18 illustrates how.

Example 5-18. Test setup to configure a web proxy

```
@BeforeEach
void setup() {
    Proxy proxy = new Proxy(); ❶
    String proxyStr = "proxy:port"; ❷
    proxy.setHttpProxy(proxyStr); ❸
    proxy.setSslProxy(proxyStr); ❹

    ChromeOptions options = new ChromeOptions();
    options.setAcceptInsecureCerts(true); ❺
    options.setProxy(proxy); ❻

    driver = WebDriverManager.chromedriver().capabilities(options).create();
}
```

❶ We create an instance of the class `Proxy`.

❷ The syntax required to specify a proxy is `host:port`.

❸ We specify the proxy is used for HTTP connections.

❹ We also specify the proxy is used for HTTPS connections.

❺ Although not mandatory, it is typically required to accept insecure certificates.

❻ We set the proxy as a capability. This line is equivalent to `options.setCapabil`
`ity(CapabilityType.PROXY, proxy);`.

 "Capture Network Traffic" on page 296 shows how to use a third-party library to capture network traffic by using a web proxy in a Selenium WebDriver test.

Log Gathering

The Selenium WebDriver API allows gathering different log sources. This feature is enabled using capabilities, although it is supported only in Chromium-based browsers at the time of this writing. Example 5-19 presents a test setup that enables gathering browser logs (i.e., console messages). This snippet also contains the test logic, in which we need to invoke `driver.manage().logs()` to gather the log list.

Example 5-19. Test gathering browser log using Chrome

```
@BeforeEach
void setup() {
    LoggingPreferences logs = new LoggingPreferences();
    logs.enable(LogType.BROWSER, Level.ALL); ❶

    ChromeOptions options = new ChromeOptions();
    options.setCapability(CapabilityType.LOGGING_PREFS, logs); ❷

    driver = WebDriverManager.chromedriver().capabilities(options).create();
}

@Test
void testBrowserLogs() {
    driver.get(
            "https://bonigarcia.dev/selenium-webdriver-java/console-logs.html"); ❸

    LogEntries browserLogs = driver.manage().logs().get(LogType.BROWSER); ❹
    Assertions.assertThat(browserLogs.getAll()).isNotEmpty(); ❺
    browserLogs.forEach(l -> log.debug("{}", l)); ❻
}
```

❶ We enable gathering all levels of browser logs.

❷   We set the `loggingPrefs` capability.

❸   We open a practice page that logs several traces in the browser console.

❹   We gather all the logs and filter them by browser (console traces).

❺   We verify the number of traces is not zero.

❻   We display each log in the standard output.

 Log gathering is not available in the W3C WebDriver specification at the time of writing. Nevertheless, it has been implemented in some drivers such as chromedriver or msedgedriver (i.e., Chrome and Edge), but it is unavailable in others, such as geckodriver (i.e., Firefox).

Get User Media

WebRTC (*https://webrtc.org*) is a set of standard technologies that allow exchanging real-time media using web browsers. This technology allows the creation of audio- and video conferencing web applications using JavaScript APIs on the client side. The practice site contains a web page that gets user media (microphone and webcam) using the *getUserMedia* JavaScript API. Like in other APIs, and for the sake of security and privacy, a browser pop-up asks for permission before accessing the user media. Figure 5-10 shows the sample web page when prompting this dialog.

Figure 5-10. Practice site prompting the user media permission pop-up

We use capabilities to grant access to the user media in the Selenium WebDriver API. The syntax of these capabilities is the same in Chrome and Edge (see Example 5-20) but different in Firefox (see Example 5-21).

Example 5-20. Test setup granting synthetic user media in Chrome

```
@BeforeEach
void setup() {
    ChromeOptions options = new ChromeOptions();
    options.addArguments("--use-fake-ui-for-media-stream"); ❶
    options.addArguments("--use-fake-device-for-media-stream"); ❷

    driver = WebDriverManager.chromedriver().capabilities(options).create();
}
```

❶ Argument to allow accessing user media (audio and video).

❷ Argument to fake user media using a synthetic video (green spinner) and audio (a beep per second). You can see this video in Figure 5-11.

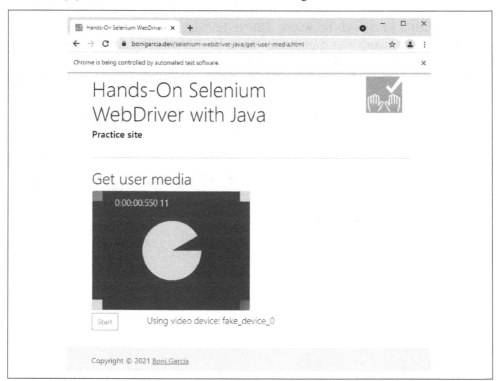

Figure 5-11. Practice site using synthetic user media in Chrome

Example 5-21. Test setup granting synthetic user media in Firefox

```
@BeforeEach
void setup() {
    FirefoxOptions options = new FirefoxOptions();
    options.addPreference("media.navigator.permission.disabled", true); ❶
    options.addPreference("media.navigator.streams.fake", true); ❷

    driver = WebDriverManager.firefoxdriver().capabilities(options)
            .create();
}
```

❶ Preference to access the user media.

❷ Preference to fake the user media using a synthetic video (with changing color background) and audio (constant beep). You can see this video in Figure 5-12.

Figure 5-12. Practice site using synthetic user media in Firefox

Loading Insecure Pages

When web browsers try to load a web page using HTTPS (Hypertext Transfer Protocol Secure) but the certificate on the server side is invalid, the browser warns the user about it. Examples of invalid certificates are self-signed, revoked, or cryptographically unsafe certificates. Figure 5-13 shows a screenshot of this warning in Chrome.

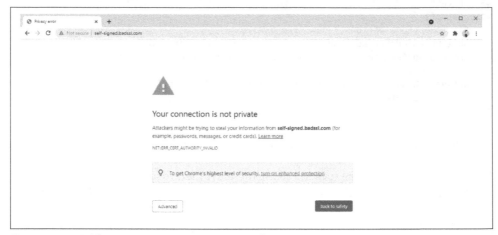

Figure 5-13. Web page using an insecure certificate

This issue does not necessarily imply a security concern. It might happen during the development of a website, for example, when using a self-signed certificate. For this reason, the Selenium WebDriver API allows disabling the certificate checks using the `acceptInsecureCerts` capability. This capability is the same in Chrome, Edge, and Firefox. Example 5-22 shows a test setup in which this capability is enabled using Chrome. This snippet also contains a test opening an insecure website.

Example 5-22. Test of a web application that uses an insecure certificate

```
@BeforeEach
void setup() {
    ChromeOptions options = new ChromeOptions();
    options.setAcceptInsecureCerts(true); ❶

    driver = WebDriverManager.chromedriver().capabilities(options).create();
}

@Test
void testInsecure() {
    driver.get("https://self-signed.badssl.com/"); ❷

    String bgColor = driver.findElement(By.tagName("body"))
            .getCssValue("background-color");
    Color red = new Color(255, 0, 0, 1);
    assertThat(Color.fromString(bgColor)).isEqualTo(red); ❸
}
```

❶ We enable the capability to allow insecure certificates.

❷ We open a website using an insecure certificate (self-signed in this case).

❸ If the website is loaded, the body background should be red.

Localization

In software engineering, *localization* refers to the process of adapting an application to meet the culture and the language (called *locale*) of its end users. Localization is sometimes written as *l10n* (10 is the number of letters between *l* and *n* in the English word localization). The most usual localization activity is translating the text displayed in an application UI to different languages. In addition, other UI aspects can be adjusted depending on the locale, such as the currencies (euros, dollars, etc.), systems of measurement (e.g., metric or imperial systems), or number and date format.

L10n is part of a broader concept called *internationalization* (i18n), which is the process of designing and developing an application that enables easy l10n for heterogeneous target audiences. Common practices to enable i18n are using Unicode for text encoding or adding CSS support for vertical text or non-Latin typographies.

Localization testing is a form of nonfunctional testing where a SUT is verified for specific locale settings. The Selenium WebDriver API allows us to make localization testing based on the browser language by setting the capability `intl.accept_languages`. This capability allows you to specify the locale identifier, such as *en_US* for American English or *es_ES* for European Spanish, to name a few. Example 5-23 shows a test setup that configures this capability in Chrome. We can use the same syntax in Edge, although we specify this capability as a preference in Firefox (see Example 5-24).

Example 5-23. Test that uses a preferred locale for Chrome

```
String lang;

@BeforeEach
void setup() {
    lang = "es-ES";
    ChromeOptions options = new ChromeOptions();
    Map<String, Object> prefs = new HashMap<>();
    prefs.put("intl.accept_languages", lang); ❶
    options.setExperimentalOption("prefs", prefs);

    driver = WebDriverManager.chromedriver().capabilities(options).create();
}

@Test
void testAcceptLang() {
    driver.get(
```

```
                    "https://bonigarcia.dev/selenium-webdriver-java/multilanguage.html"); ❷

        ResourceBundle strings = ResourceBundle.getBundle("strings",
                Locale.forLanguageTag(lang)); ❸
        String home = strings.getString("home");
        String content = strings.getString("content");
        String about = strings.getString("about");
        String contact = strings.getString("contact");

        String bodyText = driver.findElement(By.tagName("body")).getText();
        assertThat(bodyText).contains(home).contains(content).contains(about)
                .contains(contact); ❹
}
```

❶ We specify European Spanish as the preferred language in Chrome.

❷ We open a practice page that supports multilanguage (English and Spanish).

❸ We read the text translations using a resource bundle. You can find these strings
   in the file strings_es.properties (and strings_en.properties) in the project
   folder src/test/resources.

❹ We assert that the document body contains all the expected strings.

Example 5-24. Test setup that specifies a preferred locale for Firefox

```
@BeforeEach
void setup() {
    lang = "es-ES";
    FirefoxOptions options = new FirefoxOptions();
    options.addPreference("intl.accept_languages", lang);

    driver = WebDriverManager.firefoxdriver().capabilities(options)
            .create();
}
```

There is a second alternative to practice localization testing with Selenium Web-
Driver. Instead of changing the preferred language (which determines the HTTP
header accept-language), we can change the default language of the web browser. If
that HTTP header is not present, multilanguage applications will use the browser language alternatively. The Selenium WebDriver API allows changing the browser
language with a simple argument called --lang, specified as browser capability. This
argument is interoperable in Chrome, Edge, and Firefox. Example 5-25 shows how to
set the browser language to American English using WebDriver capabilities.

Example 5-25. Test setup that changes the browser language in Chrome

```
@BeforeEach
void setup() {
    lang = "en-US";
    ChromeOptions options = new ChromeOptions();
    options.addArguments("--lang=" + lang);

    driver = WebDriverManager.chromedriver().capabilities(options).create();
}
```

Incognito

Incognito mode ensures that browsers run in a clean state. This mode allows private browsing, i.e., running isolated from the main session and user data. The Selenium WebDriver API enables the execution of browsers in incognito mode using capabilities. For Chrome and Edge, this mode is activated using the `--incognito` argument (see Example 5-26), while in Firefox, we use the `-private` preference (see Example 5-27).

Example 5-26. Test setup for using Chrome in incognito mode

```
@BeforeEach
void setup() {
    ChromeOptions options = new ChromeOptions();
    options.addArguments("--incognito");

    driver = WebDriverManager.chromedriver().capabilities(options).create();
}
```

Example 5-27. Test setup for using Firefox in incognito mode

```
@BeforeEach
void setup() {
    FirefoxOptions options = new FirefoxOptions();
    options.addArguments("-private");

    driver = WebDriverManager.firefoxdriver().capabilities(options)
            .create();
}
```

Edge in Internet Explorer Mode

Edge offers built-in support for the Microsoft legacy browser, i.e., Internet Explorer (IE). This way, to create a Selenium WebDriver test that uses Edge in IE mode, we need first to enable the IE mode in Edge. As shown in Figure 5-14, this option is enabled in Edge settings → Default browser → Allow sites to be reloaded in Internet

Explorer mode. Then, we can use the Selenium WebDriver API as illustrated in Example 5-28.

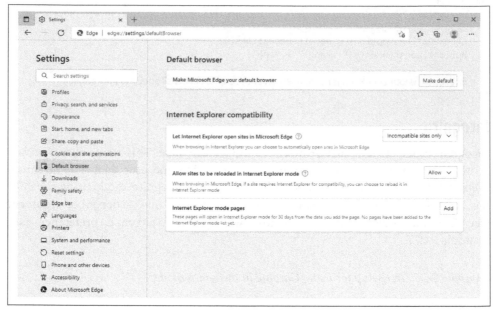

Figure 5-14. Browser setup to enable Edge in IE mode

Example 5-28. Test setup to use Edge in IE mode

```
@BeforeAll
static void setupClass() {
    assumeThat(IS_OS_WINDOWS).isTrue(); ❶
    WebDriverManager.iedriver().setup(); ❷
}

@BeforeEach
void setup() {
    Optional<Path> browserPath = WebDriverManager.edgedriver()
            .getBrowserPath(); ❸
    assumeThat(browserPath).isPresent();

    InternetExplorerOptions options = new InternetExplorerOptions();
    options.attachToEdgeChrome(); ❹
    options.withEdgeExecutablePath(browserPath.get().toString()); ❺

    driver = new InternetExplorerDriver(options); ❻
}
```

❶ We assume that the test is executed in Windows since IE mode is not supported on other operating systems.

❷ We use WebDriverManager to manage IEDriver (the driver required by Internet Explorer).

❸ We use WebDriverManager to discover the path of Edge.

❹ We use IE options to specify that we use Edge in IE mode.

❺ We set the previously discovered Edge path on the IE options.

❻ We create the driver instance to use Internet Explorer (which will actually be Edge in IE mode).

The Chrome DevTools Protocol

Chrome DevTools (*https://developer.chrome.com/docs/devtools*) is a set of web developer tools for Chromium-based web browsers, such as Chrome and Edge. These tools allow inspecting, debugging, or profiling these browsers, among other functions. The Chrome DevTools Protocol (CDP) (*https://chromedevtools.github.io/devtools-protocol*) is a communication protocol that allows the manipulation of the Chrome DevTools by external clients. Firefox implements a subset of the CDP to support automation tools like Selenium WebDriver.

There are two ways to use CDP in Selenium WebDriver. As of version 4, Selenium WebDriver provides the interface `HasDevTools` for sending CDP commands to the browser. This interface is implemented by `ChromiumDriver` (used for Chrome and Edge) and `FirefoxDriver` (for Firefox). This mechanism is quite powerful since it provides direct access to the CDP with Selenium WebDriver. Nevertheless, it has a relevant limitation since it is tied to both the browser type and version.

For this reason, the Selenium WebDriver API provides a second way to use the CDP, based on a set of wrapper classes built on top of CDP for advanced manipulation of the browsers. These wrappers allow different operations, such as network traffic interception or basic and digest authentication. The following subsection explains these wrappers. After that, I present several examples for using the CDP commands directly.

CDP Selenium Wrappers

The Selenium WebDriver API contains a group of helper classes that wraps some of the CDP commands. These classes aim to provide a friendly API enabling advanced features for Selenium WebDriver tests.

Network interceptor

The first wrapper class built on top of CDP is called `NetworkInterceptor`. This class allows stubbing the backend requests, intercepting network traffic, and returning pre-canned responses. This feature might help to simplify complex end-to-end tests by mocking external calls with fast, straightforward responses. To instantiate `Network Interceptor`, we need to specify parameters in its constructor (see Example 5-29):

- A `WebDriver` object that implements the CDP (i.e., `ChromeDriver` or `EdgeDriver`)
- A `Route` object to map the network requests to responses

Example 5-29. Test intercepting network traffic using NetworkInterceptor

```
@Test
void testNetworkInterceptor() throws Exception {
    Path img = Paths
            .get(ClassLoader.getSystemResource("tools.png").toURI());  ❶
    byte[] bytes = Files.readAllBytes(img);

    try (NetworkInterceptor interceptor = new NetworkInterceptor(driver,
            Route.matching(req -> req.getUri().endsWith(".png"))
                    .to(() -> req -> new HttpResponse()
                            .setContent(Contents.bytes(bytes))))) {  ❷
        driver.get("https://bonigarcia.dev/selenium-webdriver-java/");  ❸

        int width = Integer.parseInt(driver.findElement(By.tagName("img"))
                .getAttribute("width"));
        assertThat(width).isGreaterThan(80);  ❹
    }
}
```

❶ We load a local image stored as a test resource in the Java project.

❷ We create a network interceptor instance, creating a route for all the requests ending in `.png`, and stubbing this request with a new response, in this case sending the content of the previous picture.

❸ We open the practice site.

❹ If the interception works as expected, the image on the page should have a width higher than the original logo.

A `DevToolsException` will be thrown if a browser different than Chrome or Edge (such as Firefox) is used with previous code.

Basic and digest authentication

HTTP provides two built-in mechanisms for recognizing a user's identity, called *basic* and *digest* authentication. Both methods allow specifying the user's credential using a pair of values: username and password. The difference between them is how they communicate the credentials. On the one hand, the digest authentication method sends encrypted credentials by applying a hash function to username and password. On the other hand, basic authentication uses Base64 to encode (not encrypt) the credentials.

Selenium WebDriver provides the interface `HasAuthentication` to seamlessly implement basic and digest authentication. Example 5-30 shows a test using Chrome and basic authentication. You can use the exact mechanism with Edge and digest authentication (see the complete test in the example repository (*https://github.com/bonigarcia/selenium-webdriver-java*)).

Example 5-30. Test using basic authentication with Chrome

```
@Test
void testBasicAuth() {
    ((HasAuthentication) driver)
            .register(() -> new UsernameAndPassword("guest", "guest")); ❶

    driver.get("https://jigsaw.w3.org/HTTP/Basic/"); ❷

    WebElement body = driver.findElement(By.tagName("body"));
    assertThat(body.getText()).contains("Your browser made it!"); ❸
}
```

❶ We cast the driver object to `HasAuthentication` and register the credentials (username and password).

❷ We open a website protected with basic authentication.

❸ We verify the page content is available.

When using other browsers (such as Firefox), we cannot cast the driver object to `HasAuthentication`. Nevertheless, there is a general way to send the credentials in the URL using the syntax `protocol://username:password@domain`. Example 5-31 demonstrates this use.

Example 5-31. Test using basic authentication and Firefox

```
@Test
void testGenericAuth() {
    driver.get("https://guest:guest@jigsaw.w3.org/HTTP/Basic/");

    WebElement body = driver.findElement(By.tagName("body"));
    assertThat(body.getText()).contains("Your browser made it!");
}
```

CDP Raw Commands

As of version 4, Selenium WebDriver provides the interface HasDevTools for using the CDP directly. This interface is implemented by ChromiumDriver (used for Chrome and Edge) and FirefoxDriver (for Firefox). To use this feature, we first need to open a CDP session (i.e., a WebSocket connection between the client and the browser) using the method createSession() of a DevTools instance. Example 5-32 shows the recommended structure for using CDP in Selenium WebDriver tests. As you can see, the CDP session is created in the test setup and closed in the teardown. Each test will use the class attribute devTools to interact with the Chrome DevTools.

Example 5-32. Test structure to use Chrome DevTools

```
WebDriver driver;

DevTools devTools; ❶

@BeforeEach
void setup() {
    driver = WebDriverManager.chromedriver().create();
    devTools = ((ChromeDriver) driver).getDevTools(); ❷
    devTools.createSession(); ❸
}

@AfterEach
void teardown() {
    devTools.close(); ❹
    driver.quit();
}
```

❶ We declare a DevTools class attribute.

❷ We get the DevTools instance from the driver object. In this example (and the rest), I use ChromeDriver (although EdgeDriver instances would also be valid).

❸ We create a CDP session to interact with Chrome DevTools in the test logic.

---

❹ After each test and before quitting the WebDriver session, we terminate the CDP session.

The following subsections present several examples that illustrate the potential of DevTools in WebDriver tests. In these examples, we use an instance of `DevTools` for sending CDP commands using the method `send()`. The Selenium WebDriver API provides various commands that allow different operations for testing web applications, such as emulating network conditions, handling HTTP headers, blocking URLs, etc.

 The Selenium WebDriver tests using the raw CDP commands (as explained in the following subsections) are tied to a given browser version. You can see this version by inspecting the import clauses (e.g., `import org.openqa.selenium.devtools.v96.*;`) in the complete tests available in the examples repository.

Emulate network conditions

The CDP allows the emulation of different networks (such as mobile 2G/3G/4G, WiFi, or Bluetooth, among others) and conditions (e.g., latency or throughput). This feature can be helpful to test the behavior of web applications under specific connectivity parameters. Example 5-33 shows a test using this feature. As you can see, this test sends two CDP commands:

`Network.enable()`
To activate network tracking. This command has three optional arguments:

    `Optional<Integer> maxTotalBufferSize`
        Maximum buffer size (in bytes) for network payloads.

    `Optional<Integer> maxResourceBufferSize`
        Maximum buffer size (in bytes) for single resources.

    `Optional<Integer> maxPostDataSize`
        Longest post body size (in bytes).

`Network.emulateNetworkConditions()`
To activate network emulation. The emulated conditions are specified using the following parameters:

    `Boolean offline`
        To emulate no connection to the internet. `Number latency`: Minimum latency (in ms) from request to response.

Number downloadThroughput

> Maximal download throughput (in bytes/sec). -1 disables download throttling.

Number uploadThroughput

> Maximal upload throughput (in bytes/sec). -1 disables upload throttling.

Optional<ConnectionType> connectionType

> Emulated connection technology. The enumeration ConnectionType accepts the following options: NONE, CELLULAR2G, CELLULAR3G, CELLULAR4G, BLUE TOOTH, ETHERNET, WIFI, WIMAX, and OTHER.

Example 5-33. Test emulating network conditions

```
@Test
void testEmulateNetworkConditions() {
    devTools.send(Network.enable(Optional.empty(), Optional.empty(),
            Optional.empty())); ❶
    devTools.send(Network.emulateNetworkConditions(false, 100, 50 * 1024,
            50 * 1024, Optional.of(ConnectionType.CELLULAR3G))); ❷

    long initMillis = System.currentTimeMillis(); ❸
    driver.get("https://bonigarcia.dev/selenium-webdriver-java/"); ❹
    Duration elapsed = Duration
            .ofMillis(System.currentTimeMillis() - initMillis); ❺
    log.debug("The page took {} ms to be loaded", elapsed.toMillis());

    assertThat(driver.getTitle()).contains("Selenium WebDriver");
}
```

❶ We activate network tracking (without tuning any network parameter).

❷ We emulate a mobile 3G network with 50 KBps as download and upload bandwidth.

❸ We get a system timestamp before loading a web page.

❹ We load the index page of the practice site.

❺ We calculate the required time to load this page.

Network monitoring

We can also use the CDP to monitor network traffic when interacting with web pages. Example 5-34 shows a test using this feature. This test uses the method add Listener() of a DevTools object to trace HTTP requests and responses.

Example 5-34. Test monitoring HTTP requests and responses

```java
@Test
void testNetworkMonitoring() {
    devTools.send(Network.enable(Optional.empty(), Optional.empty(),
            Optional.empty()));

    devTools.addListener(Network.requestWillBeSent(), request -> {
        log.debug("Request {}", request.getRequestId());
        log.debug("\t Method: {}", request.getRequest().getMethod());
        log.debug("\t URL: {}", request.getRequest().getUrl());
        logHeaders(request.getRequest().getHeaders());
    }); ❶

    devTools.addListener(Network.responseReceived(), response -> {
        log.debug("Response {}", response.getRequestId());
        log.debug("\t URL: {}", response.getResponse().getUrl());
        log.debug("\t Status: {}", response.getResponse().getStatus());
        logHeaders(response.getResponse().getHeaders());
    }); ❷

    driver.get("https://bonigarcia.dev/selenium-webdriver-java/");
    assertThat(driver.getTitle()).contains("Selenium WebDriver");
}

void logHeaders(Headers headers) {
    log.debug("\t Headers:");
    headers.toJson().forEach((k, v) -> log.debug("\t\t{}:{}", k, v));
}
```

❶ We create a listener for HTTP requests and log the captured data in the console.

❷ We create a listener for HTTP responses and log the captured data in the console.

Full-page screenshot

Another possible use of the CDP is making screenshots of a full page (i.e., capture the content page beyond the viewport). Example 5-35 demonstrates this feature in Chrome.

Example 5-35. Test making a full-page screenshot using CDP in Chrome

```java
@Test
void testFullPageScreenshotChrome() throws IOException {
    driver.get(
            "https://bonigarcia.dev/selenium-webdriver-java/long-page.html"); ❶
    WebDriverWait wait = new WebDriverWait(driver, Duration.ofSeconds(10));
    wait.until(ExpectedConditions.presenceOfNestedElementsLocatedBy(
            By.className("container"), By.tagName("p"))); ❷
```

```
GetLayoutMetricsResponse metrics = devTools
        .send(Page.getLayoutMetrics());
Rect contentSize = metrics.getContentSize(); ❸
String screenshotBase64 = devTools
        .send(Page.captureScreenshot(Optional.empty(), Optional.empty(),
                Optional.of(new Viewport(0, 0, contentSize.getWidth(),
                        contentSize.getHeight(), 1)),
                Optional.empty(), Optional.of(true))); ❹
Path destination = Paths.get("fullpage-screenshot-chrome.png");
Files.write(destination, Base64.getDecoder().decode(screenshotBase64)); ❺

assertThat(destination).exists(); ❻
}
```

❶ We load the practice page containing a long text (and therefore, its content goes beyond the standard viewport).

❷ We wait until the paragraphs are loaded.

❸ We get the page layout metrics (to calculate the page dimensions).

❹ We send the CDP command to make a screenshot beyond the page viewport. As a result, we obtain the screenshot as a string in Base64.

❺ We decode the Base64 content into a PNG file.

❻ We assert the PNG file exists at the end of the test.

This feature is available in other browsers with a full implementation of the CDP, such as Chrome or Edge. Nevertheless, it might not be available in others like Firefox. Luckily, Firefox supports the same characteristic through the method getFullPage ScreenshotAs() available in FirefoxDriver objects. Example 5-36 shows a test using this method and Firefox.

Example 5-36. Test making a full-page screenshot using Firefox

```
@Test
void testFullPageScreenshotFirefox() throws IOException {
    driver.get(
            "https://bonigarcia.dev/selenium-webdriver-java/long-page.html");
    WebDriverWait wait = new WebDriverWait(driver, Duration.ofSeconds(10));
    wait.until(ExpectedConditions.presenceOfNestedElementsLocatedBy(
            By.className("container"), By.tagName("p")));

    byte[] imageBytes = ((FirefoxDriver) driver)
            .getFullPageScreenshotAs(OutputType.BYTES); ❶
    Path destination = Paths.get("fullpage-screenshot-firefox.png");
    Files.write(destination, imageBytes);
```

```
        assertThat(destination).exists();
}
```

❶ We make the whole page screenshot. As with the regular screenshots (see Table 4-2 in Chapter 4), the output type can be FILE, BASE64, or BYTES. We use the latter to get the screenshot as a byte array.

Performance metrics

CDP allows gathering runtime performance metrics, such as number of documents loaded, number of DOM nodes, time to load DOM, and script duration, among many others. Example 5-37 shows a test gathering these metrics and showing them in the standard output.

Example 5-37. Test gathering performance metrics

```
@Test
void testPerformanceMetrics() {
    devTools.send(Performance.enable(Optional.empty())); ❶
    driver.get("https://bonigarcia.dev/selenium-webdriver-java/");

    List<Metric> metrics = devTools.send(Performance.getMetrics()); ❷
    assertThat(metrics).isNotEmpty();
    metrics.forEach(metric -> log.debug("{}: {}", metric.getName(),
            metric.getValue()));
}
```

❶ We enable collecting metrics.

❷ We gather all metrics.

Extra headers

CDP allows additional headers at the HTTP level. To that aim, we need to send the command Network.setExtraHTTPHeaders() in a CDP session. Example 5-38 shows a test that uses this command to add the HTTP header Authorization, for sending credentials (username and password) in a web page that requires basic authentication to log in.

Example 5-38. Test adding extra HTTP headers

```
@Test
void testExtraHeaders() {
    devTools.send(Network.enable(Optional.empty(), Optional.empty(),
            Optional.empty()));
```

```
String userName = "guest";
String password = "guest";
Map<String, Object> headers = new HashMap<>();
String basicAuth = "Basic " + new String(Base64.getEncoder()
        .encode(String.format("%s:%s", userName, password).getBytes()));
headers.put("Authorization", basicAuth); ❶
devTools.send(Network.setExtraHTTPHeaders(new Headers(headers))); ❷

driver.get("https://jigsaw.w3.org/HTTP/Basic/"); ❸
String bodyText = driver.findElement(By.tagName("body")).getText();
assertThat(bodyText).contains("Your browser made it!"); ❹
}
```

❶ We encode the username and password in Base64.

❷ We create the authorization header.

❸ We open a web page protected with basic authentication.

❹ We verify that the page is correctly displayed.

Block URLs

CDP provides the ability to block given URLs in a session. Example 5-39 provides a test blocking the practice web page logo URL. If you run this test and inspect the browser during the execution, you will discover that this logo is not displayed on the page.

Example 5-39. Test blocking a URL

```
@Test
void testBlockUrl() {
    devTools.send(Network.enable(Optional.empty(), Optional.empty(),
            Optional.empty()));

    String urlToBlock =
            "https://bonigarcia.dev/selenium-webdriver-java/img/hands-on-icon.png";
    devTools.send(Network.setBlockedURLs(ImmutableList.of(urlToBlock))); ❶

    devTools.addListener(Network.loadingFailed(), loadingFailed -> {
        BlockedReason reason = loadingFailed.getBlockedReason().get();
        log.debug("Blocking reason: {}", reason);
        assertThat(reason).isEqualTo(BlockedReason.INSPECTOR);
    }); ❷

    driver.get("https://bonigarcia.dev/selenium-webdriver-java/");
    assertThat(driver.getTitle()).contains("Selenium WebDriver");
}
```

❶ We block a given URL.

❷ We create a listener to trace the failed events.

Device emulation

Another feature provided by CDP is the ability to emulate mobile devices (e.g., smartphones, tablets). Example 5-40 illustrates this usage. This test first overrides the user agent by sending the command `Network.setUserAgentOverride()`. Then, it emulates the device metrics sending the command `Emulation.setDeviceMetrics Override`.

Example 5-40. Test emulating a mobile device

```java
@Test
void testDeviceEmulation() {
    // 1. Override user agent (Apple iPhone 6)
    String userAgent = "Mozilla/5.0 (iPhone; CPU iPhone OS 8_0 like Mac OS X)"
            + "AppleWebKit/600.1.3 (KHTML, like Gecko)"
            + "Version/8.0 Mobile/12A4345d Safari/600.1.4";
    devTools.send(Network.setUserAgentOverride(userAgent, Optional.empty(),
            Optional.empty(), Optional.empty())); ❶

    // 2. Emulate device dimension
    Map<String, Object> deviceMetrics = new HashMap<>();
    deviceMetrics.put("width", 375);
    deviceMetrics.put("height", 667);
    deviceMetrics.put("mobile", true);
    deviceMetrics.put("deviceScaleFactor", 2);
    ((ChromeDriver) driver).executeCdpCommand(
            "Emulation.setDeviceMetricsOverride", deviceMetrics); ❷

    driver.get("https://bonigarcia.dev/selenium-webdriver-java/");
    assertThat(driver.getTitle()).contains("Selenium WebDriver");
}
```

❶ We override the user agent for emulating an Apple iPhone 6.

❷ We override the device screen parameters.

Console listeners

CDP allows you to implement listeners to monitor console events, i.e., a web page JavaScript log and error traces. Example 5-41 shows the test. This test uses a web page in the practice site that intentionally traces several JavaScript messages (using the commands `console.log()`, `console.error()`, etc.) and also throws a JavaScript exception.

Example 5-41. Test listening to console events

```
@Test
void testConsoleListener() throws Exception {
    CompletableFuture<ConsoleEvent> futureEvents = new CompletableFuture<>();
    devTools.getDomains().events()
            .addConsoleListener(futureEvents::complete); ❶

    CompletableFuture<JavascriptException> futureJsExc = new CompletableFuture<>();
    devTools.getDomains().events()
            .addJavascriptExceptionListener(futureJsExc::complete); ❷

    driver.get(
            "https://bonigarcia.dev/selenium-webdriver-java/console-logs.html"); ❸

    ConsoleEvent consoleEvent = futureEvents.get(5, TimeUnit.SECONDS); ❹
    log.debug("ConsoleEvent: {} {} {}", consoleEvent.getTimestamp(),
            consoleEvent.getType(), consoleEvent.getMessages()); ❺

    JavascriptException jsException = futureJsExc.get(5,
            TimeUnit.SECONDS); ❻
    log.debug("JavascriptException: {} {}", jsException.getMessage(),
            jsException.getSystemInformation());
}
```

❶ We create a listener for console events.

❷ We create another listener for JavaScript errors.

❸ We open the practice page that writes messages in the browser console.

❹ We wait a maximum of five seconds until a console event is received.

❺ We write the information on the received console event in the standard output.

❻ We repeat the same procedure for the JavaScript exceptions.

Geolocation override

Another feature provided by CDP is the ability to override the geolocation coordinates handled by the hosting device. Example 5-42 demonstrates how to do it. This test sends the command `Emulation.setGeolocationOverride()`, which accepts three optional arguments: latitude, longitude, and accuracy.

Example 5-42. Test overriding location coordinates

```java
@Test
void testGeolocationOverride() {
    devTools.send(Emulation.setGeolocationOverride(Optional.of(48.8584),
            Optional.of(2.2945), Optional.of(100))); ❶

    driver.get(
            "https://bonigarcia.dev/selenium-webdriver-java/geolocation.html"); ❷
    driver.findElement(By.id("get-coordinates")).click();

    WebDriverWait wait = new WebDriverWait(driver, Duration.ofSeconds(5));
    WebElement coordinates = driver.findElement(By.id("coordinates"));
    wait.until(ExpectedConditions.visibilityOf(coordinates));
}
```

❶ We override the geographical location using the coordinates of the Eiffel Tower (Paris, France).

❷ We open a practice web page that accesses the device location and displays the coordinates to the user.

Manage cookies

CDP also allows managing web cookies. Example 5-43 shows a test reading the cookies of a practice page that manages some cookies.

Example 5-43. Test managing cookies

```java
@Test
void testManageCookies() {
    devTools.send(Network.enable(Optional.empty(), Optional.empty(),
            Optional.empty()));
    driver.get(
            "https://bonigarcia.dev/selenium-webdriver-java/cookies.html");

    // Read cookies
    List<Cookie> cookies = devTools.send(Network.getAllCookies()); ❶
    cookies.forEach(cookie -> log.debug("{}={}", cookie.getName(),
            cookie.getValue()));
    List<String> cookieName = cookies.stream()
            .map(cookie -> cookie.getName()).sorted()
            .collect(Collectors.toList());
    Set<org.openqa.selenium.Cookie> seleniumCookie = driver.manage()
            .getCookies();
    List<String> selCookieName = seleniumCookie.stream()
            .map(selCookie -> selCookie.getName()).sorted()
            .collect(Collectors.toList());
    assertThat(cookieName).isEqualTo(selCookieName); ❷
```

```
// Clear cookies
devTools.send(Network.clearBrowserCookies()); ❸
List<Cookie> cookiesAfterClearing = devTools
        .send(Network.getAllCookies());
assertThat(cookiesAfterClearing).isEmpty(); ❹

driver.findElement(By.id("refresh-cookies")).click();
}
```

❶ We read all the cookies of a web page.

❷ We verify that the cookies read using the CDP command and the cookies read with the Selenium WebDriver API (using getCookies();) are the same.

❸ We remove all cookies.

❹ We verify there are no cookies at this point.

Load insecure pages

CDP also allows you to load unsafe web pages (i.e., web pages that use HTTPS, but whose certificate is not valid). Example 5-44 illustrates this feature.

Example 5-44. Test loading an insecure web page

```
@Test
void testLoadInsecure() {
    devTools.send(Security.enable()); ❶
    devTools.send(Security.setIgnoreCertificateErrors(true)); ❷
    driver.get("https://expired.badssl.com/");

    String bgColor = driver.findElement(By.tagName("body"))
            .getCssValue("background-color");
    Color red = new Color(255, 0, 0, 1);
    assertThat(Color.fromString(bgColor)).isEqualTo(red); ❸
}
```

❶ We enable tracking security.

❷ We ignore certificate errors.

❸ We verify the page is correctly loaded.

Location Context

The Selenium WebDriver API provides the interface `LocationContext` for mocking the geolocation coordinates of the user device. This interface is implemented by `ChromeDriver`, `EdgeDriver`, and `OperaDriver`. Therefore, these drivers can invoke the method `setLocation()` to specify custom coordinates (latitude, longitude, and altitude). Example 5-45 shows a basic test using this feature.

Example 5-45. Test setting custom geolocation coordinates through LocationContext

```
@Test
void testLocationContext() {
    LocationContext location = (LocationContext) driver; ❶
    location.setLocation(new Location(27.5916, 86.5640, 8850)); ❷

    driver.get(
            "https://bonigarcia.dev/selenium-webdriver-java/geolocation.html"); ❸
    driver.findElement(By.id("get-coordinates")).click();

    WebDriverWait wait = new WebDriverWait(driver, Duration.ofSeconds(5));
    WebElement coordinates = driver.findElement(By.id("coordinates"));
    wait.until(ExpectedConditions.visibilityOf(coordinates)); ❹
}
```

❶ We cast the driver object to `LocationContext` (only possible for Chrome, Edge, or Opera).

❷ We open a practice page where the geolocation coordinates are displayed to the end user.

❸ We set a custom location, in this case, the coordinates of Mount Everest (on the Nepal-China border).

❹ We assert the coordinates are visible on the page.

Web Authentication

The Web Authentication API (also known as *WebAuthn*) is a W3C specification (*https://www.w3.org/TR/webauthn-2*) that allows servers to register and authenticate users using public key cryptography instead of passwords. Major browsers (Chrome, Firefox, Edge, and Safari) have supported WebAuthn since January 2019. These browsers allow credential creation and assertion using U2F (Universal 2nd Factor) tokens, which are Universal Serial Bus (USB) or Near-Field Communication (NFC) secure devices.

In the classic web authentication approach, users send their username and password to the server using a web form. In WebAuthn, the web server uses the Web Authentication API to prompt the user to create a private-public key pair (known as a *credential*). The private key is stored securely on the user's device, and the public key is sent to the server. Then, the server can use that public key to validate user identity.

As of version 4, Selenium WebDriver supports *WebAuthn* out of the box. To that aim, the Selenium WebDriver API provides the interface `HasVirtualAuthenticator`. Instead of using secure physical devices, this interface allows us to use virtual authenticators. Although the `RemoteWebDriver` class implements this interface, at the time of this writing, this mechanism is supported only in Chromium-based browsers, i.e., Chrome and Edge. Example 5-46 shows a test using the Web Authentication API.

Example 5-46. Test using WebAuthn

```
@Test
void testWebAuthn() {
    driver.get("https://webauthn.io/"); ❶
    HasVirtualAuthenticator virtualAuth = (HasVirtualAuthenticator) driver; ❷
    VirtualAuthenticator authenticator = virtualAuth
            .addVirtualAuthenticator(new VirtualAuthenticatorOptions()); ❸

    String randomId = UUID.randomUUID().toString();
    driver.findElement(By.id("input-email")).sendKeys(randomId); ❹
    WebDriverWait wait = new WebDriverWait(driver, Duration.ofSeconds(20));
    driver.findElement(By.id("register-button")).click(); ❺
    wait.until(ExpectedConditions.textToBePresentInElementLocated(
            By.className("popover-body"), "Success! Now try logging in"));

    driver.findElement(By.id("login-button")).click(); ❻
    wait.until(ExpectedConditions.textToBePresentInElementLocated(
            By.className("main-content"), "You're logged in!")); ❼

    virtualAuth.removeVirtualAuthenticator(authenticator); ❽
}
```

❶ We open a website protected with the Web Authentication API.

❷ We cast the driver object to `HasVirtualAuthenticator`.

❸ We create and register a new virtual authenticator.

❹ We send a random identifier in the web form.

❺ We submit that identifier and wait until it is received.

❻ We click the button to log in.

❼ We verify the authentication has been correctly performed.

❽ We remove the virtual authenticator.

Print Page

Selenium WebDriver allows printing web pages to PDF documents. To do that, the Selenium WebDriver API provides the interface `PrintsPage`. This interface is inherited by the class `RemoteWebDriver`, and therefore, it is available for all browsers supported by Selenium WebDriver. Nevertheless, there are slight differences when using one or another browser. For instance, printing pages is possible when using Chrome and Edge only if the browser is started in headless mode. For Firefox, this restriction is not required, and we can use Firefox as usual. Example 5-47 shows the test logic for printing a web page to PDF. You can find the complete tests for Firefox and headless Chrome/Edge in the examples repository (*https://github.com/bonigarcia/selenium-webdriver-java*).

Example 5-47. Test printing a web page to PDF

```
@Test
void testPrint() throws IOException {
    driver.get("https://bonigarcia.dev/selenium-webdriver-java/");
    PrintsPage pg = (PrintsPage) driver; ❶
    PrintOptions printOptions = new PrintOptions();
    Pdf pdf = pg.print(printOptions); ❷

    String pdfBase64 = pdf.getContent(); ❸
    assertThat(pdfBase64).contains("JVBER"); ❹

    byte[] decodedImg = Base64.getDecoder()
            .decode(pdfBase64.getBytes(StandardCharsets.UTF_8)); ❺
    Path destinationFile = Paths.get("my-pdf.pdf");
    Files.write(destinationFile, decodedImg); ❻
}
```

❶ We cast the driver object to `PrintsPage`.

❷ We print the current web page to PDF using the default configuration.

❸ We get the content of the PDF in Base64.

❹ We verify this content contains the file signature (the "magic word" `JVBER`).

❺ We convert the Base64 to a raw byte array.

❻ We write the PDF content (byte array) to a local file.

WebDriver BiDi

The WebDriver BiDi (*https://w3c.github.io/webdriver-bidi*) is a W3C draft that defines the bidirectional WebDriver protocol. Instead of the strict command/response format of the WebDriver protocol, BiDi introduces a WebSocket connection between driver and browser to enable bidirectional communication. This way, WebDriver BiDi will allow different operations using a fast bidirectional transport (i.e., without polling the browser to get responses).

In Selenium WebDriver, the aim is that BiDi will be a standardized replacement in the long run for advanced operations currently supported by CDP. For example, the Selenium WebDriver API supports implementing event listeners through the `HasLog Events` interface. This interface works on top of CDP at the time of this writing. Nevertheless, it will use BiDi internally in future Selenium WebDriver releases, providing more robust cross-browser compatibility. `HasLogEvents` allows implementing listeners for the following events:

`domMutation`
> To capture events about changes in the DOM. Example 5-48 shows a test implementing a listener for these events.

`consoleEvent`
> To capture events about changes in the browser console, such as JavaScript traces. Example 5-49 shows a second test implementing this type of listener.

Example 5-48. Test implementing a listener for DOM mutation events

```
@Test
void testDomMutation() throws InterruptedException {
    driver.get("https://bonigarcia.dev/selenium-webdriver-java/");

    HasLogEvents logger = (HasLogEvents) driver; ❶
    JavascriptExecutor js = (JavascriptExecutor) driver;

    AtomicReference<DomMutationEvent> seen = new AtomicReference<>();
    CountDownLatch latch = new CountDownLatch(1);
    logger.onLogEvent(CdpEventTypes.domMutation(mutation -> {
        seen.set(mutation);
        latch.countDown();
    })); ❷

    WebElement img = driver.findElement(By.tagName("img"));
    String newSrc = "img/award.png";
    String script = String.format("arguments[0].src = '%s';", newSrc);
    js.executeScript(script, img); ❸
```

```
assertThat(latch.await(10, TimeUnit.SECONDS)).isTrue(); ❹
assertThat(seen.get().getElement().getAttribute("src"))
        .endsWith(newSrc); ❺
}
```

❶ We cast the driver object to `HasLogEvents`. This cast is only possible for Chrome and Edge.

❷ We create a listener for DOM mutation events. This test expects to capture only one event, synchronized using a countdown latch.

❸ We force a DOM mutation by executing JavaScript to change an image source.

❹ We verify the event occurs at most in 10 seconds.

❺ We check the image source has changed.

Example 5-49. Test implementing a listener for console events

```
@Test
void testConsoleEvents() throws InterruptedException {
    HasLogEvents logger = (HasLogEvents) driver;

    CountDownLatch latch = new CountDownLatch(4);
    logger.onLogEvent(CdpEventTypes.consoleEvent(consoleEvent -> {
        log.debug("{} {}: {}", consoleEvent.getTimestamp(),
                consoleEvent.getType(), consoleEvent.getMessages());
        latch.countDown();
    })); ❶

    driver.get(
            "https://bonigarcia.dev/selenium-webdriver-java/console-logs.html"); ❷

    assertThat(latch.await(10, TimeUnit.SECONDS)).isTrue();
}
```

❶ We create a listener for console events. This test expects to capture four events synchronized using a countdown latch.

❷ We open the practice web page, which logs several messages in the JavaScript console.

Summary and Outlook

This chapter presented a practical overview of the Selenium WebDriver API features that are not interoperable among browsers. First, you discovered how to use capabilities to run browsers in headless mode, change the page loading strategy, use web extensions, or manage browser pop-ups (e.g., geolocation, notifications, or getting user media), among other capabilities. Then, you learned that Selenium WebDriver provides different ways to interact with web browsers using the CDP. This mechanism allows incorporating a lot of powerful features in our Selenium WebDriver tests, such as emulating network conditions, basic and digest authentication, network monitoring, handling HTTP headers, or blocking URLs, to name a few. Then, you discovered other browser-specific features, such as location context, web authentication (WebAuthn), and printing web pages to PDF documents. Finally, you learned about WebDriver BiDi, a draft standardization that defines bidirectional communication with browsers for automation purposes. BiDi is in an early stage at the time of this writing. The aim is that Selenium WebDriver will support different standard features on top of BiDi in future releases.

The next chapter concludes our journey with the Selenium WebDriver API. The chapter explains how to use this API to control remote browsers. These browsers can be hosted on Selenium Grid, a cloud provider (e.g., Sauce Labs, BrowserStack, or CrossBrowserTesting), or executed in Docker containers.

CHAPTER 6

Remote WebDriver

So far, the examples explained in this book use web browsers locally installed on the machine that executes the tests. This chapter covers another relevant feature of the Selenium WebDriver API, i.e., the ability to use remote browsers (i.e., installed in other hosts). First, we review the architecture that allows using remote browsers in Selenium WebDriver. Second, we study Selenium Grid, a networked infrastructure that provides remote browsers for Selenium WebDriver tests. Third, we analyze some of the most relevant cloud providers, i.e., companies that provide managed services for automated testing. Finally, we explore how to use Docker to support the browser infrastructure for Selenium.

Selenium WebDriver Architecture

As introduced in Chapter 1, Selenium WebDriver is a library that allows controlling web browsers programmatically. The automation is based on the native capabilities of each browser. Therefore, we need to place a binary file called a *driver* between the script (typically, a test) using the Selenium WebDriver API and the browser. The examples you have seen so far in this book use local browsers, i.e., browsers installed in the same machine that executes the test that uses the Selenium WebDriver API. Figure 6-1 illustrates this approach. In this case, and when using the Java language binding of the Selenium WebDriver API, we need to create an instance of `Chrome Driver` to control Chrome, `FirefoxDriver` for Firefox, etc.

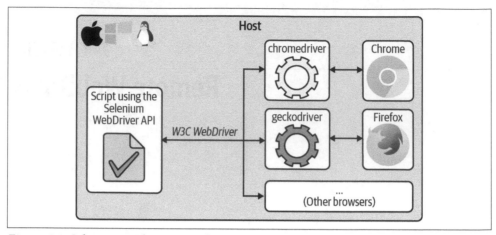

Figure 6-1. Selenium WebDriver architecture using local browsers

The communication protocol that supports this process is called W3C WebDriver. This standard protocol is based on JSON messages over HTTP. Thanks to this, the Selenium WebDriver architecture can be distributed to different interconnected computers (*hosts*). Figure 6-2 shows a schematic representation of a remote architecture.

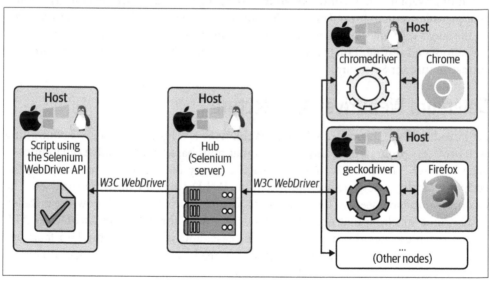

Figure 6-2. Selenium WebDriver architecture using remote browsers

In this case, the Selenium WebDriver API sends W3C WebDriver messages to a server-side component usually called *Selenium Server*. This server acts as a proxy of the client requests to other hosts that provide web browsers where the automation happens. This remote architecture eases cross-browser testing (i.e., verifying web applications in multiple browser types, versions, or operating systems) and parallel test execution.

Creation of RemoteWebDriver Objects

The Selenium WebDriver API provides the class RemoteWebDriver to control remote browsers. As shown in Figure 2-2, this class is the parent of the rest of the WebDriver classes that drive local browsers (i.e., ChromeDriver, FirefoxDriver, etc.). This way, you can use RemoteWebDriver objects in the same way we have previously studied in this book.

RemoteWebDriver Constructor

There are different ways to instantiate a RemoteWebDriver object. The most common way is to invoke its constructor by passing two arguments: the URL of the Selenium Server and the required capabilities. As shown in Figure 5-1, these capabilities are objects that inherit from the Capabilities interface (e.g., ChromeOptions, Firefox Options, etc.). Example 6-1 shows a test setup. You can find the complete test in this book's code repository (*https://github.com/bonigarcia/selenium-webdriver-java*).

> There is a second RemoteWebDriver constructor, which accepts only one parameter for the desired capabilities. In this case, the Selenium Server URL is read from the Java system property webdriver.remote.server. You can find an example of this feature in the examples repository.

Example 6-1. Instantiation of a RemoteWebDriver object using the constructor

```
@BeforeEach
void setup() throws MalformedURLException {
    URL seleniumServerUrl = new URL("http://localhost:4444/"); ❶
    assumeThat(isOnline(seleniumServerUrl)).isTrue(); ❷

    ChromeOptions options = new ChromeOptions(); ❸
    driver = new RemoteWebDriver(seleniumServerUrl, options); ❹
}
```

❶ We create a Java URL object with the Selenium Server address.

❷ We assume this URL is online. For that, we create an AssertJ assumption by invoking the static method isOnline available on WebDriverManager. As a result, the test is skipped when the Selenium Server is offline.

❸ We instantiate a ChromeOptions object to specify the required capabilities.

❹ We invoke the RemoteWebDriver constructor using the Selenium Server URL and the Chrome options as arguments.

We use a ChromeOptions object without any particular setup to specify the required capabilities in the previous example. In other words, we request to use a remote Chrome browser using its default behavior. Nevertheless, we could use this object to configure specific capabilities (e.g., headless browser, page loading strategies, device emulation, etc.) as explained in Chapter 5. Moreover, since capabilities are internally handled using key-value pairs that encapsulate specific browser aspects, we can manage individual capabilities invoking the method options.setCapability(key, value);. The Selenium WebDriver API provides the class CapabilityType to specify the key of these capabilities. This class has a set of public attributes that can be used as a key in the setCapability() method. Table 6-1 shows some of these attributes.

Table 6-1. CapabilityType attributes

Attribute	Capability name	Description
BROWSER_NAME	browserName	Browser name (e.g., chrome, firefox, or msedge)
PLATFORM_NAME	platformName	Platform name (e.g., WINDOWS, LINUX, MAC, ANDROID, IOS, among others)
BROWSER_VERSION	browserVersion	Browser version
SUPPORTS_JAVASCRIPT	javascriptEnabled	Enable or disable JavaScript execution
PAGE_LOAD_STRATEGY	pageLoadStrategy	Page loading strategy (normal, eager, or none)

An alternative way to specify the required capabilities in a RemoteWebDriver object is using an instance of DesiredCapabilities. Table 6-2 summarizes the methods provided by these objects.

Table 6-2. DesiredCapabilities methods

Method	Return	Description
setBrowserName(String browserName)	void	Specify the browser name
setVersion(String version)	void	Specify the browser version
setPlatform(Platform platform)	void	Specify the platform name

Method	Return	Description
setJavascriptEnabled(boolean javascriptEnabled)	void	Enable or disable JavaScript execution
setAcceptInsecureCerts(boolean acceptInsecureCerts)	void	Enable or disable loading insecure pages
acceptInsecureCerts()	void	Enable loading insecure pages
merge(Capabilities extraCapabilities)	DesiredCapabilities	Merge with another capabilities object

 DesiredCapabilities is still supported by Selenium WebDriver 4 since there is a lot of existing code relying on this feature. Nevertheless, the recommended way to specify capabilities is using browser-specific options (e.g., ChromeOptions, FirefoxOptions, etc.).

RemoteWebDriver Builder

A second way to create RemoteWebDriver objects is using the built-in builder available in the Selenium WebDriver API. Example 6-2 demonstrates how, using Edge as the remote browser.

Example 6-2. Instantiation of a RemoteWebDriver object using the builder

```
@BeforeEach
void setup() throws MalformedURLException {
    URL seleniumServerUrl = new URL("http://localhost:4444/");
    assumeThat(isOnline(seleniumServerUrl)).isTrue();

    driver = RemoteWebDriver.builder().oneOf(new EdgeOptions())
            .address(seleniumServerUrl).build();
}
```

WebDriverManager Builder

Alternatively, we can also use WebDriverManager to create an instance of RemoteWebDriver. To that aim, we need to invoke the method remoteAddress() of a given manager to pass the Selenium Server URL. Example 6-3 shows a test setup using this feature and Firefox as the remote browser.

Example 6-3. Instantiation of a RemoteWebDriver object using WebDriverManager

```
@BeforeEach
void setup() throws MalformedURLException {
    URL seleniumServerUrl = new URL("http://localhost:4444/");
```

```
    assumeThat(isOnline(seleniumServerUrl)).isTrue();

    driver = WebDriverManager.firefoxdriver()
            .remoteAddress(seleniumServerUrl).create();
}
```

Selenium-Jupiter

As usual, Selenium-Jupiter uses the parameter resolution feature provided by Jupiter. This way, and concerning remote browsers, you need to declare a test (or constructor) parameter using the type `RemoteWebDriver`. Then, the following Selenium-Jupiter annotations allow configuring the remote browser:

`@DriverUrl`
> Annotation used to identify the Selenium Server URL. Alternatively, the annotation `@EnabledIfDriverUrlOnline` allows specifying this URL, and at the same time, disables the test if that URL is not responding.

`@DriverCapabilities`
> Annotation used to configure the desired capabilities.

Example 6-4 shows a Selenium-Jupiter test using a remote Chrome provided by a local Selenium Server. This test will be skipped when the URL `http://localhost:4444/` is offline.

Example 6-4. Using a RemoteWebDriver object in Selenium-Jupiter test

```
@EnabledIfDriverUrlOnline("http://localhost:4444/")
@ExtendWith(SeleniumJupiter.class)
class RemoteChromeSelJupTest {

    @DriverCapabilities
    ChromeOptions options = new ChromeOptions();

    @Test
    void testRemote(RemoteWebDriver driver) {
        driver.get("https://bonigarcia.dev/selenium-webdriver-java/");
        assertThat(driver.getTitle()).contains("Selenium WebDriver");
    }

}
```

 The `RemoteWebDriver` instantiation modes described in this section are equivalent from a functional point of view. In other words, these objects work in the same way. The difference between them is the provided *syntactic sugar* (i.e., the style and expressiveness).

Selenium Grid

As introduced in Chapter 1, Selenium Grid is a subproject of the Selenium suite that allows creating a networked infrastructure for remote browsers accessible with the W3C WebDriver protocol. Selenium Grid allows running parallel tests across different machines and different browsers. To that aim, Selenium Grid provides a Selenium Server that you can control using an instance of `RemoteWebDriver`. There are three ways to run Selenium Grid:

Standalone
> A single host acts as Selenium Server and supplies the browsers in this mode. It provides a simple way to run Selenium WebDriver tests in remote browsers.

Hub-nodes
> A potential problem of the standalone mode is the scalability (since the Selenium Server and the browsers are executed in the same home). Thus, the hub-nodes architecture defines two types of components to solve this issue. First, one host acts as *hub* (or Selenium Server). Then, one or most hosts are registered as *nodes* in the hub, providing browsers to be controlled with Selenium WebDriver. This architecture was introduced in Chapter 1 (see Figure 1-2).

Fully distributed
> The standalone and the hub-nodes approaches are centralized architectures that can degrade performance when the number of incoming requests increases. As of Selenium 4, Selenium Grid provides a fully distributed mode that implements load balancing mechanisms to solve this bottleneck.

The following subsections provide more details about these modes and explain how to set up each approach.

Standalone

The standalone is the simplest approach for a Selenium Grid infrastructure. We can execute this mode using the shell and Java code.

From the shell

First, we can use the shell and the Selenium Grid binary distribution to launch it. Selenium Grid is developed in Java, and each release is distributed as a self-contained JAR file with all its dependencies (also known as *uber-JAR* or *fat-JAR*). You can download this fat-JAR from the Selenium download page (*https://www.selenium.dev/down loads*).

The Selenium Server automatically detects the drivers (e.g., chromedriver, geckodriver, etc.) available in the system in the standalone mode. To that aim, it looks for these drivers in the PATH environment variable. As usual, we can manage these driver managers manually. Nevertheless, it is recommended to use WebDriverManager to resolve the drivers automatically. Thus, and as explained in Appendix B, WebDriver-Manager can be used as a CLI tool. WebDriverManager CLI is distributed as a fat-JAR, available for download on GitHub (*https://github.com/bonigarcia/webdriver manager/releases*).

To illustrate this, Example 6-5 shows the shell commands required to resolve chrome-driver and geckodriver in a Linux machine with WebDriverManager CLI. Then, we use the Selenium Grid fat-JAR to start a standalone grid. Notice that these commands are executed in the same folder. This way, the drivers downloaded with WebDriver-Manager are available for Selenium Grid.

Example 6-5. Commands to resolve drivers with WebDriverManager CLI and to start Selenium Grid in standalone mode using the shell

```
boni@linux:~/grid$ java -jar webdrivermanager-5.0.3-fat.jar resolveDriverFor chrome ❶
[INFO] Using WebDriverManager to resolve chrome
[DEBUG] Detecting chrome version using online commands.properties
[DEBUG] Running command on the shell: [google-chrome, --version]
[DEBUG] Result: Version=94.0.4606.71
[DEBUG] Latest version of chromedriver according to
    https://chromedriver.storage.googleapis.com/LATEST_RELEASE_94 is 94.0.4606.61
[INFO] Using chromedriver 94.0.4606.61 (resolved driver for Chrome 94)
[INFO] Reading https://chromedriver.storage.googleapis.com/ to seek
    chromedriver
[DEBUG] Driver to be downloaded chromedriver 94.0.4606.61
[INFO] Downloading https://chromedriver.storage.googleapis.com/94.0.4606.61/
    chromedriver_linux64.zip
[INFO] Extracting driver from compressed file chromedriver_linux64.zip
[INFO] Driver location: /home/boni/grid/chromedriver

boni@linux:~/grid$ java -jar webdrivermanager-5.0.3-fat.jar resolveDriverFor firefox ❷
[INFO] Using WebDriverManager to resolve firefox
[DEBUG] Detecting firefox version using online commands.properties
[DEBUG] Running command on the shell: [firefox, -v]
[DEBUG] Result: Version=92.0.0.7916
[DEBUG] Getting driver version for firefox92 from online versions.properties
[INFO] Using geckodriver 0.30.0 (resolved driver for Firefox 92)
[INFO] Reading https://api.github.com/repos/mozilla/geckodriver/releases to
    seek geckodriver
[DEBUG] Driver to be downloaded geckodriver 0.30.0
[INFO] Downloading https://github.com/mozilla/geckodriver/releases/download/
    v0.30.0/geckodriver-v0.30.0-linux64.tar.gz
[INFO] Extracting driver from compressed file geckodriver-v0.30.0-linux64.tar.gz
[INFO] Driver location: /home/boni/grid/geckodriver

boni@linux:~/grid$ java -jar selenium-server-4.0.0.jar standalone ❸
INFO [LogManager$RootLogger.log] - Using the system default encoding
INFO [OpenTelemetryTracer.createTracer] - Using OpenTelemetry for tracing
INFO [NodeOptions.getSessionFactories] - Detected 8 available processors
```

```
INFO [NodeOptions.discoverDrivers] - Discovered 2 driver(s)
INFO [NodeOptions.report] - Adding Chrome for {"browserName": "chrome"} 8 times
INFO [NodeOptions.report] - Adding Firefox for {"browserName": "firefox"} 8 times
INFO [Node.<init>] - Binding additional locator mechanisms: name, id, relative
INFO [LocalDistributor.add] - Added node 41045bd8-ec7e-43c9-84bd-f63f7aca59ed
    at http://192.168.56.1:4444. Health check every 120s
INFO [GridModel.setAvailability] - Switching node 41045bd8-ec7e-43c9-84bd-
    f63f7aca59ed (uri: http://192.168.56.1:4444) from DOWN to UP
INFO [Standalone.execute] - Started Selenium Standalone 4.0.0 (revision
    3a21814679): http://192.168.56.1:4444
```

❶ We use WebDriverManager CLI to resolve chromedriver.

❷ We use WebDriverManager CLI to resolve geckodriver (the driver required for
   Firefox).

❸ We start Selenium Grid in standalone mode in the same folder (which contains
   chromedriver and geckodriver).

After these commands, the standalone Selenium Server listens to incoming HTTP
requests in port 4444 of the localhost. Therefore, we can create an instance of Remote
WebDriver using that URL (e.g., http://localhost:4444/ if the test executes in the
same host) and the required capabilities (for Chrome or Firefox, in this case). For
instance, as follows:

```
WebDriver driver = new RemoteWebDriver("http://localhost:4444/",
        new ChromeOptions());
```

 In Selenium Grid 3, the default Selenium Server URL is http://
localhost:4444/wd/hub. In Selenium Grid 4, although this URL
should also work, the path /wd/hub is no longer required.

Another helpful feature provided by Selenium Grid is its *web console*. This console is
a web UI accessible in the Selenium Server URL that allows monitoring of the available browsers registered in the grid and the sessions in execution.

Figure 6-3 shows a screenshot of the console of the previous standalone grid. Notice
that in this case, the standalone Selenium Server can serve up to eight concurrent sessions (the same number of the available processors in the machine running the grid)
of Chrome and Firefox.

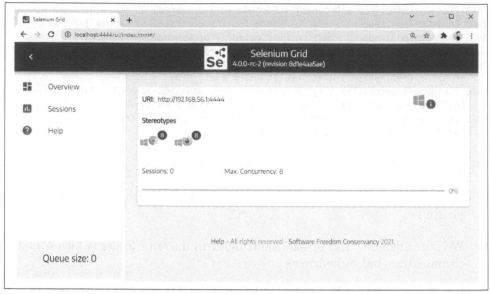

Figure 6-3. Selenium Grid console

From Java code

An alternative way to start Selenium Grid is using Java. In addition to the fat-JAR, Selenium Grid is released to Maven Central using `org.seleniumhq.selenium` as groupId and `selenium-grid` as artifactId. This way, we need to resolve its coordinates in our project setup (Maven or Gradle) to use it in our Java project (see Appendix B for the configuration details). Example 6-6 demonstrates how to start Selenium Grid in standalone mode from a Java test case.

Example 6-6. Test starting Selenium Grid in standalone mode

```
static URL seleniumServerUrl;

@BeforeAll
static void setupAll() throws MalformedURLException {
    int port = PortProber.findFreePort();              ❶
    WebDriverManager.chromedriver().setup();           ❷
    Main.main(
            new String[] { "standalone", "--port", String.valueOf(port) });  ❸

    seleniumServerUrl = new URL(
            String.format("http://localhost:%d/", port));  ❹
}

@BeforeEach
void setup() {
```

```
        driver = new RemoteWebDriver(seleniumServerUrl, new ChromeOptions()); ❺
}
```

❶ We find a free port on the localhost. For that, we use the class `PortProber`, available on Selenium WebDriver API.

❷ We use WebDriverManager to resolve chromedriver since the standalone grid to be started will serve Chrome browsers.

❸ We start Selenium Grid in standalone mode, calling its `main` method.

❹ We create a Java URL using the port previously selected.

❺ We create an instance of `RemoteWebDriver`. As usual, we use this object in the test logic to invoke the Selenium WebDriver API and control the browser (see the examples repository for the entire class).

Hub-nodes

The classic architecture of Selenium Grid involves two types of hosts: the hub (i.e., the Selenium Server) and a group of nodes. Like in the standalone mode, we can use the Selenium Grid fat-JAR to start this mode in the shell. First, we start the hub in a host. Then, we register one or more nodes in the same or different host. Example 6-7 shows the execution of these commands in a Windows console.

Example 6-7. Command to start Selenium Grid in hub-nodes mode using the shell

```
C:\grid>java -jar selenium-server-4.0.0.jar hub ❶
INFO [LogManager$RootLogger.log] - Using the system default encoding
INFO [OpenTelemetryTracer.createTracer] - Using OpenTelemetry for tracing
INFO [BoundZmqEventBus.<init>] - XPUB binding to [binding to tcp://*:4442,
    advertising as tcp://192.168.56.1:4442], XSUB binding to [binding to
    tcp://*:4443, advertising as tcp://192.168.56.1:4443]
INFO [UnboundZmqEventBus.<init>] - Connecting to tcp://192.168.56.1:4442 and
    tcp://192.168.56.1:4443
INFO [UnboundZmqEventBus.<init>] - Sockets created
INFO [UnboundZmqEventBus.<init>] - Event bus ready
INFO [Hub.execute] - Started Selenium Hub 4.0.0 (revision 3a21814679):
    http://192.168.56.1:4444
INFO [Node.<init>] - Binding additional locator mechanisms: relative, name, id
INFO [LocalDistributor.add] - Added node 98c35075-e5f0-4168-be97-c277e4f40d8d
    at http://192.168.56.1:5555. Health check every 120s
INFO [GridModel.setAvailability] - Switching node 98c35075-e5f0-4168-be97-
    c277e4f40d8d (uri: http://192.168.56.1:5555) from DOWN to UP


C:\grid>java -jar selenium-server-4.0.0.jar node ❷
```

```
INFO [LogManager$RootLogger.log] - Using the system default encoding
INFO [OpenTelemetryTracer.createTracer] - Using OpenTelemetry for tracing
INFO [UnboundZmqEventBus.<init>] - Connecting to tcp://*:4442 and tcp://*:4443
INFO [UnboundZmqEventBus.<init>] - Sockets created
INFO [UnboundZmqEventBus.<init>] - Event bus ready
INFO [NodeServer.createHandlers] - Reporting self as: http://192.168.56.1:5555
INFO [NodeOptions.getSessionFactories] - Detected 8 available processors
INFO [NodeOptions.discoverDrivers] - Discovered 2 driver(s)
INFO [NodeOptions.report] - Adding Chrome for {"browserName": "chrome"} 8 times
INFO [NodeOptions.report] - Adding Firefox for {"browserName": "firefox"} 8
    times
INFO [Node.<init>] - Binding additional locator mechanisms: relative, name, id
INFO [NodeServer$1.start] - Starting registration process for node id
    98c35075-e5f0-4168-be97-c277e4f40d8d
INFO [NodeServer.execute] - Started Selenium node 4.0.0 (revision
    3a21814679): http://192.168.56.1:5555
INFO [NodeServer$1.lambda$start$1] - Sending registration event...
INFO [NodeServer.lambda$createHandlers$2] - Node has been added
```

❶ We start the hub. By default, this server listens to W3C WebDriver HTTP requests in port 4444 and TCP ports 4442 and 4443 for registering nodes.

❷ In a second console, we register the node(s). In this example, this command is executed in the same host as the hub. Moreover, it supposes that the required drivers (e.g., chromedriver and geckodriver) are already resolved (as in Example 6-5). To start nodes from another host, we would need to invoke the following command:

```
java -jar selenium-server-4.0.0.jar node --hub http://<hub>:4444
```

In the same way as the standalone mode, you can start a hub-nodes grid using Java code. For that, you need to change the parameters to invoke the Selenium Grid main class following the same syntax of the CLI commands for hub and nodes.

Fully Distributed

As of version 4, we can execute a Selenium Grid infrastructure following a fully distributed architecture. The decisive aspect of this approach is scalability. Specialized nodes take care of different automation and infrastructure management aspects in this mode. These nodes are:

Router
Node acting as a single entry point to the Grid. This component listens to W3C WebDriver commands from Selenium scripts.

Session Queue

Node that stores the new session requests. These incoming sessions wait to be read by the *Distributor*.

Distributor

Node aware of all nodes and their capabilities. It asks for new session requests to the *Session Queue* in regular intervals.

Event Bus

Component that provides a message-oriented communication channel among several members of the Grid architecture. This communication is represented with dotted lines in Figures 6-4 and 6-5.

Session Map

It keeps the relation of the WebDriver sessions and the nodes where the sessions are being executed.

Node(s)

Hosts that provide web browsers (and their corresponding drivers) for automation based on Selenium WebDriver.

 In a hub-nodes architecture, the hub aggregates the responsibilities of the Router, Session Queue, Distributor, Event Bus, and Session Map of the fully distributed mode.

The following subsections provide details about the most relevant processes in a fully distributed Selenium Grid: node registration, new session, and other WebDriver commands.

Node registration

The first process required to operate a distributed Selenium Grid is registering one or more nodes. To that aim, nodes need to register their capabilities in the Distributor. Figure 6-4 illustrates this process, composed of three steps:

1. A node sends a message through the Event Bus to announce its capabilities.

2. This message reaches the Distributor, which stores the relationship between nodes and capabilities.

3. The Distributor double-checks that the node exists by exchanging HTTP messages (solid line) with the source node.

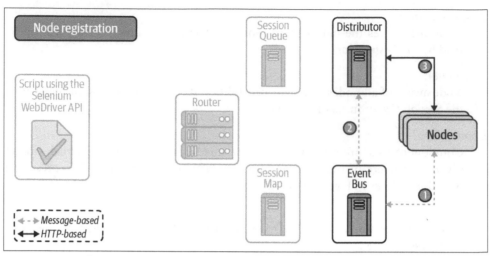

Figure 6-4. Node registration in a Selenium Grid distributed architecture

New session

At some point, a script (typically a test case) will try to start a new session to drive a browser automatically. Figure 6-5 describes the communication required to carry out this process in a fully distributed Selenium Grid, namely:

1. A script/test using the Selenium WebDriver API sends a request to the Router to create a new session (i.e., to drive a browser programmatically).

2. The Router creates a new entry in the Session Queue to store this new session request.

3. The Distributor asks the Session Queue for incoming new session requests in intervals.

4. Once the Distributor discovers a new session request, it checks if a node can support this session. If the session is possible (i.e., a node previously registered in the Distributor offers the required capabilities), the Distributor creates a new session with the node.

5. The Distributor sends an HTTP message to the Session Map to store the new session. The Session Map stores a unique session identifier (*session id*) that univocally associates the node executing the browser session.

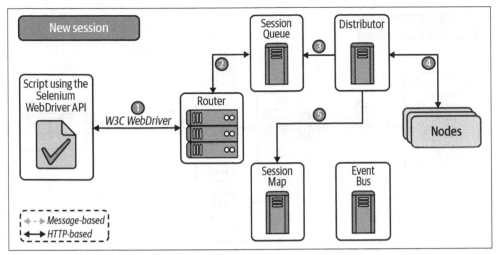

Figure 6-5. New session in a Selenium Grid distributed architecture

WebDriver commands

Once the session is established, the Selenium WebDriver API script will continue sending W3C WebDriver commands to control the web browser in the remote node. Figure 6-6 shows how this communication occurs in a distributed Selenium Grid infrastructure following these steps:

1. The script/test exchanges W3C WebDriver commands to drive the browser (e.g., open a web page, interact with web elements, etc.) in the current session.

2. Further requests to the same browser session use the same session id. The Router recognizes that a browser session is active by reading the Session Map.

3. The Router forwards the subsequent commands of the same session directly to the assigned node.

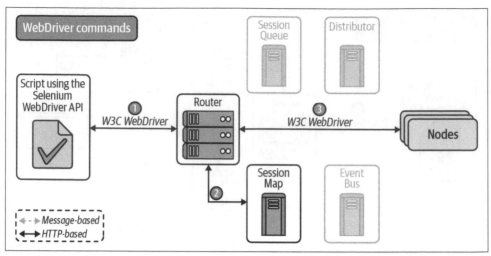

Figure 6-6. WebDriver commands in a Selenium Grid distributed architecture

Setting up a distributed grid

Like in the standalone and hub-nodes modes, we can use the Selenium Grid distribution (as a fat-JAR or regular Java dependency) to start the fully distributed architecture. Example 6-8 shows the shell command required to do this using the command line.

Example 6-8. Command to start Selenium Grid in distributed mode using the shell

```
C:\grid>java -jar selenium-server-4.0.0.jar event-bus ❶
INFO [BoundZmqEventBus.<init>] - XPUB binding to [binding to tcp://*:4442,
    advertising as tcp://192.168.56.1:4442], XSUB binding to [binding to
    tcp://*:4443, advertising as tcp://192.168.56.1:4443]
...


C:\grid>java -jar selenium-server-4.0.0.jar sessions ❷
...
INFO [SessionMapServer.execute] - Started Selenium SessionMap 4.0.0 (revision
    5fe1af712f): http://192.168.56.1:5556

C:\grid>java -jar selenium-server-4.0.0.jar sessionqueue ❸
...
INFO [NewSessionQueueServer.execute] - Started Selenium SessionQueue 4.0.0
    (revision 5fe1af712f): http://192.168.56.1:5559

C:\grid>java -jar selenium-server-4.0.0.jar distributor --sessions
    http://<session_map>:5556 --sessionqueue http://<session_queue>:5559 --bind-bus
    false ❹
...
```

```
INFO [DistributorServer.execute] - Started Selenium Distributor 4.0.0 (revision
    5fe1af712f): http://192.168.56.1:5553

C:\grid>java -jar selenium-server-4.0.0.jar router --sessions
    http://<session_map>:5556 --distributor http://<distributor_address>:5553
    --sessionqueue http://>session_queue>:5559 ❺
...
INFO [RouterServer.execute] - Started Selenium Router 4.0.0 (revision
    5fe1af712f): http://192.168.56.1:4444

C:\grid>java -jar selenium-server-4.0.0.jar node --publish-events
    tcp://<event_bus>:4442 --subscribe-events tcp://<event_bus>:4443 ❻
...
INFO [NodeOptions.discoverDrivers] - Discovered 2 driver(s)
...
INFO [NodeServer$1.lambda$start$1] - Sending registration event...
INFO [NodeServer.lambda$createHandlers$2] - Node has been added
```

❶ We start the Event Bus. By default, the Event Bus listens to TCP ports 4442 and
4443.

❷ We start the Session Map. By default, this component listens to incoming HTTP
messages in port 5556.

❸ We start the Session Queue. By default, this queue listens to HTTP in port 5559.

❹ We start the Distributor. For that, we need to specify the Session Map and Session
Queue addresses. In addition, and since we already started the Event Bus inde-
pendently, we set the flag `--bind-bus` to `false`. By default, the Distributor uses
port 5553 for the HTTP communication.

❺ We start the Router. We need to specify the URLs of the Session Map, Session
Queue, and Distributor.

❻ We start the Nodes. We need to specify the ports where the Event Bus listens to
publish-subscribe messages. Moreover, in this example, several drivers (chomedriver and geckodriver) are available in the same folder in which this command
is executed.

Observability

In software engineering, *observability* is a measure that determines the current state
of a software system based on its external outputs or signals. This way, observability
allows understanding the internal state of the system by leveraging its external indica-
tors. Observability can be critical for maintaining complex software systems and

determining the root cause of any issue. To that aim, the three pillars of observability are:

Metrics
> Measures of system performance over time, such as response time, transactions per second, or memory usage, to name a few

Logs
> Lines of text (typically timestamped) that a system produces when running a piece of code

Traces
> Representation of causally related distributed events (such as selected logs) that characterize the request flow of a given operation in a software system

Selenium Grid 4 provides different features for measuring observability. First, Selenium Grid allows tracing using the OpenTelemetry (*https://opentelemetry.io*) API. Second, Selenium Grid provides a GraphQL endpoint to run queries against the grid.

Tracing with OpenTelemetry

Tracing is an essential way of measuring observability based on the logs and metrics of a software system. Selenium Grid exposes tracing in two ways. First, we can check the log traces when executing a grid from the shell. By default, the logs at the INFO level are displayed. We can change the level using the argument `--log-level` in the shell command, for instance:

```
java -jar selenium-server-4.0.0.jar standalone --log-level FINE
```

Furthermore, Selenium Grid supports *distributed tracing* via OpenTelemetry APIs. This feature allows tracing the commands flowing through a Selenium Grid infrastructure. Distributed tracing requires two activities in this order:

1. Code instrumentation
> Selenium Grid allows exporting tracing information using the OpenTelemetry API.

2. Data collection
> For example, we can use Jaeger (*https://www.jaegertracing.io*), an open source distributed tracing platform that provides seamless integration with OpenTelemetry. It allows querying, visualizing, and collecting tracing data.

The following commands show how to set up Selenium Grid to export data to Jaeger. First, we need a Jaeger backend up and running. For that, we can download the executable binaries for the Jaeger download page (*https://www.jaegertracing.io/download*). Alternatively, we can start the server using Docker, as follows:

```
docker run --rm -it --name jaeger \
  -p 16686:16686 \ ❶
  -p 14250:14250 \ ❷
  jaegertracing/all-in-one:1.27
```

❶ We will use the URL `http://localhost:16686` to access the Jaeger UI.

❷ We will use the URL `http://localhost:14250` to collect the data (exported by Selenium Grid).

Then, we start Selenium Grid as follows:

```
java -Dotel.traces.exporter=jaeger \
  -Dotel.exporter.jaeger.endpoint=http://localhost:14250 \ ❶
  -Dotel.resource.attributes=service.name=selenium-standalone \ ❷
  -jar selenium-server-4.0.0.jar \
  --ext $(cs fetch -p \ ❸
    io.opentelemetry:opentelemetry-exporter-jaeger:1.6.0 \
    io.grpc:grpc-netty:1.41.0) \
  standalone
```

❶ We use a Jaeger endpoint to export the tracing data.

❷ We specify the service name `selenium-standalone`. We will look for this name in the Jaeger UI to visualize the gathered data (see Figure 6-7).

❸ We use Coursier (*https://get-coursier.io*) to download and generate the classpath of two required dependencies (`opentelemetry-exporter-jaeger` and `grpc-netty`).

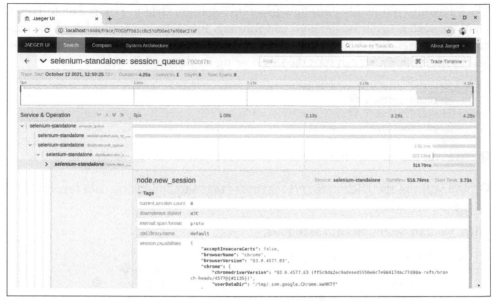

Figure 6-7. Jaeger UI showing the data gathered from Selenium Grid

GraphQL queries

GraphQL (*https://graphql.org*) is an open source data query and manipulation language for APIs. GraphQL defines a syntax to ask for data, generally from an online service. Selenium Grid 4 provides a GraphQL endpoint (`http://localhost:4444/graphql`). A simple way to make GraphQL queries to this endpoint is using curl (*https://curl.se*) from the shell. For example, and supposing that we have a Selenium Grid running in the localhost, we can send the following command to the GraphQL endpoint to get the maximum and the current number of sessions in the grid:

```
curl -X POST -H "Content-Type: application/json" --data \
    '{"query": "{ grid {maxSession, sessionCount } }"}' -s \
    http://localhost:4444/graphql
```

Configuration

You can find more details about Selenium Grid in its official documentation (*https://www.selenium.dev/documentation/grid*). For advanced configuration, there are two ways to specify a custom setup for Selenium Grid:

Using CLI options for the different aspects of Selenium Grid
    Some examples of these options are `--port` to change the default port through which the Selenium Server listens (4444 by default), or `--session-timeout`, which is the timeout in which nodes are terminated when there is no activity (three hundred seconds by default).

Using TOML (https://toml.io) files
> TOML (Tom's Obvious Minimal Language) is a configuration format designed to be human-readable. Like the CLI options, these files allow configuring the Selenium Grid parameters but using TOML notation.

Cloud Providers

As introduced in Chapter 1, a *cloud provider* in the Selenium ecosystem is a company that provides managed services (usually commercial) for automated web and mobile testing. Common services offered by cloud providers include:

Browsers as a service
> To request on-demand web browsers hosted by the providers. These browsers are usually of different types, versions, and operating systems. This feature is typically used for cross-browser automated or live testing.

Analysis capabilities
> To monitor and debug automated tests. To that aim, cloud providers typically support session recordings or rich error-reporting features.

Mobile testing
> To request emulated (and real) mobile devices on different platforms, such as Android and iOS.

Visual testing
> Automatically inspect the UI and ensure that end users have a correct visual experience.

Examples of current cloud providers for Selenium are Sauce Labs (*https://sauce labs.com*), BrowserStack (*https://www.browserstack.com*), LambdaTest (*https://www.lambdatest.com*), CrossBrowserTesting (*https://crossbrowsertesting.com*), Moon Cloud (*https://aerokube.com/moon-cloud*), TestingBot (*https://testingbot.com*), Perfecto (*https://www.perfecto.io*), or Testinium (*https://testinium.com*). All these companies offer specific services with different pricing plans. Their common aspect is that each cloud provider maintains a Selenium Server endpoint that we can use in `Remote WebDriver` tests. Example 6-9 illustrates how to use one of them (concretely, Sauce Labs) to create a `WebDriver` object. You can find equivalent tests for other cloud providers (BrowserStack, LambdaTest, CrossBrowserTesting, Perfecto, and Testinium) in the examples repository (*https://github.com/bonigarcia/selenium-webdriver-java*). These tests allow using remote browsers managed by the cloud providers.

Example 6-9. Test setup for using Sauce Labs

```
@BeforeEach
void setup() throws MalformedURLException {
    String username = System.getProperty("sauceLabsUsername"); ❶
    String accessKey = System.getProperty("sauceLabsAccessKey");
    assumeThat(username).isNotEmpty(); ❷
    assumeThat(accessKey).isNotEmpty();

    MutableCapabilities capabilities = new MutableCapabilities();
    capabilities.setCapability("username", username); ❸
    capabilities.setCapability("access_key", accessKey);
    capabilities.setCapability("name", "My SauceLabs test"); ❹
    capabilities.setCapability("browserVersion", "latest"); ❺

    ChromeOptions options = new ChromeOptions();
    options.setCapability("sauce:options", capabilities); ❻
    URL remoteUrl = new URL(
            "https://ondemand.eu-central-1.saucelabs.com:443/wd/hub"); ❼

    driver = new RemoteWebDriver(remoteUrl, options); ❽
}
```

❶ To use Sauce Labs, we need a valid account. In other words, we need credentials in the form of a username and access key. To avoid hardcoding these credentials in our test logic, I use Java system properties in this test. These properties can be informed in the execution command (e.g., `mvn test -DsauceLabsUsername =myname -DsauceLabsAccessKey=mykey`). An alternative way to specify this data is using environment variables (e.g., `String username = System.getenv ("SAUCELABS_USERNAME");`).

❷ We skip this test (using assumptions) when the username or the key is unavailable.

❸ We need to include the username and the key as Selenium capabilities.

❹ We can specify a custom label to identify this test in the Sauce Labs dashboard (see Figure 6-8).

❺ We use the latest version of a given browser (Chrome, as specified in the following line).

❻ We use a custom label called `sauce:options` to select the required capabilities in the Sauce Labs cloud.

❼ We use the Sauce Labs public endpoint as a remote URL. Sauce Labs provides endpoints in different regions. In this example, I use the EU Central data center.

Other possibilities are US West (*https://ondemand.us-west-1.saucelabs.com/wd/hub*), US East (*https://ondemand.us-east-1.saucelabs.com/wd/hub*), or Asia-Pacific Southeast (*https://ondemand.apac-southeast-1.saucelabs.com*).

❽ We use both the URL and the capabilities to create an instance of `RemoteWeb Driver`.

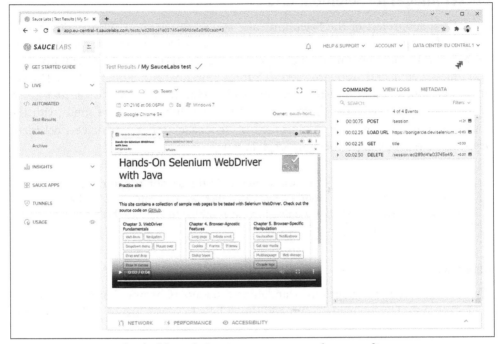

Figure 6-8. Sauce Labs dashboard showing an automated test result

Browsers in Docker Containers

Docker (*https://www.docker.com*) is an open source platform that allows creating, deploying, and running applications as lightweight, portable containers. The Docker platform is made up of two main components:

- Docker Engine (*https://docs.docker.com/engine*), an application that allows creating and running containers in a host. Docker Engine is a client-server application composed of three elements:

  — A server implemented as a daemon process (`dockerd`)

  — A REST API used by application clients to instruct the daemon

  — A CLI tool (the `docker` command)

- Docker Hub (*https://hub.docker.com*), a cloud service for distributing containers.

In Selenium, Docker can be a relevant technology to support the browser infrastructure required for automated tests based on Selenium WebDriver. The following subsections explain the alternatives for executing browsers in Docker containers.

Docker Images for Selenium Grid

An official subproject of the Selenium suite is docker-selenium (*https://github.com/SeleniumHQ/docker-selenium*). This project maintains Docker images for the different Selenium Grid components (i.e., standalone, hub, nodes, router, distributor, session queue, etc.) and web browsers (Chrome, Firefox, and Edge). These Docker images are open source and released on Docker Hub (*https://hub.docker.com/u/selenium*). A simple way to use these images is to start them using the shell (with the `docker` command) and use an instance of `RemoteWebDriver` to drive *dockerized* browsers. The following subsections explain how.

 The commands and tests presented in this section suppose Docker is available in your system. In other words, you need to have installed a Docker Engine in your machine to execute these examples properly.

Standalone

We can find Selenium images for standalone browsers (Chrome, Firefox, and Edge) in Docker Hub. The following command shows how to start Chrome in Docker using the shell.

```
docker run -d -p 4444:4444 --shm-size="2g" selenium/standalone-chrome:latest
```

This command starts the Docker image `selenium/standalone-chrome:latest`, i.e., the latest version of Chrome available in Docker Hub. Alternatively, we can use a fixed Chrome version (e.g., `selenium/standalone-chrome:94.0`). The Docker container is started in detached mode (using the -d flag) using a shared memory of 2 GB (`--shm-size="2g"`). This figure is a value known to work well, although you can change it depending on your resources or specific needs. Finally, the internal container port 4444 is mapped to the same port of the host where the command is executed (`-p 4444:4444`). We can then use the following Java command to instantiate a `WebDriver` object that uses this dockerized Chrome:

```
WebDriver driver = new RemoteWebDriver("http://localhost:4444/",
        new ChromeOptions());
```

Moreover, when using Selenium Grid, we can use Docker containers for registering nodes. The following command shows how to start a Selenium Grid in standalone mode using a node with Firefox in Docker:

```
java -jar selenium-server-4.0.0.jar node -D selenium/standalone-firefox:latest
    '{"browserName": "firefox"}'
```

Hub-nodes

We can easily start Selenium Grid in the hub-nodes mode using the official Selenium Docker images. The following commands show how to do it in the shell.

```
docker network create grid ❶

docker run -d -p 4442-4444:4442-4444 --net grid \
    --name selenium-hub selenium/hub:4.0.0 ❷

docker run -d --net grid -e SE_EVENT_BUS_HOST=selenium-hub --shm-size="2g" \
    -e SE_EVENT_BUS_PUBLISH_PORT=4442   -e SE_EVENT_BUS_SUBSCRIBE_PORT=4443 \
    selenium/node-chrome:4.0.0 ❸

docker network rm grid ❹
```

❶ First, we create a Docker network called grid. This network allows communication between hub and node(s) using their hostnames (e.g., selenium-hub).

❷ We start the Selenium Hub. We need to map ports 4444 (for the Selenium Server URL) and 4442-4443 (for registering nodes).

❸ We register nodes. In this command, we use Chrome (selenium/node-chrome). Other browsers can be registered in the hub using other Docker images (e.g., selenium/node-firefox or selenium/node-edge).

❹ If not required anymore, we can remove the grid network at the end.

Further features

The project docker-selenium provides a wide variety of features. I recommend you take a look at its README (*https://github.com/SeleniumHQ/docker-selenium*) for more details. Here is a summary of these features:

Docker Compose scripts
    These scripts allow starting Selenium Grid hub-nodes and the fully distributed mode effortlessly.

Video recording
    We can record the desktop session of the browsers in the nodes using another Docker container.

Dynamic grid
>This allows us to start Docker containers on demand.

Deploying to Kubernetes
>Kubernetes (*https://kubernetes.io*) is an open source container-orchestration system that automates the deployment and management of containerized applications. We can use Kubernetes to deploy the Selenium Docker containers.

Advanced container configuration
>This can be used, for instance, to specify Selenium or Java custom configuration.

Access to the remote session
>This can be achieved using Virtual Network Computing (VNC) (a graphical desktop sharing system) and noVNC (*https://novnc.com*) (an open source web-based VNC client).

Selenoid

Selenoid (*https://aerokube.com/selenoid*) is an open source Golang implementation of a Selenium Hub. Selenoid can be seen as a lightweight Selenium Server that provides a browser infrastructure based on Docker. The Selenoid team also maintains the Docker images used by Selenoid. These images include multiple web browsers and Android devices, such as Chrome, Firefox, Edge, Opera, Safari (WebKit engine), or Chrome Mobile.

There are different ways to use Selenoid and its Docker images. A straightforward way is to use the configuration manager (a binary called `cm`) provided by the project. The following snippet shows how to start Selenoid and its UI (a web-based dashboard to monitor Selenoid):

```
./cm selenoid start ❶
./cm selenoid-ui start ❷
```

❶ We start Selenoid. The configuration manager downloads the Docker image for Selenoid and the two latest versions of several browsers (Chrome, Firefox, and Opera). Once it is started, Selenoid listens to Selenium WebDriver requests in the URL `http://localhost:4444/wd/hub`.

❷ Optionally, we can start the Selenoid UI. This UI is a web application accessible in the URL `http://localhost:8080/`. Figure 6-9 shows a screenshot of this UI during the execution of a Selenium WebDriver test. Example 6-10 shows the setup of a test that uses a Chrome browser served by Selenoid.

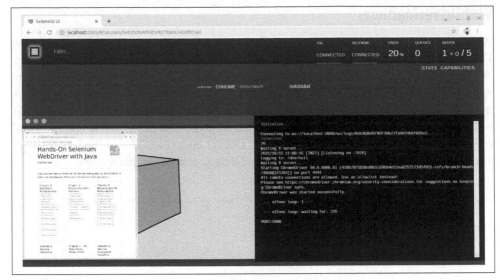

Figure 6-9. Selenoid UI during a test execution using VNC

Example 6-10. Instantiation of a RemoteWebDriver object using the constructor

```
@BeforeEach
void setup() throws MalformedURLException {
    URL seleniumServerUrl = new URL("http://localhost:4444/wd/hub");
    assumeThat(isOnline(seleniumServerUrl)).isTrue();

    ChromeOptions options = new ChromeOptions();
    Map<String, Object> selenoidOptions = new HashMap<>();
    selenoidOptions.put("enableVNC", true); ❶
    options.setCapability("selenoid:options", selenoidOptions); ❷
    driver = new RemoteWebDriver(seleniumServerUrl, options);
}
```

❶ The capability `enableVNC` is Selenoid-specific and allows us to start the docker-ized browser with VNC support (this way, we can visualize the browser session in the Selenoid UI, as illustrated in Figure 6-9).

❷ Since this capability is vendor-specific, the W3C WebDriver-compatible way to set this capability is using a custom namespace (`selenoid:options` in this case).

Further features

Selenoid provides different features and configuration capabilities. You can check its documentation (*https://aerokube.com/selenoid/latest*) for more details. These features include video recording, custom configuration, log management, or access to browser developer tools, to name a few.

WebDriverManager

As of version 5, WebDriverManager allows the effortless use of web browsers in Docker containers. To that aim, each manager (e.g., chromedriver(), firefox driver(), etc.) provides the method browserInDocker(). WebDriverManager internally pulls the Docker images and runs the container, creating a RemoteWebDriver instance when invoking the method create(). WebDriverManager uses the Docker images maintained by the Selenoid team. This way, you can use Chrome (desktop and mobile), Firefox, Edge, Opera, and Safari as Docker containers out of the box through WebDriverManager. Example 6-11 illustrates a basic test using this feature.

Example 6-11. Complete test using WebDriverManager and Chrome in Docker

```
class DockerChromeJupiterTest {

    WebDriver driver;

    WebDriverManager wdm = WebDriverManager.chromedriver().browserInDocker(); ❶

    @BeforeEach
    void setupTest() {
        assumeThat(isDockerAvailable()).isTrue(); ❷
        driver = wdm.create(); ❸
    }

    @AfterEach
    void teardown() {
        wdm.quit(); ❹
    }

    @Test
    void testDockerChrome() {
        driver.get("https://bonigarcia.dev/selenium-webdriver-java/");
        assertThat(driver.getTitle()).contains("Selenium WebDriver");
    }

}
```

❶ We get an instance of the manager for Chrome (chromedriver()). Then, using the WebDriverManager fluent API, we specify that the future WebDriver objects created with this instance (called wmd) will use Docker to execute the corresponding browser (Chrome, in this case).

❷ We assume a Docker engine is available in the machine running this test. For that, we create an AssertJ assumption by invoking the static method isDocker Available on WebDriverManager. This way, when Docker is not available, the test is skipped.

❸ In the test setup, we create the `WebDriver` instance. Internally, WebDriverManager will connect to Docker Hub to discover the latest version of Chrome available as a Docker image. This image is pulled to the local machine, the Docker container is executed, and the corresponding `RemoteWebDriver` instance is returned to the test logic.

❹ WebDriverManager allows quitting the previously created `WebDriver` instances through the method `quit()`. This method has the same effect of directly quitting the instance (`driver.quit()` in this case), and the used Docker containers are gracefully terminated.

WebDriverManager provides a fluent API to configure different aspects of the dockerized web browsers. The following snippet shows several possibilities. As usual, you can find the complete tests using these features in the examples repository for this book (*https://github.com/bonigarcia/selenium-webdriver-java*).

```
WebDriverManager wdm = WebDriverManager.firefoxdriver().browserInDocker(); ❶

WebDriverManager wdm = WebDriverManager.chromedriver().browserInDocker()
        .browserVersion("beta"); ❷

WebDriverManager wdm = WebDriverManager.chromedriver().browserInDocker()
        .enableVnc(); ❸

WebDriverManager wdm = WebDriverManager.chromedriver().browserInDocker()
        .enableRecording(); ❹
```

❶ We select a given manager to use the corresponding dockerized browser (Firefox in this case). In addition to Chrome and Firefox, the other alternatives are Edge, Opera, Safari, and Chrome Mobile.

❷ By default, WebDriverManager uses the latest version available in Docker Hub for the dockerized browser. Nevertheless, we can force the use of a given version (e.g., `94.0`). Moreover, different wildcards are valid for specifying the following versions, namely:

`latest`
> To use the latest version (default option).

`latest-N`
> To use a previous version to the stable release. For example, if we specify `latest-1` (i.e., latest version minus one), the former version to the stable release is used.

`beta`

> To use the beta version. This version is only available for Chrome and Firefox, using a fork of the Aerokube Docker images for these browsers maintained by Twilio (*https://hub.docker.com/r/twilio/selenoid*).

`dev`

> To use the development version (again, for Chrome and Firefox).

❸ Connect to the remote desktop session using VNC or noVNC. By default, WebDriverManager prints the noVNC URL in the log traces. In addition, this URL is accessible by invoking the method `wdm.getDockerNoVncUrl()`. Figure 6-10 shows a web browser that allows watching and interacting with a remote session with noVNC.

❹ To enable the session recording. At the end of the test, you can find the recording (in MP4 format) in the project root folder.

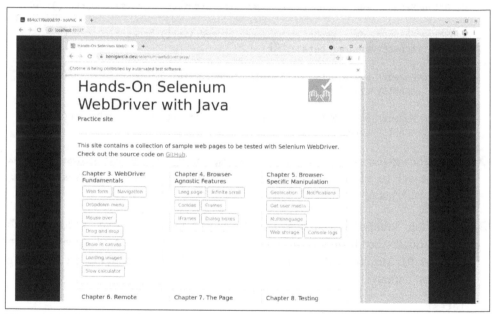

Figure 6-10. Remote desktop using noVNC of a dockerized browser started with WebDriverManager

Further features

As explained in its documentation (*https://bonigarcia.dev/webdrivermanager*), you can configure WebDriverManager in multiple ways. For instance, you can specify fine-grained aspects of dockerized browsers, such as the time zone, network, shared memory, volumes, environment variables, screen resolution, or recording output, among others. In addition, WebDriverManager can be used as a Selenium Server. This server uses the container images pulled from Docker Hub to support the browser infrastructure.

Selenium-Jupiter

Selenium-Jupiter internally uses WebDriverManager to manage and handle web browsers in Docker containers. For dockerized browsers, Selenium-Jupiter provides the annotation @DockerBrowser. You can use this annotation with WebDriver or RemoteWebDriver parameters in test methods. Example 6-12 demonstrates this feature. In this example, we use Chrome in Docker.

Example 6-12. Complete test using Selenium-Jupiter and Chrome in Docker

```
@EnabledIfDockerAvailable ❶
@ExtendWith(SeleniumJupiter.class)
class DockerChromeSelJupTest {

    @Test
    void testDockerChrome(@DockerBrowser(type = CHROME) WebDriver driver) {
        driver.get("https://bonigarcia.dev/selenium-webdriver-java/");
        assertThat(driver.getTitle()).contains("Selenium WebDriver");
    }

}
```

❶ We decorate the test class with the Selenium-Jupiter annotation @EnabledIf DockerAvailable. This annotation disables the test when Docker is not installed in the machine running the test.

The annotation @DockerBrowser allows setting different aspects and features. The following snippet illustrates some of them.

```
@DockerBrowser(type = FIREFOX) ❶

@DockerBrowser(type = CHROME, version = "beta") ❷

@DockerBrowser(type = CHROME, vnc = true) ❸

@DockerBrowser(type = CHROME, recording = true) ❹
```

❶ We can change the browser using the type attribute. The accepted values are CHROME, FIREFOX, OPERA, EDGE, SAFARI, and CHROME_MOBILE.

❷ We can change the browser version using the attribute version. Like WebDriver-Manager, Selenium-Jupiter allows specifying a fixed version value (e.g., 94.0) and using the wildcards `latest` and `latest-N`, as well as `beta` and `dev` for Chrome and Firefox.

❸ We enable access to the remote desktop session through VNC and noVNC using the attribute `vnc`.

❹ We enable the session recording with the `recording` attribute.

You can find more details, examples, and configuration capabilities of Selenium-Jupiter in its documentation (*https://bonigarcia.dev/selenium-jupiter*).

Summary and Outlook

Selenium WebDriver allows controlling remote web browsers. This feature is feasible because the underlying communication protocol (W3C WebDriver) is based on JSON messages over HTTP. This way, the components of the Selenium WebDriver architecture (Selenium Server, nodes, or client script) can be distributed (i.e., executed in different hosts). To use this feature in Java, we need to create an instance of `RemoteWebDriver`, typically passing two arguments: the Selenium Server URL and the required capabilities. We can start a Selenium Server infrastructure using Selenium Grid (in standalone, hub-nodes, or fully distributed mode). Alternatively, we can use the managed services provided by a cloud provider (such as Sauce Labs, Browser-Stack, LambdaTest, or CrossBrowserTesting, among others). Finally, we can use Docker to support a containerized infrastructure of web browsers.

This chapter concludes the second part of the book, in which you have discovered the main features of the Selenium WebDriver API. The next part of the book covers different aspects of developing end-to-end tests using the Selenium WebDriver API, starting with the Page Object Model (POM), a widely used design pattern for enhancing test maintenance and reducing code duplication in Selenium WebDriver.

Advanced Concepts

This last part covers different aspects and use cases built on top of the Selenium Web-Driver API. First, you will learn about the Page Object Model (POM), a widely used design pattern that allows the development of reusable and maintainable WebDriver tests. The following chapter explains different techniques for robust cross-browser testing, such as parameterized tests, test order, or parallel text execution. The next chapter describes how to use third-party libraries and frameworks in conjunction with Selenium WebDriver, such as Cucumber or the Spring Framework, among others. The final chapter summarizes various libraries complementary to Selenium Web-Driver, such as Appium or REST Assured. To conclude, you will discover the main features of the current alternatives of Selenium, such as Cypress, WebDriverIO, Test-Cafe, Puppeteer, and Playwright.

Advanced Chapters

CHAPTER 7

The Page Object Model (POM)

A *design pattern* is a reusable solution to a recurring problem in software engineering. This chapter presents the Page Object Model (POM), a popular design pattern used to develop Selenium WebDriver tests. The use of POM has different benefits, such as improving reusability and avoiding code duplication. POM is based on creating *page classes* for modeling the SUT UI in a single repository, which is later used from the test logic.

Motivation

Some of the biggest challenges of developing end-to-end tests with Selenium Web-Driver are *maintainability* and *flakiness*. Regarding the former, the problem might happen during the development or evolution of the SUT. The changes made in the UI can cause existing end-to-end tests to break. The maintenance costs for fixing these tests can be relevant when having a large test suite in which code duplication exists in several tests cases (e.g., when the same locators are used repeatedly in different tests).

Concerning flakiness (i.e., lack of reliability), a test is *flaky* when it has inconsistent behavior, i.e., it both passes and fails periodically under the same conditions (test logic, input data, setup, etc.). There are two major causes of test flakiness in Selenium WebDriver tests. First, the root of the problem might be the SUT. For instance, a bug in the server-side logic (e.g., a race condition) can expose erratic behavior in end-to-end tests. In this case, developers and testers should work together to detect and solve the problem, typically fixing server-side bugs. Second, the cause could be in the test itself. This is an undesirable situation that testers should avoid. There are different strategies to prevent flakiness in Selenium WebDriver tests, such as implementing a robust locator strategy (to avoid brittle tests due to responsiveness or viewport changes) or using a waiting strategy (to handle the distributed and asynchronous nature of web applications, as explained in "Waiting Strategies" on page 94).

Utilizing a design pattern like POM can help reduce code duplication and enhance maintainability issues. Moreover, we can use POM for including reusable robust locating and waiting strategies. The following section describes how to carry out the POM design pattern.

 The POM design pattern itself is not strictly a solution for test flakiness. However, as explained in the following sections, it enables the encapsulation of reusable code that prevents test unreliability.

The POM Design Pattern

The principle of the POM design pattern is to separate the logic for handling UI elements in separate classes (called *page classes*) from the test logic. In other words, we model the appearance and behavior of our SUT following an object-oriented paradigm, i.e., as *page objects*. Then, these page objects are used by Selenium WebDriver tests.

Let's look at a simple example to illustrate POM. Consider Figure 7-1, which contains a login form. As usual, this page is contained on the practice site. Example 7-1 shows a test case using *vanilla* Selenium WebDriver. In programming, we use the term "vanilla" to refer to technology used without customization from the original form. In this case, we use the standard Selenium WebDriver API, explained in Part II of this book.

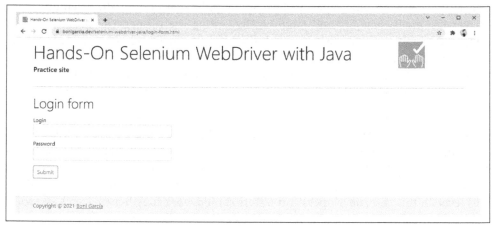

Figure 7-1. Practice web page with a login form

Example 7-1. Test using vanilla Selenium WebDriver to implement a successful login

```
@Test
void testVanillaBasicLogin() {
    driver.get(
            "https://bonigarcia.dev/selenium-webdriver-java/login-form.html");

    driver.findElement(By.id("username")).sendKeys("user");  ❶
    driver.findElement(By.id("password")).sendKeys("user");  ❷
    driver.findElement(By.cssSelector("button")).click();  ❸

    assertThat(driver.findElement(By.id("success")).isDisplayed()).isTrue();  ❹
}
```

❶ We type the word user as username in the web form.

❷ We type the same word as password in the web form.

❸ We click on the Submit button.

❹ We verify the success box is displayed.

This test is perfectly correct, but a potential problem might occur if we implement additional tests using the same web page. For instance, Example 7-2 shows another test case using vanilla Selenium WebDriver to implement a negative test (a failed login) using the same web form. This test is again sound, but together with Example 7-1, we duplicate most of the logic for locating web elements, only using different input data and the expected outcome. This way of proceeding violates one of the most relevant principles in software design: Don't Repeat Yourself (DRY). This is problematic since using the same code in different places makes maintainability harder.

Example 7-2. Test using vanilla Selenium WebDriver to implement a failed login

```
@Test
void testVanillaBasicLoginFailure() {
    driver.get(
            "https://bonigarcia.dev/selenium-webdriver-java/login-form.html");

    driver.findElement(By.id("username")).sendKeys("bad-user");
    driver.findElement(By.id("password")).sendKeys("bad-password");
    driver.findElement(By.cssSelector("button")).click();

    assertThat(driver.findElement(By.id("invalid")).isDisplayed()).isTrue();
}
```

Page Objects

Page object classes enable the separation of the code devoted to the UI, such as locators and page layout, from the test logic. We can see page classes as a single repository that encapsulates the operations or services provided by the application under test. These classes are instantiated as *page objects* in different test cases. We can implement end-to-end tests using the method exposed in these objects while avoiding code repetition.

Here is a basic example using page objects. In the following example, we refactor the test explained in the previous section (i.e., using the login form) using a page object instead of vanilla Selenium WebDriver. The first step is to create a Java class that models the login page. Example 7-3 shows a very basic implementation of this page class.

Example 7-3. Basic page class to model the practice login form

```java
public class BasicLoginPage {

    WebDriver driver; ❶

    By usernameInput = By.id("username"); ❷
    By passwordInput = By.id("password");
    By submitButton = By.cssSelector("button");
    By successBox = By.id("success");

    public BasicLoginPage(WebDriver driver) { ❸
        this.driver = driver;

        driver.get(
                "https://bonigarcia.dev/selenium-webdriver-java/login-form.html");
    }

    public void with(String username, String password) { ❹
        driver.findElement(usernameInput).sendKeys(username);
        driver.findElement(passwordInput).sendKeys(password);
        driver.findElement(submitButton).click();
    }

    public boolean successBoxPresent() { ❺
        return driver.findElement(successBox).isDisplayed();
    }

}
```

❶ We declare a WebDriver class attribute. This variable is used in the page object to implement the interaction with the web page.

❷ We declare all the required locators as additional attributes. In this case, we locate the text input for the username and password, the Submit button, and the success box.

❸ The constructor defined by this page class accepts the `WebDriver` object. We use the constructor to load the page under test.

❹ We declare a method to model the required interaction to log in, i.e., type the username and password, and click on the Submit button.

❺ We declare another method to check if the success box is visible.

Now, we can use this page class in a test case. Example 7-4 illustrates how. Notice that we create a `WebDriver` instance, as usual before each test, and quit it after each test. We use this driver as an argument in the page class constructor.

Example 7-4. Test using the basic page class to implement a succesful login

```
class BasicLoginJupiterTest {

    WebDriver driver;
    BasicLoginPage login; ❶

    @BeforeEach
    void setup() {
        driver = WebDriverManager.chromedriver().create();
        login = new BasicLoginPage(driver); ❷
    }

    @AfterEach
    void teardown() {
        driver.quit();
    }

    @Test
    void testBasicLoginSuccess() {
        login.with("user", "user"); ❸
        assertThat(login.successBoxPresent()).isTrue(); ❹
    }

}
```

❶ We declare the page class as an attribute in the test class.

❷ We create the page object, passing the `WebDriver` instance.

❸ We invoke the method with defined by the page class to make the login operation.

❹ We verify the success box is available on the resulting web page using a method provided by the page object.

This approach is a handy start for improving the maintainability of our tests because now, all the logic related to the login web page is centralized as a reusable class. Nevertheless, the code in the page classes is still brittle. For instance, imagine we need to implement a negative test for the login page, i.e., a login attempt using incorrect credentials. Example 7-5 seems a reasonable way to do that, given the current implementation of the page class. However, if you run this test, you will discover that the test fails due to a `NoSuchElementException` exception. The next section explains how to solve this potential problem by creating more robust page objects.

Example 7-5. Test using the basic page class to implement a failed login

```
@Test
void testBasicLoginFailure() {
    login.with("bad-user", "bad-password");
    assertThat(login.successBoxPresent()).isFalse();
}
```

Robust Page Objects

The example presented in the previous sections improves code maintainability since the page operations are encapsulated in a single class instead of having them scattered throughout the test suite. That said, there are different ways to enhance the previous page classes implementation. First of all, our SUT is likely to have several web pages, not only one. For this reason, a common strategy is to follow an object-oriented approach and create a *base page* class that encapsulates the common logic for all the page classes. Example 7-6 shows a Java class implementing a typical base for page classes.

Example 7-6. Example of a base class for page classes

```
public class BasePage {

    static final Logger log = getLogger(lookup().lookupClass());

    WebDriver driver;
    WebDriverWait wait;
    int timeoutSec = 5; // wait timeout (5 seconds by default)

    public BasePage(WebDriver driver) {
        this.driver = driver;
```

```java
        wait = new WebDriverWait(driver, Duration.ofSeconds(timeoutSec)); ❶
    }

    public void setTimeoutSec(int timeoutSec) { ❷
        this.timeoutSec = timeoutSec;
    }

    public void visit(String url) { ❸
        driver.get(url);
    }

    public WebElement find(By element) {
        return driver.findElement(element);
    }

    public void click(By element) {
        find(element).click();
    }

    public void type(By element, String text) {
        find(element).sendKeys(text);
    }

    public boolean isDisplayed(By locator) { ❹
        try {
            wait.until(ExpectedConditions.visibilityOfElementLocated(locator));
        } catch (TimeoutException e) {
            log.warn("Timeout of {} wait for {}", timeoutSec, locator);
            return false;
        }
        return true;
    }

}
```

❶ We define an explicit wait (WebDriverWait) attribute in the base class. We instantiate this attribute in the constructor using a default timeout value (five seconds
in this example).

❷ We create a setter method to change the default value for the wait timeout. For
instance, we might need to adjust this timeout depending on the system response
time.

❸ We create several common methods that page classes can reuse, such as visit()
(to open a web page), find() (to locate a web element), or type() (to send data
to a writable element, such as an input field).

❹ We implement a method to check if a web element is displayed or not. Notice that this method hides the complexity of waiting for this element, returning a simple boolean value that tests can use.

We use the previous base class as the parent of specific page classes. For instance, Example 7-7 shows a Java class that extends this base to implement the page class, using the login sample page in the practice site.

Example 7-7. Login page class using the previous base

```java
public class LoginPage extends BasePage {

    By usernameInput = By.id("username"); ❶
    By passwordInput = By.id("password");
    By submitButton = By.cssSelector("button");
    By successBox = By.id("success");

    public LoginPage(WebDriver driver, int timeoutSec) { ❷
        this(driver);
        setTimeoutSec(timeoutSec);
    }

    public LoginPage(WebDriver driver) { ❸
        super(driver);
        visit("https://bonigarcia.dev/selenium-webdriver-java/login-form.html");
    }

    public void with(String username, String password) { ❹
        type(usernameInput, username);
        type(passwordInput, password);
        click(submitButton);
    }

    public boolean successBoxPresent() { ❺
        return isDisplayed(successBox);
    }

}
```

❶ We define the page locators as class attributes.

❷ We define a constructor with two parameters: the WebDriver object and the time-out value (in seconds).

❸ We define another constructor that opens the web page under test.

❹ We include a method to log in using username and password as credentials. This uses the methods defined in the parent (type() and click()).

❺ We include another method to check if the success box is visible or not (using the method `isDisplayed()` defined in the base class).

Finally, we can use the page class to implement a Selenium WebDriver test. Example 7-8 shows a test using JUnit 5 (as usual, you can find the JUnit 4, TestNG, and Selenium-Jupiter flavors in the examples repository (*https://github.com/bonigar cia/selenium-webdriver-java*)).

Example 7-8. Test using the page class to implement a successful and failed login

```
class LoginJupiterTest {

    WebDriver driver;
    LoginPage login;

    @BeforeEach
    void setup() {
        driver = WebDriverManager.chromedriver().create();
        login = new LoginPage(driver); ❶
    }

    @AfterEach
    void teardown() {
        driver.quit();
    }

    @Test
    void testLoginSuccess() {
        login.with("user", "user");
        assertThat(login.successBoxPresent()).isTrue();
    }

    @Test
    void testLoginFailure() {
        login.with("bad-user", "bad-password");
        assertThat(login.successBoxPresent()).isFalse(); ❷
    }

}
```

❶ We instantiate the page object before each test.

❷ Since the page class logic is robust, we can invoke `successBoxPresent()` to implement a negative test. This method internally implements an explicit wait for the web element, which eventually returns `false` when the success box is not displayed.

Creating a Domain Specific Language (DSL)

We can push things a little more in our journey of modeling our SUT and create a complete Domain Specific Language (DSL) using the page classes. In computing, a DSL is a specialized language for a particular domain. When using the POM and Selenium WebDriver, we can see a DSL as the encapsulation of all the SUT operations and services in the methods provided by the page classes. This way, test cases use a simple, readable API provided by the page classes. These classes encapsulate all the calls to the Selenium WebDriver API to interact with the SUT.

Continuing with the example shown in the previous sections, Example 7-9 shows a base page class for the login page following a DSL approach. This base class is quite similar to Example 7-6, but in this case, this class also encapsulates the required logic to create a `WebDriver` instance.

Example 7-9. Example of base class following a DSL approach

```
public class ExtendedBasePage {

    static final Logger log = getLogger(lookup().lookupClass());

    WebDriver driver;
    WebDriverWait wait;
    int timeoutSec = 5; // wait timeout (5 seconds by default)

    public ExtendedBasePage(String browser) { ❶
        driver = WebDriverManager.getInstance(browser).create(); ❷
        wait = new WebDriverWait(driver, Duration.ofSeconds(timeoutSec));
    }

    public void setTimeoutSec(int timeoutSec) {
        this.timeoutSec = timeoutSec;
    }

    public void quit() { ❸
        if (driver != null) {
            driver.quit();
        }
    }

    // Rest of common methods: quit(), visit(URL url), find(By element), etc.

}
```

❶ We declare a `String` parameter in the base constructor. This string will be the browser name (specified in the tests).

❷ We use WebDriverManager to resolve the required driver and create the Web Driver instance. As explained in "Generic Manager" on page 353, WebDriver-Manager allows the use of a parameterized manager by invoking the method getInstance(). In this case, we use the browser name (e.g., chrome, firefox, etc.) to select the manager.

❸ We also encapsulate the method to terminate the session and close the browser.

Example 7-10 shows the page class that extends this base. As you can see, the only difference from Example 7-7 is that this page class uses a string parameter (the browser name) in the constructor.

Example 7-10. Login page class following a DSL approach

```java
public class ExtendedLoginPage extends ExtendedBasePage {

    By usernameInput = By.id("username");
    By passwordInput = By.id("password");
    By submitButton = By.cssSelector("button");
    By successBox = By.id("success");

    public ExtendedLoginPage(String browser, int timeoutSec) {
        this(browser);
        setTimeoutSec(timeoutSec);
    }

    public ExtendedLoginPage(String browser) {
        super(browser);
        visit("https://bonigarcia.dev/selenium-webdriver-java/login-form.html");
    }

    public void with(String username, String password) {
        type(usernameInput, username);
        type(passwordInput, password);
        click(submitButton);
    }

    public boolean successBoxPresent() {
        return isDisplayed(successBox);
    }

}
```

Finally, Example 7-11 shows the resulting test. Notice that this test does not contain any single call to Selenium WebDriver or WebDriverManager. The page class encapsulates all the low-level details of the interaction with the browser, exposing a high-level, readable API used in the test.

Example 7-11. Test case using POM and following a DSL approach

```
class ExtendedLoginJupiterTest {

    ExtendedLoginPage login;

    @BeforeEach
    void setup() {
        login = new ExtendedLoginPage("chrome"); ❶
    }

    @AfterEach
    void teardown() {
        login.quit(); ❷
    }

    @Test
    void testLoginSuccess() {
        login.with("user", "user");
        assertThat(login.successBoxPresent()).isTrue();
    }

    @Test
    void testLoginFailure() {
        login.with("bad-user", "bad-password");
        assertThat(login.successBoxPresent()).isFalse();
    }

}
```

❶ We instantiate the page object, simply specifying the browser type to be used (chrome in this case).

❷ As usual, we terminate the browser session after each test, but this time using a method provided by the page object.

Page Factory

Page Factory is the name given to several support classes provided by the Selenium WebDriver API to ease the implementation of page object classes. The most relevant of these support classes are:

FindBy
> Annotation used at the attribute level to identify web elements in a page.

FindAll
> Annotation that allows composing different @FindBy locators.

PageFactory

Class used to initialize all the previously declared web elements with @FindBy (and @FindAll).

CacheLookup

One downside of using the @FindBy annotation to locate web elements is that as each locator is used, the driver will try to find it on the current page. This feature is helpful in dynamic web applications. However, it would be desirable to cache the web elements in static web applications. For this reason, the annotation @CacheLookup allows caching the web elements once they are located, improving the performance of the resulting tests.

Example 7-12 shows a page class that uses these Selenium WebDriver support classes. You can find the resulting test using this page class in the repository object. This test is equivalent to Example 7-11, but uses FactoryLoginPage instead of ExtendedLogin Page for interaction with the login page.

Example 7-12. Class using the Page Factory provided by Selenium WebDriver

```
public class FactoryLoginPage extends ExtendedBasePage {

    @FindBy(id = "username")
    @CacheLookup
    WebElement usernameInput; ❶

    @FindBy(id = "password")
    @CacheLookup
    WebElement passwordInput;

    @FindBy(css = "button")
    @CacheLookup
    WebElement submitButton;

    @FindBy(id = "success")
    @CacheLookup
    WebElement successBox;

    public FactoryLoginPage(String browser, int timeoutSec) {
        this(browser);
        setTimeoutSec(timeoutSec);
    }

    public FactoryLoginPage(String browser) {
        super(browser);
        PageFactory.initElements(driver, this); ❷
        visit("https://bonigarcia.dev/selenium-webdriver-java/login-form.html");
    }
```

```
// Same logic to the page class without using the page factory
}
```

❶ We declare the web elements in the page using the `WebElement` type decorated with two annotations:

@FindBy
> To specify the locator (by `id` and `css` in this example).

@CacheLookup
> To cache the web element location results (since the web page is static and its content will not change in different calls).

❷ We invoke the `initElements` method to locate the web elements using the `Web Driver` instance.

 The Page Factory approach is only recommended when the web page tested with Selenium WebDriver is static. This approach can lead to undesirable effects such as stale web elements (i.e., old or no-longer-available elements) when using dynamic web pages.

Summary and Outlook

This chapter provided a comprehensive overview of the Page Object Model (POM) in Selenium WebDriver tests. POM is a design pattern in which we separate the logic to interact with web pages and the test code. This way, *page classes* contain the logic related to web locators and page layout, and test classes determine how to exercise and verify the SUT. The POM pattern improves the maintainability of test suites based on Selenium WebDriver since the page classes are stored in a single repository that models the SUT. This repository is used later in different test cases. We can create robust web pages using proper location and waiting strategies.

The next chapter presents specific aspects of the used unit testing frameworks (JUnit, TestNG, and Selenium-Jupiter) to improve the overall testing process with Selenium WebDriver. These features allow creating parameterized tests (for cross-browser testing), categorizing tests (for test filtering), ordering and retrying tests, or executing tests in parallel.

CHAPTER 8

Testing Framework Specifics

In the examples presented throughout this book, I have recommended embedding the calls to the Selenium WebDriver API in Java methods decorated with the annotation @Test using different unit testing frameworks: JUnit 4, JUnit 5 (alone or extended with Selenium-Jupiter), or TestNG. When executing regular tests, the difference in using one or another testing framework is minimal. Nevertheless, each testing framework has specific features for different use cases. This chapter summarizes some of these features to implement Selenium WebDriver tests. As usual, you can find the source code for this chapter in the examples repository for this book. You can use these examples to compare and choose the most convenient unit testing framework for your specific needs.

Parameterized Tests

A widespread feature commonly supported by unit testing frameworks is creating *parameterized tests*. This feature enables the execution of tests multiple times using different parameters. Although we can implement parameterized tests both with JUnit (4 and 5) and TestNG, there are significant differences among each implementation.

JUnit 4

We need to use a *test runner* called Parameterized for implementing parameterized tests in JUnit 4. A test runner in JUnit 4 is a Java class responsible for running tests. We decorate a Java class using the JUnit 4 annotation @RunWith to specify a test runner. Then, we need to use the JUnit 4 annotation @Parameters to decorate the method that provides the test parameters. There are two ways to inject these parameters into the test class: in the test class constructor or as class attributes decorated with the annotation @Parameter. Example 8-1 shows a test case where the test parameters are injected using the second technique. This example executes the same test for login into the practice site using different credentials (username and password). As a result, the message provided by the web page is different (login successful or invalid credentials).

Example 8-1. Parameterized test using JUnit 4

```
@RunWith(Parameterized.class) ❶
public class ParameterizedJUnit4Test {

    WebDriver driver;

    @Parameter(0) ❷
    public String username;

    @Parameter(1)
    public String password;

    @Parameter(2)
    public String expectedText;

    @Before
    public void setup() {
        driver = WebDriverManager.chromedriver().create();
    }

    @After
    public void teardown() {
        driver.quit();
    }

    @Parameters(name = "{index}: username={0} password={1} expectedText={2}") ❸
    public static Collection<Object[]> data() {
        return Arrays
                .asList(new Object[][] { { "user", "user", "Login successful" },
                        { "bad-user", "bad-passwd", "Invalid credentials" } }); ❹
    }

    @Test
    public void testParameterized() { ❺
        driver.get(
                "https://bonigarcia.dev/selenium-webdriver-java/login-form.html");

        driver.findElement(By.id("username")).sendKeys(username);
        driver.findElement(By.id("password")).sendKeys(password);
        driver.findElement(By.cssSelector("button")).click();

        String bodyText = driver.findElement(By.tagName("body")).getText();
        assertThat(bodyText).contains(expectedText); ❻
```

```
        }

    }
```

❶ We specify the `Parameterized` test runner for this Java class.

❷ We inject three test parameters as class attributes: username (index 0), password (index 1), and expected text (index 2).

❸ We specify the test parameter in a method that returns a collection of generic parameters (`Collection<Object[]>`).

❹ We return a collection of the three `String` sets to be used as a test parameter. The values of each entry will be injected using the previously declared three parameters (username, password, and expected text).

❺ In the test logic (that will be executed twice, once per data entry), we try to log in to the practice site using the username and password provided as parameters.

❻ We assert the expected data (which is different depending on the credentials provided as a parameter) is available in the page body.

 One of the most significant limitations of JUnit 4 is that we can use only one test runner per Java class. In other words, test runners are not composable in JUnit 4. To overcome this restriction (among others), the JUnit team released JUnit 5 in 2017.

TestNG

We can use the annotation `@DataProvider` to decorate the method that provides the test parameters in a parameterized TestNG test. As you can see in Example 8-2, this method returns a double array of general Java objects. The annotation `@Data Provider` should provide a name as an attribute. This name is later used in the `@Test` method to specify the data provider. Finally, the parameters are injected into the test method.

Example 8-2. Parameterized test using TestNG

```
public class ParameterizedNGTest {

    WebDriver driver;

    @BeforeMethod
    public void setup() {
```

```
        driver = WebDriverManager.chromedriver().create();
    }

    @AfterMethod
    public void teardown() {
        driver.quit();
    }

    @DataProvider(name = "loginData") ❶
    public static Object[][] data() {
        return new Object[][] { { "user", "user", "Login successful" },
                { "bad-user", "bad-passwd", "Invalid credentials" } };
    }

    @Test(dataProvider = "loginData") ❷
    public void testParameterized(String username, String password,
            String expectedText) { ❸
        // Same test logic than the example before
    }

}
```

❶ We create a method used as a data provider.

❷ We specify this test will use the previous data provider that we call loginData.

❸ A notable difference between JUnit 4 and TestNG regarding parameterized tests is that the parameters (username, password, and expected test in this example) are injected in TestNG as test method parameters.

JUnit 5

Jupiter (the programming and extension model of JUnit 5) provides a potent mechanism for creating parameterized tests. In a nutshell, we need two elements to implement these tests in JUnit 5:

- An argument provider, which is the data source for the parameterized tests. Table 8-1 provides a comprehensive summary of these argument providers.

- The annotation @ParameterizedTest (instead of the usual @Test annotation), which decorates the test method where the parameters are injected.

Table 8-1. Argument providers in JUnit 5

Annotation	Description	Example	Example output
@ValueSource	Array of literal values	```@ParameterizedTest
@ValueSource(strings = { "Hi", "Bye" })
void test(String argument) {
log.debug("arg: {}", argument);
}```	arg: Hi arg: Bye
@EnumSource	Constants of a Java enumeration	```@ParameterizedTest
@EnumSource(TimeUnit.class)
void test(TimeUnit argument) {
log.debug("{}", argument);
}```	NANOSECONDS MICROSECONDS MILLISECONDS SECONDS MINUTES HOURS DAYS
@MethodSource	A static method of the class that provides a Stream of values	```static IntStream intProvider() {
    return IntStream.of(0, 1);
}

@ParameterizedTest
@MethodSource("intProvider")
void test(int argument) {
    log.debug("arg: {}", argument);
    assertNotNull(argument);
}``` | arg: 0
arg: 1 |
| @CsvSource | Comma-Separated Values (CSV) within the annotation | ```@ParameterizedTest
@CsvSource({ "hello, 1", "world, 2"})
void test(String first, int second) {
    log.debug("{} and {} ", first,
            second);
}``` | hello and 1
world and 2 |
| @CsvFileSource | Values in CSV format in a file located in the classpath | ```@ParameterizedTest
@CsvFileSource(resources =
            "/input.csv")
void test(String first, int second) {
    log.debug("{} and {} ", first,
            second);
}``` | hi and 3
there and 4 |

Annotation	Description	Example	Example output
@ArgumentsSource	A class that implements the ArgumentsProvider interface	```@ParameterizedTest
@ArgumentsSource(MyArgs.class)
void test(String first, int second) {
    log.debug("{} and {} ", first,
            second);
}

public class MyArgs implements
            ArgumentsProvider {
  @Override
  public Stream<? extends
        Arguments> provideArguments(
        ExtensionContext context) {
    return Stream.of(Arguments.
        of("hi", 5), Arguments.
        of("there", 6));
  }
}``` | hi and 5
there and 6 |
| @NullSource | A single null argument | ```@ParameterizedTest
@ValueSource(strings = { "one",
                "two" })
@NullSource
void test(String argument) {
    log.debug("arg: {}", argument);
}``` | arg: one
arg: two
arg: null |
| @EmptySource | A single empty argument | ```@ParameterizedTest
@ValueSource(strings = { "three",
                "four" })
@EmptySource
void test(String argument) {
    log.debug("arg: {}", argument);
}``` | arg: three
arg: four
arg: |
| @NullAndEmptySource | A null plus an empty argument | ```@ParameterizedTest
@ValueSource(strings = { "five",
                "six" })
@NullAndEmptySource
void test(String arg) {
    log.debug("arg: {}", arg);
}``` | arg: five
arg: six
arg: null
arg: |

Example 8-3 illustrates the Jupiter version of the same parameterized test shown in the previous examples. We can use different argument providers to implement this parameterized test. In this case, we use @MethodSource to return a stream of arguments. An alternative that might fit well for this test is using @CsvSource to embed the input data and expected outcome as CSV format.

Example 8-3. Parameterized test using JUnit 5

```
class ParameterizedJupiterTest {

    WebDriver driver;

    @BeforeEach
    void setup() {
        driver = WebDriverManager.chromedriver().create();
    }

    @AfterEach
    void teardown() {
        driver.quit();
    }

    static Stream<Arguments> loginData() { ❶
        return Stream.of(Arguments.of("user", "user", "Login successful"),
                Arguments.of("bad-user", "bad-passwd", "Invalid credentials"));
    }

    @ParameterizedTest ❷
    @MethodSource("loginData") ❸
    void testParameterized(String username, String password,
            String expectedText) { ❹
        // Same test logic than the examples before
    }

}
```

❶ We define a static method to be used as an argument provider in @MethodSource.

❷ Instead of a regular @Test, we implement a parameterized test.

❸ The argument provider is linked to the data provided by the loginData method.

❹ The parameters are injected in the test method.

Selenium-Jupiter

You can use the same approach for implementing JUnit 5 parameterized tests when using Selenium-Jupiter. The only difference is that you delegate the creation and disposal of WebDriver objects with Selenium-Jupiter. Example 8-4 demonstrates how to implement the same test explained in the previous sections (i.e., parameterized login) but using Selenium-Jupiter.

Example 8-4. Parameterized test using JUnit 5 with Selenium-Jupiter

```
@ExtendWith(SeleniumJupiter.class)
class ParameterizedSelJupTest {

    static Stream<Arguments> loginData() {
        return Stream.of(Arguments.of("user", "user", "Login successful"),
                Arguments.of("bad-user", "bad-passwd", "Invalid credentials"));
    }

    @ParameterizedTest
    @MethodSource("loginData")
    void testParameterized(String username, String password,
            String expectedText, ChromeDriver driver) { ❶
        // Same test logic than the examples before
    }

}
```

❶ When using different parameter resolvers in a Jupiter test, by convention, we must first declare the parameters injected due to `@ParameterizedTest`, and then the parameter injected by extensions (Selenium-Jupiter in this case, for `Web Driver` objects).

Cross-Browser Testing

Cross-browser testing is a kind of functional testing in which we verify that a web application works as expected using different types of web browsers. A possible way to implement cross-browser tests is through parameterized tests using the browser type (i.e., Chrome, Firefox, Edge, etc.) as the test parameter. The following sections describe how to use the unit testing framework capabilities for parameterized testing applied to cross-browser testing. We will use local browsers (Chrome, Firefox, and Edge) in these examples. An alternative way to carry out cross-browser testing is to use remote browsers (from a Selenium Server, cloud provider, or Docker), as explained in Chapter 6.

JUnit 4

Example 8-5 shows a cross-browser test implemented with JUnit 4. We use WebDriverManager to ease the parameterization. As explained in "Generic Manager" on page 353, WebDriverManager can use one or another manager depending on the value of a parameter. This parameter can be a `WebDriver` class, an enumeration, or the browser name. We use the latter in the following examples (although you can find the alternative methods in the examples repository (*https://github.com/bonigarcia/selenium-webdriver-java*)).

Example 8-5. Cross-browser testing using JUnit 4

```
@RunWith(Parameterized.class)
public class CrossBrowserJUnit4Test {

    WebDriver driver;

    @Parameter(0)
    public String browserName;

    @Parameters(name = "{index}: browser={0}")
    public static Collection<Object[]> data() {
        return Arrays.asList(
                new Object[][] { { "chrome" }, { "edge" }, { "firefox" } }); ❶
    }

    @Before
    public void setup() {
        driver = WebDriverManager.getInstance(browserName).create(); ❷
    }

    @After
    public void teardown() {
        driver.quit();
    }

    @Test
    public void testCrossBrowser() { ❸
        driver.get("https://bonigarcia.dev/selenium-webdriver-java/");
        assertThat(driver.getTitle()).contains("Selenium WebDriver");
    }

}
```

❶ We specify three browsers using their names.

❷ We use the WebDriverManager generic manager, using these browser names as
the parameters. An alternative way to select one or another browser is using the
generic manager without parameters (i.e., with the method .getInstance(), as
explained in "Generic Manager" on page 353) and then parameterize the test (or
the suite) using the Java system property wdm.defaultBrowser (for instance,
when running it with Maven or Gradle).

❸ This test is executed three times, using a different browser (Chrome, Edge, and
Firefox) each time.

TestNG

Example 8-6 shows the same cross-browser test, this time using TestNG. In this case, the test parameter (the browser name) is injected into the test method.

Example 8-6. Cross-browser testing using TestNG

```
public class CrossBrowserNGTest {

    WebDriver driver;

    @DataProvider(name = "browsers")
    public static Object[][] data() {
        return new Object[][] { { "chrome" }, { "edge" }, { "firefox" } };
    }

    @AfterMethod
    public void teardown() {
        driver.quit();
    }

    @Test(dataProvider = "browsers")
    public void testCrossBrowser(String browserName) {
        driver = WebDriverManager.getInstance(browserName).create(); ❶

        driver.get("https://bonigarcia.dev/selenium-webdriver-java/");
        assertThat(driver.getTitle()).contains("Selenium WebDriver");
    }

}
```

❶ We need to create the WebDriver instance in the test logic since the test parameters are injected in the test method when using TestNG.

JUnit 5

Example 8-7 shows the same cross-browser test following the Jupiter model. Again, we use WebDriverManager to create the WebDriver instance, using the browser name as a parameter. Since these parameters are strings, we use @ValueSource as an argument provider.

Example 8-7. Cross-browser testing using JUnit 5

```
class CrossBrowserJupiterTest {

    WebDriver driver;

    @AfterEach
```

```
    void teardown() {
        driver.quit();
    }

    @ParameterizedTest
    @ValueSource(strings = { "chrome", "edge", "firefox" })
    void testCrossBrowser(String browserName) {
        driver = WebDriverManager.getInstance(browserName).create();   ❶

        driver.get("https://bonigarcia.dev/selenium-webdriver-java/");
        assertThat(driver.getTitle()).contains("Selenium WebDriver");
    }

}
```

❶ In Jupiter, the parameters in parameterized tests are injected in the test methods.
    For this reason, we need to create the driver instance in the test logic.

Selenium-Jupiter

Selenium-Jupiter provides a complementary feature for creating cross-browser tests,
called *test templates*. Test templates are a special kind of parameterized test supported
by Jupiter in which an extension collects the parameters. Selenium-Jupiter uses this
feature to provide a comprehensive way to specify different browser aspects (such as
type, version, arguments, and capabilities) using a custom JSON notation called a
browser scenario in Selenium-Jupiter jargon. You can find more details about this feature in the Selenium-Jupiter documentation (*https://bonigarcia.dev/selenium-jupiter/
#template-tests*).

Example 8-8 shows a sample browser scenario. This JSON is stored in a file called
browsers.json, the default name used by a template test. Example 8-9 shows a template test using this browser scenario.

Example 8-8. Browser scenario for a test template in Selenium-Jupiter

```
{
    "browsers": [
        [
            {
                "type": "chrome"   ❶
            }
        ],
        [
            {
                "type": "edge",   ❷
                "arguments" : [
                    "--headless"
                ]
```

```
            }
        ],
        [
            {
                "type": "firefox-in-docker",  ❸
                "version": "93"
            }
        ]
    ]
}
```

❶ This browser scenario contains three browsers. The first one is a local Chrome.

❷ The second browser is a local Edge in headless mode.

❸ The third browser is Firefox 93, executed in a Docker container.

Example 8-9. Cross-browser testing using test templates in JUnit 5 with Selenium-Jupiter

```
@EnabledIfDockerAvailable ❶
@ExtendWith(SeleniumJupiter.class)
class CrossBrowserJsonSelJupTest {

    @TestTemplate ❷
    void testCrossBrowser(WebDriver driver) { ❸
        driver.get("https://bonigarcia.dev/selenium-webdriver-java/");
        assertThat(driver.getTitle()).contains("Selenium WebDriver");
    }

}
```

❶ We use this Selenium-Jupiter annotation to skip the test when Docker is unavailable (since one of the browsers defined in the scenario uses Docker).

❷ We need to decorate the test method using `@TestTemplate` instead of the usual `@Test` annotation.

❸ We use the generic `WebDriver` to inject the driver instances. Alternatively, `Remote WebDriver` is also valid for test templates.

Categorizing and Filtering Tests

A common need when basing a test suite on Selenium WebDriver (especially when the number of tests is high) is to execute only a group of tests. There are different ways to achieve single or group test execution. When using an IDE to run tests, we can select the specific test(s) to be executed. When using the command line, there are other mechanisms we can use to select these tests.

At first glance, we can use the filtering mechanisms provided by the build tools. For instance, Maven and Gradle allow including or excluding tests based on the test classes and method names. The basic syntax for these commands is introduced in Appendix C. Table 8-2 shows several common examples using these commands. Notice that the wildcard * is used in these examples to match any character in the test class name.

Table 8-2. Examples of Maven and Gradle commands for including and excluding tests

Description	Maven	Gradle
Run tests starting with the word *Hello*	`mvn -B test` `    -Dtest=Hello*`	`gradle test` `    --tests Hello*`
Run tests that contain *Basic* or *Timeout*	`mvn test` `    -Dtest=*Basic*,*Timeout*`	`gradle test` `    --tests *Basic* --tests *Timeout*`
Run tests except those starting with *Firefox*	`mvn test` `    -Dtest=!*Firefox*`	`gradle test` `    -PexcludeTests=**/*Firefox*`
Run tests except those starting with *Docker* or containing *Remote*	`mvn test` `    -Dtest=!Docker*,!*Remote*`	`gradle test` `    -PexcludeTests=**/Docker*,**/*Remote*`

In addition to the build tool, we can use built-in features provided by the unit testing frameworks for categorizing (also known as grouping or tagging) and filtering tests based on those categories. The following subsections explain how.

JUnit 4

JUnit 4 provides the annotation @Category to group tests. We need to specify one or more Java classes as attributes in this annotation. Then we can use these classes to select and execute the tests belonging to one or more categories. Example 8-10 shows a basic class using this feature.

Example 8-10. Test using categories and JUnit 4

```
public class CategoriesJUnit4Test {

    WebDriver driver;

    @Before
    public void setup() {
        driver = WebDriverManager.chromedriver().create();
    }

    @After
```

```
    public void teardown() {
        driver.quit();
    }

    @Test
    @Category(WebForm.class) ❶
    public void testCategoriesWebForm() {
        driver.get(
                "https://bonigarcia.dev/selenium-webdriver-java/web-form.html");
        assertThat(driver.getCurrentUrl()).contains("web-form");
    }

    @Test
    @Category(HomePage.class) ❷
    public void tesCategoriestHomePage() {
        driver.get("https://bonigarcia.dev/selenium-webdriver-java/");
        assertThat(driver.getCurrentUrl()).doesNotContain("web-form");
    }

}
```

❶ WebForm is an empty interface available in the examples repository.

❷ HomePage is another empty interface available in the examples repository.

Then we can use the command line to execute tests based on their groups. For instance, the following commands show the Maven and Gradle command for running the tests that belong to the HomePage category.

```
mvn test -Dgroups=
    io.github.bonigarcia.webdriver.junit4.ch08.categories.HomePage
gradle test -Pgroups=
    io.github.bonigarcia.webdriver.junit4.ch08.categories.HomePage
```

We can combine this filtering with the Maven and Gradle support for selecting tests based on the class name. For instance, the following commands execute those tests belonging to the HomePage category but only in the test class CategoriesJUnit4Test.

```
mvn test -Dtest=CategoriesJUnit4Test -DexcludedGroups=
    io.github.bonigarcia.webdriver.junit4.ch08.categories.HomePage
gradle test --tests CategoriesJUnit4Test -PexcludedGroups=
    io.github.bonigarcia.webdriver.junit4.ch08.categories.HomePage
```

TestNG

TestNG also allows grouping tests. Example 8-11 demonstrates a basic use of this feature. In summary, the @Test annotation allows specifying string labels for these groups.

Example 8-11. Test using groups and TestNG

```java
public class CategoriesNGTest {

    WebDriver driver;

    @BeforeMethod(alwaysRun = true) ❶
    public void setup() {
        driver = WebDriverManager.chromedriver().create();
    }

    @AfterMethod(alwaysRun = true)
    public void teardown() {
        driver.quit();
    }

    @Test(groups = { "WebForm" }) ❷
    public void testCategoriesWebForm() {
        driver.get(
                "https://bonigarcia.dev/selenium-webdriver-java/web-form.html");
        assertThat(driver.getCurrentUrl()).contains("web-form");
    }

    @Test(groups = { "HomePage" }) ❸
    public void tesCategoriestHomePage() {
        driver.get("https://bonigarcia.dev/selenium-webdriver-java/");
        assertThat(driver.getCurrentUrl()).doesNotContain("web-form");
    }

}
```

❶ We set to `true` the attribute `alwaysRun` to indicate that the setup and teardown methods are not filtered during test execution.

❷ We assign the group name `WebForm` to the first test of this class.

❸ We set the group name `HomePage` to the second test.

Then we can use the command line to filter the test execution based on these categories. The following snippet first shows how to execute the test that belongs to the HomePage group. The second illustrates how to combine this grouping with the Maven and Gradle filtering mechanism based on the class name.

```
mvn test -Dgroups=HomePage
gradle test -Pgroups=HomePage

mvn test -Dtest=CategoriesNGTest -DexcludedGroups=HomePage
gradle test --tests CategoriesNGTest -PexcludedGroups=HomePage
```

JUnit 5

The Jupiter programming model provides a way to group tests based on custom labels called *tags*. We use the annotation @Tag for that purpose. Example 8-12 illustrates this feature.

Example 8-12. Test using tags and JUnit 5

```java
class CategoriesJupiterTest {

    WebDriver driver;

    @BeforeEach
    void setup() {
        driver = WebDriverManager.chromedriver().create();
    }

    @AfterEach
    void teardown() {
        driver.quit();
    }

    @Test
    @Tag("WebForm") ❶
    void testCategoriesWebForm() {
        driver.get(
                "https://bonigarcia.dev/selenium-webdriver-java/web-form.html");
        assertThat(driver.getCurrentUrl()).contains("web-form");
    }

    @Test
    @Tag("HomePage") ❷
    void testCategoriesHomePage() {
        driver.get("https://bonigarcia.dev/selenium-webdriver-java/");
        assertThat(driver.getCurrentUrl()).doesNotContain("web-form");
    }

}
```

❶ We mark the first test using the label WebForm.

❷ We categorize the second test using the HomePage tag.

We can use these tags to include or exclude tests when executing tests using the command line. The following commands show several examples for Maven and Gradle:

```
mvn test -Dgroups=HomePage
gradle test -Pgroups=HomePage

mvn test -Dtest=CategoriesNGTest -DexcludedGroups=HomePage
gradle test --tests CategoriesNGTest -PexcludedGroups=HomePage
```

Ordering Tests

The test execution order is unknown beforehand in the unit testing frameworks used in this book. Nevertheless, there are mechanisms to select a given execution order. One possible use of this feature in the Selenium WebDriver arena is to reuse the same browser session (i.e., use the same WebDriver instance) by different tests, interacting with the SUT in a given order. The following examples demonstrate this use case for JUnit 4, TestNG, JUnit 5, and JUnit 5 plus Selenium-Jupiter.

JUnit 4

JUnit 4 provides the annotation @FixMethodOrder to establish the test execution. This annotation accepts an enumeration called MethodSorters, which is composed of the following values:

NAME_ASCENDING
> Sorts the test methods by the method name in lexicographic order

JVM
> Leaves the test methods in the order returned by the JVM

DEFAULT
> Sorts the test methods in a deterministic, but not predictable, order

Example 8-13 shows a complete test case in which the tests are executed using the method name.

Example 8-13. Ordering tests using JUnit 4

```
@FixMethodOrder(MethodSorters.NAME_ASCENDING) ❶
public class OrderJUnit4Test {

    static WebDriver driver;

    @BeforeClass ❷
    public static void setup() {
        driver = WebDriverManager.chromedriver().create();
    }

    @AfterClass ❸
    public static void teardown() {
        driver.quit();
```

```
    }

    @Test ❹
    public void testA() {
        driver.get(
                "https://bonigarcia.dev/selenium-webdriver-java/navigation1.html");
        assertBodyContains("Lorem ipsum");
    }

    @Test
    public void testB() {
        driver.findElement(By.linkText("2")).click();
        assertBodyContains("Ut enim");
    }

    @Test
    public void testC() {
        driver.findElement(By.linkText("3")).click();
        assertBodyContains("Excepteur sint");
    }

    void assertBodyContains(String text) {
        String bodyText = driver.findElement(By.tagName("body")).getText();
        assertThat(bodyText).contains(text);
    }

}
```

❶ We use the annotation @FixMethodOrder at the class level to fix the order of the tests available in this class.

❷ We create the driver instance before all tests (since we want to use the WebDriver session in all the tests).

❸ We quit the driver instance after all tests. Therefore, we finish the session after the last test of this class.

❹ Since the test names are lexicographically ordered (testA, testB, and testC), the test execution will follow this sequence.

TestNG

A simple way to order tests in TestNG is using an incremental priority for each test. Example 8-14 demonstrates this feature, by using the attribute priority in the @Test annotation.

Example 8-14. Ordering tests using TestNG

```java
public class OrderNGTest {

    static WebDriver driver;

    @BeforeClass
    public static void setup() {
        driver = WebDriverManager.chromedriver().create();
    }

    @AfterClass
    public static void teardown() {
        driver.quit();
    }

    @Test(priority = 1)
    public void testA() {
        // Test logic
    }

    @Test(priority = 2)
    public void testB() {
        // Test logic
    }

    @Test(priority = 3)
    public void testC() {
        // Test logic
    }

}
```

JUnit 5

Jupiter provides the annotation `@TestMethodOrder` for ordering tests. This annotation can be configured using the following ordering implementations:

`DisplayName`
   Sorts test methods alphanumerically based on their display names.

`MethodName`
   Sorts test methods alphanumerically based on their names.

`OrderAnnotation`
   Sorts test methods based on the numeric values specified using the `@Order` annotation. Example 8-15 shows a test using this method.

`Random`
   Orders test methods pseudorandomly.

Example 8-15. Ordering tests using JUnit 5

```
@TestMethodOrder(OrderAnnotation.class)
class OrderJupiterTest {

    static WebDriver driver;

    @BeforeAll
    static void setup() {
        driver = WebDriverManager.chromedriver().create();
    }

    @AfterAll
    static void teardown() {
        driver.quit();
    }

    @Test
    @Order(1)
    void testA() {
        // Test logic
    }

    @Test
    @Order(2)
    void testB() {
        // Test logic
    }

    @Test
    @Order(3)
    void testC() {
        // Test logic
    }

}
```

Selenium-Jupiter

As usual, tests using Selenium-Jupiter also use the Jupiter programming model; therefore, these features (such as test ordering) also are valid for Selenium-Jupiter tests. Example 8-16 shows the same test as before, using Selenium-Jupiter for the driver instantiation. By default, the driver objects are created before each test and terminated after each test. Selenium-Jupiter provides the annotation @SingleSession to change this behavior, creating the driver instance before all tests, and closing the session after all tests.

Example 8-16. Ordering tests using JUnit 5 with Selenium-Jupiter

```
@ExtendWith(SeleniumJupiter.class)
@TestMethodOrder(OrderAnnotation.class)
@SingleSession
class OrderSelJupTest {

    WebDriver driver;

    OrderSelJupTest(ChromeDriver driver) {
        this.driver = driver;
    }

    @Test
    @Order(1)
    void testA() {
        // Test logic
    }

    @Test
    @Order(2)
    void testB() {
        // Test logic
    }

    @Test
    @Order(3)
    void testC() {
        // Test logic
    }

}
```

Failure Analysis

Failure analysis (also known as *troubleshooting*) is the process of gathering and analyzing data to discover the cause of a failure. This process can be challenging for Selenium WebDriver tests because the whole system is tested, and the underlying root
causes of a failed test can be multiple. For instance, the cause of a failure in an end-to-
end test might be the client-side (frontend) logic, the server-side (backend) logic, or
even the integration with other components (e.g., database or external services).

We can use different techniques to help developers and testers in the failure analysis
process. A typical way to do this is to detect when a test has failed and, before termi-
nating the driver session, gather some data to discover the cause. The following assets
can help in this process:

Screenshots

A picture of the web application UI after a test failure might help determine the failure cause. "Screenshots" on page 112 explains how to use the Selenium Web-Driver API to make screenshots.

Browser log

The JavaScript console can be another potential source of information when an error occurs. "Log Gathering" on page 168 explains how to carry out this log gathering.

Session recordings

We can easily record the browser session when using browsers in Docker containers. "Browsers in Docker Containers" on page 219 explains how to do this with WebDriverManager and Selenium-Jupiter.

The following subsections provide basic examples for making browser screenshots of failed tests. To that aim, we need to relay in the unit testing specific features to detect failed tests.

JUnit 4

JUnit allows tuning the default behavior of tests by using *rules*. A test class defines a rule by decorating a class attribute with the @Rule annotation. Table 8-3 summarizes the rules provided out of the box by JUnit 4.

Table 8-3. Rules in JUnit 4

Rule	Description	Example

ErrorCollector	Allows the execution of a test to continue when exceptions happen (while collecting these exceptions)	```@Rule public ErrorCollector collector = new ErrorCollector();```
		
		 ```@Ignore @Test public void test() { collector.checkThat("a", equalTo("b")); collector.checkThat(1, equalTo(2)); }```

Rule	Description	Example

ExternalResource	Provides a base class to set up and tear down an external resource before each test	<pre>private Resource resource;
		
		@Rule
		public ExternalResource rule =
		        new ExternalResource() {
		    @Override
		    protected void before() throws Throwable {
		        resource = new Resource();
		        resource.open();
		    }
		
		    @Override
		    protected void after() {
		        resource.close();
		    }
		};</pre>

TestName	Makes the current test name available for test methods	<pre>@Rule
		public TestName name = new TestName();
		
		@Test
		public void testA() {
		    assertThat("testA")
		        .isEqualTo(name.getMethodName());
		}</pre>

TemporaryFolder	Allows for the creation of temporary files and folders	<pre>@Rule
		public TemporaryFolder folder =
		        new TemporaryFolder();
		
		@Test
		public void test() throws IOException {
		    File file = folder.newFile("myfile.txt");
		}</pre>

Timeout	Applies a timeout to all test methods in a class	<pre>@Rule
		public Timeout timeout =
		        new Timeout(10, SECONDS);
		
		@Test
		public void test() {
		    while (true);
		}</pre>

Rule	Description	Example

TestWatcher	Allows the capture of several execution phases of a test: starting, succeeded, failed, skipped, and finished.	```
		@Rule
		public TestWatcher watcher =
		        new TestWatcher() {
		    @Override
		    protected void succeeded(Description d) {
		        log.debug("Test succeeded: {}",
		            d.getMethodName());
		    }
		
		    @Override
		    protected void failed(Throwable e,
		            Description d) {
		        log.debug("Test failed: {}",
		            d.getMethodName());
		    }
		};
		``

We can use the `TestWatcher` rule to gather data for failure analysis with JUnit 4. Example 8-17 shows a test that captures a screenshot when the test fails. Example 8-18 contains the implementation for this rule. As noted earlier, we make a browser screenshot. The logic to make this screenshot is available in Example 8-19.

Example 8-17. Analyzing failed tests using JUnit 4

```java
public class FailureJUnit4Test {

    static WebDriver driver;

    @Rule
    public TestRule testWatcher = new FailureWatcher(driver); ❶

    @BeforeClass
    public static void setup() {
        driver = WebDriverManager.chromedriver().create();
    }

    @AfterClass
    public static void teardown() {
        driver.quit();
    }

    @Test
    public void testFailure() {
        driver.get("https://bonigarcia.dev/selenium-webdriver-java/");
        fail("Forced error"); ❷
    }

}
```

❶ We define the rule at the class level, passing the driver instance as a parameter.

❷ We force this test to fail to make the screenshot of the browser using the rule.

Example 8-18. Analyzing failed tests using JUnit 4

```java
public class FailureWatcher extends TestWatcher {

    FailureManager failureManager;

    public FailureWatcher(WebDriver driver) {
        failureManager = new FailureManager(driver); ❶
    }

    @Override
    public void failed(Throwable throwable, Description description) { ❷
        failureManager.takePngScreenshot(description.getDisplayName());
    }

}
```

❶ We encapsulate the logic for failure analysis in a separate class.

❷ We override the method triggered when the test fails. In this case, we simply use the failure manager instance to make a screenshot.

Example 8-19. Analyzing failed tests using JUnit 4

```java
public class FailureManager {

    static final Logger log = getLogger(lookup().lookupClass());

    WebDriver driver;

    public FailureManager(WebDriver driver) {
        this.driver = driver;
    }

    public void takePngScreenshot(String filename) { ❶
        TakesScreenshot ts = (TakesScreenshot) driver;
        File screenshot = ts.getScreenshotAs(OutputType.FILE);
        Path destination = Paths.get(filename + ".png");

        try {
            Files.move(screenshot.toPath(), destination);
        } catch (IOException e) {
            log.error("Exception moving screenshot from {} to {}", screenshot,
                    destination, e);
        }
```

```
    }

}
```

❶ We take the screenshot as a PNG file, stored with a file name passed as a parameter.

TestNG

TestNG provides several *listeners* out of the box. These listeners are classes that capture different events of the test lifecycle. For instance, the ITestResult listener allows you to monitor the status and result of a test. As Example 8-20 shows, we can easily use this listener to implement failure analysis in a Selenium WebDriver test.

Example 8-20. Analyzing failed tests using TestNG

```
public class FailureNGTest {

    WebDriver driver;

    @BeforeMethod
    public void setup() {
        driver = WebDriverManager.chromedriver().create();
    }

    @AfterMethod
    public void teardown(ITestResult result) { ❶
        if (result.getStatus() == ITestResult.FAILURE) { ❷
            FailureManager failureManager = new FailureManager(driver); ❸
            failureManager.takePngScreenshot(result.getName());
        }

        driver.quit();
    }

    @Test
    public void testFailure() {
        driver.get("https://bonigarcia.dev/selenium-webdriver-java/");
        fail("Forced error");
    }

}
```

❶ We declare an ITestResult parameter in the method for test teardown.

❷ We read the status of the test.

❸ In case of failure, we create an instance of the failure manager (we use the same logic described in Example 8-19) for creating a screenshot.

JUnit 5

In JUnit 5, the Jupiter extension model replaced and improved the former test lifecycle management of JUnit 4 based on rules. As introduced in Chapter 2, the extension model provided by Jupiter allows adding new features on the top of the Jupiter programming model. This way, a Jupiter extension is a Java class that implements one or several *extension points*, which are interfaces that allow different types of operations in the Jupiter programming model. Table 8-4 summarizes the extension points provided by Jupiter.

Table 8-4. Jupiter extension points

Category	Description	Extension point(s)
Test lifecycle callbacks	To include custom logic during the test lifecycle	BeforeAllCallback BeforeEachCallback BeforeTestExecutionCallback AfterTestExecutionCallback AfterEachCallback AfterAllCallback
Parameter resolution	To inject parameters in test methods or constructors	ParameterResolver
Test templates	To implement tests using @TestTemplate	TestTemplateInvocationContextProvider
Conditional test execution	To enable or disable tests depending on custom conditions	ExecutionCondition
Exception handling	To handle exceptions during the test and its lifecycle	TestExecutionExceptionHandler LifecycleMethodExecutionExceptionHandler
Test instance	To create and process test class instances	TestInstanceFactory TestInstancePostProcessor TestInstancePreDestroyCallback
Intercepting invocations	To intercept calls to test code (and decide whether or not these calls proceed)	InvocationInterceptor

A convenient extension point for implementing failure analysis is `AfterTestExecutionCallback`, since it allows including custom logic immediately after an individual test has been executed. Example 8-21 provides a Jupiter test using a custom annotation (see Example 8-22) implementing this extension point.

Example 8-21. Analyzing failed tests using JUnit 5

```java
class FailureJupiterTest {

    static WebDriver driver;

    @RegisterExtension
    FailureWatcher failureWatcher = new FailureWatcher(driver); ❶

    @BeforeAll
    static void setup() {
        driver = WebDriverManager.chromedriver().create();
    }

    @AfterAll
    static void teardown() {
        driver.quit();
    }

    @Test
    void testFailure() {
        driver.get("https://bonigarcia.dev/selenium-webdriver-java/");
        fail("Forced error"); ❷
    }

}
```

❶ We use the `FailureWatcher` extension for the tests available in this class. We pass the driver instance as an argument.

❷ We force a failure to make the extension take the browser screenshot.

Example 8-22. Analyzing failed tests using JUnit 5

```java
public class FailureWatcher implements AfterTestExecutionCallback { ❶

    FailureManager failureManager;

    public FailureWatcher(WebDriver driver) {
        failureManager = new FailureManager(driver);
    }

    @Override
    public void afterTestExecution(ExtensionContext context) throws Exception { ❷
        if (context.getExecutionException().isPresent()) { ❸
            failureManager.takePngScreenshot(context.getDisplayName()); ❹
        }
    }

}
```

❶ This extension implements a single extension point: `AfterTestExecution Callback`.

❷ This extension point must override this method, which is executed immediately after each test.

❸ We check if an execution exception is present.

❹ If so, we take a screenshot using the `WebDriver` instance.

Selenium-Jupiter

Selenium-Jupiter is a Jupiter extension that, among other features, allows making browser screenshots effortlessly. Example 8-23 demonstrates this feature.

Example 8-23. Analyzing failed tests JUnit 5 with Selenium-Jupiter

```
class FailureSelJupTest {

    @RegisterExtension
    static SeleniumJupiter seleniumJupiter = new SeleniumJupiter();

    @BeforeAll
    static void setup() {
        seleniumJupiter.getConfig().enableScreenshotWhenFailure(); ❶
    }

    @Test
    void testFailure(ChromeDriver driver) {
        driver.get("https://bonigarcia.dev/selenium-webdriver-java/");
        fail("Forced error");
    }

}
```

❶ Selenium-Jupiter takes a browser screenshot in the case of failed tests simply by using this configuration capability.

Retrying Tests

As explained in Chapter 7, test *flakiness* (i.e., lack of reliability) is a well-known issue in end-to-end tests. As testers, we sometimes need to identify a *flaky* test (i.e., a test that passes or fails under the same conditions), and for that, we retry a given test to check whether its result is consistent. Thus, we might want a mechanism to retry tests in case of failure. This section explains how to carry out this process using the different unit testing frameworks.

JUnit 4

We need to use a custom JUnit 4 rule for retrying failed tests. Example 8-24 shows a test using an example of this kind of rule, and Example 8-25 contains the source code of that rule.

Example 8-24. Retrying tests using JUnit 4

```java
public class RandomCalculatorJUnit4Test {

    static WebDriver driver;

    @Rule
    public RetryRule retryRule = new RetryRule(5); ❶

    @BeforeClass
    public static void setup() {
        driver = WebDriverManager.chromedriver().create(); ❷
    }

    @AfterClass
    public static void teardown() {
        driver.quit();
    }

    @Test
    public void testRandomCalculator() {
        driver.get(
          "https://bonigarcia.dev/selenium-webdriver-java/random-calculator.html"); ❸
        // 1 + 3
        driver.findElement(By.xpath("//span[text()='1']")).click(); ❹
        driver.findElement(By.xpath("//span[text()='+']")).click();
        driver.findElement(By.xpath("//span[text()='3']")).click();
        driver.findElement(By.xpath("//span[text()='=']")).click();

        // ... should be 4
        String result = driver.findElement(By.className("screen")).getText();
        assertThat(result).isEqualTo("4"); ❺
    }

}
```

❶ We declare the retrying rule as a test attribute.

❷ We use the same browser for all the repetitions.

❸ We open a practice web page called *random calculator*. This page has been designed to produce incorrect results a given percentage of the time (50% by default). Then the calculator works perfectly after a configurable number of times (five by default).

❹   We use the calculator GUI to make an essential arithmetic operation.

❺   We verify the result. There is a 50% probability of getting an incorrect result for the first five attempts.

Example 8-25. JUnit 4 rule for retrying failed tests

```java
public class RetryRule implements TestRule { ❶

    static final Logger log = getLogger(lookup().lookupClass());

    int maxRetries;

    public RetryRule(int maxRetries) {
        this.maxRetries = maxRetries; ❷
    }

    @Override
    public Statement apply(Statement base, Description description) { ❸
        return new Statement() {
            @Override
            public void evaluate() throws Throwable {
                Throwable throwable = null;
                for (int i = 0; i < maxRetries; i++) { ❹
                    try {
                        base.evaluate();
                        return;
                    } catch (Throwable t) { ❺
                        throwable = t;
                        log.debug("{}: run {} failed",
                                description.getDisplayName(), i + 1);
                    }
                }
                log.debug("{}: giving up after {} failures",
                        description.getDisplayName(), maxRetries);
                throw throwable; ❻
            }
        };
    }
}
```

❶   We implement the generic interface for JUnit 4 rules, i.e., `TestRule`.

❷   This rule accepts an integer value in its constructor, used to determine the maximum number of retries.

❸ We need to override the method `apply`, which allows manipulation of the test lifecycle.

❹ We repeat the test execution in a loop, repeated a maximum number of times equal to the number of retries.

❺ In case of error during test execution, we get the exception object and repeat the test execution.

❻ If this line is reached, it means the test has been repeated the maximum number of times.

TestNG

TestNG provides a custom capability for implementing test retries. As shown in Example 8-26, we use the attribute `retryAnalyzer` of a `@Test` annotation to enable this feature. Example 8-27 shows the implementation for that retries analyzer.

Example 8-26. Retrying tests using TestNG

```
@Test(retryAnalyzer = RetryAnalyzer.class)
public void testRandomCalculator() {
    // Same logic than the example before
}
```

Example 8-27. Test analyzer for TestNG

```
public class RetryAnalyzer implements IRetryAnalyzer { ❶

    static final int MAX_RETRIES = 5; ❷

    int retryCount = 0;

    @Override
    public boolean retry(ITestResult result) { ❸
        if (retryCount <= MAX_RETRIES) { ❹
            retryCount++;
            return true;
        }
        return false;
    }
}
```

❶ We need to implement a TestNG listener called `IRetryAnalyzer` to implement a retry analyzer.

❷ We cannot parameterize this class; therefore, we declare the maximum retries number within the class (as a constant, in this case).

❸ We need to override the method `retry`. This method returns a boolean value that determines if the test is retried or not in case of failure.

❹ The logic to determine this value is an accumulator that checks if the retries threshold is reached.

JUnit 5

We need to use the extension model previously explained (see Table 8-4) for retrying failed tests. Instead of reinventing the wheel, we can use an existing open source Jupiter extension for this aim. To retry tests, and as introduced in Chapter 2, there are various alternatives: JUnit Pioneer (*https://junit-pioneer.org*) or rerunner-jupiter (*https://github.com/artsok/rerunner-jupiter*). Example 8-28 shows a test using the latter.

Example 8-28. Retrying tests using JUnit 5

```
@RepeatedIfExceptionsTest(repeats = 5) ❶
void testRandomCalculator() {
    // Same logic as the example before
}
```

❶ Simply decorating a test with this annotation, we repeat the test a maximum number of times (five in this case) in case of failure.

Selenium-Jupiter

Tests using Selenium-Jupiter can also use other extensions. Example 8-29 shows how to use rerunner-jupiter in a Selenium-Jupiter test.

Example 8-29. Retrying tests JUnit 5 with Selenium-Jupiter

```
@SingleSession ❶
@ExtendWith(SeleniumJupiter.class)
class RandomCalculatorSelJupTest {

    @RepeatedIfExceptionsTest(repeats = 5)
    void testRandomCalculator(ChromeDriver driver) {
        // Same logic than the example before
    }

}
```

❶ We reuse the same browser for all the possible repetitions.

Parallel Test Execution

The time required to execute a Selenium WebDriver test suite (especially if the number of tests is high) can be considerable. The reason for this slowness is that a regular Selenium WebDriver test starts a new browser each time, and as a result, the overall execution time rises. A possible solution to this problem is to execute tests in parallel. There are different ways to achieve this parallelization. First, we can use the built-in capabilities for parallel execution provided by the build tools (Maven or Gradle). Second, we can use the features provided by the unit testing frameworks (JUnit 4 or 5, and TestNG) to that aim. The following subsections explain all these options.

Maven

Maven offers different mechanisms for parallel execution. First, Maven allows building modules of multimodule projects in parallel. For that, we need to invoke the Maven command from the command line using the option -T. This option accepts two types of arguments for parallelization: using a fixed number of threads or using a factor multiplied by the number of available CPU cores in your system. The following snippet shows an example of each type:

```
mvn test -T 4 ❶
mvn test -T 1C ❷
```

❶ It executes the test of a multimodule project (e.g., the examples repository) in parallel using four threads.

❷ It executes the test of a multimodule project using the same number of threads as the CPU cores (for example, four threads in a quad-core system).

In addition, the plug-in used to execute unit tests in Maven (called *Surefire*) provides two ways to run tests in parallel. The first is multithreading inside a single JVM process. To enable this mode, we need to specify different configuration parameters, such as:

parallel
  To configure the level of granularity for parallelism. The possible values for this parameter are methods (to execute test methods in separate threads), classes (for test classes), suites (for test suites), suitesAndClasses (for test suites and classes), suitesAndMethods (for test suites and methods), and all (to execute every test in separate threads).

threadCount
  To define the maximum number of threads for parallelism.

---

useUnlimitedThreads
To allow an unlimited number of threads.

There are two ways to specify these configuration parameters. First, we can configure them directly on the Maven configuration file (i.e., the pom.xml file). Example 8-30 demonstrates how. In addition, we can specify these parameters as system properties when using the command line, for example:

```
mvn test -Dparallel=classesAndMethods -DthreadCount=4
```

Example 8-30. Maven Surefire configuration sample for parallel execution

```xml
<build>
    <plugins>
        <plugin>
            <groupId>org.apache.maven.plugins</groupId>
            <artifactId>maven-surefire-plugin</artifactId>
            <version>${maven-surefire-plugin.version}</version>
            <configuration>
                <parallel>classesAndMethods</parallel>
                <threadCount>4</threadCount>
            </configuration>
        </plugin>
    </plugins>
</build>
```

The second way to implement parallelism with Maven Surefire is *forking*, i.e., creating multiple JVM processes. This option can be helpful if we need to prevent thread-level concurrency issues since different processes do not share memory space, as happens in multithreading. As a drawback, forking consumes more memory and has lower performance. To enable forking, we need to use the forkCount configuration property (again, in the pom.xml or as a system property) to a value higher than one (i.e., the number of JVM process to be created). For example, the following command executes the tests of a Maven project using four JVM processes:

```
mvn test -DforkCount=4
```

Gradle

Gradle also provides several ways to execute tests in parallel. First, it allows executing tasks in parallel in a multimodule project. There are two ways to enable this mode. First, by setting the property org.gradle.parallel=true in the configuration file gradle.properties. Second, using the option --parallel in the command, for example:

```
gradle test --parallel
```

In addition, we can use the configuration property `maxParallelForks` in the Gradle configuration file to specify the maximum number of test processes to start in parallel. By default, Gradle executes a single test class at a time. We change this default behavior by setting a value higher than one for this parameter. In addition to a fixed value, we can specify the number of available CPU cores in your system:

```
maxParallelForks = Runtime.runtime.availableProcessors()
```

In the example repository, this property is enabled conditionally using a profile called `parallel` (see Appendix C). Therefore, we can use this profile using the command line:

```
gradle test -Pparallel
```

JUnit 4

JUnit provides a basic way to execute tests in parallel through the class `Parallel Computer`. This class accepts two boolean parameters in its constructor to enable parallel test execution of classes and methods, respectively. Example 8-31 shows a test using this class.

Example 8-31. Parallel test execution using JUnit 4

```
public class ParallelJUnit4Suite {

    @Test
    public void runInParallel() {
        Class<?>[] classes = { Parallel1JUnit4Test.class,
                Parallel2JUnit4Test.class }; ❶
        JUnitCore.runClasses(new ParallelComputer(true, true), classes); ❷
    }

}
```

❶ We specify which test classes are executed in parallel.

❷ We enable parallel test execution for test classes and methods.

TestNG

A common way to specify parallel execution for tests in TestNG is through the configuration file `testng.xml`. The most relevant attributes to enable this mode in TestNG are:

`parallel`
Specifies the mode for running tests in parallel. The alternatives are `methods`, `tests`, and `classes`.

threadcount
    Sets the default maximum number of threads for running tests in parallel.

Example 8-32 shows a basic configuration of `testng.xml` for test parallelism.

Example 8-32. Parallel test configuration for TestNG

```
<!DOCTYPE suite SYSTEM "https://testng.org/testng-1.0.dtd">
<suite name="parallel-suite" parallel="classes" thread-count="2">
    <test name="parallel-tests">
        <classes>
            <class name=
                "io.github.bonigarcia.webdriver.testng.ch08.parallel.Parallel1NGTest"/>
            <class name=
                "io.github.bonigarcia.webdriver.testng.ch08.parallel.Parallel2NGTest"/>
        </classes>
    </test>
</suite>
```

We can use Maven or Gradle in the command line to run the previous parallel test suite:

```
mvn test -Dsurefire.suiteXmlFiles=src/test/resources/testng.xml
gradle test -Psuite=src/test/resources/testng.xml
```

JUnit 5

JUnit 5 allows different ways to execute tests in parallel. The following list summarizes the most relevant configuration parameters for this purpose:

`junit.jupiter.execution.parallel.enabled`
    Boolean flag to enable test parallelism (`false` by default).

`junit.jupiter.execution.parallel.mode.classes.default`
    To run test classes in parallel. The possible values are `same_thread` for single threaded execution (by default) and `concurrent` for parallel execution.

`junit.jupiter.execution.parallel.mode.default`
    To run test methods in parallel. The possible values are the same as before (for test classes).

There are two ways to specify these parameters. First, in the configuration file `junit-platform.properties` (that should be available in the project classpath). Example 8-33 shows sample content of this file. Second, by using system properties and the command line. The following commands (Maven/Gradle) show how:

```
mvn test -Djunit.jupiter.execution.parallel.enabled=true
gradle test -Djunit.jupiter.execution.parallel.enabled=true
```

Example 8-33. Parallel test execution using JUnit 5

```
junit.jupiter.execution.parallel.enabled = true
junit.jupiter.execution.parallel.mode.default = same_thread
junit.jupiter.execution.parallel.mode.classes.default = same_thread
```

In addition, the Jupiter programming model provides the annotation @Execution to change the parallelization mode for test classes or methods. This annotation can be used at the class level or method level and accepts two values: ExecutionMode.CONCUR RENT (for parallel execution) and ExecutionMode.SAME_THREAD (for single-thread execution). Example 8-34 shows the structure of a test class contained in the example repository. Supposing that the parallel test is enabled (as in Example 8-33), this class will be executed in parallel together with other tests that allow parallelization.

Example 8-34. Parallel test execution using JUnit 5

```
@Execution(ExecutionMode.CONCURRENT)
class Parallel1JupiterTest {

    // Test logic

}
```

Test Listeners

A common need in the testing process is to keep track of the different stages of test execution. Unit testing frameworks thus provide a feature known as a *test listener*. Test listeners can be seen as utilities that modify the default test behavior by performing custom actions at multiple stages of the test execution cycle. As usual, each unit testing framework provides its own implementation for these test listeners.

JUnit 4

In JUnit 4, test listeners include custom operations when tests are started, passed, finished, failed, skipped, or ignored. The first step for implementing a JUnit 4 listener is to create a Java class that extends the RunListener class. In this class, you can override several methods (e.g., testRunStarted, testIgnored, testFailure, etc.) for including additional logic in the different steps of the test lifecycle. Example 8-35 shows basic implementation of a JUnit 4 test listener. This listener simply displays a message in the standard output about the test stage.

Example 8-35. Test listener using JUnit 4

```
public class MyTestListener extends RunListener {

    static final Logger log = getLogger(lookup().lookupClass());

    @Override
    public void testStarted(Description description) throws Exception {
        super.testStarted(description);
        log.debug("testStarted {}", description.getDisplayName());
    }

    @Override
    public void testFailure(Failure failure) throws Exception {
        super.testFailure(failure);
        log.debug("testFailure {} {}", failure.getException(),
                failure.getMessage());
    }

    // Other listeners

}
```

A common way to register a test listener in JUnit 4 is to create a custom runner and use that runner in test classes. Example 8-36 shows a custom test runner registering the previous listener. Example 8-37 shows a test skeleton using this runner.

Example 8-36. Test listeners using JUnit 4

```
public class MyTestRunner extends BlockJUnit4ClassRunner { ❶

    public MyTestRunner(Class<?> clazz) throws InitializationError {
        super(clazz);
    }

    @Override
    public void run(RunNotifier notifier) {
        notifier.addListener(new MyTestListener()); ❷
        super.run(notifier); ❸
    }
}
```

❶   We extend `Blockjunit4classrunner`, the default test runner in JUnit 4.

❷   We register our custom test listener.

❸   We call the parent to continue using the default test runner.

Example 8-37. Test listeners using JUnit 4

```
@RunWith(MyTestRunner.class) ❶
public class ListenersJUnit4Test {

    // Test logic

}
```

❶ We decorate test classes using the JUnit 4 annotation `@RunWith` and our custom runner.

TestNG

TestNG provides the interface `ITestListener` for implementing test listeners. The classes implementing this interface can override methods for the different stages of the TestNG lifecycle, such as `onTestSuccess`, `onTestFailure`, or `onTestSkipped`, among others. Example 8-38 shows a sample class implementing this interface. In this example, the listener methods log a message in the standard output. Example 8-39 shows a test using this listener.

Example 8-38. Test listener using TestNG

```
public class MyTestListener implements ITestListener {

    static final Logger log = getLogger(lookup().lookupClass());

    @Override
    public void onTestStart(ITestResult result) {
        ITestListener.super.onTestStart(result);
        log.debug("onTestStart {}", result.getName());
    }

    @Override
    public void onTestFailure(ITestResult result) {
        ITestListener.super.onTestFailure(result);
        log.debug("onTestFailure {}", result.getThrowable());
    }

    // Other listeners

}
```

Example 8-39. Test listeners using TestNG

```
@Listeners(MyTestListener.class) ❶
public class ListenersNGTest {

    // Test logic

}
```

❶ We use the TestNG annotation `@Listeners` to specify that all the tests in this class use our custom test listener.

JUnit 5

As previously discussed (see Table 8-4), Jupiter provides a wide variety of extension points for including custom logic in the JUnit 5 test lifecycle. In addition to this extension model, JUnit 5 allows the implementation of test listeners to keep track of several test execution stages, such as test started, skipped, or finished. This feature is available through the JUnit Launcher API, which is the API for discovering, filtering, and executing tests in the JUnit Platform (see Figure 2-4).

To create a test listener in JUnit 5, we need to implement the `TestExecutionListener` interface. A class implementing this interface can override different methods to be notified of events that occur during test execution. Example 8-40 contains a basic class implementing this interface. These kinds of listeners are registered in JUnit 5 using a standard Java service loader mechanism. For that, we need to create a file called `/META-INF/services/org.junit.platform.launcher.TestExecutionListen er` in the project classpath, and write the fully qualified name of the test listener we want to register (e.g., `io.github.bonigarcia.webdriver.jupiter.ch08.listeners .MyTestListener` for Example 8-40). Note that this file is not included in the examples repository to avoid intruding on the whole test suite.

Example 8-40. Test listeners using JUnit 5

```
public class MyTestListener implements TestExecutionListener {

    static final Logger log = getLogger(lookup().lookupClass());

    @Override
    public void executionStarted(TestIdentifier testIdentifier) {
        TestExecutionListener.super.executionStarted(testIdentifier);
        log.debug("Test execution started {}", testIdentifier.getDisplayName());
    }

    @Override
    public void executionSkipped(TestIdentifier testIdentifier, String reason) {
        TestExecutionListener.super.executionSkipped(testIdentifier, reason);
```

```
        log.debug("Test execution skipped: {}", reason);
    }

    @Override
    public void executionFinished(TestIdentifier testIdentifier,
            TestExecutionResult testExecutionResult) {
        TestExecutionListener.super.executionFinished(testIdentifier,
                testExecutionResult);
        log.debug("Test execution finished {}",
                testExecutionResult.getStatus());
    }

}
```

 Interface `TestExecutionListener` belongs to the JUnit Platform Launcher API; therefore, to use it, we need to include this API as an extra dependency in our project. Appendix C explains the required Maven and Gradle setup for that.

Disabled Tests

Unit testing frameworks allow disabling (i.e., skipping in test execution) entire test classes or individual test methods programmatically. The following subsections explain the differences between JUnit 4, TestNG, JUnit 5, and Selenium-Jupiter.

JUnit 4

JUnit 4 provides the annotation `@Ignore` to disable tests. This annotation can be used at the class or method level. Optionally, we can include a message in the annotation to specify the reason for disabling. Example 8-41 contains a disabled test.

Example 8-41. Disabled tests using JUnit 4

```
@Ignore("Optional reason for disabling")
@Test
public void testDisabled() {
    // Test logic
}
```

TestNG

TestNG allows disabling tests in two ways. First, we can use the annotation `@Ignore` for test classes or methods. Second, we can use the `enabled` attribute of the `@Test` annotation. Example 8-42 illustrates both methods.

Example 8-42. Disabled tests using TestNG

```
@Ignore("Optional reason for disabling")
@Test
public void testDisabled1() {
    // Test logic
}

@Test(enabled = false)
public void testDisabled2() {
    // Test logic
}
```

JUnit 5

The Jupiter programming model provides various annotations for disabling tests based on different conditions. Table 8-5 summarizes these annotations, and Example 8-43 provides a basic example using some of these annotations.

Table 8-5. Jupiter annotations for disabling tests

Annotation(s)	Description
@Disabled	To disable test class or method
@DisabledOnJre @EnabledOnJre	To disable/enable depending on the Java version
@DisabledOnJreRange @EnabledOnJreRange	To disable/enable depending on a range of Java versions
@DisabledOnOs @EnabledOnOs	To disable/enable depending on the operating system (e.g., Windows, Linux, macOS, etc.)
@DisabledIfSystemProperty @DisabledIfSystemProperties @EnabledIfSystemProperty @EnabledIfSystemProperties	To disable/enable depending on the value of system properties
@DisabledIfEnvironmentVariable @DisabledIfEnvironmentVariables @EnabledIfEnvironmentVariable @EnabledIfEnvironmentVariables	To disable/enable depending on the value of an environment variable
@DisabledIf @EnabledIf	To disable/enable based on the boolean return of a custom method

Example 8-43. Disabled tests using JUnit 5

```
@Disabled("Optional reason for disabling")  ❶
@Test
public void testDisabled1() {
    // Test logic
}
```

```
@DisabledOnJre(JAVA_8) ❷
@Test
public void testDisabled2() {
    // Test logic
}

@EnabledOnOs(MAC) ❸
@Test
public void testDisabled3() {
    // Test logic
}
```

❶ We skip this test always.

❷ We skip this test in the case of using Java 8.

❸ We skip this test in any operating system different than macOS.

Selenium-Jupiter

Selenium-Jupiter provides additional annotations to disable tests conditionally
depending on specific conditions of Selenium WebDriver tests. These conditions are
browser availability, Docker availability, and URL online (i.e., it returns a 200
response code when requesting the URL with the GET HTTP method). Example 8-44
shows several tests using these annotations.

Example 8-44. Disabled tests using JUnit 5 with Selenium-Jupiter

```
@EnabledIfBrowserAvailable(SAFARI) ❶
@Test
void testDisabled1(SafariDriver driver) {
    // Test logic
}

@EnabledIfDockerAvailable ❷
@Test
void testDisabled2(@DockerBrowser(type = CHROME) WebDriver driver) {
    // Test logic
}

@EnabledIfDriverUrlOnline("http://localhost:4444/") ❸
@Test
void testDisabled3(
        @DriverCapabilities("browserName=chrome") WebDriver driver) {
    // Test logic
}
```

❶ This test is skipped if Safari is unavailable in the system.

❷ This test is skipped if Docker is unavailable in the system.

❸ This test is skipped if a Selenium Server URL is not online. If so, the test is executed, and the previous URL is used to create an instance of `RemoteWebDriver`. To specify the required capabilities, we use the annotation `@DriverCapabilities` in this test (as explained in Chapter 6).

Summary and Outlook

This chapter presented some of the most relevant specific features of the testing framework used in this book (i.e., JUnit 4, TestNG, JUnit 5, and Selenium-Jupiter) for developing Selenium WebDriver tests. First, you learned how to implement parameterized tests. This feature can be convenient for cross-browser testing (i.e., using different browsers for web testing). Then, you learned how to categorize tests and use these categories to include or exclude them from test execution. You continued by comprehending mechanisms for failure analysis (e.g., make a browser screenshot when a test fails), retrying tests, or executing tests in parallel. Finally, you discovered how to implement test listeners and the different mechanisms for disabling tests.

In the next chapter, you will learn how to integrate Selenium WebDriver with different third-party utilities for implementing advanced end-to-end tests. You will discover how to download files from web applications, capture traffic without using CDP (e.g., in Firefox), test nonfunctional requirements (such as performance, security, or accessibility), handle different input data, improve test reporting, and integrate with existing frameworks such as Spring or Cucumber.

Third-Party Integrations

This chapter introduces different third-party technologies (such as libraries or frameworks) that we can use with Selenium WebDriver. We need to use these technologies when the Selenium WebDriver API is insufficient to carry out specific tasks. This is the case for file downloading, in which we need to use a third-party utility to wait until the files are correctly downloaded or, alternatively, use an HTTP client to control the download. We also capture the HTTP traffic using a third-party proxy.

Another scenario in which we need to use external utilities with Selenium WebDriver is when implementing nonfunctional tests, such as performance, security, accessibility, or A/B testing. We can also use third-party libraries to develop Selenium WebDriver tests using a fluent API, generate fake test data, or improve test reporting. Finally, we can integrate relevant frameworks such as Cucumber for Behavior Driven Development (BDD) or the Spring Framework (for developing web applications). We will go through all of these uses in this chapter.

 To use the third-party utilities presented in this chapter, you must first include the required dependencies in your project. You can find the details for resolving each dependency using Maven and Gradle in Appendix C.

File Download

Selenium WebDriver has limited support for file downloading because its API does not expose download progress. In other words, we can use Selenium WebDriver to download files from web applications, but we cannot control the required time to copy these files into the local file system. For this reason, we can use third-party libraries to enhance the experience of web downloads with Selenium WebDriver. There are different alternatives to this aim. The following subsections explain how.

Using Browser-Specific Capabilities

We can use browser-specific capabilities (as we did in Chapter 5) to configure several parameters for file downloading, such as the target folder. This approach is convenient since these features are available in the Selenium WebDriver API out of the box, but it also has several disadvantages. First, it is incompatible with different browser types (Chrome, Firefox, etc.). In other words, the required capabilities are distinct for individual browsers. Second, and more importantly, we do not have the control to track download progress. To solve this problem, we need to use a third-party library. In this book, I propose using the open source library Awaitility (*http://www.awaitil ity.org*).

Awaitility is a popular library that provides features to handle asynchronous operations. This way, it provides a fluent API for managing threads, timeouts, and concurrency issues. In the case of downloading files with Selenium WebDriver, we use the Awaitility API to wait until the downloaded files are stored in the file system. Example 9-1 shows an example using Chrome and Awaitility. Example 9-2 shows the equivalent test setup when using Firefox.

Example 9-1. Test download files using Chrome and Awaitility

```
class DownloadChromeJupiterTest {

    WebDriver driver;

    File targetFolder;

    @BeforeEach
    void setup() {
        targetFolder = new File(System.getProperty("user.home"), "Downloads"); ❶
        Map<String, Object> prefs = new HashMap<>();
        prefs.put("download.default_directory", targetFolder.toString()); ❷
        ChromeOptions options = new ChromeOptions();
        options.setExperimentalOption("prefs", prefs);

        driver = WebDriverManager.chromedriver().capabilities(options).create();
    }

    @AfterEach
    void teardown() {
        driver.quit();
    }

    @Test
    void testDownloadChrome() {
```

```
        driver.get(
                "https://bonigarcia.dev/selenium-webdriver-java/download.html");  ❸

        driver.findElement(By.xpath("(//a)[2]")).click();  ❹
        driver.findElement(By.xpath("(//a)[3]")).click();

        ConditionFactory await = Awaitility.await()
                .atMost(Duration.ofSeconds(5));  ❺
        File wdmLogo = new File(targetFolder, "webdrivermanager.png");
        await.until(() -> wdmLogo.exists());  ❻

        File wdmDoc = new File(targetFolder, "webdrivermanager.pdf");
        await.until(() -> wdmDoc.exists());  ❼
    }

}
```

❶ We specify a folder to save the downloaded files. Nevertheless, you should be aware that Chrome allows only certain directories for download. For example, it allows the download directory (and subfolder) but forbids employing other paths, such as the desktop folder or the home directory.

❷ We use a Chrome preference to specify the target folder.

❸ We use a web page available on the practice site to download different files by clicking on buttons (see Figure 9-1).

❹ We click on two of the buttons available on the page. As a result, the browser starts downloading two files: a PNG picture and a PDF document, respectively.

❺ We use Awaitility to configure a wait timeout of five seconds.

❻ We wait until the first file is in the file system.

❼ We also wait until the second file is downloaded.

Example 9-2. Test setup for downloading files using Firefox

```
@BeforeEach
void setup() {
    FirefoxOptions options = new FirefoxOptions();
    targetFolder = new File(".");  ❶
    options.addPreference("browser.download.dir",
            targetFolder.getAbsolutePath());  ❷
    options.addPreference("browser.download.folderList", 2);  ❸
    options.addPreference("browser.helperApps.neverAsk.saveToDisk",
            "image/png, application/pdf");  ❹
    options.addPreference("pdfjs.disabled", true);  ❺
```

```
driver = WebDriverManager.firefoxdriver().capabilities(options)
        .create();
}
```

❶ Firefox allows specifying any folder for downloading files. In this case, we use the
    local project folder.

❷ We use a Firefox preference to specify a custom download directory.

❸ We need to set to 2 the preference `browser.download.folderList` to select a
    custom download folder. The other possible values are 0 to download files into
    the user desktop and 1 to use the download folder (default value).

❹ We specify the content types that Firefox will not ask to save in the local file
    system.

❺ We disable the previsualization of PDF files.

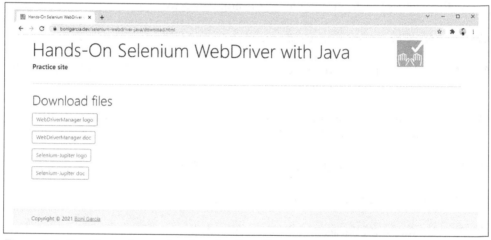

Figure 9-1. Practice web page for downloading file

Using an HTTP Client

An alternative mechanism to download files with Selenium WebDriver is to use an
HTTP client library. I propose using Apache HttpClient (*https://hc.apache.org/
httpcomponents-client-5.1.x*), since WebDriverManager internally uses this library,
and therefore, you can use it as a transitive dependency in your project. Example 9-3
shows a complete test case that downloads several files with Apache HttpClient from
the practice site. Notice that in this case, it is not necessary to explicitly wait until the

file download finishes since Apache HttpClient handles the HTTP responses synchronously.

Example 9-3. Test download files using an HTTP client

```
class DownloadHttpClientJupiterTest {

    WebDriver driver;

    @BeforeEach
    void setup() {
        driver = WebDriverManager.chromedriver().create();
    }

    @AfterEach
    void teardown() {
        driver.quit();
    }

    @Test
    void testDownloadHttpClient() throws IOException {
        driver.get(
                "https://bonigarcia.dev/selenium-webdriver-java/download.html"); ❶

        WebElement pngLink = driver.findElement(By.xpath("(//a)[2]")); ❷
        File pngFile = new File(".", "webdrivermanager.png");
        download(pngLink.getAttribute("href"), pngFile); ❸
        assertThat(pngFile).exists();

        WebElement pdfLink = driver.findElement(By.xpath("(//a)[3]")); ❹
        File pdfFile = new File(".", "webdrivermanager.pdf");
        download(pdfLink.getAttribute("href"), pdfFile);
        assertThat(pdfFile).exists();
    }

    void download(String link, File destination) throws IOException {
        try (CloseableHttpClient client = HttpClientBuilder.create().build()) { ❺
            HttpUriRequestBase request = new HttpGet(link);
            try (CloseableHttpResponse response = client.execute(request)) { ❻
                FileUtils.copyInputStreamToFile(
                        response.getEntity().getContent(), destination); ❼
            }
        }
    }
}
```

❶ We use the practice web page again for downloading files.

❷ We click on a button to download a file.

❸ We refactor the common logic for downloading files in the class method download.

❹ We repeat the operation for a second file to be downloaded.

❺ We create an Apache HTTPClient instance inside a try-with-resources. This client is automatically closed at the end of the statement scope.

❻ We use another try-with-resources statement to send an HTTP request to the provided URL and, as a result, get an HTTP response.

❼ We copy the resulting file in the local file system.

Capture Network Traffic

"Network monitoring" on page 182 and "Network interceptor" on page 178 explain how to use browser-specific capabilities to capture the HTTP traffic between Selenium WebDriver and the web application under test. The drawback of this mechanism is that it is only available in browsers that support CDP. Nevertheless, we can use a third-party proxy for other browsers. In this book, I propose you use Browser-Mob (*https://bmp.lightbody.net*) proxy for this purpose.

BrowserMob is an open source proxy that allows manipulating HTTP traffic using a Java library. Example 9-4 shows a complete test using this proxy in a Selenium Web-Driver test. In this example, we use the BrowserMob proxy to intercept the HTTP traffic between the test and the target website, tracing this traffic (request-response) as logging traces.

Example 9-4. Test capturing network traffic through BrowserMob proxy

```
class CaptureNetworkTrafficFirefoxJupiterTest {

    static final Logger log = getLogger(lookup().lookupClass());

    WebDriver driver;

    BrowserMobProxy proxy;

    @BeforeEach
    void setup() {
        proxy = new BrowserMobProxyServer(); ❶
        proxy.start(); ❷
        proxy.newHar(); ❸
        proxy.enableHarCaptureTypes(CaptureType.REQUEST_CONTENT,
                CaptureType.RESPONSE_CONTENT); ❹
```

```
        Proxy seleniumProxy = ClientUtil.createSeleniumProxy(proxy); ❺
        FirefoxOptions options = new FirefoxOptions();
        options.setProxy(seleniumProxy); ❻
        options.setAcceptInsecureCerts(true); ❼

        driver = WebDriverManager.firefoxdriver().capabilities(options)
                .create();
    }

    @AfterEach
    void teardown() {
        proxy.stop(); ❽
        driver.quit();
    }

    @Test
    void testCaptureNetworkTrafficFirefox() {
        driver.get("https://bonigarcia.dev/selenium-webdriver-java/");
        assertThat(driver.getTitle()).contains("Selenium WebDriver");

        List<HarEntry> logEntries = proxy.getHar().getLog().getEntries();
        logEntries.forEach(logEntry -> { ❾
            log.debug("Request: {} - Response: {}",
                    logEntry.getRequest().getUrl(),
                    logEntry.getResponse().getStatus());
        });
    }

}
```

❶   We create an instance of a BrowserMob.

❷   We start this proxy.

❸   We capture the HTTP traffic using HAR (HTTP Archive), a JSON-based file for-
      mat used to capture and export this traffic.

❹   We enable capturing the exchanged HTTP requests and responses.

❺   We transform the BrowserMob server into a Selenium WebDriver proxy.

❻   We set this proxy as a browser option (in this case, for Firefox).

❼   We need to allow insecure certificates since the communication with the proxy is
      done using HTTP (and not HTTPS).

❽   We stop the proxy after the test.

❾ We use the proxy instance to gather the HTTP traffic (requests and responses). We use a logger to write this information in the standard output in this basic example.

Nonfunctional Testing

As explained in Chapter 1, Selenium WebDriver is primarily used to assess the functional requirements of web applications. In other words, testers use the Selenium WebDriver API to verify that a web application under test behaves as expected. Nevertheless, we can leverage this API to test nonfunctional requirements, i.e., quality attributes such as performance, security, accessibility, etc. A common strategy to accomplish this goal is to integrate with specific third-party utilities. The following subsections explain different integrations with Selenium WebDriver for nonfunctional testing.

Performance

Performance testing evaluates the responsiveness and stability of a SUT under a particular workload. Instead of Selenium WebDriver, testers usually adopt specific tools like Apache JMeter (*https://jmeter.apache.org*) for performance testing. Apache JMeter is an open source tool that allows sending multiple HTTP requests to a given URL endpoint while measuring the response time and other metrics. Although the direct integration between Selenium WebDriver and Apache JMeter is not trivial, we can leverage an existing Selenium WebDriver test as a JMeter test plan (i.e., the series of steps that JMeter executes). The benefit of this approach is that the resulting JMeter test plan will mimic the same user workflow used in the Selenium WebDriver test, reusing the same HTTP traffic the browser makes (e.g., for JavaScript libraries, CSS, etc.). To that aim, I propose the following procedure:

1. Use the BrowserMob proxy (introduced in the previous section) to capture the exchanged network traffic in Selenium WebDriver as a HAR file.

2. Convert the resulting HAR file to a JMeter test plan. Test plans in JMeter are stored as XML-based files with the extension JMX.

3. Load the JMX test plan in JMeter and tune it for simulating concurrent users and including result listeners

4. Run the test plan and evaluate the results.

Example 9-5 shows a complete test case that implements the first step. As you can see, the required login to start and create the HAR file is done before and after each test. You can use this approach to leverage existing functional tests (i.e., the logic in the @Test methods) as performance tests (to be executed in JMeter).

Example 9-5. Test creating a HAR file

```
class HarCreatorJupiterTest {

    WebDriver driver;

    BrowserMobProxy proxy;

    @BeforeEach
    void setup() {
        proxy = new BrowserMobProxyServer(); ❶
        proxy.start();
        proxy.newHar();
        proxy.enableHarCaptureTypes(CaptureType.REQUEST_CONTENT,
                CaptureType.RESPONSE_CONTENT);

        Proxy seleniumProxy = ClientUtil.createSeleniumProxy(proxy);
        ChromeOptions options = new ChromeOptions();
        options.setProxy(seleniumProxy);
        options.setAcceptInsecureCerts(true);

        driver = WebDriverManager.chromedriver().capabilities(options).create();
    }

    @AfterEach
    void teardown() throws IOException {
        Har har = proxy.getHar(); ❷
        File harFile = new File("login.har");
        har.writeTo(harFile);

        proxy.stop();
        driver.quit();
    }

    @Test
    void testHarCreator() {
        driver.get(
                "https://bonigarcia.dev/selenium-webdriver-java/login-form.html");

        driver.findElement(By.id("username")).sendKeys("user");
        driver.findElement(By.id("password")).sendKeys("user");
        driver.findElement(By.cssSelector("button")).click();
        String bodyText = driver.findElement(By.tagName("body")).getText();
        assertThat(bodyText).contains("Login successful");
    }

}
```

❶ We start BrowserMob before the test and configure it in the WebDriver session.

❷ We get the HAR file after the test and write it as a local file.

After running the previous test, we get a HAR file called login.har. Now, we need to convert it to a JMeter test plan. There are different alternatives to do that. You can find several programs (e.g., in Ruby or Java) that make this job freely available on the web. Also, you can use online converters services, such as the BlazeMeter JMX Converter (*https://converter.blazemeter.com*). In this example, I use this online service and open the resulting JMX test plan in JMeter. At this point, you can tune the JMeter configuration at your convenience (you can find further information about JMeter in its official user manual (*https://jmeter.apache.org/usermanual/index.html*)). For instance, Figure 9-2 shows the JMeter GUI after loading the resulting JMX test plan plus the following changes:

- Increase the number of concurrent users to one hundred (in the "Thread Group" tab)

- Include some result listeners, such as "Aggregate Graph" and "Graph Results

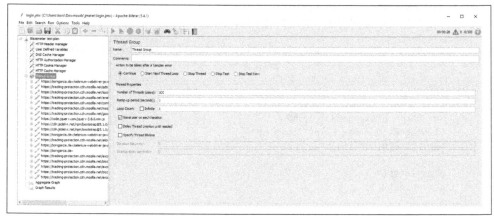

Figure 9-2. JMeter GUI loading the resulting test plan

Now, we can run the test plan with JMeter (for example, clicking on the button with a green triangle in the JMeter GUI). As a result, a load of one hundred concurrent users is generated following the interactions initially developed as a Selenium WebDriver test (Example 9-5). Figure 9-3 shows the results for the previously added listeners.

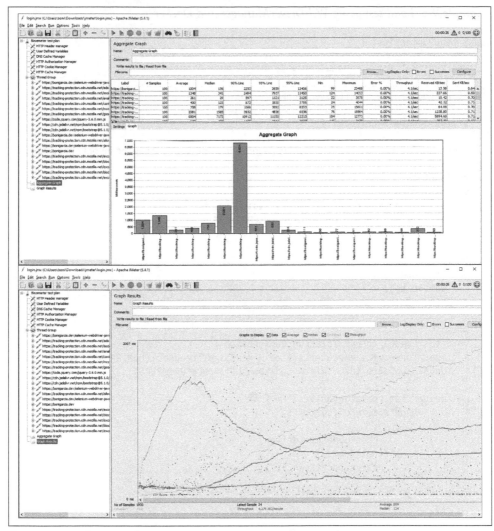

Figure 9-3. JMeter results

Using browsers to generate the load

Using tools like JMeter is convenient for many performance testing scenarios for web applications. Nevertheless, this approach is unsuitable when you need actual browsers to recreate the complete user workflow (e.g., in videoconferencing web apps). In that case, a possible solution is to use WebDriverManager in conjunction with Docker. Example 9-6 demonstrates this use. As you can see in this test, WebDriverManager allows creating a list of `WebDriver` instances simply by specifying the size as a parameter in the `create()` method. Then, for example, we can use standard Java to exercise the web application under test in parallel using a thread pool.

Example 9-6. Load test using WebDriverManager and Docker

```java
class LoadJupiterTest {

    static final int NUM_BROWSERS = 5;

    final Logger log = getLogger(lookup().lookupClass());

    List<WebDriver> driverList;

    WebDriverManager wdm = WebDriverManager.chromedriver().browserInDocker(); ❶

    @BeforeEach
    void setupTest() {
        assumeThat(isDockerAvailable()).isTrue(); ❷
        driverList = wdm.create(NUM_BROWSERS); ❸
    }

    @AfterEach
    void teardown() {
        wdm.quit();
    }

    @Test
    void testLoad() throws InterruptedException {
        ExecutorService executorService = newFixedThreadPool(NUM_BROWSERS); ❹
        CountDownLatch latch = new CountDownLatch(NUM_BROWSERS);

        driverList.forEach((driver) -> { ❺
            executorService.submit(() -> {
                try {
                    checkHomePage(driver);
                } finally {
                    latch.countDown();
                }
            });
        });

        latch.await(60, SECONDS); ❻
        executorService.shutdown();
    }

    void checkHomePage(WebDriver driver) {
        log.debug("Session id {}", ((RemoteWebDriver) driver).getSessionId());
        driver.get("https://bonigarcia.dev/selenium-webdriver-java/");
        assertThat(driver.getTitle()).contains("Selenium WebDriver");
    }

}
```

❶ We create an instance of the Chrome manager, using Docker to execute the browsers as containers.

❷ We assume that Docker is installed in the machine running this test. Otherwise, the test is skipped.

❸ We create a WebDriver list (containing five instances in this example).

❹ We create a thread pool using the same size as the WebDriver list.

❺ We use the thread pool to execute in parallel the SUT assessment.

❻ We wait until each parallel evaluation finishes. We use a synchronization method based on a counter latch to do that.

Security

A relevant organization in the software security domain is OWASP (*https://owasp.org*) (Open Web Application Security Project), a nonprofit foundation that promotes open solutions to improve software security. One of the most popular OWASP projects is the Zed Attack Proxy (ZAP). OWASP ZAP (*https://www.zaproxy.org*) is an open source web application security scanner used to implement *vulnerability assessment* (i.e., look for security issues) or *penetration testing* (i.e., a simulated cyberattack) to find exploitable web application vulnerabilities.

We can use OWASP ZAP as a standalone desktop application. Figure 9-4 shows a screenshot of its GUI.

Figure 9-4. OWASP ZAP GUI

This GUI provides different features for automated scans to detect security threats that a web application might face, such as SQL injection, cross-site scripting (XSS), or cross-site request forgery (CSRF), to name a few.

In addition to the standalone application, we can integrate a Selenium WebDriver test with ZAP. Example 9-7 provides a test case illustrating this integration. The steps required to execute this test properly are:

1. Start OWAS ZAP in the localhost. By default, OWASP starts a proxy that listens to port 8080. You can change this port using the OWASP GUI using the menu option Tools → Options → Local Proxies.

2. Disable the API key (or copy its value in the Selenium WebDriver test). You can change this value in the menu option Tools → Options → API.

3. Implement a Selenium WebDriver test that uses OWASP ZAP as a proxy (like Example 9-7).

4. Execute the Selenium WebDriver test. At this point, you should see the generated vulnerability report in the ZAP GUI.

Example 9-7. Test using OWASP ZAP as security scanner

```
class SecurityJupiterTest {

    static final Logger log = getLogger(lookup().lookupClass());

    static final String ZAP_PROXY_ADDRESS = "localhost"; ❶
    static final int ZAP_PROXY_PORT = 8080;
    static final String ZAP_API_KEY = "<put-api-key-here-or-disable-it>"; ❷

    WebDriver driver;

    ClientApi api;

    @BeforeEach
    void setup() {
        String proxyStr = ZAP_PROXY_ADDRESS + ":" + ZAP_PROXY_PORT;
        assumeThat(isOnline("http://" + proxyStr)).isTrue();

        Proxy proxy = new Proxy(); ❸
        proxy.setHttpProxy(proxyStr);
        proxy.setSslProxy(proxyStr);

        ChromeOptions options = new ChromeOptions();
        options.setAcceptInsecureCerts(true);
        options.setProxy(proxy);

        driver = WebDriverManager.chromedriver().capabilities(options).create();
```

```
        api = new ClientApi(ZAP_PROXY_ADDRESS, ZAP_PROXY_PORT, ZAP_API_KEY); ❹
    }

    @AfterEach
    void teardown() throws ClientApiException {
        if (api != null) {
            String title = "My ZAP report";
            String template = "traditional-html";
            String description = "This is a sample report";
            String reportfilename = "zap-report.html";
            String targetFolder = new File("").getAbsolutePath();
            ApiResponse response = api.reports.generate(title, template, null,
                    description, null, null, null, null, null, reportfilename,
                    null, targetFolder, null); ❺
            log.debug("ZAP report generated at {}", response.toString());
        }
        if (driver != null) {
            driver.quit();
        }
    }

    @Test
    void testSecurity() {
        driver.get(
                "https://bonigarcia.dev/selenium-webdriver-java/web-form.html");
        assertThat(driver.getTitle()).contains("Selenium WebDriver");
    }

}
```

❶ We configure the address and port where the ZAP local proxy is listening.

❷ If the ZAP API key is not disabled, we need to set its value here.

❸ We configure ZAP as a Selenium WebDriver proxy.

❹ We interact with ZAP using its API.

❺ After the test, we create an HTML report with vulnerabilities found during the
    execution of the Selenium WebDriver test. Figure 9-5 shows a screenshot of this
    report.

We can also use OWASP ZAP as a standalone GUI, as introduced
previously. The potential benefit of the integration with Selenium
WebDriver could be reusing existing functional tests for assessing
security or automated security assessment (e.g., a regression test
suite executed by a CI server).

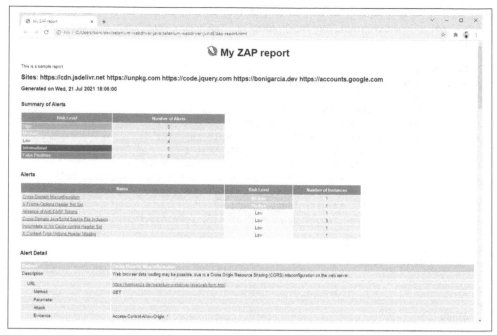

Figure 9-5. Report generated by ZAP after executing a Selenium WebDriver test

Accessibility

Digital accessibility refers to the ability of users with disabilities to effectively use software systems such as websites, mobile apps, etc. An essential reference in this domain is the Web Content Accessibility Guidelines (*https://www.w3.org/WAI/standards-guidelines/wcag*) (WCAG), which are a set of standard recommendations created by the W3C Web Accessibility Initiative (*https://www.w3.org/WAI*) (WAI) that explain how to make web content more accessible to people with disabilities.

There are several methods to test the accessibility of web applications. The most common approach consists of checking the WCAG recommendations. To that aim, we can use automated accessibility scanners like Axe (*https://www.deque.com/axe*), an open source engine for automated accessibility testing of web applications following WCAG rules. Axe provides seamless integration with the Java bindings of Selenium WebDriver using a helper library (*https://github.com/dequelabs/axe-core-maven-html*). Example 9-8 shows a test using this library.

Example 9-8. Test using Axe to generate an accessibility report

```
@Test
void testAccessibility() {
    driver.get("https://bonigarcia.dev/selenium-webdriver-java/");
    assertThat(driver.getTitle()).contains("Selenium WebDriver");
```

```
    Results result = new AxeBuilder().analyze(driver); ❶
    List<Rule> violations = result.getViolations(); ❷
    violations.forEach(rule -> {
        log.debug("{}", rule.toString()); ❸
    });
    AxeReporter.writeResultsToJsonFile("testAccessibility", result); ❹
}
```

❶   We analyze the current WebDriver session with Axe. This way, all pages loaded in
     the browser will be scanned by Axe.

❷   We get a report of the accessibility violations found.

❸   We log each violation in the standard output. In this example, the found issues
     are:

     color-contrast
          Elements must have sufficient color contrast.

     heading-order
          Heading levels should only increase by one.

     image-alt
          Images must have alternate text.

     link-name
          Links must have discernible text.

❹   We write the results as a local JSON file.

A/B Testing

A/B testing is a form of usability evaluation that compares variations of the same
application to discover which one is more effective to its end users. Different commercial products facilitate advanced features for A/B tests in Selenium WebDriver
tests. For example, Applitools Eyes (*https://applitools.com/products-eyes*) provides an
automated visual comparison of multiple web page variations. Another option is
Optimizely (*https://www.optimizely.com*), a company that provides tools for custom-
izing and experimenting with A/B testing.

Another way to carry out A/B testing is to use the vanilla Selenium WebDriver API
and custom conditions for the different variations of a web page. Example 9-9 shows
a basic test following a manual approach for a multivariant web page. Notice that this
test shows a simple way to implement an A/B test based on assessing the different
page variations.

Example 9-9. Basic A/B test using Selenium WebDriver

```
@Test
void testABTesting() {
    driver.get(
            "https://bonigarcia.dev/selenium-webdriver-java/ab-testing.html"); ❶
    WebDriverWait wait = new WebDriverWait(driver, Duration.ofSeconds(10));
    WebElement header = wait.until(
            ExpectedConditions.presenceOfElementLocated(By.tagName("h6")));

    if (header.getText().contains("variation A")) { ❷
        assertBodyContains(driver, "Lorem ipsum");
    } else if (header.getText().contains("variation B")) {
        assertBodyContains(driver, "Nibh netus");
    } else {
        fail("Unknown variation");
    }
}

void assertBodyContains(WebDriver driver, String text) {
    String bodyText = driver.findElement(By.tagName("body")).getText();
    assertThat(bodyText).contains(text);
}
```

❶ We open a multivariant practice web page. The content of this page is randomly loaded 50% of the time.

❷ We check the page variations are as expected.

Fluent API

As introduced in Chapter 1, Selenium is the foundation technology for other frameworks and libraries. For instance, we can find several libraries wrapping Selenium WebDriver to expose a fluent API for creating end-to-end tests for web applications. An example of this kind of library is Selenide (*https://selenide.org*), an open source (MIT license) library that defines a concise fluent API on top of Selenium WebDriver. Selenide provides several benefits, such as automated waiting for web elements or support for AJAX applications.

A relevant difference of a Selenide test compared to Selenium WebDriver is that Selenide handles the WebDriver objects internally. For that, it uses WebDriverManager to resolve the required driver (e.g., chromedriver, geckodriver, etc.), holding the Web Driver instance in a separate thread that is closed at the end of the test. As a result, the required test boilerplate related to the creation and termination of WebDriver objects is not required. Example 9-10 demonstrates this feature by showing a basic Selenide test.

Example 9-10. Test using Selenide

```
class SelenideJupiterTest {

    @Test
    void testSelenide() {
        open("https://bonigarcia.dev/selenium-webdriver-java/login-form.html"); ❶

        $(By.id("username")).val("user"); ❷
        $(By.id("password")).val("user");
        $("button").pressEnter(); ❸
        $(By.id("success")).shouldBe(visible)
                .shouldHave(text("Login successful")); ❹
    }

}
```

❶ We use the static method open provided by Selenide to navigate a given URL. By default, Selenide uses a local Chrome, although the browser can be changed using a configuration class (e.g., Configuration.browser = "firefox";) or using a Java system property (e.g., -Dselenide.browser=firefox).

❷ The Selenide method $ allows you to locate web elements by CSS selector or using Selenium WebDriver By locators. This line of code uses the latter to type text into an input field.

❸ We locate another web element, this time by CSS selector, and click on it.

❹ We verify that the web element for successful login is present on the page and contains the expected text.

Test Data

A relevant part of any test case is the test data, i.e., the input data used to exercise the SUT. The selection of suitable test data is paramount for implementing effective tests. Differing techniques in classic testing theory for test data selection include:

Equivalence partitioning
    The process of testing by dividing all possible input test data into value sets that we assume to be processed in the same way.

Boundary testing
    The process of testing between extreme ends or between partitions of the input values. The basic idea of this approach is to select the representative limit values in an input domain (for example, below the minimum, minimum, just above the

minimum, nominal, just below the maximum, maximum, and above the maximum value).

These approaches can be impractical in end-to-end testing since the required number of tests (and the resulting execution time) to carry out these strategies can be enormous. Alternatively, we typically select some representative test data manually to verify the *happy path* (i.e., *positive* testing), and optionally, some test data for unexpected conditions (*negative* testing).

Another alternative for selecting test data is using *fake* data, i.e., random data of different domains, such as personal names, surnames, addresses, countries, emails, phone numbers, etc. A simple alternative to this aim is using Java Faker (*https://dius.github.io/java-faker*), a port of the popular faker (*https://github.com/faker-ruby/faker*) Ruby gem. Example 9-11 shows a test using this library. This test uses fake data to submit a web form available on the practice site. Figure 9-6 shows this web page after submitting the form with that fake data.

Example 9-11. Test using Java Faker to generate different types of fake data

```java
@Test
void testFakeData() {
    driver.get(
            "https://bonigarcia.dev/selenium-webdriver-java/data-types.html");

    Faker faker = new Faker(); ❶

    driver.findElement(By.name("first-name")) ❷
            .sendKeys(faker.name().firstName());
    driver.findElement(By.name("last-name"))
            .sendKeys(faker.name().lastName());
    driver.findElement(By.name("address"))
            .sendKeys(faker.address().fullAddress());
    driver.findElement(By.name("zip-code"))
            .sendKeys(faker.address().zipCode());
    driver.findElement(By.name("city")).sendKeys(faker.address().city());
    driver.findElement(By.name("country"))
            .sendKeys(faker.address().country());
    driver.findElement(By.name("e-mail"))
            .sendKeys(faker.internet().emailAddress());
    driver.findElement(By.name("phone"))
            .sendKeys(faker.phoneNumber().phoneNumber());
    driver.findElement(By.name("job-position"))
            .sendKeys(faker.job().position());
    driver.findElement(By.name("company")).sendKeys(faker.company().name());

    driver.findElement(By.tagName("form")).submit();

    List<WebElement> successElement = driver
            .findElements(By.className("alert-success"));
```

```
        assertThat(successElement).hasSize(10); ❸

        List<WebElement> errorElement = driver
                .findElements(By.className("alert-danger"));
        assertThat(errorElement).isEmpty(); ❹
}
```

❶   We create an instance of Java Faker.

❷   We send random data of different types (name, address, country, etc.).

❸   We verify that the data is submitted correctly.

❹   We check there are no errors on the page.

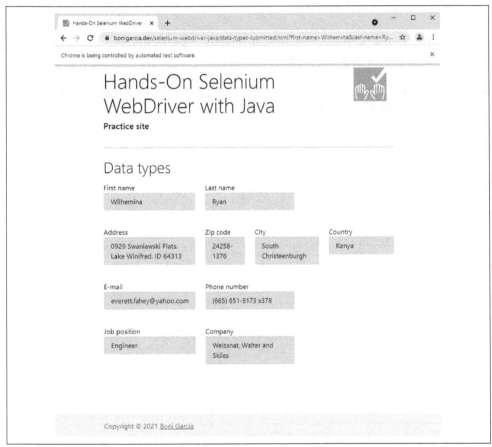

Figure 9-6. Practice page using fake data

Reporting

A *test report* is a document that summarizes the results after executing a test suite. This document typically contains the number of tests executed plus their verdicts (pass, fail, skip) and execution time. There are different ways to obtain a test report in our Java project. For example, when using Maven, we can create a basic test report using the following commands:

```
mvn test ❶
mvn surefire-report:report-only ❷
mvn site -DgenerateReports=false ❸
```

❶ We execute the test with Maven. As a result, the Maven Surefire plug-in generated a set of XML files in the `target` folder. These files contain the results of the test execution.

❷ We convert the XML reports into an HTML report. You can find this HTML report in your project folder `target/site`.

❸ We force a copy of the CSS and images required in the HTML report. Figure 9-7 shows a screenshot of this report.

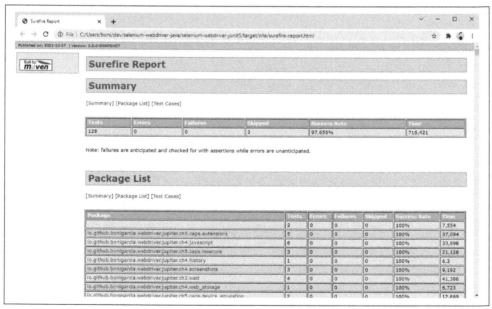

Figure 9-7. Test report generated with Maven

We can also generate an equivalent report using Gradle. After executing a test suite with this build tool, Gradle automatically generates an HTML report in the folder build/reports. Figure 9-8 shows an example of the test report generated for executing a group of tests (using the shell command `gradle test --tests Hello*`).

Figure 9-8. Test report generated with Gradle

In addition to Maven and Gradle, we can use existing reporting libraries to create richer reports. A possible alternative is Extent Reports (*https://www.extentreports.com*), a library to create interactive test reports. Extent Reports provides professional (commercial) and community (open source) editions. Example 9-12 shows a test using the latter.

Example 9-12. Test using Extent Reports to generate an HTML report

```
class ReportingJupiterTest {

    WebDriver driver;

    static ExtentReports reports;

    @BeforeAll
    static void setupClass() {
        reports = new ExtentReports();                                    ❶
        ExtentSparkReporter htmlReporter = new ExtentSparkReporter(
                "extentReport.html");
        reports.attachReporter(htmlReporter);                            ❷
    }

    @BeforeEach
    void setup(TestInfo testInfo) {
        reports.createTest(testInfo.getDisplayName());                   ❸
        driver = WebDriverManager.chromedriver().create();
```

```
    }

    @AfterEach
    void teardown() {
        driver.quit();
    }

    @AfterAll
    static void teardownClass() {
        reports.flush();
    }

    // Test methods ❹

}
```

❶ We create an instance of the test reporter.

❷ We configure it to generate an HTML report.

❸ After each test, we create an entry in the test report using the test name as an identifier. In JUnit 5, we use `TestInfo`, a built-in parameter resolver that allows retrieving information about the current test.

❹ As usual, you can find the complete source code in the examples repository (*https://github.com/bonigarcia/selenium-webdriver-java*). In particular, this class has two test methods. Figure 9-9 shows the resulting test report generated when this test class is executed.

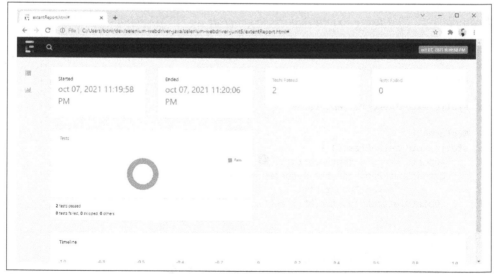

Figure 9-9. Test report generated with Extent Reports

An inconvenience of Extent Reports is that we need to add each test explicitly to the reporter. A possible solution to this problem is using custom test listeners (as explained in "Test Listeners" on page 282) to group the common logic for reporting.

Another possible library for generating rich test reports is Allure (*http://allure.qatools.ru*), an open source reporting framework for generating test reports for different programming languages, including Java, Python, and JavaScript, among others. A notable difference between Allure and Extent Reports is that Allure uses a test listener configured in the build tool Maven or Gradle (see Appendix C for further details about this configuration). This way, we did not need to change our test suite for generating Allure reports. Table 9-1 summarizes the necessary commands to create Allure reports with Maven and Gradle.

Table 9-1. Maven and Gradle commands to generate test reports with Allure

Maven	Gradle	Description
mvn test	gradle test	Run test cases
mvn allure:report	gradle allureReport	Create the reports on the target folder
mvn allure:serve	gradle allureServe	Open the HTML report using a local web server (as shown in Figure 9-10)

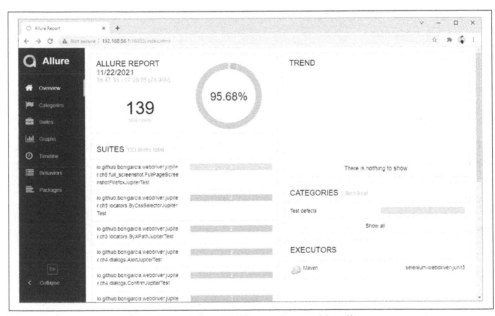

Figure 9-10. Test report generated with Allure and served locally

Behavior Driven Development

As introduced in Chapter 1, Behavior Driven Development (BDD) is a software methodology that promotes the development and testing of software systems using high-level user scenarios. Different tools implement the BDD methodology. One of the most popular is Cucumber (*https://cucumber.io*). Cucumber executes tests based on user stories written in *Gherkin*, a human-readable notation based on natural languages (e.g., English and others). Gherkin was designed to be used by nonprogrammers (e.g., customers or end users), and its main keywords are listed next (see the Gherkin user manual (*https://cucumber.io/docs/gherkin*) for further information):

Feature
> High-level description of the software feature tested.

Scenario
> Concrete test that illustrates a business rule. Scenarios describe different pieces of information (called *steps* in the Gherkin jargon), such as:

> *Given*
>> Preconditions and initial state

> *When*
>> User actions

> *And*
>> Additional user actions

> *Then*
>> Expected outcome

Example 9-13 shows a Gherkin feature containing two scenarios for a test login (successful and failed).

Example 9-13. Gherkin scenarios for login into the practice site

```
Feature: Login in practice site ❶

  Scenario: Successful login ❷
    Given I use "Chrome" ❸
    When I navigate to
        "https://bonigarcia.dev/selenium-webdriver-java/login-form.html" ❹
    And I log in with the username "user" and password "user" ❺
    And I click Submit
    Then I should see the message "Login successful" ❻

  Scenario: Failure login ❼
    Given I use "Chrome"
    When I navigate to
```

```
    "https://bonigarcia.dev/selenium-webdriver-java/login-form.html"
And I log in with the username "bad-user" and password "bad-password"
And I click Submit
Then I should see the message "Invalid credentials"
```

❶ Feature description

❷ First scenario (login successful)

❸ Browser to be used

❹ Web page URL

❺ Set of actions (type credentials and click the Submit button)

❻ Expected message

❼ Second scenario (login failed)

To run Gherkin scenarios as test cases, we must first create the corresponding *step definitions*. A step definition is a *glue code* that exercises the SUT using the information specified in the scenario. In Java, we use annotations (such as @Given, @Then, @When, or @And) to decorate methods implementing each step. These annotations contain a string value to map each step definition and the parameters. Example 9-14 shows a step definition for the Gherkin scenario defined on Example 9-13. We use the Selenium WebDriver API to implement the required actions for navigation, web element interaction, etc.

Example 9-14. Steps to log in to the practice site with Cucumber

```
public class LoginSteps {

    private WebDriver driver;

    @Given("I use {string}") ❶
    public void iUse(String browser) {
        driver = WebDriverManager.getInstance(browser).create();
    }

    @When("I navigate to {string}") ❷
    public void iNavigateTo(String url) {
        driver.get(url);
    }

    @And("I log in with the username {string} and password {string}") ❸
    public void iLogin(String username, String password) {
        driver.findElement(By.id("username")).sendKeys(username);
```

```
        driver.findElement(By.id("password")).sendKeys(password);

    }

    @And("I click Submit") ❹
    public void iPressEnter() {
        driver.findElement(By.cssSelector("button")).click();
    }

    @Then("I should see the message {string}") ❺
    public void iShouldSee(String result) {
        try {
            String bodyText = driver.findElement(By.tagName("body")).getText();
            assertThat(bodyText).contains(result);
        } finally {
            driver.quit();
        }
    }

}
```

❶ We use the first step to create a WebDriver instance.

❷ We open the URL.

❸ We type the credentials.

❹ We click on the Submit button.

❺ We verify that the expected message is on the page.

Finally, we need to run our step definition as a test case. As usual, we create that test using a unit testing framework. This test is unit testing framework-dependent in the integration with Cucumber. In other words, the required code is different in JUnit 4 (see Example 9-15), JUnit 5 (see Example 9-16), and TestNG (see Example 9-17). The resulting tests are executed in the usual way (i.e., using the shell or an IDE).

 Selenium-Jupiter does not provide any additional features for integrating with Cucumber, so the default JUnit 5 procedure is the same in the Selenium-Jupiter project in the examples repository.

Example 9-15. Cucumber test using JUnit 4

```
@RunWith(Cucumber.class) ❶
@CucumberOptions(features = "classpath:io/github/bonigarcia", glue = {
        "io.github.bonigarcia" }) ❷
public class CucumberTest {

}
```

❶ We use the Cucumber runner to execute the step definitions as test cases.

❷ We specify the location of the Gherkin scenarios. In this case, the feature is the folder io/github/bonigarcia in the project classpath (concretely, in the src/ test/resources folder). This annotation also specified the initial package to search the glue code (i.e., the steps definition).

Example 9-16. Cucumber test using JUnit 5

```
@Suite ❶
@IncludeEngines("cucumber") ❷
@SelectClasspathResource("io/github/bonigarcia") ❸
@ConfigurationParameter(key = GLUE_PROPERTY_NAME, value = "io.github.bonigarcia") ❹
public class CucumberTest {

}
```

❶ We need to use the JUnit 5 suite module to run Cucumber tests.

❷ We include the Cucumber engine in the JUnit Platform.

❸ We specify the path for features within the project classpath.

❹ We set the initial package to search the glue code.

Example 9-17. Cucumber test using TestNG

```
@CucumberOptions(features = "classpath:io/github/bonigarcia", glue = {
        "io.github.bonigarcia" }) ❶
public class CucumberTest extends AbstractTestNGCucumberTests { ❷

}
```

❶ We specify the location of the Gherkin scenarios and the package to search the glue code.

❷ We extend a TestNG parent test class for Cucumber tests.

Web Frameworks

Web frameworks are software frameworks designed to support the development of web applications and services. One of the most popular frameworks for the Java language is the Spring Framework (*https://spring.io*). Spring is an open source framework for building Java applications, including enterprise web applications and services. The core technology of Spring is known as *Inversion of Control* (IoC), which is a procedure to create instances outside the class in which these objects are used. These objects, called *beans* or *components* in the Spring jargon, are later injected on demand as dependencies by the Spring IoC container.

The following examples show basic tests that verify a local web application created with Spring-Boot (*https://spring.io/projects/spring-boot*), a subproject of the Spring portfolio that simplifies the development of Spring-based applications thanks to convention over configuration and autodiscovery features. In addition, Spring-Boot provides an embedded web server to ease the development of web applications. The integration with Selenium WebDriver in this kind of project facilitates the testing process of Spring-based web applications by deploying automatically in the embedded web server per test case.

The code to integrate Spring-Boot with Selenium WebDriver and the unit testing frameworks used in this book is different. Example 9-18 shows a test integrating Spring-Boot and JUnit 4. Example 9-19 shows the differences when using TestNG, Example 9-20 illustrates how to use JUnit 5, and finally, Example 9-21 shows a Spring test based on JUnit 5 with Selenium-Jupiter.

Example 9-18. Test using Spring-Boot and JUnit 4

```
@RunWith(SpringRunner.class) ❶
@SpringBootTest(classes = SpringBootDemoApp.class,
        webEnvironment = SpringBootTest.WebEnvironment.RANDOM_PORT) ❷
public class SpringBootJUnit4Test {

    private WebDriver driver;

    @LocalServerPort ❸
    protected int serverPort;

    @Before
    public void setup() {
        driver = WebDriverManager.chromedriver().create();
    }

    @After
    public void teardown() {
        driver.quit();
    }
```

```
    @Test
    public void testSpringBoot() {
        driver.get("http://localhost:" + serverPort);
        String bodyText = driver.findElement(By.tagName("body")).getText();
        assertThat(bodyText)
                .contains("This is a local site served by Spring-Boot");
    }

}
```

❶ We use the Spring runner in JUnit 4.

❷ We use a Spring-Boot annotation for tests to define the Spring-Boot class name. Also, we specify the web application is deployed using a random available port.

❸ We inject the web application port as a class attribute.

Example 9-19. Test using Spring-Boot and TestNG

```
@SpringBootTest(classes = SpringBootDemoApp.class,
        webEnvironment = SpringBootTest.WebEnvironment.RANDOM_PORT) ❶
public class SpringBootNGTest extends AbstractTestNGSpringContextTests { ❷

    // Same logic as the previous test

}
```

❶ We use the annotation @SpringBootTest in the same way in JUnit 4.

❷ We extend a TestNG parent to run this test using the Spring context.

Example 9-20. Test using Spring-Boot and JUnit 5

```
@ExtendWith(SpringExtension.class) ❶
@SpringBootTest(classes = SpringBootDemoApp.class,
        webEnvironment = SpringBootTest.WebEnvironment.RANDOM_PORT) ❷
class SpringBootJupiterTest {

    // Same logic as the previous test

}
```

❶ We use the JUnit 5 Spring extension to integrate the Spring context in a Jupiter test.

❷ We use Spring-Boot to start our Spring application context as in the previous examples.

Example 9-21. Test using Spring-Boot and JUnit 5 plus Selenium-Jupiter

```
@ExtendWith({ SeleniumJupiter.class, SpringExtension.class }) ❶
@SpringBootTest(classes = SpringBootDemoApp.class,
        webEnvironment = SpringBootTest.WebEnvironment.RANDOM_PORT)
class SpringBootSelJupTest {

    @LocalServerPort
    protected int serverPort;

    @Test
    void testSpringBoot(ChromeDriver driver) { ❷
        driver.get("http://localhost:" + serverPort);
        String bodyText = driver.findElement(By.tagName("body")).getText();
        assertThat(bodyText)
                .contains("This is a local site served by Spring-Boot");
    }

}
```

❶ In the case of Selenium-Jupiter, we use two JUnit 5 extensions (for Spring and Selenium WebDriver).

❷ As usual in Selenium-Jupiter, we use the JUnit 5 parameter resolution mechanism to declare the type of `WebDriver` instance we use in this test.

Summary and Outlook

This chapter provided a practical overview for integrating different technologies (such as tools, libraries, and frameworks) in the development of end-to-end tests for web applications with Selenium WebDriver. First, we used Awaitility (a library to handle asynchronous operations) for waiting until files are downloaded with Selenium WebDriver. An alternative library to execute the same use case (i.e., downloading files) is Apache HttpClient. Then, we used the BrowserMob proxy to intercept the HTTP traffic exchanged by a Selenium WebDriver test. The next group of technologies focused on enabling nonfunctional testing with Selenium WebDriver: BrowserMob (to create a JMeter test plan for performance testing), OWASP ZAP (for security testing), and Axe (for accessibility testing). Then, we used the fluent API provided by Selenide, Java Faker, to create fake test data for Selenium WebDriver tests, and Extent Reports and Allure to generate rich test reports. Finally, we discovered how to integrate Cucumber (a BDD framework) and Spring (a Java and web framework) with Selenium WebDriver.

The next chapter concludes this book by presenting complementary frameworks to Selenium WebDriver, namely REST Assured (for testing REST services) and Appium (for testing mobile applications). Finally, the chapter presents several popular alternatives to Selenium WebDriver in the browser automation space: Cypress, WebDriverIO, TestCafe, Puppeteer, and Playwright.

Beyond Selenium

This chapter closes this book by presenting several complementary technologies to Selenium. First, we analyze the basics of mobile apps and introduce Appium, a popular testing framework for mobile testing. Then, you will learn how to test REST (REpresentational State Transfer) services with an open source Java library called REST Assured. Finally, you will be introduced to alternative tools to Selenium WebDriver for implementing end-to-end tests for web applications, namely: Cypress, WebDriverIO, TestCafe, Puppeteer, and Playwright.

Mobile Apps

Mobile applications (usually called mobile apps, or simply apps) are software applications designed to run on mobile devices, such as smartphones, tablets, or wearables. There are two principal operating systems for mobile devices:

Android (https://www.android.com)
> An open source (Apache 2.0 license) mobile operating system based on a modified version of Linux. It was initially developed by a startup named Android, acquired by Google in 2005.

iOS (https://www.apple.com/ios)
> A proprietary mobile operating system created by Apple exclusively for its hardware (e.g., iPhone, iPad, or Watch).

A common way to classify mobile apps is as follows:

Native apps
> Mobile apps developed for a particular mobile operating system (e.g., Android or iOS).

Web-based apps
> Web applications rendered into a mobile browser (e.g., Chrome, Safari, or Firefox Mobile). These apps are typically designed to be *responsive* (i.e., adaptable to different screen sizes and viewports).

Hybrid apps
> Mobile applications developed using client-side web standards (i.e., HTML, CSS, and JavaScript) and deployed to mobile devices using a native container called *webview*. Examples of frameworks that enable the development of hybrid apps are Ionic (*https://ionicframework.com*), React Native (*https://reactnative.dev*), or Flutter (*https://flutter.dev*).

Progressive web apps (PWAs)
> Web applications built with modern web standard APIs (for installability, responsiveness, etc.) intended to work on multiple platforms, including desktop and mobile devices.

Mobile Testing

Testing is an essential process in the development of mobile apps. Mobile testing involves different challenges such as hardware compatibility, network connectivity, or operating system specifics. Different approaches to carry out mobile testing include:

Using desktop browsers with mobile emulation
> We can use Selenium WebDriver for this type of mobile testing. To that aim, you can use browser-specific features (as explained in "Device Emulation" on page 153) or use the CDP with Chromium-based browsers (as explained in "Device emulation" on page 187).

Using virtual devices
> There are two types of virtual mobile devices:

> *Emulators*
>> Desktop applications that virtualize all aspects of mobile devices, including the hardware and the operating system.

> *Simulators*
>> Desktop apps that mimic certain features of a mobile operating system. They are primarily intended for iOS since Android devices are emulated easily.

Using real devices
> Using actual devices and their native Android or iOS APIs in real conditions.

Appium

Appium (*https://appium.io*) is an open source test automation framework for mobile apps. Appium provides a cross-platform API that allows testing native, hybrid, and mobile web apps for iOS and Android on virtual or real devices. Furthermore, Appium enables automated testing for desktop applications on Windows and macOS.

The story of Appium started in 2011 when Dan Cuellar created an automation tool for iOS applications developed in C# called iOSAuto. He met Jason Huggins (the co-creator of Selenium) during the SeleniumConf 2012 in London. Jason contributed to the project by adding a web server and using the WebDriver wire protocol over HTTP, making iOSAuto compatible with any Selenium WebDriver client. They changed the project name to Appium (the *Selenium for Apps*). In January 2013, Sauce Labs decided to support Appium and provide more developer power. The new team rewrote Appium using Node.js since it is a well-known, efficient framework for the server side.

As depicted in Figure 10-1, Appium follows a client-server architecture. Appium is a web server that exposes a REST API that carries out an automated session on mobile or desktop apps. To that aim, the Appium server receives incoming requests from clients, executes those commands on target devices/apps, and responds with an HTTP response representing the command execution result. Appium client libraries communicate with the Appium server using the Mobile JSON Wire Protocol (an official draft extension to the original WebDriver protocol). The Appium server and its client also use the W3C Webdriver specification. There are different Appium client libraries. Table 10-1 summarizes these libraries, both officially maintained by the Appium project and community.

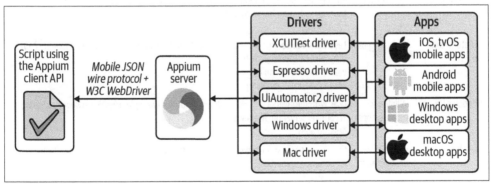

Figure 10-1. Appium architecture

Table 10-1. Appium client libraries

Name	Language	License	Maintainer	Website
Appium java-client	Java	Apache 2.0	Appium team	*https://github.com/appium/java-client*
Appium ruby_lib	Ruby	Apache 2.0	Appium team	*https://github.com/appium/ruby_lib*
Appium Python Client	Python	Apache 2.0	Appium team	*https://github.com/appium/python-client*
appium-dotnet-driver	C#	Apache 2.0	Appium team	*https://github.com/appium/appium-dotnet-driver*
WebdriverIO	JavaScript (Node.js)	MIT	WebdriverIO team	*https://webdriver.io*
web2driver	JavaScript (browser)	Apache 2.0	HeadSpin	*https://github.com/projectxyzio/web2driver*
Appium library for RobotFramework	Python	Apache 2.0	Serhat Bolsu	*https://github.com/serhatbolsu/robotframework-appiumlibrary*

In Appium, the support for the automation of a particular platform is provided by a component called *driver* in Appium jargon. These drivers were tightly coupled with the Appium Server in version 1. Nevertheless, in Appium 2 (the latest version of Appium at the time of this writing), these drivers are segregated from the Appium Server (see Figure 10-1) and are installed separately.

Table 10-2. Appium drivers

Name	Target	Description	Repository
XCUITest Driver	iOS and tvOS apps	Leverages Apple's XCUITest libraries to enable automation	*https://github.com/appium/appium-xcuitest-driver*
Espresso Driver	Android apps	Enables automation through Espresso (a testing framework for Android)	*https://github.com/appium/appium-espresso-driver*
UiAutomator2 Driver	Android apps	Leverages Google UiAutomator2 technology to enable automation on an Android device or emulator	*https://github.com/appium/appium-uiautomator2-driver*
Windows Driver	Windows desktop apps	Uses WinAppDriver, a WebDriver server for Windows desktop apps	*https://github.com/appium/appium-windows-driver*
Mac Driver	macOS desktop apps	Uses Apple's XCTest framework for automating macOS applications	*https://github.com/appium/appium-mac2-driver*

A basic Appium test

This section presents a basic test case using Appium server 2 and the Appium Java client. For simplicity, I use the UiAutomator2 Driver and an emulated Android device. The SUT will be a web application, concretely, the practice site used throughout this book. The calls to the Appium Java clients are embedded in the different unit testing frameworks used in the rest of the examples (i.e., JUnit 4 and 5, TestNG, and Selenium-Jupiter). As usual, you can find the complete source code in the examples repository. The requisites for running this test are:

1. Install Appium server 2.

2. Install UiAutomator2 Driver.

3. Install Android SDK (i.e., the official software development kit for Android). You can easily install this SDK by installing Android Studio (*https://devel oper.android.com/studio*) on your computer.

4. Create an Android Virtual Device (AVD) using the AVD Manager in Android Studio. Figure 10-2 shows the menu option to open this tool, and Figure 10-3 shows the virtual device used in the test (a Nexus 5 mobile phone using the Android API level 30).

5. Start the virtual device and Appium server.

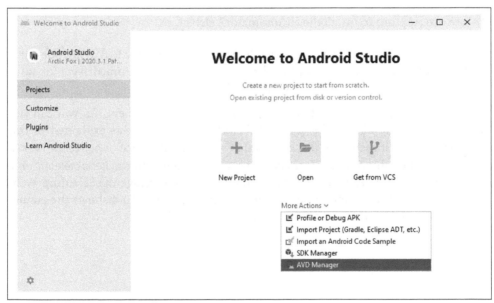

Figure 10-2. Android Studio

Figure 10-3. AVD Manager

As explained previously, the Appium server is a Node.js application. Therefore, you need Node.js installed in your system to run Appium. The following commands summarize how to install the Appium server 2 and the UiAutomator2 Driver, and how to start the Appium server:

```
npm install -g appium@next ❶
appium driver install uiautomator2 ❷
appium --allow-insecure chromedriver_autodownload ❸
```

❶ We use npm (the default package manager for Node.js) to install Appium 2.

❷ We use Appium to install the UiAutomator2 Driver.

❸ We start the Appium server (by default, it listens to port 4723). We include a flag to let Appium manage the required browser drivers (e.g., chromedriver) for automating web applications (just like in Selenium WebDriver).

Example 10-1 shows a complete test using the Appium Java client. As you can see, this test is quite similar to the regular Selenium WebDriver tests explained in this book. The main difference, in this case, is that we use an instance of `AppiumDriver`, a class provided by the Appium Java client. This class extends to the `RemoteWebDriver` class of the Selenium WebDriver API. Therefore, we can leverage the Selenium WebDriver API to test web applications on mobile devices. Figure 10-4 shows the emulated mobile device (a Nexus 5) during this test.

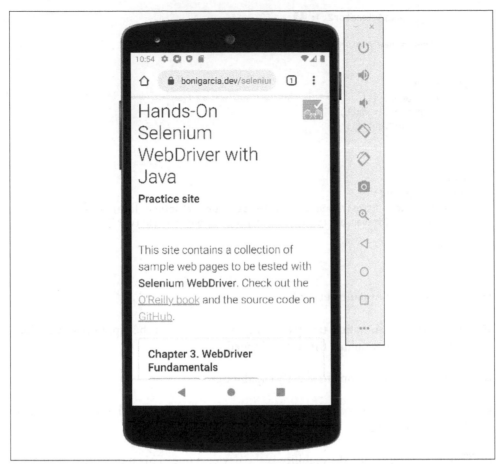

Figure 10-4. Android device

Example 10-1. Test using Appium Java client

```
class AppiumJupiterTest {

    WebDriver driver;

    @BeforeEach
    void setup() throws MalformedURLException {
        URL appiumServerUrl = new URL("http://localhost:4723"); ❶
        assumeThat(isOnline(new URL(appiumServerUrl, "/status"))).isTrue(); ❷

        ChromeOptions options = new ChromeOptions(); ❸
        options.setCapability(MobileCapabilityType.PLATFORM_NAME, "Android"); ❹
        options.setCapability(MobileCapabilityType.DEVICE_NAME,
                "Nexus 5 API 30"); ❺
        options.setCapability(MobileCapabilityType.AUTOMATION_NAME,
```

```
            "UiAutomator2");  ❻

        driver = new AppiumDriver(appiumServerUrl, options);  ❼
    }

    @AfterEach
    void teardown() {
        if (driver != null) {
            driver.quit();
        }
    }

    @Test
    void testAppium() {
        driver.get("https://bonigarcia.dev/selenium-webdriver-java/");  ❽
        assertThat(driver.getTitle()).contains("Selenium WebDriver");
    }

}
```

❶ We specify the Appium server URL.

❷ We make an assumption using the endpoint /status of the Appium server URL. If this URL is not online, the test is skipped.

❸ We use Chrome options to specify capabilities.

❹ The first mandatory capability when using Appium is the platform name (Android in this case).

❺ The following required capability is the device name. This name must match the name defined in the AVD manager (see Figure 10-3).

❻ The last mandatory capability is the driver name (UiAutomator2 in this case).

❼ We create an instance of AppiumDriver using the Appium server URL and the browser options.

❽ We use the driver object to exercise the SUT as usual.

REST Services

REST (REpresentational State Transfer) is an architectural style for designing distributed services. Roy Fielding coined this term in his 2000 doctoral dissertation. REST is a popular way of creating web services on top of the HTTP protocol.

REST follows a client-server architecture. The server handles a set of *resources*, listening for incoming requests made by clients. These resources are the building blocks of REST services and define the type of information transferred. Each resource is identified uniquely. In HTTP, we use URLs (also known as *endpoints*) for accessing individual resources. Each resource has a representation, a machine-readable explanation of the current state of a resource. We use a data-interchange format for defining representations, such as JSON, YAML, or XML. REST services expose a set of *actions* on the resources, such as CRUD (create, retrieve, update, and delete). We can use the HTTP methods (the so-called *verbs*) to map REST actions. Table 10-3 summarizes the HTTP methods used to create REST services. Finally, we can use the HTTP status codes to identify the response associated with REST actions. Table 10-4 summarizes the typical HTTP status codes used in REST. Figure 10-5 shows a sequence of requests and responses of an example REST service that uses different HTTP methods and response codes.

Table 10-3. HTTP methods for creating REST services

HTTP Method	Description
GET	Read a resource
POST	Send a new resource to the server
PUT	Update a resource
DELETE	Eliminate a resource
PATCH	Partially update a resource
HEAD	Ask if a given resource exists without returning any of its representations
OPTIONS	Retrieve the available verbs for a given resource

Table 10-4. HTTP status codes for creating REST services

Status Code	Description
200 OK	The request was successful, and the content requested was returned (e.g., in a GET request).
201 Created	The resource was created (e.g., in a POST or PUT request).
204 No content	The action was successful, but no content was returned. This status code is useful in actions that do not require a response body (e.g., in a DELETE request).
301 Moved permanently	The resource was moved to another location.
400 Bad request	The request has some problems (e.g., missing parameters).
401 Unauthorized	The requested resource is not accessible for the user that made the request.
403 Forbidden	The resource is not accessible, but unlike 401, authentication will not affect the response.
404 Not found	The provided endpoint does not identify any resource.
405 Method not allowed	The used verb is not allowed (e.g., when using PUT in a read-only resource).
500 Internal server error	Generic unexpected condition in the server side.

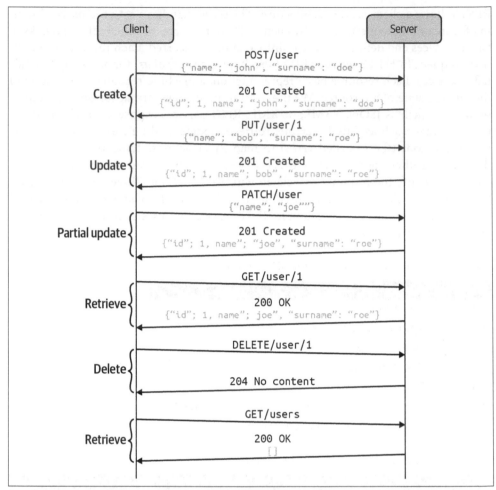

Figure 10-5. Example of a REST service

REST Assured

REST APIs are ubiquitous. As usual, it is highly recommended to implement automated tests for verifying these services, for instance, by using REST Assured (*https://rest-assured.io*). REST Assured is a popular open source (Apache 2.0 license) Java library for testing REST services. It provides a fluent API for testing and validating REST services. A convenient way to create readable assertions with REST Assured is to generate POJOs (Plain Old Java Objects) to map the REST responses (e.g., in JSON format) as Java classes. Then, we can use a library like AssertJ to verify the expected conditions using the accessors (i.e., the getter methods) of these POJOs. Example 10-2 shows a test case using this approach. Example 10-3 contains the POJO used in this test.

Example 10-2. Test using REST Assured

```
class RestJupiterTest {

    @Test
    void testRest() {
        HttpBinGet get = RestAssured.get("https://httpbin.org/get").then()
                .assertThat().statusCode(200).extract().as(HttpBinGet.class); ❶

        assertThat(get.getHeaders()).containsKey("Accept-Encoding"); ❷
        assertThat(get.getOrigin()).isNotBlank(); ❸
    }

}
```

❶ We use REST Assured to request an online public REST service using the GET HTTP method. This line also verifies the expected status code (200) and converts the response payload (in JSON) to a Java class (shown in Example 10-3).

❷ We assert the header list (using the corresponding accessor method) contains a given key value.

❸ We assert that the origin is not blank.

Example 10-3. POJO class for testing a REST service

```
public class HttpBinGet {

    public Map<String, String> args; ❶
    public Map<String, String> headers;
    public String origin;
    public String url;

    // Getters and setters ❷

}
```

❶ This POJO defines a set of attributes to map the JSON response payload using Java.

❷ We define accessors (getters) and mutators (setters) for each class attribute. Modern IDEs allow generating these methods automatically from the class attributes.

Alternatives to Selenium

Selenium is currently the leading technology for implementing end-to-end tests. Nevertheless, it is not the only alternative available. This section provides an overview of other frameworks and libraries that also allow implementing end-to-end tests for web applications. In addition, the following subsections also review the main pros and cons of each of these alternatives. In my opinion, Selenium is still the reference solution for end-to-end testing since it is built to promote web standards (i.e., the W3C WebDriver and WebDriver BiDi) to support the automation process and, therefore, it guarantees cross-browser compatibility.

Cypress

Cypress (*https://www.cypress.io*) is a JavaScript end-to-end automated testing framework. As illustrated in Figure 10-6, the Cypress architecture consists of a Node.js process plus a tool called *Test Runner* executed in a browser.

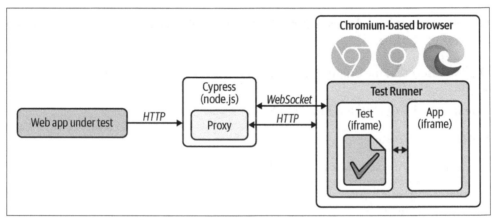

Figure 10-6. Cypress architecture

The Test Runner is an interactive web application that embeds a test based on Mocha (*https://mochajs.org*) (a JavaScript unit testing framework) plus the web application under test as two iframes. Test code and the application code run in the same browser tab (i.e., in the same JavaScript loop). The Node.js process communicates with the Test Runner using a WebSocket. Finally, the Node.js process is a proxy for the HTTP traffic between the Test Runner and the web application under test.

The Cypress Test Runner is open source, licensed under the terms of the MIT license. The Cypress team also provides commercial support for advanced features. One of them is the Cypress Dashboard, a cloud-managed web application that allows tracking the tests executed in Test Runner. Table 10-5 summarizes some of the most relevant pros and cons of Cypress.

Table 10-5. Cypress pros and cons

Pros	Cons
• Automatic waiting and fast execution, since the test and the application run in the same browser • Live reload (the Test Runner automatically keeps track of changes in the tests)	• Only some browsers supported: Firefox and Chromium-based (including Chrome, Edge, and Electron), but not other browsers like Safari or Opera • Since the application is executed in a browser iframe, certain operations are not allowed (e.g., drive different browsers or multiple tabs)

The following commands show how to install Cypress locally and execute it. After executing these commands, you will see the Cypress GUI (like in Figure 10-7). You can use this GUI to execute tests with Cypress.

```
npm install cypress ❶
npx cypress open ❷
```

❶   We can use npm (the default package manager in Node.js) for installing Cypress.

❷   We can use npx (an npm package runner) for running the Cypress process.

Figure 10-7. Cypress GUI

By default, in the Cypress GUI, you can find introductory test examples in the folders 1-getting-started and 2-advanced-examples. In addition, we can create new tests using the button New Spec File. For instance, Example 10-4 shows a brand-new basic test using Cypress (i.e., a *hello world* in Cypress). This test is called hello-world-cypress.spec.js (the extension spec.js is used by default in Mocha tests), and it is stored in the path cypress/integration of the Cypress installation. Figure 10-8 shows a screenshot of the Cypress Test Runner during the execution of this test.

Example 10-4. Hello world test using Cypress

```
describe('Hello World with Cypress', () => {
   it('Login in the practice site', () => {
      cy.visit('https://bonigarcia.dev/selenium-webdriver-java/login-form.html') ❶

      cy.get('#username').type('user') ❷
      cy.get('#password').type('user')
      cy.contains('Submit').click() ❸
      cy.contains('Login successful') ❹

      cy.screenshot("hello-world-cypress") ❺
   })
})
```

❶   We open the login page in the practice site.

❷   We type the correct credentials (username and password).

❸   We click on the Submit button.

❹   We verify the resulting page contains the message for successful login.

❺   We make a browser screenshot.

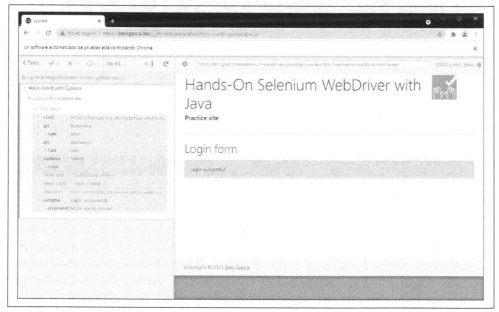

Figure 10-8. Cypress Test Runner

WebDriverIO

WebDriverIO (*https://webdriver.io*) is an automated testing framework for web and mobile applications. It is entirely open source (MIT license) and based on web standards such as the W3C WebDriver protocol. Figure 10-9 illustrates its architecture. WebDriverIO is written in JavaScript and runs on Node.js. It uses several *services* to support automation: chromedriver (for local Chrome browsers), Selenium Server (for other browsers), Appium Server (for mobile devices), Chrome DevTools (for Chromium-based local browsers using the CDP), and cloud providers (such as Sauce Labs, BrowserStack, or TestingBot). These services manipulate the corresponding browsers and mobile devices. Table 10-6 summarizes some of the pros and cons of WebDriverIO.

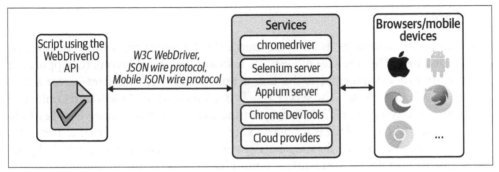

Figure 10-9. WebDriverIO architecture

Table 10-6. WebDriverIO pros and cons

Pros	Cons
• Support for multiple browsers and mobile devices • Works with different testing and reporting frameworks • Based on web standards	• Only available using JavaScript

The following `npm` command installs WebDriverIO locally. This installer displays a command-line wizard that asks for several options, such as the services (chomedriver, Selenium Server, Appium Server, CDP, or cloud providers), testing framework (Mocha, Jasmine, or Cucumber), or reporter tool (JUnit or Allure, among others):

```
npm init wdio .
```

When the previous command finishes, we can create our custom tests. For instance, Example 10-5 shows a basic WebDriverIO using Mocha. We locate this test under the folder `test` of the project scaffolding and run it through the following command:

```
npx wdio run ./wdio.conf.js
```

Example 10-5. Hello world test using WebDriverIO

```
describe('Hello World with WebDriverIO', () => {
   it('Login in the practice site', async () => {
      await browser.url(
            `https://bonigarcia.dev/selenium-webdriver-java/login-form.html`);

      await $('#username').setValue('user');
      await $('#password').setValue('user');
      await $('button[type="submit"]').click();
      await expect($('#success')).toHaveTextContaining('Login successful');
      await browser.saveScreenshot('hello-world-webdriverio.png');
   });
});
```

TestCafe

TestCafe (*https://testcafe.io*) is an open source (MIT license) cross-browser automation testing tool. The core idea of TestCafe is to avoid external drivers to support the automation process and emulate the user actions using a hybrid client-server architecture (see Figure 10-10). The server side is implemented in Node.js and contains a *proxy* that intercepts the HTTP traffic with the web application under test. TestCafe tests are also written as Node.js scripts and are executed on the server side. The *automation scripts* that emulate the user activity run on the client side on the tested page in the browser. Table 10-7 summarizes some advantages and limitations of TestCafe.

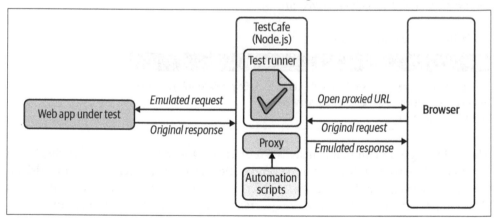

Figure 10-10. TestCafe architecture

Table 10-7. TestCafe pros and cons

Pros	Cons
• Full cross-browser support (since TestCafe only launches browsers, it can automate any browser)	• It supports only JavaScript and TypeScript • Some actions cannot be automated since it is not possible with JavaScript

We can install TestCafe easily using `npm`. Then, we can use the TestCafe CLI tool to run TestCafe scripts from the command line. The following snippet illustrates how:

```
npm install -g testcafe ❶
testcafe chrome helloworld-testcafe.js ❷
```

❶ We install TestCafe globally.

❷ We start a TestCafe basic script (Example 10-6) using Chrome as a browser.

Example 10-6. Hello world test using TestCafe

```
import { Selector } from 'testcafe';

fixture`Hello World with TestCafe`
   .page`https://bonigarcia.dev/selenium-webdriver-java/login-form.html`;
test('Login in the practice site', async t => {
   await t
      .typeText('#username', 'user')
      .typeText('#password', 'user')
      .click('button[type="submit"]')
      .expect(Selector('#success').innerText).eql('Login successful')
      .takeScreenshot();
});
```

Puppeteer

Puppeteer (*https://pptr.dev*) is an open source (MIT license) Node.js library that provides a high-level API to control Chromium-based browsers over the DevTools Protocol. Puppeteer is maintained by the Chrome DevTools team at Google. Figure 10-11 illustrates the architecture of Puppeteer. Table 10-8 presents the main advantages and drawbacks of Puppeteer.

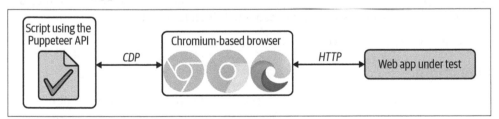

Figure 10-11. Puppeteer architecture

Table 10-8. Puppeteer pros and cons

Pros	Cons
• Fast execution and comprehensive automation capabilities (due to direct communication with the browser using CDP)	• Limited cross-browser support (only Chromium-based browsers, although there is experimental Firefox support at the time of writing) • Supports only JavaScript and TypeScript

We can install Puppeteer using npm. Then, we need to use Node.js to run Puppeteer tests (for instance, Example 10-7). The following snippet shows these commands:

```
npm install puppeteer
node helloword-puppeteer.js
```

Example 10-7. Hello world test using Puppeteer

```
const puppeteer = require('puppeteer');

(async () => {
    const browser = await puppeteer.launch(); ❶
    const page = await browser.newPage();

    await page.goto('https://bonigarcia.dev/selenium-webdriver-java/login-form.html');
    await page.type('#username', 'user');
    await page.type('#password', 'user');
    await page.click('button[type="submit"]');
    await page.waitForXPath('//*[contains(text(), "Login successful")]');
    await page.screenshot({ path: 'helloword-puppeteer.png' });

    await browser.close();
})();
```

❶ Puppeteer runs browsers in headless mode by default. It can be configured to use nonheadless browsers simply by changing this statement to:

```
const browser = await puppeteer.launch({ headless: false });
```

Playwright

Playwright (*https://playwright.dev*) is an open source (Apache 2.0 license) library for browser automation supported by Microsoft. Playwright originally started as a Node.js library. In addition to JavaScript, it now supports other programming languages, namely Python, Java, and .NET C#.

Playwright supports three types of web engines: Chromium, Firefox, and WebKit (i.e., the web browser engine used by Safari). The idea of supporting these engines is that they cover most of the browser market. Thus, the Playwright team maintains a patched version of these browsers that expose the necessary capabilities to enable the automation. These patched versions provide an event-driven architecture to access different internal browser processes (e.g., the render, network, browser, or service worker processes). Figure 10-12 illustrates this architecture. Table 10-9 contains some of the most relevant pros and cons for Playwright.

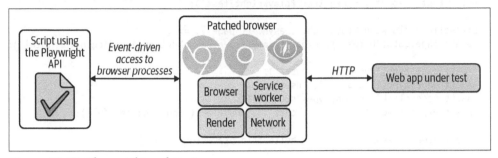

Figure 10-12. Playwright architecture

Table 10-9. Playwright pros and cons

Pros	Cons
• Autowaiting for elements to be ready • Multilanguage API • Provides a test generator by recording user actions in the browser • Allows browser session recording • Intercepts network traffic for stubbing and mocking	• Uses patched browser versions instead of actual releases

To use Playwright, we need first to install the patched browser binaries. We can use npm to that aim. The following command downloads the proper browser binaries for Chromium, Firefox, and WebKit for the operating system running this command (Windows, Linux, and macOS are supported):

```
npm install -D playwright
```

Then we can implement Playwright scripts using one supported API. For instance, when using the JavaScript API, we can use a third-party test runner (e.g., Jest, Jasmine, Mocha, etc.) or use the Playwright Test (i.e., the test runner provided by the Playwright team). To use the latter, we need to install it as follows:

```
npm install -D @playwright/test
```

Example 10-8 contains a basic Playwright JavaScript test to be executed with the Playwright runner. This command supposes that this test (called `helloworld-playwright.spec.mjs`) is located under the `tests` directory. We can invoke the Playwright runner as shown in the following snippet to run this test. This command runs Playwright tests in headless mode by default. To run browsers in nonheadless mode, you need to include the flag `--headed` at the of the command:

```
npx playwright test
```

Example 10-8. Hello world test using Playwright

```
const { test, expect } = require('@playwright/test');

test('Hello World with Playwright', async ({ page }) => {
    await page.goto('https://bonigarcia.dev/selenium-webdriver-java/login-form.html');

    await page.type('#username', 'user');
    await page.type('#password', 'user');
    await page.click('button[type="submit"]');
    await expect(page.locator('#success')).toHaveText('Login successful');

    await page.screenshot({ path: 'helloworld-playwright.png' });
});
```

Summary and Final Remarks

Web development is a heterogeneous discipline that involves many different technologies, such as client side, server side, or integration with external services, to name a few. For this reason, this chapter introduced two complementary technologies for Selenium that can be helpful in testing web applications: Appium (an open source test automation framework for mobile apps) and REST Assured (an open source Java library for testing REST services). You also learned the basics of alternative tools for implementing end-to-end tests for web applications, namely Cypress, WebDriverIO, TestCafe, Puppeteer, and Playwright. Although these alternatives deliver remarkable advantages compared to Selenium (e.g., automated waiting), in my opinion, Selenium provides a more comprehensive automation model since it is built on top of web standards, such as the W3C WebDriver and WebDriver BiDi. In addition, the Selenium project actively participates in the deelopment of these specifications.

This chapter concludes your journey through the development of end-to-end tests with Selenium. The next step is to put all the knowledge presented in this book into practice in your projects. This way, you can build your custom automation framework for your team, project, company, etc. There are many decisions you need to make, such as the project setup (e.g., Maven, Gradle), unit testing framework (e.g., JUnit, TestNG), browser infrastructure (e.g., Docker, cloud providers), and integration with third-party utilities. To deal with all of this complexity, as a final word, I recommend you play with the provided examples in this book. In other words: clone the repository, run the tests, and edit the code to fulfill your needs. I will maintain the GitHub repo after the book is published. And remember: it is an open source software project, so feel free to create a pull request to improve it if you want to contribute.

What's New in Selenium 4

This appendix provides a summary of the novelties available in Selenium 4. The aim of this content is twofold. First, it enumerates the new features in the core components of the Selenium suite (i.e., WebDriver, Driver, and IDE), providing a link to the book chapter that explains each aspect. In addition, this appendix describes other aspects of the Selenium project that changed with Selenium 4, such as documentation and governance. The second objective is to identify the deprecated parts and the corresponding new features when migrating from Selenium 3 to 4.

Selenium WebDriver

The first stable version of Selenium WebDriver 4.0.0 was released on October 13, 2021. Table A-1 summarizes the most relevant new features in this version compared with the former stable version (i.e., Selenium WebDriver 3.141.59).

Table A-1. Novelties in Selenium WebDriver 4

Feature	Description	Chapter	Section
Full adoption of W3C WebDriver	Standard communication protocol between the Selenium WebDriver API and the drivers	Chapter 1	"Selenium WebDriver" on page 5
Relative locators	Location strategy based on the proximity of other web elements	Chapter 3	"Relative Locators" on page 76
Pinned scripts	Attach a piece of JavaScript to a WebDriver session	Chapter 4	"Pinned Scripts" on page 108
Element screenshots	Capture screenshots of web elements (instead of the entire page)	Chapter 4	"WebElement Screenshots" on page 115
Shadow DOM	Seamless access to a shadow tree	Chapter 4	"The Shadow DOM" on page 118
Open new windows and tabs	Improved way to navigate to different windows and tabs	Chapter 4	"Tabs and Windows" on page 129

Feature	Description	Chapter	Section
Decorators	Wrappers for `WebDriver` objects for implementing event listeners	Chapter 4	"Event Listeners" on page 138
Chrome DevTools Protocol	Native access to the DevTools in Chromium-based browsers (e.g., Chrome and Edge)	Chapter 5	"The Chrome DevTools Protocol" on page 177
Network interception	Stubbing out the backend requests and intercepting network traffic	Chapter 5	"Network interceptor" on page 178
Basic authentication	Simplified API for basic and digest authentication	Chapter 5	"Basic and digest authentication" on page 179
Full-page screenshots	Capture the full content of a web page	Chapter 5	"Full-page screenshot" on page 183
Location context	Mock geolocation coordinates	Chapter 5	"Location Context" on page 191
Print to PDF	Save web pages as PDF documents	Chapter 5	"Print Page" on page 193
WebDriver BiDi	Bidirectional communication between driver and browser	Chapter 5	"WebDriver BiDi" on page 194

Migration Guide

This section summarizes the changes you need to make to migrate an existing codebase that uses Selenium WebDriver 3 to version 4.

Locators

The utility methods to find elements (`FindsBy` interfaces) have been removed in Selenium WebDriver 4. Table A-2 compares the old and new API for finding Web Elements in Selenium WebDriver. You can find more details about this feature in "Locating WebElements" on page 59.

Table A-2. Migration of web element location in Selenium WebDriver 4

Selenium WebDriver 3	Selenium WebDriver 4
`driver.findElementByTagName("tagName");`	`driver.findElement(By.tagName("tagName"));`
`driver.findElementByLinkText("link");`	`driver.findElement(By.linkText("link"));`
`driver`	`driver.findElement(By`
`    .findElementByPartialLinkText("partLink");`	`    .partialLinkText("partLink"));`
`driver.findElementByName("name");`	`driver.findElement(By.name("name"));`
`driver.findElementById("id");`	`driver.findElement(By.id("id"));`
`driver.findElementByClassName("class");`	`driver.findElement(By.className("class"));`
`driver.findElementByCssSelector("css");`	`driver.findElement(By.cssSelector("css"));`
`driver.findElementByXPath("xPath");`	`driver.findElement(By.xpath("xPath"));`

User gestures

The class `Actions` allows emulating complex user gestures (such as drag and drop, hovering, mouse movements, etc.). As illustrated in Table A-3, the API exposed by this class has been simplified in Selenium WebDriver 4. "User Gestures" on page 86 contains further information and examples about this class.

Table A-3. Migration of the Actions class in Selenium WebDriver 4

Selenium WebDriver 3	Selenium WebDriver 4

`actions.moveToElement(webElement).click();`
`actions.moveToElement(webElement).doubleClick();`
`actions.moveToElement(webElement).contextClick();`
`actions.moveToElement(webElement).clickAndHold();`
`actions.moveToElement(webElement).release();`
	`actions.click(webElement);`
	`actions.clickAndHold(webElement);`
	`actions.contextClick(webElement);`
	`actions.doubleClick(webElement);`
	`actions.release(webElement);`

Waits and timeouts

The parameters to specify timeouts have switched from `TimeUnit` to `Duration`. Table A-4 describes this change. You can see more detail in "Waiting Strategies" on page 94 and "Timeouts" on page 110.

Table A-4. Migration of waits and timeouts in Selenium WebDriver 4

Selenium WebDriver 3	Selenium WebDriver 4

`new WebDriverWait(driver, 3).`
`    until(ExpectedConditions.`
`    elementToBeClickable(By.id("id")));`
	`new WebDriverWait(driver,`
	`    Duration.ofSeconds(3)).until(`
	`    ExpectedConditions.`
	`    elementToBeClickable(By.id("id")));`

`Wait<WebDriver> wait =`
`    new FluentWait<WebDriver>(driver)`
`    .withTimeout(30, TimeUnit.SECONDS)`
`    .pollingEvery(5, TimeUnit.SECONDS)`
`    .ignoring(NoSuchElementException.class);`
	`Wait<WebDriver> wait =`
	`    new FluentWait<WebDriver>(driver)`
	`    .withTimeout(Duration.ofSeconds(30))`
	`    .pollingEvery(Duration.ofSeconds(5))`
	`    .ignoring(NoSuchElementException.class);`

`driver.manage().timeouts()`
`    .implicitlyWait(10, TimeUnit.SECONDS);`
`driver.manage().timeouts()`
`    .setScriptTimeout(3, TimeUnit.MINUTES);`
`driver.manage().timeouts()`
`    .pageLoadTimeout(30, TimeUnit.SECONDS);`
	`driver.manage().timeouts()`
	`    .implicitlyWait(Duration.ofSeconds(10));`
	`driver.manage().timeouts()`
	`    .scriptTimeout(Duration.ofMinutes(3));`
	`driver.manage().timeouts()`
	`    .pageLoadTimeout(Duration.ofSeconds(30));`

Event listeners

In Selenium WebDriver 3, we used the class `EventFiringWebDriver` to create event listeners. This class is deprecated in Selenium WebDriver 4, and instead, the class `EventFiringDecorator` is recommended. Table A-5 summarizes this change. "Event Listeners" on page 138 contains a complete example of this feature.

Table A-5. Migration of event listeners in Selenium WebDriver 4

Selenium WebDriver 3	Selenium WebDriver 4

`EventFiringWebDriver newDriver =`
`    new EventFiringWebDriver(originalDriver);`
`wrapper.register(myListener);`
	`WebDriver newDriver =`
	`    new EventFiringDecorator(myListener)`
	`    .decorate(originalDriver);`

Capabilities

The static methods for selecting different browser types have been removed in Selenium WebDriver 4. Instead, we should use browser-specific options. Table A-6 summarizes this change. "Browser Capabilities" on page 145 contains more details and examples.

Table A-6. Migration of desired capabilities in Selenium WebDriver 4

Selenium WebDriver 3	Selenium WebDriver 4

DesiredCapabilities caps =
    DesiredCapabilities.chrome();
	ChromeOptions options =
	    new ChromeOptions();

DesiredCapabilities caps =
    DesiredCapabilities.edge();
	EdgeOptions options =
	    new EdgeOptions();

DesiredCapabilities caps =
    DesiredCapabilities.firefox();
	FirefoxOptions options =
	    new FirefoxOptions();

DesiredCapabilities caps =
    DesiredCapabilities.internetExplorer();
	InternetExplorerOptions options =
	    new InternetExplorerOptions();

DesiredCapabilities caps =
    DesiredCapabilities.safari();
	SafariOptions options =
	    new SafariOptions();

DesiredCapabilities caps =
    DesiredCapabilities.chrome();
	ChromeOptions options =
	    new ChromeOptions();

Then, the WebDriver constructors based on capabilities are deprecated instead of browser-specific options. Table A-7 shows an example of this process. You can find examples using this constructor "Browser Capabilities" on page 145.

Table A-7. Migration of WebDriver instantiation using capabilities in Selenium WebDriver 4

Selenium WebDriver 3	Selenium WebDriver 4
WebDriver driver = new ChromeDriver(caps);	WebDriver driver = new ChromeDriver(options);

Moreover, how capabilities are merged has changed in Selenium WebDriver 4. In Selenium WebDriver 3, it was possible to combine capabilities by mutating the calling object. This process is different in Selenium WebDriver 4, in which the merge operation needs to be assigned. Table A-8 provides an example of this change.

Table A-8. Migration of merging capabilities in Selenium WebDriver 4

Selenium WebDriver 3	Selenium WebDriver 4

MutableCapabilities caps =
    new MutableCapabilities();
 caps.setCapability("platformName",
    "Linux");
 ChromeOptions options =
    new ChromeOptions();
 options.setHeadless(true);
 options.merge(caps);
	MutableCapabilities caps =
	    new MutableCapabilities();
	 caps.setCapability("platformName",
	    "Linux");
	 ChromeOptions options =
	    new ChromeOptions();
	 options.setHeadless(true);
	 options = options.merge(caps);

Finally, the `BrowserType` interface has been deprecated in favor of the new `Browser` interface. Table A-9 illustrates the difference between these interfaces when specifying capabilities. You can find more details about this aspect in "Creation of RemoteWebDriver Objects" on page 199.

Table A-9. Migration of capabilities in Selenium WebDriver 4

Selenium WebDriver 3	Selenium WebDriver 4

`caps.setCapability("browserName",`
    `BrowserType.CHROME);`
	`caps.setCapability("browserName",`
	    `Browser.CHROME);`

Selenium Grid

Selenium Grid 4 has been completely rewritten from scratch. The new codebase has been created with all the learning from Selenium Grid 3, improving its source code maintainability. Selenium Grid 4 supports the classical mode implemented in version 3, i.e., the standalone and the hub-nodes architecture. In addition, Selenium Grid provides a fully distributed architecture to improve its overall performance and scalability. Finally, Selenium Grid 4 uses modern infrastructure technologies such as Docker, Kubernetes, or distributed tracing using OpenTelemetry.

"Selenium Grid" on page 6 provides an introduction to Selenium Grid. Then, "Selenium Grid" on page 203 explains the details of the different modes of Selenium Grid (i.e., standalone, hub-nodes, and fully distributed), and how to use it from Selenium WebDriver tests.

Migration guide

When using Selenium Grid as a Java dependency and bumping to version 4, in addition to the version upgrade, you should know that the project coordinates changed in Selenium Grid 4. Previously, the `artifactId` was `selenium-server`. This value has changed to `selenium-grid` in Selenium Grid 4. Table A-10 contains the new coordinates of Selenium Grid 4 in Maven and Gradle.

Table A-10. Migration of Selenium Grid 4 as Maven and Gradle dependency

Selenium WebDriver 3	Selenium WebDriver 4

`<dependency>`
`  <groupId>org.seleniumhq.selenium</groupId>`
`  <artifactId>selenium-server</artifactId>`
`  <version>3.141.59</version>`
`</dependency>`
	`<dependency>`
	`  <groupId>org.seleniumhq.selenium</groupId>`
	`  <artifactId>selenium-grid</artifactId>`
	`  <version>4.0.0</version>`
	`</dependency>`

`testImplementation("org.seleniumhq.selenium:`
    `selenium-server:3.141.59")`
	`testImplementation("org.seleniumhq.selenium:`
	    `selenium-grid:4.0.0")`

Selenium IDE

Selenium IDE is introduced in "Selenium IDE" on page 8. Some of the new features available as of Selenium 4 are:

Backup element selectors
> Selenium IDE records multiple locators (e.g., by id, XPath, or CSS selector) for each element. This way, if the test execution does not locate an element using the first locator, it will fall back to the following until it is found.

Control flows
> Selenium IDE enhances script execution using conditionals (i.e., `if`, `else`, `else if`, and `end`) and loops (i.e., `do`, `while`, `times`, and `forEach`) .

Code export
> Selenium IDE allows exporting the recording to several Selenium WebDriver binding languages (i.e., C#, Java, JavaScript, Python, and Ruby) and unit testing frameworks (i.e., NUnit, xUnit, JUnit, Mocha, pytest, and RSpec).

Plug-ins
> We can extend the Selenium IDE (e.g., introducing new commands or third-party integration) using custom add-ons.

Other Novelties

The official Selenium documentation has been significantly improved with Selenium 4. The new site is available on *https://www.selenium.dev*, and it covers the Selenium subprojects (WebDriver, IDE, and Grid), user guide, blog, support, and other project information.

Last but not least, Simon Stewart, the cocreator of Selenium WebDriver and Selenium project lead since 2009, stepped down as leader of the Selenium project on October 27, 2021. You can find the current project structure (composed of the project leadership committee, technical leadership committee, and Selenium committers and triggers) and governance (i.e., model, philosophy, project roles, decision-making process, etc.) on the Selenium website (*https://www.selenium.dev/project*).

Driver Management

As discussed in Chapter 1, driver management involves three steps: download, setup, and maintenance. Manual driver management is costly in terms of effort and potentially problematic regarding maintainability. For this reason, I use WebDriverManager to carry out this process in an automated and automaintained manner in all the examples of this book. For completeness, this appendix also describes the involved steps (download, setup, and maintenance) in manual driver management.

WebDriverManager: Automated Driver Management

WebDriverManager (*https://bonigarcia.dev/webdrivermanager*) is an open source Java library that manages the drivers required by Selenium WebDriver (e.g., chromedriver, geckodriver, msedgedriver, etc.) in an automated manner. WebDriverManager provides a set of *managers* for different browsers, namely Chrome, Firefox, Edge, Opera, Chromium, and Internet Explorer.

WebDriverManager internally executes a *resolution algorithm* to manage the drivers required by each browser. This algorithm aims to automatically discover, download, set up, and maintain these drivers.

Figure B-1 represents this algorithm in the context of the methodology implemented by WebDriverManager. For each manager (e.g., `chromedriver()`, `firefoxdriver()`, etc.), the resolution algorithm works as follows:

1. WebDriverManager tries to find the browser version (e.g., Chrome) installed in the local machine. For that, it uses an internal knowledge database called *commands database*. This database contains a list of shell commands (in different operating systems) that allow discovering the browser versions (e.g., `google-chrome --version` in Linux).

2. Using the found major browser version (e.g., Chrome 89), WebDriverManager determines the correct driver version (e.g., chromedriver 89.0.4389.23). I call this process *version resolution*. To ease this process, several driver maintainers (i.e., chromedriver and msedgedriver) publish the specific driver version in their online repositories using simple text files (e.g., *https://chromedriver.storage.googleapis.com/LATEST_RELEASE_89*). Unfortunately, this information is not available for other drivers, such as geckodriver or operadriver. For this reason, WebDriverManager uses another internal knowledge database (called *versions database*) to keep the association between the versions of browsers and drivers. Both versions and commands databases synchronize their values using an online master reference stored on GitHub.

3. WebDriverManager downloads the specific driver for the local operating system (Windows, Linux, or macOS) and stores it in the local file system in the *driver cache* (by default, in the path ~/.cache/selenium).

4. Finally, WebDriverManager exports the downloaded driver path using the proper Java system property (e.g., webdriver.chrome.driver).

For the sake of performance and maintainability, WebDriverManager internally uses a *resolution cache*. This cache (by default stored in the driver cache as a properties file) keeps the relationship between the resolved driver versions. This relationship is valid following a *time-to-live* (TTL) approach. The default value of this TTL is one day for drivers (e.g., chromedriver 89.0.4389.23) and one hour for browsers (e.g., Chrome 89). The resolution algorithm resolves drivers using the cached files in the subsequent invocations (this usually happens in a Selenium WebDriver test suite). Then, when a TTL expires, the resolution algorithm tries to resolve a new driver release. Finally, when a different browser version is detected, WebDriverManager downloads the new driver (if required). Thanks to this process, the version compliance of browser and driver is guaranteed even for evergreen browsers.

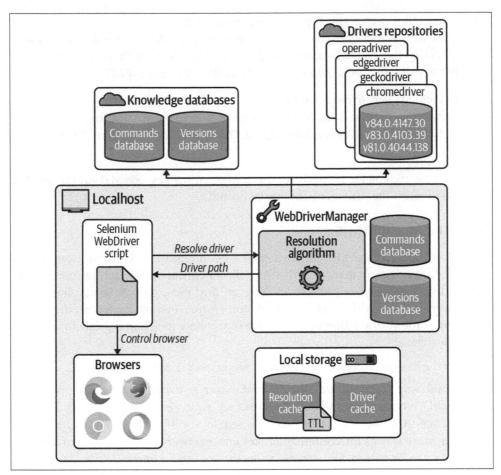

Figure B-1. WebDriverManager methodology

Generic Manager

In addition to the browser-specific managers (e.g., `chromedriver()`, `firefox driver()`, etc.), WebDriverManager provides a *generic* manager, i.e., a manager that can be parameterized to act as a specific manager (for Chrome, Firefox, etc.). This feature is available using the method `getInstance()` of the WebDriverManager API. There are different options to invoke this method:

`getInstance(Class<? extends WebDriver> webDriverClass)`
> Where `webDriverClass` is a class of the `WebDriver` hierarchy, such as `Chrome Driver.class`, `FirefoxDriver.class`, etc.

getInstance(DriverManagerType driverManagerType)

> Where driverManagerType is an enumeration provided by WebDriverManager to identify the available managers. The possible values of this enumeration are CHROME, FIREFOX, EDGE, OPERA, CHROMIUM, IEXPLORER, and SAFARI.

getInstance(String browserName)

> Where browserName is the browser name as case-insensitive string. The possible values are Chrome, Firefox, Edge, Opera, Chromium, IExplorer, and Safari.

getInstance()

> When no parameter is specified, the configuration key wdm.defaultBrowser is used to select the manager (Chrome by default).

Advanced Configuration

WebDriverManager provides different ways of configuration. First, you can use its Java API through each manager. This API allows concatenating several methods to specify custom options or preferences. You can find the complete description of the WebDriverManager API in its documentation (*https://bonigarcia.dev/webdriverman ager*). For example, the following command shows how to set up a proxy for the network connection:

```
WebDriverManager.chromedriver().proxy("server:port").setup();
```

The second way to configure WebDriverManager is using Java system properties. Each WebDriverManager API method has an equivalent configuration key. For instance, the API method cachePath() (used to specify the driver cache folder) works the same way as the configuration key wdm.cachePath. These types of configuration keys can be passed, for example, using the command line:

```
mvn test -Dwdm.cachePath=/custom/path/to/driver/cache
```

Finally, you can also use environment variables to configure WebDriverManager. The variable names derive from each configuration key (e.g., wdm.cachePath), converting them to uppercase and replacing the symbol . with _ (e.g., WDM_CACHEPATH). This mechanism can be convenient for configuring global parameters at the operating system level.

Other Uses

In addition to serving as a Java dependency, WebDriverManager can be used in other ways, namely:

As a command-line interface (CLI) tool
> This mode allows you to resolve drivers (e.g., chromedriver, geckodriver). In addition, this mode allows you to execute browsers in Docker containers and interact with them through a remote desktop session.

As a server
> The WebDriverManager Server is based on HTTP and offers two types of services. First, it exposes a simple RESTlike API to resolve drivers. Second, it acts as a regular Selenium Server, and therefore, you can use it with different language bindings than Java.

As a Java agent
> In this case, and using the JVM instrumentation API, WebDriverManager uses the Java instrumentation API to check the objects being created in the JVM. When WebDriver objects are instantiated (`ChromeDriver`, `FirefoxDriver`, etc.), the required manager is used to resolve its driver (`chromedriver`, `geckodriver`, etc.). Thanks to this approach, you can get rid of the WebDriverManager call from your tests.

Manual Driver Management

This section describes how to manually implement the driver management process (download, setup, and maintenance).

Download

The first step for driver management is to download the proper driver. Table B-1 shows the websites to obtain the drivers for the main browsers. You need to find the correct driver version and platform (Windows, Linux, macOS) for the browser you plan to use. Regarding the version, the Chrome and Edge (although not Firefox, unfortunately) maintainers follow the same versioning schema for drivers and browsers to ease this process. So, for instance, if you use Chrome or Edge 91.x, you also need to use chromedriver and msedgedriver 91.x. You will find the specific driver version in the documentation provided on the websites. For instance, to use Chrome 91, you need to download ChromeDriver 91.0.4472.19.

Table B-1. Java system properties to set up drivers

Browser	Driver	Download website
Chrome/Chromium	chromedriver	*https://chromedriver.chromium.org/downloads*
Edge	msedgedriver	*https://developer.microsoft.com/en-us/microsoft-edge/tools/webdriver*
Firefox	geckodriver	*https://github.com/mozilla/geckodriver/releases*

Setup

Once you have the required driver for your WebDriver script, you need to set it up correctly. There are two ways to carry out this process. The first one is adding the driver location (the full path or the parent folder that contains the driver) to your PATH environmental variable (*env*). The PATH env is standard in Unix-like (e.g., Linux and macOS) and Windows operating systems. This environmental variable allows specifying a set of folders where the operating system locates executable programs. The way we configure PATH (and other environmental variables) depends on the specific operating system. For example, in Windows systems, we can do it using its GUI (Control Panel → System → Advanced → Environment Variables). In a Unix-like system, we can use the command line to carry out this process, for instance, using the following command (or equivalent):

```
export PATH=$PATH:/path/to/drivers >> ~/.profile
```

The second way to set up the driver is using *Java system properties*, which are configuration attributes (in the form of name/value) passed to the JVM. Table B-2 summarizes the names for the main drivers in Selenium WebDriver. The value for these properties is the full path of a given driver (e.g., /path/to/drivers/chromedriver).

Table B-2. Java system properties to set up drivers

Browser	Driver	Java system property name
Chrome/Chromium	chromedriver	webdriver.chrome.driver
Edge	msedgedriver	webdriver.edge.driver
Firefox	geckodriver	webdriver.gecko.driver

There are two ways to configure these properties: the command line (passing the system property using the -Dname=value syntax) or Java code. For example, Example B-1 shows the Maven and Gradle commands to execute all the tests of a given project while passing the properties to set up the drivers for Chrome, Edge, and Firefox. Then, Example B-2 shows how to make the same configuration, but this time using Java.

Example B-1. Maven and Gradle commands to configure system properties in the command line

```
mvn test -Dwebdriver.chrome.driver=/path/to/drivers/chromedriver
mvn test -Dwebdriver.edge.driver=/path/to/drivers/msedgedriver
mvn test -Dwebdriver.gecko.driver=/path/to/drivers/geckodriver

gradle test -Dwebdriver.chrome.driver=/path/to/drivers/chromedriver
gradle test -Dwebdriver.edge.driver=/path/to/drivers/msedgedriver
gradle test -Dwebdriver.gecko.driver=/path/to/drivers/geckodriver
```

Example B-2. Java commands to configure system properties

```
System.setProperty("webdriver.chrome.driver", "/path/to/drivers/chromedriver");
System.setProperty("webdriver.edge.driver", "/path/to/drivers/msedgedriver");
System.setProperty("webdriver.gecko.driver", "/path/to/drivers/geckodriver");
```

Maintenance

Last but not least, the final step of driver management is to maintain these drivers. This maintenance is necessary because evergreen browsers (such as Chrome, Edge, or Firefox) upgrade themselves automatically. Although appealing from a user perspective, this automated upgrade is problematic for Selenium WebDriver scripts where the driver management is manual. In this case, driver and browser compatibility is not guaranteed in the long run.

A specific driver (e.g., chromedriver version 84.0.4147.30) is typically compatible with a given browser version (e.g., Chrome 84). Eventually, this compatibility is not guaranteed because of the automatic upgrade. As a result, a Selenium WebDriver script based on this driver stops working (i.e., the test is said to be broken). In practice, Selenium WebDriver developers experience this problem when tests fail because of driver and browser incompatibility. For instance, when using Chrome as a browser, a broken test due to driver incompatibility reports the following error message: "this version of chromedriver only supports Chrome version N" (where N is the latest version of Chrome supported by a particular version of chromedriver). To illustrate this problem, Figure B-2 shows the worldwide search interest of that error message on Google during 2019 and 2020, together with the release date of the different Chrome versions in this period. As you can see, the interest over time concerning this error message is related to some Chrome releases.

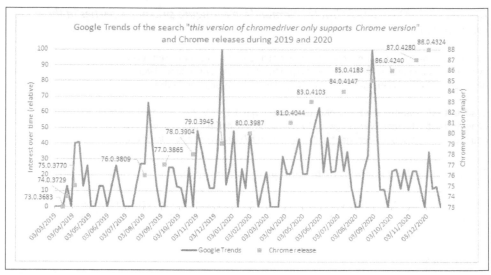

Figure B-2. Worldwide relative interest over time of the search term "this version of chromedriver only supports chrome version" in Google Trends together with the release dates of Chrome during 2019 and 2020

Summary

Selenium WebDriver is a library that allows you to control web browsers programmatically. The automation is based on the native capabilities of each browser. Therefore, we need to place a platform-dependent binary file called *driver* between the script/test using the Selenium WebDriver API and the browser. Some examples of drivers are chromedriver (for Chrome), geckodriver (for Firefox), and msedgedriver (for Edge). This appendix presented the driver management process. This process has three steps (download, setup, and maintenance), and it can be done either manually or automatically. By default, I recommend you use an automated driver management approach. To that aim, the reference tool in Java is WebDriverManager.

Examples Repository Setup

The examples repository (*https://github.com/bonigarcia/selenium-webdriver-java*) is a vital ingredient of this book as it contains all the covered examples and the complete configuration of Maven and Gradle. In addition, this repo uses several services provided by GitHub, such as:

GitHub Pages (https://pages.github.com)
> A service that allows hosting public websites configured straight from a GitHub repository. I use a simple website linked to the examples repository to showcase web pages used as SUT in the Selenium WebDriver test examples: *https://bonigar cia.dev/selenium-webdriver-java*. As you can see, it contains different HTML pages using Bootstrap (*https://getbootstrap.com*) as a CSS framework.

GitHub Actions (https://github.com/features/actions)
> A CI/CD build server for GitHub repositories. I use this service to build and test the whole repo with each new commit. You can see the details about the workflow configuration at the end of this section.

Dependabot (https://github.com/dependabot)
> A bot that automatically updates the project dependencies. When this bot detects a new version for any Maven and Gradle dependencies (see the following subsection for more details), it creates a pull request with the corresponding update.

In the rest of this appendix, you will find the configuration details for the examples repository. This configuration includes the Maven and Gradle dependencies declaration and other aspects, and it should be sufficient for standard projects using Selenium WebDriver. In addition, the final part of this appendix explains how to configure the logging libraries, Dependabot, and GitHub Actions (to build and test the project following a CI approach).

Project Layout

Figure C-1 shows the schematic representation of the examples repository layout.

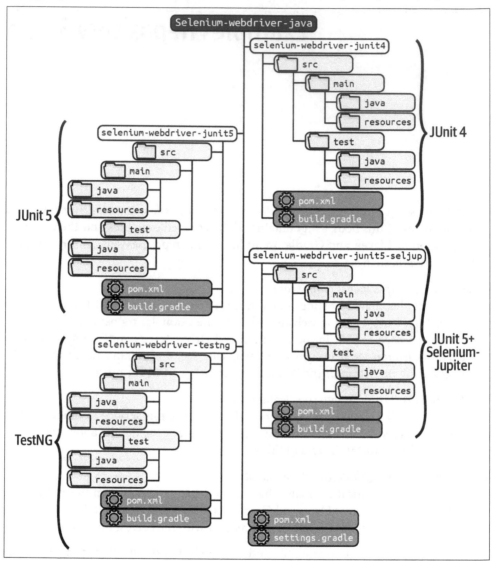

Figure C-1. Layout of the examples repository (hosted on GitHub)

Since I am providing each example in four flavors (JUnit 4, JUnit 5, JUnit 5 plus Selenium-Jupiter, and TestNG), the configuration in both Maven and Gradle is based on *multiprojects*. This way, the examples repository has four modules, one per testing framework: `selenium-webdriver-junit4`, `selenium-webdriver-junit5`, `selenium-webdriver-junit5-seljup`, and `selenium-webdriver-testng`. In Maven, the multiproject setup is in the `pom.xml` located in the root folder, and in the file `settings.gradle` in Gradle.

As you can see in Figure C-1, each module has the same structure. You can find the test source code in `src/test/java` folder. I use Java packages to divide the examples per chapter (e.g., `io.github.bonigarcia.webdriver.jupiter.ch02.helloworld`). Then, each project needs its own Logback configuration file. I use the general configuration file (i.e., `logback.xml`) placed under the folder `src/main/resources`. I follow this convention since it is quite usual to use logging also for the application, and in case you plan to reuse this project structure, this is the standard approach. Finally, at the root of each subproject, you can find the specific configuration file for Maven (`pom.xml`) and Gradle (`build.gradle`). You can find the declaration for the dependencies in these files, as explained in the following section.

Maven

A core concept in Maven is the *build lifecycle*, the name given to the process of building and distributing a particular project. There are three standard build lifecycles in Maven: `default` (for project deployment), `clean` (for project cleaning), and `site` (for documentation). These build lifecycles have a list of *build phases*, wherein each phase represents a stage in the lifecycle. The primary phases of the `default` lifecycle are:

validate
: Assess the project is correct and all necessary information is available.

compile
: Compile the source code.

test
: Execute test using a unit testing framework.

package
: Bundle the compiled code into a distributable format, such as a Java ARchive (JAR) file.

verify
: Execute further tests (typically integration or other high-level tests).

install
: Install the package into the local repository.

deploy
: Install the package into a remote repository or server.

We can use the shell to invoke Maven, using the command mvn. For instance, the following command invokes the clean lifecycle (i.e., clean the target folder and all its content) and then it invokes in cascade all the phases of the default lifecycle until package (i.e., validate, compile, test, and finally, package):

```
mvn clean package
```

Another core element in Maven is the concept of *plug-ins*. A plug-in is a built-in artifact that executes the phases mentioned above. In this book, we are particularly interested in testing. Therefore, we focus on the phases test and verify and their corresponding plug-ins: maven-surefire-plugin and maven-failsafe-plugin, respectively. Table C-1 summarizes the main differences between these two plug-ins.

Table C-1. Differences between the Surefire and Failsafe Maven plug-ins

	maven-surefire-plugin	maven-failsafe-plugin
Description	Maven plug-in to execute tests before packaging	Maven plug-in to execute tests after packaging
Classic use	Unit tests	Integration (and other high-level) tests
Basic command	mvn test	mvn verify
Type	Default plug-in (i.e., we can use it without declaring it in the pom.xml)	Not default plug-in (i.e., we need to declare it in the pom.xml to use it)
Used version	Defined internally in Maven	Latest available version
Test name pattern	**/Test*.java **/*Test.java **/*Tests.java **/*TestCase.java	**/IT*.java **/*IT.java **/*ITCase.java

For simplicity, I use only maven-surefire-plugin for executing tests in the examples repository. Although these tests are not a unit (in fact, they are end-to-end), it is not a problem to run them with maven-surefire-plugin (i.e., after compilation and before packaging). Table C-2 summarizes the basic commands to run tests from the shell using this plug-in.

Table C-2. Basic commands for running tests with maven-surefire-plugin

Command	Description
mvn test	Run all tests in the project
mvn test -Dtest=MyClass	Run all tests in a single class
mvn test -Dtest=MyClass#myMethod	Run a single test in a single class

Nevertheless, if you want to use maven-failsafe-plugin to execute tests, you need to use the setup shown in Example C-1 in your pom.xml file. Finally, you can run the tests using the command mvn verify (i.e., run tests after packaging).

Example C-1. Required Maven configuration for using `maven-failsafe-plugin`

```
<build>
    <plugins>
        <plugin>
            <groupId>org.apache.maven.plugins</groupId>
            <artifactId>maven-failsafe-plugin</artifactId>
            <executions>
                <execution>
                    <goals>
                        <goal>integration-test</goal>
                        <goal>verify</goal>
                    </goals>
                </execution>
            </executions>
        </plugin>
    </plugins>
</build>
```

Common Setup

Example C-2 contains the common parts of the Maven configuration in the examples repository.

Example C-2. Common Maven dependencies in the examples repository

```
<properties>
    <java.version>1.8</java.version>  ❶
    <maven.compiler.target>${java.version}</maven.compiler.target>
    <maven.compiler.source>${java.version}</maven.compiler.source>
</properties>

<dependencies>  ❷
    <dependency>
        <groupId>org.slf4j</groupId>
        <artifactId>slf4j-api</artifactId>
        <version>${slf4j.version}</version>
    </dependency>
    <dependency>
        <groupId>ch.qos.logback</groupId>
        <artifactId>logback-classic</artifactId>
        <version>${logback.version}</version>
    </dependency>

    <dependency>
        <groupId>org.seleniumhq.selenium</groupId>
        <artifactId>selenium-java</artifactId>
        <version>${selenium.version}</version>
        <scope>test</scope>
    </dependency>
    <dependency>
```

```
        <groupId>org.assertj</groupId>
        <artifactId>assertj-core</artifactId>
        <version>${assertj.version}</version>
        <scope>test</scope>
    </dependency>
    <dependency>
        <groupId>io.github.bonigarcia</groupId>
        <artifactId>webdrivermanager</artifactId>
        <version>${wdm.version}</version>
        <scope>test</scope>
    </dependency>
</dependencies>

<build>
    <plugins>
        <plugin> ❸
            <groupId>org.apache.maven.plugins</groupId>
            <artifactId>maven-surefire-plugin</artifactId>
            <version>${maven-surefire-plugin.version}</version>
        </plugin>
    </plugins>
</build>
```

❶ We use Java 8 in this project.

❷ We specify the common dependencies. On the one hand, we declare Selenium
    WebDriver, AssertJ, and WebDriverManager using the test scope. This way, we
    can use these dependencies only from the test logic (i.e., Java classes under the
    src/test/java folder). On the other hand, the scope of Simple Logging Facade
    for Java (SLF4J) and Logback is missing, and therefore Maven uses the default,
    which is compile. This means we can use these dependencies from both the
    application and the test logic. Finally, notice we use Maven properties to declare
    the dependency versions (e.g., ${selenium.version}). You can find the precise
    version in the online repository.

❸ We need to declare a specific version of maven-surefire-plugin. As explained in
    Table C-1, the version used for this plug-in is defined internally by Maven. But to
    make the most of this plug-in, we need to specify a newer version.

JUnit 4

In a Maven project using JUnit 4 as the unit testing framework, we also need to
declare the following dependency:

```
<dependency>
    <groupId>junit</groupId>
    <artifactId>junit</artifactId>
    <version>${junit4.version}</version>
```

```
        <scope>test</scope>
    </dependency>
```

JUnit 5

Although JUnit 5 is a modular framework, we can declare a single dependency to use the Jupiter programming model in a Maven project. As you can see in the snippet below, this artifact is called `junit-jupiter`, and it transitively pulls the following JUnit 5 artifacts:

`junit-jupiter-api`
> For developing tests

`junit-jupiter-engine`
> For executing tests in the JUnit Platform

`junit-jupiter-params`
> For developing parameterized tests (see Chapter 8)

```
<dependencies>
    <dependency>
        <groupId>org.junit.jupiter</groupId>
        <artifactId>junit-jupiter</artifactId>
        <version>${junit5.version}</version>
        <scope>test</scope>
    </dependency>
</dependencies>
```

Selenium-Jupiter

When using Jupiter in conjunction with Selenium-Jupiter, in addition to the previous artifacts (`junit-jupiter` and `maven-surefire-plugin`), we need to include the coordinates of Selenium-Jupiter (see the next code sample). In this case, we can remove the coordinates of WebDriverManager since Selenium-Jupiter transitively pulls it.

```
<dependency>
    <groupId>io.github.bonigarcia</groupId>
    <artifactId>selenium-jupiter</artifactId>
    <version>${selenium-jupiter.version}</version>
    <scope>test</scope>
</dependency>
```

TestNG

Finally, the coordinates we need to include in our `pom.xml` to use TestNG are:

```
<dependency>
    <groupId>org.testng</groupId>
    <artifactId>testng</artifactId>
    <version>${testng.version}</version>
```

```
    <scope>test</scope>
  </dependency>
```

Although not used in the examples repository, TestNG tests can also be executed on the JUnit Platform. If you want to enable this mode, you need to add the TestNG engine for the JUnit Platform to your project setup. You can see more information about that on the TestNG engine page (*https://github.com/junit-team/testng-engine*).

Other Dependencies

This book explains other dependencies used in conjunction with Selenium Web-Driver. Table C-3 summarizes these dependencies and the chapter in which they are presented.

Table C-3. Dependencies for third-party integration in the example repository

Dependency	Chapter	groupId	artifactId
HtmlUnitDriver	Chapter 1	org.seleniumhq.selenium	htmlunit-driver
Selenium Grid	Chapter 6	org.seleniumhq.selenium	selenium-grid
rerunner-jupiter	Chapter 8	io.github.artsok	rerunner-jupiter
JUnit Platform Launcher	Chapter 8	org.junit.platform	junit-platform-launcher
Awaitility	Chapter 9	org.awaitility	awaitility
BrowserMob	Chapter 9	net.lightbody.bmp	browsermob-core
OWASP ZAP Client API	Chapter 9	org.zaproxy	zap-clientapi
Axe Selenium Integration	Chapter 9	com.deque.html.axe-core	selenium
Selenide	Chapter 9	com.codeborne	selenide
JavaFaker	Chapter 9	com.github.javafaker	javafaker
Extent Reports	Chapter 9	com.aventstack	extentreports
Allure	Chapter 9	io.qameta.allure	io.qameta.allure allure-junit5 allure-testng
Cucumber Java	Chapter 9	io.cucumber	cucumber-java
Cucumber JUnit 4, 5 or TestNG	Chapter 9	io.cucumber	cucumber-junit cucumber-junit-platform-engine cucumber-testng
Spring-Boot Web	Chapter 9	org.springframework.boot	spring-boot-starter-web
Spring-Boot Test	Chapter 9	org.springframework.boot	spring-boot-starter-test
Appium Java client	Chapter 10	io.appium	java-client
REST Assured	Chapter 10	io.rest-assured	rest-assured

In addition, the plug-ins statement needs some extra setup for using some of these third-party dependencies. The following snippet shows this new setup.

```
<build>
    <plugins>
        <plugin>
            <groupId>org.apache.maven.plugins</groupId>
            <artifactId>maven-surefire-plugin</artifactId>
            <version>${maven-surefire-plugin.version}</version>
            <!-- The following setup is required only when using Allure --> ❶
            <configuration>
                <properties>
                    <property>
                        <name>listener</name>
                        <value>io.qameta.allure.junit4.AllureJunit4</value> ❷
                    </property>
                </properties>
            </configuration>
            <!-- /Allure -->
        </plugin>
        <plugin> ❸
            <groupId>io.qameta.allure</groupId>
            <artifactId>allure-maven</artifactId>
            <version>${allure-maven.version}</version>
        </plugin>
        <plugin> ❹
            <groupId>org.springframework.boot</groupId>
            <artifactId>spring-boot-maven-plugin</artifactId>
            <version>${spring-boot.version}</version>
        </plugin>
    </plugins>
</build>
```

❶ This setup (from this line to `<!-- /Allure -->`) is required only if you plan to use Allure to generate a test report. If you do not use it, you can safely remove it from your project.

❷ The listener class changes for the different unit testing frameworks:

  - `io.qameta.allure.junit4.AllureJunit4` for JUnit 4

  - `io.qameta.allure.junit5.AllureJunit5` for JUnit 5 (and JUnit 5 plus Selenium-Jupiter)

  - No listener is required for TestNG

❸ In addition to the listener, the Allure plug-in is required when using this reporter tool.

❹ The Spring-Boot plug-in is recommended when using Spring-Boot.

Gradle

Each Gradle project is composed of several *tasks*. Each task represents an atomic piece of work within the build. Typical examples of tasks in a Java project are:

compileJava
> Compiles the application logic (i.e., Java classes in the folder src/main/java).

processResources
> Copies the application resources (i.e., files in the folder src/main/resources) into the output folder (build).

compileTestJava
> Compiles the test logic (i.e., Java classes in the folder src/test/java).

processTestResources
> Copies the test resources (i.e., files in the folder src/test/resources) into the output folder.

test
> Runs the tests using JUnit or TestNG. Table C-4 summarizes common commands to run Gradle tests in the shell.

clean
> Deletes the project output folder and its content.

Table C-4. Basic commands for running tests with Gradle

Command	Description
gradle test	Run all tests in the project
gradle test --rerun-tasks	Run all tests in the project (even if everything is up-to-date)
gradle test --tests MyClass	Run all tests in a single class
gradle test --tests MyClass.MyMethod	Run a single test in a single class

Example C-3 contains the common configuration for all the subprojects of the examples repository. I explain the relevant parts of this snippet next.

Example C-3. Common setup for Gradle projects

```
plugins {
    id "java" ❶
}

compileTestJava { ❷
    sourceCompatibility = 1.8
    targetCompatibility = 1.8
```

```
        options.compilerArgs += "-parameters"
}

test {
    testLogging { ❸
        events "passed", "skipped", "failed"
        showStandardStreams = true
    }

    systemProperties System.properties ❹

    if (project.hasProperty("excludeTests")) { ❺
        "$excludeTests".split(",").each { excludeTests ->
            exclude excludeTests
        }
    }

    if (project.hasProperty("parallel")) { ❻
        maxParallelForks = Runtime.runtime.availableProcessors()
    }

    ext.failedTests = [] ❼

    tasks.withType(Test) {
        afterTest { TestDescriptor descriptor, TestResult result ->
            if(result.resultType ==
                    org.gradle.api.tasks.testing.TestResult.ResultType.FAILURE) {
                failedTests << ["${descriptor.className}::${descriptor.name}"]
            }
        }
    }

    gradle.buildFinished {
        if(!failedTests.empty){
            println "Failed test(s) for ${project.name}:"
            failedTests.each { failedTest ->
                println failedTest
            }
        }
    }
}

repositories {
    mavenCentral() ❽
}

dependencies { ❾
    implementation("org.slf4j:slf4j-api:${slf4jVersion}")
    implementation("ch.qos.logback:logback-classic:${logbackVersion}")

    testImplementation("org.seleniumhq.selenium:selenium-java:${seleniumVersion}")
    testImplementation("org.assertj:assertj-core:${assertjVersion}")
```

```
        testImplementation("io.github.bonigarcia:webdrivermanager:${wdmVersion}")
}
```

❶ Since we are implementing a Java project, we need to declare the `java` plug-in (*https://docs.gradle.org/current/userguide/java_plugin.html*).

❷ For compiling the tests, we use Java 8.

❸ Although not mandatory, we force writing the test logs in the standard output.

❹ This allows passing Java system properties in the command line (as explained in Example B-1).

❺ This clause allows using the property `excludeTests` at the command line to exclude some tests. For instance, the following command excludes those tests starting with the word Docker: `gradle test -PexcludeTests=**/Docker*`

❻ These lines allow running tests in parallel using the command `gradle test -Pparallel`.

❼ The following clauses gather the failed test in the property `failedTests` and display this information in the standard output at the end of the test suite execution.

❽ We use Maven Central (*https://search.maven.org*) to pull dependencies.

❾ The common dependencies are Selenium WebDriver, AssertJ, WebDriverManager (for tests), and SLF4J and Logback (for the whole project).

JUnit 4

The specific setup for JUnit 4 is as follows:

```
test {
    useJUnit() { ❶
        if (project.hasProperty("groups")) {
            includeCategories "$groups"
        }
        if (project.hasProperty("excludedGroups")) {
            excludeCategories "$excludedGroups"
        }
    }
}

dependencies { ❷
    testImplementation("junit:junit:${junit4Version}")
}
```

❶ We use an extra configuration to allow filtering tests using the class name (see "Categorizing and Filtering Tests" on page 256).

❷ We include the JUnit 4 dependency.

JUnit 5

When using JUnit 5, we need to specify the `junit-jupiter` artifact (like in Maven, it depends on `junit-jupiter-api` `junit-jupiter-engine`, and `junit-jupiter-params`). In addition, we need to select the JUnit Platform for executing by using the clause `useJUnitPlatform()` in the `test` task setup.

```
test {
    useJUnitPlatform() {
        if (project.hasProperty("groups")) {
            includeTags "$groups"
        }
        if (project.hasProperty("excludedGroups")) {
            excludeTags "$excludedGroups"
        }
    }
}

dependencies {
    testImplementation("org.junit.jupiter:junit-jupiter:${junit5Version}")
}
```

Selenium-Jupiter

If you use Selenium-Jupiter, in addition to the previous configuration for JUnit 5, you need to include the following dependency. In this case, we can remove WebDriver-Manager since it is pulled transitively by Selenium-Jupiter.

```
dependencies {
    testImplementation("io.github.bonigarcia:selenium-jupiter:${selJupVersion}")
}
```

TestNG

Finally, for using TestNG as the unit testing framework, we need to include the following setup:

```
test {
    useTestNG() {
        if (project.hasProperty("groups")) { ❶
            includeGroups "$groups"
        }
        if (project.hasProperty("excludedGroups")) {
            excludeGroups "$excludedGroups"
```

```
        }
    }

    scanForTestClasses = false ❷
}

dependencies { ❸
    testImplementation("org.testng:testng:${testNgVersion}")
}
```

❶ We include these statements to allow filtering by class name.

❷ This property needs to be set to false to match the include and exclude patterns in the filtering process.

❸ We include the TestNG dependency.

Other Dependencies

We need to include additional dependencies in the Gradle setup to use third-party libraries. Table C-3 (in the previous section) summarizes the coordinates for these dependencies and the chapter in which they are presented. In addition, a couple of additional plug-ins are required in the Gradle setup (for using Allure and Spring-Boot, respectively). For using Allure, you also need to define an extra repository, as follows:

```
plugins {
    id "io.qameta.allure"
    id "org.springframework.boot"
}

repositories {
    maven {
        url "https://plugins.gradle.org/m2/"
    }
}
```

Logging

I use two logging libraries in the examples repository:

Logback (https://logback.qos.ch)
    This is the actual logging framework (also called *logger*). Logback is used by many relevant Java projects, such as Spring Framework and Groovy, to name a couple.

Simple Logging Facade for Java (SLF4J) (https://www.slf4j.org)
This is a popular utility based on the facade design pattern that decouples the underlying logger. It supports the main logging frameworks (e.g., Logback, Log4j, or SimpleLogger, among others). As summarized in Table C-5, SLF4J defines five logging levels depending on the severity of the message.

Table C-5. Log levels in SLF4J

Log level	Description
ERROR	Used to report flaws in our application.
WARN	Something unexpected happened, but it does not affect the expected application behavior.
INFO	Informative messages, such as the application entered a given state, etc.
DEBUG	Information for diagnosing and troubleshooting.
TRACE	Finest-grained information. We use this level only in exceptional cases where we need a complete understanding of what is happening in our application.

As usual, to use these libraries, we need to resolve the corresponding dependencies (see next section for details in Maven and Gradle). Then, we need to configure Logback properly. For that, we need to include an XML configuration file in our project classpath. If we are configuring the logging for the whole project (i.e., application plus test logic), the name of this file should be `logback.xml`. In this case, it should be available within the application resources, typically under the `src/main/resources` folder (see next section for further information about the project layout). If we are logging only for tests, the name of the configuration file is `logback-test.xml` and is stored within the tests resources (e.g., in `src/test/resources` folder).

The syntax in both cases (`logback.xml` and `logback-test.xml`) is the same. Example C-4 shows an example of a configuration file. This XML file sets the pattern for each logging line, composed by the timestamp, the thread name, the trace level, the source (package, class name, and code line), and the message. In this example, INFO is the default logging level. This way, every trace of this level or more severe ones (i.e., WARN, ERROR, and FATAL) is displayed, but not the following (i.e., DEBUG and TRACE). In addition, the traces from the package `io.github.bonigarcia` (used in the test examples, WebDriverManager, and Selenium-Jupiter) is DEBUG.

Example C-4. Logback configuration file

```
<?xml version="1.0" encoding="UTF-8"?>
<configuration>
    <appender name="STDOUT" class="ch.qos.logback.core.ConsoleAppender">
        <encoder>
            <pattern>%d{yyyy-MM-dd HH:mm:ss} [%thread] %-5level %logger{36}.%M\(%line\)
                - %msg%n</pattern>
        </encoder>
```

```
    </appender>

    <logger name="io.github.bonigarcia" level="DEBUG" />

    <root level="INFO">
       <appender-ref ref="STDOUT" />
    </root>

</configuration>
```

The final step is using a variable for logging in our Java classes. To that aim, we can use the code of Example C-5. This snippet provides a handy way to get the current class using reflection through the method lookup(). Then, we declare the variable for logging (called log in this example) and using the SLF4J's method getLogger(). Finally, we can use the variable log in any method of this class to log messages of different levels.

Example C-5. Example of logging messages

```
static final Logger log = getLogger(lookup().lookupClass());

log.info("This is an informative message");
log.debug("This is a debugging message");
```

GitHub Actions

I use GitHub Actions as the CI server for the examples repository (*https://github.com/ bonigarcia/selenium-webdriver-java/actions*). This way, each time I commit a new change to the repo, GitHub Actions builds the project and executes all the tests. Example C-6 shows the configuration to carry out this process.

Example C-6. GitHub Actions workflow configuration

```
name: build

on: ❶
  push:
    branches: [ master ]
  pull_request:
    branches: [ master ]

env: ❷
  DISPLAY: :99
  WDM_GITHUBTOKEN: ${{ secrets.WDM_GITHUBTOKEN }}

jobs:
  tests: ❸
    runs-on: ${{ matrix.os }}
```

```
strategy:
  matrix:
    os: [ ubuntu-latest, windows-latest, macos-latest ]
    java: [ 8 ]

steps: ❹
- name: Checkout GitHub repo
  uses: actions/checkout@v2
- name: Set up Java
  uses: actions/setup-java@v2
  with:
    distribution: 'temurin'
    java-version: ${{ matrix.java }}
- name: Start Xvfb
  run: Xvfb :99 &
- name: Test with Maven
  run: mvn -B test
- name: Test with Gradle
  run: ./gradlew test
```

❶ The events that trigger the workflow are push (new commits in the repository) and pull_request (commits proposed by other developers).

❷ Two environment variables are required:

DISPLAY

> The browsers controlled by Selenium WebDriver, by default, need to be executed in an operating system with a graphical user interface. On the other side, the Linux distributions available in GitHub Actions are *headless* (i.e., without a graphical user interface). Thus, we use Xvfb (X virtual framebuffer) to run WebDriver tests on these Linux distributions. Xvfb is an in-memory display server for Unix-like systems that requires the declaration of the environment variable DISPLAY with the screen number for the graphical system in Linux (X11).

WDM_GITHUBTOKEN

> GitHub hosts some of the drivers required by Selenium WebDriver (e.g., geckodriver or operadriver). When external clients (like WebDriverManager) make many consecutive requests to GitHub, it eventually returns an HTTP error response (403, forbidden) due to its rate limit. WebDriverManager can make authenticated requests using a *personal access token* to avoid this problem. Figure C-2 shows the permissions granted to this token in the examples repository. All in all, this environment variable exports the value of this token. I keep the actual value of this token as a GitHub repository secret.

❸ For the sake of completeness, I execute the workflow in three different operating systems: Ubuntu (i.e., Linux), Windows, and macOS, using Java 8 in all of them.

❹ The workflow has five steps:

1. Check out the repository.
2. Set up Java 8 using Eclipse Adoptium (*https://adoptium.net*).
3. Start X virtual framebuffer.
4. Run all tests with Maven.
5. Run all tests with Gradle.

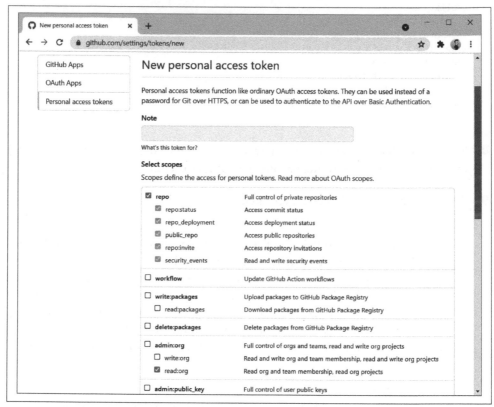

Figure C-2. Permissions of the GitHub personal access token used in the examples repository

Dependabot

To configure Dependabot, we need to include a file called `dependabot.yml` in the folder `.github` of our repository. Example C-7 shows this content in the examples repository.

Example C-7. Dependabot configuration

```
version: 2
updates:
- package-ecosystem: maven ❶
  directory: "/"
  schedule:
    interval: daily
    time: '06:00'
  open-pull-requests-limit: 99

- package-ecosystem: gradle ❷
  directory: "/"
  schedule:
    interval: daily
    time: '06:00'
  open-pull-requests-limit: 99

- package-ecosystem: github-actions ❸
  directory: "/"
  schedule:
    interval: daily
    time: '06:00'
  open-pull-requests-limit: 99
```

❶ We check daily the updates for the Maven dependencies.

❷ We check daily the updates for the Gradle dependencies.

❸ We check daily the updates for the GitHub Actions setup.

Summary

All the examples presented in this book are available in a public GitHub repository (*https://github.com/bonigarcia/selenium-webdriver-java*). This appendix showed the fine-grained configuration details for the build tools (Maven and Gradle), dependencies (Selenium WebDriver, JUnit, TestNG, Selenium-Jupiter, WebDriverManager, etc.), logging (Logback and SLF4J), and other services (GitHub Actions, GitHub Pages, and Dependabot).

Index

DevOps (development and operations), 24
DevTools (see Chrome DevTools Protocol (CDP))
devTools class attribute, 180
DevToolsException exception, 179
dialog boxes, 133-136
digest authentication, 179
directory structure for project, 32-34
disabling tests, 286-289
dismiss() method, 134, 135
DISPLAY env variable, 375
distributed mode, Selenium Grid, 203, 208-213
distributed tracing, 214
Distributor node, 209-211, 213
DOC (Depended-On Component), 27
Docker containers
    about, 14
    for browser infrastructure support, 14, 31, 219-228
    Docker Engine in, 14, 31, 219, 224
    Docker Hub in, 14, 220
    and docker-selenium, 14, 220-222
    and images for remote browsers, 220-222, 224
    launching, 220-221
    Selenium-Jupiter with, 227-228
    Selenoid with, 222-223
    WebDriverManager with, 224-227
    with WebManager for load testing, 301-303
@DockerBrowser annotation, 227
dockerized browsers, 220, 223, 225-227
documentation, Selenium, 15, 350
DOM (Document Object Model)
    function and structure of, 59-61
    listener for event changes in, 194-195
    shadow DOM in, 118-120
    with XPath, 69
Domain Specific Language (DSL), 240-242
domMutation events, 194-195
done callback, 109
doubleClick() method, 88-89
downloading drivers, 355
drag and drop, 90-91
dragAndDrop() method, 87, 91
dragAndDropBy() method, 87, 91
driver cache, 352
driver management, 12
    (see also WebDriverManager)

automation of, 11-12, 30, 36, 204, 351-355, 358
    manual, 11, 355-357
    steps in procedure of, 11, 36, 355-357
driver.manage().logs(), 168-169
driver.quit() method, 225
@DriverCapabilities annotation, 202, 289
drivers
    about, 358
    in Appium, 328
    architecture of, 5-6, 197-199
    automatic browser updates and, 11, 30, 357
    and browser session identification, 58
    downloading, 355
    maintenance of, 11, 357
    and Selenium WebDriver, 5
        (see also Selenium WebDriver API)
    setting up, 356
    versions of, 11, 120, 351-352, 355
    WebDriver hierarchy of classes of, 35, 137, 199
    WebDriverManager resolution of, 55-57, 150, 152, 204-205, 241, 351-354
@DriverURL annotation, 202
dropdown lists, 125-128
DRY (Don't Repeat Yourself) with code, 233
DSL (Domain Specific Language), 240-242
Duration timeout argument, 96, 98, 347
dynamic grid, docker-selenium, 222

E

eager page loading strategy, 151
Eclipse IDE, 44, 96, 138
ecosystem, Selenium, 10-16
    browser infrastructure in, 14
    community in, 15
    driver managers in, 11-12
    frameworks in, 12-14
    language bindings in, 10
    locator tools for web elements in, 12
ecosystems, software, 10
Edge
    capabilities, overview of, 145-147, 348
    CDP and, 177
        (see also Chrome DevTools Protocol (CDP))
    as Chromium-based browser, 146, 153-155, 177, 180, 192
    cross-browser testing with, 252-256

test report creation in, 312, 315
wrapper file, 34
gradlew and gradlew.bat, 34
GraphQL queries, 216
groupId, 34
grouping CSS selector, 67
grouping tests, 257-260, 371-372
GUI (Graphical User Interface)
    of Cypress, 337
    with date picker example, 78-80
    of JMeter test plan, 300-301
    of OWASP ZAP, 303
    with Selenium IDE, 8
GUI testing, 20

H

Hammant, Paul, 3
Hanrigou, Philippe, 6
HAR (HTTP Archive), 297-300
HasAuthentication interface, 179
HasDevTools interface, 177, 180
HasExtensions interface, 159
HashMap object, 154, 155, 161
HasLogEvents interface, 194-195
HasVirtualAuthenticator interface, 192
headers, additional, 185
headless browsers, 147-150, 342, 343
hidden input text, locating, 66, 69
hierarchy, WebDriver, 35
history, browser, 117
HTML
    attributes, 62-66, 81
    color picker in, 106
    frames and iframes in, 128
    link text for, 66
    for locating WebElements, 59-61, 63-65
    reports in, 312-315
    tags, 59-61, 63, 66, 81, 92, 125
HtmlUnit, 32, 48, 367
HTTP
    cookies and, 120
    error messages from, 375
    and headers, 185
    methods for creating REST services, 333
    network traffic, 296-298
    requests and responses, monitoring, 182
    status codes for creating REST services, 333
    URLs as endpoints in, 333
    user agent specification in, 155

web proxies and, 166-168
HTTP Archive (HAR), 297-300
HTTP client library, 294-296
HTTPS, 168, 171, 190
Hub (Selenium Server), 7, 199, 201-203, 205, 221, 222, 227, 339
hub-nodes mode, Selenium Grid, 7, 203, 207-209, 221
Huggins, Jason, 3, 327
hybrid apps, 326

I

Id, HTML attribute, 62-65
identification of project, 34
IDEs (Integrated Development Environments), 8-10, 30, 44, 46, 256, 335, 350
i18n (internationalization), 173
iframes, navigating web pages with, 128, 131
@Ignore annotation, 286
ignoring() method, 98
impersonation, user, 82-86
implicit waits, 94-96, 105, 110
inclusion and exclusion of tests, 257-260, 370
incognito argument and mode, 175
infinite scroll page, 105
INFO log level, 205, 207, 214, 373
initElements() method, 244
input devices, 82-86
input elements/data, 83-85, 128, 309-312
insecure pages, loading, 171-173, 190
installExtension() method, 159
Integrated Development Environments (IDEs), 8-10, 30, 44, 46, 256, 335, 350
integration testing, 17
intercepting invocations extension, 41, 271
internationalization (i18n), 173
Internet Explorer, 5, 32, 37, 175-177, 351
intl.accept_languages capability, 173-175
InvalidArgumentException exception, 84, 143
Inversion of Control (IoC), 320
IretryAnalyzer listener, 276
isDisplayed() method, 61, 239
isDockerAvailable() method, 224
isEnabled() method, 61
isOnline() method, 200
isSelected() method, 61, 86
ITestListener interface, 284

setHeadless(true) method, 147
setLocation() method, 191
settings.gradle, 34
setup in testing, xUnit family, 25-26
setup() method, 37, 46
shadow DOM, 118-120, 345
shadow host, 118, 120
shadow root, 118, 120
shell, launching from, 204-205, 207, 212-213, 220-221
simulation of mobile devices, 153-155, 187, 326
@SingleSession annotation, 264
SLF4J (Simple Logging Facade for Java), 372-374
sliders, range, 84
slow calculator example, wait time with, 97
SmalltalkUnit (SUnit), 24
software design principles, 232-233
software for end-to-end testing, 29-32
software project development
    build tools for, 31
    CI practice and, 22
    community resources for, 15
    dependencies for, 34-44, 359
    with DevOps for teams, 24
    lifecycle of, 21
    project layout for, 32-34, 360, 368
    web frameworks for, 320
source code
    in examples repository, 22, 32, 361
    loading extensions from, 158-160
Spring portfolio, 320
Spring-Boot, 320-322, 367, 372
@SpringBootTest annotation, 321
src/main/java, 33, 368
src/main/resources, 33, 361, 368, 373
src/test/java, 33, 361, 364, 368
src/test/resources, 33, 368, 373
stacked levels of testing, 16, 17
standalone mode, Selenium Grid, 203-207, 220
step definitions in Gherkin, 317-319
Stewart, Simon, 4, 350
storage, web, 137
stress testing, 20
string script argument, 102
structural testing, 19, 21
submit() method, 61
successBoxPresent() method, 239
SUnit (SmalltalkUnit), 24

Surefire plug-in, 278, 312, 362
SUT (System Under Test)
    about, 16
    challenges with, 231
    in end-to-end testing, 17
    with four-phase structure, 25-26
    improving design of, 231, 232, 236, 240, 244
switchTo() method, 57, 129-131
synchronous JavascriptExecutor scripts, 102-108
synthetic user media, 170-171
system testing, 17, 27
System Under Test (SUT) (see SUT (System Under Test))
SystemUtils class, 93

T

tabs, navigating web pages with, 128, 129, 345
@Tag annotation, 260
tag name, HTML, 59-61, 63, 66, 81, 92
tagging tests, 257-260
takeScreenshot(), 140
TakesScreenshot interface, 112, 115
target folders, specifying, 292-293
TargetLocator interface and methods, 129
TDD (Test Driven Development), 21
teams, project software and, 24
teardown in testing, 25, 83, 270
teardown() method, 56
@Test annotation, 40, 42, 245, 258, 262, 276, 286
test classes, 244
test data selection, 309-312
test doubles, 17
Test Driven Development (TDD), 21
test engine API, 38-40
test grouping (TestNG), 43
test instance extension, 271
Test Last Development (TLD), 21
test launcher API, 38
test lifecycle callbacks extension, 41, 42, 271
test lifecycles, 38, 40, 43, 276, 282-286
test listeners, 270, 282-286, 315
test logic, 46, 57, 232, 254, 364
test pyramid, 17
Test Runner, Cypress, 336, 337
test runners, 245-247, 282-284, 343
test setup, 25-26, 37, 46
test skeletons of builders, 54-57

X

XPath (XML Path Language), 62, 69-73, 80-82, 85, 89, 97
XPInstall file, 158
xUnit (unit testing family), 24-26

Xvfb (X virtual framebuffer), 375

Z

ZAP (Zed Attack Proxy), 303
zipFolder(Path) method, 160

About the Author

Boni García (*https://bonigarcia.dev*) is a visiting professor at Universidad Carlos III de Madrid (UC3M) in Spain. He is passionate about software engineering with an emphasis on automated testing. He is the author of more than 45 publications, including international conferences, journals, book chapters, and the book *Mastering Software Testing with JUnit 5* (Packt). He is the creator and maintainer of different open source projects related to Selenium, including WebDriverManager (a well-known helper library for Selenium WebDriver in Java) and Selenium-Jupiter (a JUnit 5 extension for Selenium WebDriver).

He presented his PhD dissertation, focused on automated web navigation and testing, in 2011. The reference implementation of this work used Selenium IDE and Remote Control as foundational tools. He continued researching automated testing from 2013 to 2020, participating in the open source projects Kurento, OpenVidu, and ElasTest. In this period, he adopted Selenium WebDriver as the fundamental framework to assess WebRTC applications and Quality of Experience. Currently, he continues working actively with Selenium. His latest publications focus on the Selenium ecosystem and automated driver management in Selenium WebDriver. He started to collaborate with Sauce Labs as an open source engineer in 2022.

Colophon

The animal on the cover of *Hands-On Selenium WebDriver with Java* is a crested shriketit (*Falcunculus frontatus*). Endemic to mainland Australia, these striking birds can be found in eucalyptus forests and woodlands, forested gullies, and along rivers in drier areas. This species can sometimes be located by listening for its repeated plaintive whistle, but as it often imitates other birds, identification can be difficult.

The crested shriketit is a medium-sized bird with a black-and-white striped head, a small crest, and a short bill with a hooked tip. It has wide, rounded wings and a square, slightly forked tail. The males are larger than females, and can also be distinguished by their black throats (females have olive green throats). The shriketit mainly feeds on insects, but sometimes also consumes fruit and seeds. The bird acquires food by using its strong beak to tear at or probe tree bark for insects. Shriketits usually forage alone, but can be found in pairs, groups of up to five individuals (usually a family group), or in mixed feeding flocks with other insect-eating birds.

The breeding season of a crested shriketit usually lasts from August to January. The male shriketit selects a nest site in a high fork of a eucalyptus tree, attracting the female to him with quivering and waving wings. The female builds a deep cone-shaped nest from dry grass and bark strips, covering the outside with spider webs, moss, and lichen. The male helps collect materials, and both sexes incubate the eggs and feed the young. The incubation period lasts about 20 days. Two broods may be raised in a season, and the young birds often remain with their parents until the beginning of the next breeding season. The nests are often parasitized by various cuckoo species.

Among all the species of the crested shriketit, the northern subspecies, *whitei*, is the one most at threat of extinction. It is endangered in Western Australia, occurring in such low densities in some areas that populations may not be able to renew themselves and are isolated from each other. More importantly, the hot and widespread fires in the dry season decrease the ability of insects to establish themselves under the bark, hence reducing the shriketit's main source of food. The western subspecies, *leucogaster*, is also near-threatened and is affected by land clearing in the wheat belt. The eastern subspecies, *frontatus*, is adversely threatened by urban development. Many of the animals on O'Reilly covers are endangered; all of them are important to the world.

The cover illustration is by Karen Montgomery, based on an antique line engraving from *Lydekker's Royal Natural History*. The cover fonts are Gilroy Semibold and Guardian Sans. The text font is Adobe Minion Pro; the heading font is Adobe Myriad Condensed; and the code font is Dalton Maag's Ubuntu Mono.

O'REILLY®

Learn from experts.
Become one yourself.

Books | Live online courses
Instant Answers | Virtual events
Videos | Interactive learning

Get started at oreilly.com.

Milton Keynes UK
Ingram Content Group UK Ltd.
UKHW010918130924
448262UK00004BA/5

9 781098 110000